This study provides Canada's first comprehensive, integrated treatment of the emergence and development of key communication sectors: telegraph, telephones, cable TV, broadcasting, communication satellites, and electronic publishing. By focusing on real institutions, actual (and frequently predatory) business practices, and law and regulatory policies, in both historical and contemporary perspectives, Babe helps demystify current communication issues.

He provides a realistic basis on which to devise policies respecting such current controversies as:

- rate rebalancing and the erosion of universal telephone service;
- integration of responsibilities for content and carriage in electronic publishing;
- privatization of communication sectors;
- monopoly vs. competition in telecommunications;
- conglomerate ownership of public utilities;
- public funding of new technological ventures such as videotex, communication satellites, and ISDN (Integrated Services Digital Network);
- the performance of regulatory agencies in constraining monopolistic abuses.

Stressing the flexibility of communication 'technologies' on the one hand, and the element of corporate power on the other, Babe reintroduces the principle of corporate/governmental responsibility for communication outcomes, a principle that has been largely drowned out by the shrill cries of 'Information Revolution.'

ROBERT E. BABE is a professor in the Department of Communication, University of Ottawa. He is the author of *Cable Television and Telecommunications in Canada: An Economic Analysis* and *Canadian Television Broadcasting Structure, Performance and Regulation*, and co-author of *Broadcasting Policy and Copyright Law*.

ROBERT E. BABE

Telecommunications in Canada: Technology, Industry, and Government

UNIVERSITY OF TORONTO PRESS
Toronto Buffalo London

© University of Toronto Press 1990
Toronto Buffalo London
Printed in Canada

ISBN 0-8020-5831-0 (cloth)
ISBN 0-8020-6738-7 (paper)

∞

Printed on acid-free paper

Canadian Cataloguing in Publication Data

Babe, Robert E., 1943–
    Telecommunications in Canada

    Includes bibliographical references.
    ISBN 0-8020-5831-0 (bound) ISBN 0-8020-6738-7 (pbk.)

    1. Telecommunication – Canada – History.
    2. Telecommunication policy – Canada – History.
    I. Title.

    HE7815.B32 1989   384'.0971   C89-095147-0

This book has been published with the assistance of the Canada Council
and the Ontario Arts Council under their block grant programs.

To Walter Adams

Contents

xi Contents

Preface and Acknowledgments

The idea for this book was conceived several years ago during a brief but invaluable stint as public servant in the federal Department of Communications. There I learned how senior policy-makers become embroiled in 'firefighting.' A cursory reading of u.s. and Canadian telecommunications history, even at that time, however, persuaded me that the 'burning' issues of the day most frequently are but replays of the past; for a full and adequate understanding of current concerns historical perspective is essential.

Of course no policy issue can be construed in a vacuum – that is, in the complete absence of some context or other. Since the period of my public service, however, it has gradually dawned on me that as context our policy-makers are wont to substitute myth in the place of history.

Myth is always ahistorical. It makes appear as 'natural,' 'exogenous,' or 'inevitable' those circumstances and developments which are in fact contingent.

A chief aim of this book is to restore what Roland Barthes has termed 'the soiling trace of origin or choice' to current issues in Canadian telecommunications. By recovering a sense of history Canadian telecommunications can be demythologized and a deeper, truer understanding of the subject emerge.

An exception during my bureaucratic employment to that pervasive ahistorical and mythical posturing in the Department of Communications was Fred G. Bigham. As graduate student, Fred had himself researched Canadian telecommunications history, and he most graciously afforded me the fruits of that labour, an encouraging, indeed auspicious, debut for my own work. Subsequently, as director of the Cost Inquiry at the CRTC, Fred enthusiastically responded to many solicitations for documentation, even consenting to read an early draft of this book, supplying most valued commentary.

Speaking of origins, I most gratefully and affectionately acknowledge guidance and instruction of Walter Adams, distinguished university professor and president emeritus, Michigan State University. Walter Adams initiated me to the study of institutional economics (political economy), and encouraged me to adopt a critical perspective towards neoclassical micro-economic analysis. The present book continues very much in the tradition of political economy. Over the years Walter Adams has retained keen interest in my life and work and has provided much encouragement and support for this endeavour.

Despite years of research and consulting in the telecommunications field it is unlikely I would ever have actually begun composition had not two distinguished professors and former colleagues from Simon Fraser University, William H. Melody and Dallas W. Smythe, in 1984 agreed to be co-authors. With the prospect of such wise and experienced collaboration, I was finally able to muster the resolve to begin writing. That circumstances were such that in the end I pursued the project on my own in no way lessens my indebtedness to them.

Conversations over the years with both Professors Melody and Smythe undoubtedly inform this manuscript, as have their comments on previous drafts. But particular note must be made of a seminal lecture delivered by Dallas Smythe to the Studies in Communication and Information Technology symposium, Queen's University, on 8 April 1986. The topic was 'Technology as myth.'

Joe Schmidt, vice-president of regulatory and governmental matters, CNCP Telecommunications, is another to whom I am much indebted. I first made his acquaintance in 1973 as consultant to the Manitoba government on provincial telecommunications. Although Manitoba Telephone System, a provincial Crown corporation, was then eyeing warily CNCP's operations in the province (as it continues to do), Joe Schmidt was most forthcoming in responding to all requests for data, a feature that has characterized our dealings ever since. In addition, he too read an earlier draft of this book, passing on detailed, informed, and critical commentary, on occasion even steering me from factual error, for which I am most grateful.

My primary research assistant was Emmanuel Mankumah. Although working for me but briefly, Emmanuel pried loose valuable documentation concerning both the early years of telephone competition and Bell Canada's incursions into radio broadcasting, his research substantiating one of the major threads of this book.

Special thanks are afforded Professors Gertrude Robinson of McGill, Ian Parker of the University of Toronto, and Vincent Mosco of Carleton, all of whom provided encouragement, advice and support when much needed.

Others whose aid over the years I am pleased to acknowledge include Andy Thurswalden, Richard Starr, Garry Steeves, Robert Bulger, Kenneth Wyman, Sy Berger, Bruce Olsen, Ken Hancock, Stephannie Sykes, Dennis Wardrop, Gary Hauch, Gordon Henderson, Don Braden, Steve McRae, Dr. Hans van Baeyer, Christian Elwes, Gordon Kaiser, Andrew Roman, G.D. Zimmerman, Antoine Zalatan, Herschel Hardin, and students of my 1987–8 policy seminar at the University of Ottawa.

Heather Durant, my typist for a decade, cheerfully and faithfully transformed a scarcely legible scrawl into a manuscript of elegant appearance. And Virgil Duff, managing editor at University of Toronto Press, deserves accolades for his continuing faith in a project experiencing many vicissitudes along the way.

Finally, much love and thanks to Jane, for support, understanding, and advice.

In acknowledging indebtedness one unfortunately runs the risk of implicating others in one's own folly. Let it be understood clearly that all deficiencies in what follows are those of the author alone.

University of Ottawa
May 1989

PART I

Introduction

1

Mythologies of Canadian Telecommunications

PATTERN RECOGNITION

'There are eight million stories in the naked city; this has been one of them.' So ended each episode of a once popular u.s. television series.

It is doubtful that there are more than a handful of distinctly different stories of Canadian telecommunications. None the less, the author is aware that what follows can be but one.[1]

Other books on our topic, although not numerous, have appeared. Mostly they have been 'living histories'[2] that have tried to place the reader in the period; describe the adventures, misadventures, tricks, and heroism of the personalities; recount anecdotes, humorous and otherwise; describe the evolution of an industrial art; and even, perhaps, detect interrelations between the social customs and the industrial techniques ('technologies') as they changed. That approach, which I term 'living history,' can certainly be interesting, lively and informative; but it must also be largely non-analytical. By stressing the uniqueness of incidents and personalities, little emphasis can be afforded underlying themes and recurring patterns.

There is, of course, a second approach.

Marshall McLuhan was fond of recounting as parable Edgar Allan Poe's 'Descent into the Maelstrom.'[3] Poe's sailor went out fishing and, in the late afternoon, the tide turning, found himself caught in a great eddy. Unable to row out of it, he began studying closely the action of the timbers and other debris. Some were sucked down, never to re-emerge, but others resurfaced. As McLuhan told the story the sailor would have drowned had he not detached his attention from the particularities of the whirlpool's action to perceive repeating occurrences. Choosing wisely to attach himself to one of these recurring forms, he was saved. McLuhan called this tactic 'pattern recognition.'

So too with this present study. Many years of research and consulting in Canadian telecommunications, as well as fruitful instruction from experts in this and other disciplines, have enabled me to detect historical patterns, presented here. The intent is not so much to give the reader a 'feel' for the times or to construct 'living history' (although that approach certainly is not ignored) as it is to detect, describe, and analyse patterns – recurrences over the past 150 years that, by their very frequency of reappearance, may be expected to continue resurfacing. This book is first and foremost one of pattern recognition.

In another sense, the current approach is not unlike 'living history,' for haven't some of the major corporate players in Canadian telecommunications been around a good long time? Historical analysis reveals a consistent 'corporate personality' as strategies for problem-solving are repeated. From myriad incidents, details, and circumstances, constancy emerges.

Today it is particularly important to recognize the constants or patterns in the historical development of Canadian telecommunications. Much of the current thinking of our all-too-often ahistorically minded policy-makers is shrouded in misconception, even myth.

Roland Barthes once wrote: 'Myth deprives the object of which it speaks of all History. In it, history evaporates ... Nothing is produced, nothing is chosen: all one has to do is to possess these new objects from which all soiling trace of origin or choice has been removed. This miraculous evaporation of history is another form of a concept common to most bourgeois myths: *the irresponsibility of man.*'[4]

At the most basic level this book is an analytical history of telecommunications in Canada, from inception to present, emphasizing what is too often omitted in industrial histories – namely, the role of corporate and governmental power in implementing industrial devices and processes and in structuring industries. The seventeen chapters forming the body of this work can be read on their own as a political/economic treatise on telecommunications in this country. But historical analysis serves additionally the broader purpose of demystification. Juxtaposed with current myths adumbrated below, the present history reintroduces the 'soiling trace of origin or choice,' re-establishing thereby human responsibility. In no sense did the industrial arts ('technologies') introduce themselves. They did not descend from the clouds, nor did they make 'natural' any particular industrial structure. Rather, our communication industries took shape and developed through the agency of and the struggle for human power.

Dispelling myths, past and present, is important simply to set the record straight. But more than that, this task is vital for our future well-being because Canada's policy-makers are now preparing agendas and setting trajectories to carry us into the twenty-first century.

The remainder of this first chapter identifies and critiques some of the most prevalent myths of our day relating to the field of Canadian telecommunications. What follows thereafter will be an exercise in demythologizing, as patterns are presented to help undermine the myths now adumbrated.

THE FIRST MYTH: TECHNOLOGICAL NATIONALISM

Canada is a country that 'exists by reason of communication.'[5] So declared Harry J. Boyle in 1970 as vice-chairman of the Canadian Radio-Television Commission (CRTC, now the Canadian Radio-television and Telecommunications Commission). Mr Boyle's has been but one of many voices to have articulated that proposition. Here are some others: From the federal *White Paper on Broadcasting* in 1966: 'Broadcasting may well be regarded as the central nervous system of Canadian nationhood.'[6] And from Communications Minister Gérard Pelletier in 1973: 'The existence of Canada as a political and social entity has always been heavily dependent upon effective systems of east/west communication.' (The minister added that Canadian telecommunications have helped counterbalance 'the strong north/south pull of continentalism.'[7])

As one might expect, the recurring theme of 'technological nationalism' – nationhood through deployment of industrial devices – has had important policy repercussions. Intent on legitimizing substantial governmental financial aid to develop a Canadian satellite system, then Deputy Minister of Communications A.E. Gotlieb in 1969 remarked: '[The satellite] will introduce a new dimension into life in the North and thereby make it much more possible for that part of Canada to be a single, national, cohesive whole by integrating the more remote areas into the common whole.'

He continued: 'I hate to use clichés, but I think there is an analogy with the railway here. When it was opened up, I imagine very, very few people lived at the end of the line where the last spike was driven, but the very fact this facility went in, I think, transformed the character of the country.'[8]

More recently this doctrine of 'technological nationalism' has attained expression in an important discussion paper from the Department of Communications. The following is a brief extract:

Communications have always played a central role in Canada's history. From the fur trade of the seventeenth and eighteenth centuries, to the canals and railways of the nineteenth, from the broadcasting networks, airlines and highways to the telephone and satellite systems of the twentieth, communications technologies have helped Canadians reach new frontiers, settle and develop the wilderness, and build both a society and culture that are unique in the world for the degree to which they depend on good communications systems.[9]

So ingrained in the Canadian imagination has been this purported link between Canadian nationhood on the one hand and media of communication on the other that Arthur Kroker wrote recently: 'The Canadian identity is, and always has been, fully integral to the question of technology ... Technological nationalism ... has always been the essence of the Canadian state, and, most certainly, the locus of the Canadian identity.'[10]

One factor contributing to the notion that Canadian nationhood is indelibly linked to deployment of communication devices is this country's vast but sparsely settled geographic expanse. Canada occupies a land mass of 3.6 million square miles (9.2 million square kilometres) spanning seven time zones, facing on three oceans, and stretching at its deepest point 2800 miles north and south and 4000 miles east and west. But inhabiting the vast tracts of land are merely 26 million people, mostly concentrated along the 4000-mile-long border with the United States.

Moreover, cultural and linguistic diversities have tended to produce barriers and tensions, helping thwart political integration. Hence, Hallman and Hindley have written:

Against this mosaic of regions and languages and cultures, against the inequalities of the economy, communication has a special importance in Canadian life. Without the roads and railways, without the airlines, the centrifugal forces of the Canadian environment are difficult to keep in balance. Without the national broadcasting services in both French and English, the full character of the country, its regions and its particularities could not be expressed to the community as a whole. Perhaps the main responsibility of Canadian broadcasting is to create for Canadians the shared experience of living together in the second largest country in the world.[11]

History too plays a part. After all, were not canals and railways instrumental in forging an independent state amidst powerful continentalist pressures? Writing in 1870, three years after Ontario, Quebec, New Brunswick, and Nova Scotia entered into Confederation, Sir John A. Macdonald cautioned: 'The United States Government are resolved to do all they can short of war to get possession of the western territory, and we must take immediate and vigorous steps to counteract them. One of the first things to be done is to show unmistakably our resolve to build the Pacific Railway.'[12] For many, apparently, it is but a short step to extrapolate early experiences with transportation onto modern systems of electronic telecommunications.

Such analogizing is not, however, completely without merit. On occasion communication media have indeed been purposefully and successfully deployed in aid of nation-building. A full decade before construction of the Pacific Railway, for example, the Canadian government built 1300 miles of telegraph between the Lakehead and Edmonton, helping promote political integration in British North America.[13] Broadcasting too, upon publication in 1929 of the Aird Royal Commission's report,[14] came to be regarded as essential for achieving and promoting cultural and political sovereignty; the federal government responded quickly to Aird's call by establishing in 1932 the Canadian Radio Broadcasting Commission as chosen instrument for that purpose.

Far more common, however, has been the tendency for communication media to be deployed in manners supportive of continental integration; indeed, it may be fairly said that Canada as a nation persists despite, not because of, communication media.[15] Such is one theme of this book.

Canadian broadcasting is perhaps the starkest illustration. In spite of legislated pronouncements requiring the broadcasting system to contribute to Canadian unity and be an expression of Canadian identity,[16] 78 per cent of prime time programs diffused and rediffused by licensed Canadian television and cable television undertakings originate in the United States. Indeed, foreign programming accounts for 76 per cent of prime time viewing by English-speaking Canadians.[17]

Nor is television broadcasting by any means the sole reason for contending that Canada persists despite, not because of, electronic communication. From the inception of the Canadian telegraph, as another illustration, integration between the Canadian and u.s. industries was close. Most frequently telegraph lines were constructed to link a Canadian centre with important u.s. metropolises, sometimes even precluding for years thereafter direct connections to other Canadian communities and provinces. Early in the history of the Canadian industry, the dominant company (Montreal Telegraph) entered into a continental cartel as a full-fledged member; exclusive territories were apportioned, prices fixed, and connections with non-members restricted. Then, by 1881, virtually all the Canadian industry had tumbled into u.s. hands, only hesitatingly to re-emerge under Canadian ownership with the inception of Canadian Pacific Telegraphs a few years later.

The Canadian telephone industry, by and large, has followed a similar trend. Within four years of the first telephone conversation, control over both the patent and a Canada-wide charter had been sent south of the border. Nor did Bell Canada, even today this country's largest telephone company, fully extricate itself from u.s. control until the mid-1970s.

Turning to 'new technologies,' we see that satellite communication, while residing under Canadian ownership since inception, is exemplary of what Harold Innis termed 'space binding media,' helping efface local culture by facilitating the spread of 'global consciousness.' Cable television, yet another of the new technologies, has had similar effect. Likewise, computer networks extend the hegemony of transnational corporations, speeding instructions from headquarters to distant localities and then facilitating data retrieval and processing.

Widespread belief in the doctrine of Canadian technological nationalism is thus hard to fathom, and the three major sections of this book attempt to set the record straight on the first of our myths. The telegraph is studied in chapters 3 to 5; the telephone in chapters 6 to 15; and broadcasting and 'new technologies' in chapters 16 to 19.

THE SECOND MYTH: TECHNOLOGICAL DEPENDENCE

There is a second and possibly more virulent myth running through the Canadian policy literature. The doctrine of technological nationalism postulates that Canadians have purposefully deployed systems of communication for nation-building, but, paradoxically, the myth of technological dependence asseverates that we have few options in deploying industrial techniques. The industrial arts in this perspective are outcomes of a necessary, indeed evolutionary, process of ever-expanding reach.

More precisely the myth of technological dependence encompasses dual doctrines of *technological imperative* and *technological determinism*. The former holds that the march of engineered artefacts is necessary, 'in the order of things,' subject to little human direction or control. The latter posits that all important human phenomena – cultures, distribution of power, belief systems, industrial structures, and so forth – are explainable by the evolution of these same industrial devices. Stated thus starkly, the doctrines seem incredible, and the reader is justified in questioning whether such beliefs are widely held at all. Note, however, some extracts from official government-policy documents.

The first example of the doctrine of the technological imperative is from the Therrien committee, reporting to the Canadian Radio-television and Telecommunications Commission (CRTC) in 1980 on the extension of broadcasting to the North: 'This new technological universe is no longer to be regarded as visionary; it already taking shape at a pace that is inexorable.'[18]

This report, prepared under the direction of the late Réal Therrien, then a CRTC commissioner, is of particular importance to Canadian broadcasting because it laid the foundation for distribution by satellite of television signals, not only to northern and remote communities but to cable systems in the populous southern regions, enabling the former to become more completely 'integrated' into the Canadian cultural mainstream while permitting southern audiences to avail themselves of yet more U.S.-originated programming. In the committee's view, these developments were 'inexorable.'

Other examples abound. In 1981 the Department of Communications published a book by two senior officials, Shirley Serafini and Michel Andrieu, which acknowledged a number of problems inhering in an information revolution. National sovereignty, the authors advised, may be eroded as information devices meld countries politically and economically; and national culture may be enfeebled as centrally produced information products blanket the globe through satellites and related terrestrial machinery. Possibilities of continued and indeed increasing structural unemployment as a result of automated information processes were acknowledged and declared particularly disconcerting; likewise, the erosion of both privacy and civil liberties and the depersonalization of communications ('electronic hermit').[19] Whether the authors were correct in their prognostications is beside the main point here; for present purposes what is most pertinent was their declination to offer advice how these perceived fall-outs could be mitigated, for, 'Like the industrial revolution, the information revolution is unavoidable.'[20]

For Serafini and Andrieu this information revolution is a 'world wide phenomenon causing structural changes in the economies of all countries, regardless of national differences in institutional arrangements or public policies.'[21] Being unavoidable it should therefore, in their view, be embraced and promoted: 'Canada has no choice but to promote vigorously introduction of the new technology ... A nationalist approach based strictly on homegrown technology is bound to fail ... The only strategy with a chance of success is one which attempts to take advantage of the benefits of the technology with respect to devising new products and improving productivity. Any attempt to slow down the revolution out of concern for possible employment effects will backfire.'[22]

This information revolution, according to Serafini and Andrieu, touches 'virtually every aspect of our economic, social, cultural and political life as a people.'[23] None the less, they also declare 'the new information technology [to be] "a solution in search of problems."'[24] The irony is inescapable.

Potential benefits are not slighted, however; to the contrary, new goods and services, wider availability of information, opportunities for greater job satisfaction, and elimination of dangerous jobs[25] are cited as likely outcomes. None the less, the authors make no attempt to weigh these perceived benefits against the disruption and dislocation also envisaged. Proceeding with caution, in their view, is simply not an option; we face 'the technological imperative itself.'[26]

Subsequently, Francis Fox, in official capacity as minister of communications, reiterated these themes, concluding that 'Regardless of whether one approves or disapproves of these developments, it is clear that Canada has no option but to vigorously embrace the development and dissemination of these technologies.'[27]

This theme of technological imperative recurs often in publications from the federal Department of Communications. Here is an example from the recent *Communications for the Twenty-First Century*:

In the past three or four decades we have come to rely progressively on the creation, communication and consumption of information as a source of jobs, wealth and social progress, and less on the exploitation of raw materials and physical labour. This trend will almost certainly continue into the foreseeable future ... Canada's transition to an information society is, to paraphrase Clemençeau, too important an issue to be left to the specialists. The changes in economic and social life which the information society will bring about should be of concern to every Canadian, since they will affect the way we live, the way we work, how we are educated, how we use our leisure time and how we interact with others in our communities, across the country and throughout the world.[28]

Of course, social, political, economic, and cultural changes, related to advances in communication media, *are* occurring. Canada *is* becoming an information economy: upwards of 50 per cent of the workforce now have electronic work-stations with which to interact;[29] so-called 'producer service industries' (business management, accounting, legal, finance, consulting, etc.), all heavily dependent upon the production and exchange of information, are of much greater relative importance to the economy than hitherto; banking is now an interconnected electronic information processing/distribution system; regional and national businesses are giving way increasingly to global enterprises, a trend facilitated by improved telecommunications. That changes such as these have occurred and are continuing seems incontestable. The critique presented here, rather, is at a deeper level.

For what is omitted in the Canadian government's policy literature on the information revolution is reference to the factors lying behind its 'imminence' – for example, the billions upon billions of dollars spent annually by governments to fuel this same information revolution. One searches in vain the Canadian policy literature for material linking military procurement to telecommunication innovations, despite the fact that the world's leading defence contractors, almost without exception, specialize in electronics or aerospace.[30] The civil activities of these military suppliers span the globe, encompassing communications hardware and software, carriage, and content. The literature is silent too on the enhancement through sophisticated telecommunications of transnationals' ability to bypass domestic regulations on data.[31] Rather, it is content to propagate the myth of inexorability.

Not only is Canada's future as an information economy said to be set, but so is the transformation of many hitherto important cultural, political, and social relationships. Our Department of Communications claims 'this new information technology [to be] a "transformative" technology that will radically change the way we work and live.'[32] And note how well the august Science Council of Canada melds the doctrines – of technological imperative and technological determinism (our term, used to encapsulate the notion of engineered devices determining culture, belief systems, industrial and social structures, and so forth) – in the following pithy paragraph: 'Current advances in microelectronics are causing a worldwide technological revolution which *all* societies *must* accommodate. This revolution may cause fundamental changes in human thought and action.'[33]

Likewise, in 1971 the Telecommission (an official task force on the future of telecommunications in Canada) declared: 'Technology has fundamentally transformed the human condition twice before [reference being to the Agricultural and Industrial revolutions] ... How the third technological revolution will *shape our ends* is still far from clear but its nature and substance are already becoming familiar ... Ours is ... a society built upon and shaped by technology.'[34]

One finds here no hint that procedures, machines, and equipment are introduced by *people* – particularly by agglomerations (corporations and governments) – and only in being wielded do they 'shape our ends.' How different a reading would be given to the information revolution if the foregoing extract were to read: 'Twice before, certain privileged people invested heavily to introduce and deploy industrial equipment and procedures in ways that fundamentally transformed the human condition ... How governments and mega-corporations are currently reshaping our ends is still far from clear, but the nature and substance of these changes are already becoming familiar. Ours is ... a society built upon and shaped by mega-corporations.'

Like *Instant World*, DOC's *Communications for the Twenty-First Century* also boldly proclaims: 'Like all industrialized countries, Canada is in the midst of a profound shift in the foundations of economic and social life.'[35]

Why are all industrialized countries experiencing such a profound shift, if they are? Who decreed this to be so? The answer most always given is 'Technology.'

Again, announcing a new broadcasting policy for Canada in 1983, the Department of Communications declared: 'The new broadcasting environment is simply one facet of that sweeping, international movement. Based on the proliferation of new technologies and computer-communications services for the creation of knowledge and transmission of information, this "information revolution" is now taking Canada into a new, cultural, economic and social world where there are few existing rules.'[36]

There are in these declarations, and others like them,[37] scarcely veiled allusions to the doctrine of technological determinism. In each, 'technology' is said to be imposing *new* rules, *new* goals, *new* values, *new* ethics, implying that it is retrogressive and futile to apply old criteria, old goals, and old values and ethics to direct, shape, or modify deployment of 'new technologies.' The 'good,' in other words, is neither given nor is it to be discovered; values are mutable, and imposed by exogenously evolving 'technology.'

Again, in the foregoing extracts, 'change,' 'technology,' the 'new broadcasting environment,' the 'revolution,' and the 'technological universe' are presented as being active; humans adapt. Canadians 'have no option' but to run the race and implement with haste the 'new technologies' even though, the authors assert, there will be dramatic and unforeseen political, social, and cultural consequences. Such posture mythologizes 'technology' by effacing all 'soiling trace of origin or choice.'

Openness to and inevitability of an infinite future with neither horizons nor boundaries; transcendence beyond anachronistic 'folk' categories like right and wrong, good and evil; the finality of becoming – these all are Nietzschean notions[38] and constitute an essential, albeit implicit, philosophical underpinning of the information revolution. This particular philosophical outlook, however, gives rise to what Jacques Ellul has aptly termed the 'insidious ethics of adaptation.' Ellul writes: 'Since technique is a fact, we should adapt ourselves to it. Consequently, anything that hinders technique ought to be eliminated, and thus adaptation itself becomes a moral criterion.'[39]

In the concluding chapter we shall review the genesis of this 'self-propelling' information revolution and postulate some reasons for its so successful propagation. For the present, it is sufficient to point out that the dual doctrines of technological dependence (technological imperative and technological determinism) deflect attention away from the wielders of industrial techniques. In contrast, this book redirects our gaze and understanding – away from the myth of 'technology' and onto the underlying motivators: the wielders of industrial equipment, products, and processes. It is in this regard that the present work is most essentially an exercise in demystification, for it reintroduces the 'soiling trace of origin or choice.'

The present work contends further that a dialectic of dominance and dependence is key to comprehending deployment of communication contrivances in the telecommunications field. Dominance and dependence through devices for communicating are crucial to our understanding developments in the industrial arts, industrial structures, and even international relations. 'Technology' is here viewed as a mythic cover-up, sometimes consciously invoked but often unobtrusively taken for granted as part of our culture, whereby some – the controllers of technique – exert power over others – customers, employees, rivals, and even governments.

Historical awareness is essential for dispelling today's myths of technological dependence. By refusing to neglect power, greed, and the struggle for dominance in the historical account of the emergence and development of Canadian communications, this book challenges the current mythology that Canada is entering an information revolution *because of* some engineering inexorability. This myth successfully laid to rest, it follows that future cultural, political, and social consequences ensuing from applications of industrial technique should be ascribed to human agents, not to some autonomous, impersonal process. Unfortunately, human responsibility for outcomes is currently being obscured by the shrill cry of 'information revolution.'

A THIRD MYTH: TECHNOLOGY AND INDUSTRIAL STRUCTURING

Less sweeping but still in keeping with technological determinism are these three claims: that efficient and existing industrial structures hinge on underlying technique (the doctrine of 'natural monopoly,' for example, recently recast as 'uneconomic bypass');[40] that publishing, telegraphs, telephones, and broadcasting for many years constituted separate industries *because of* unique, underlying industrial arts; and that industrial applications of scientific knowledge ('technological evolution') are now *forcing* convergence among these industrial sectors.[41]

With respect to natural monopoly in Canadian telephones and telegraphs, detailed historical account reveals that machines and equipment per se had little if any impact in structuring industries. On the contrary, patterns of control over these devices explain fully the emergence and sustenance of monopoly, and what was true in the past remains true today. Recurrent restrictive industrial practices that were conceived with the birth of the electric telegraph, that were finely honed in the early years of telephony, and that persist in Canadian telecommunications to this day include: predatory pricing, merger, inflated acquisition prices, manipulation of corporate form, intimidation, deception, anti-competitive cross-subsidy, refusal to interconnect, vertical integration, exclusionary reciprocity agreements, collusive deals, 'public relations,' and politicking.

The temptation to point out the striking parallels between the early history of Canadian telecommunications and current issues/tactics is, for stylistic reasons, resisted in the following chapters. Although these parallels will become obvious enough as the book unfolds, it is perhaps appropriate to cite a few examples here, which, with an array of others, may be located in the text. The current refusal of telephone companies to interconnect CNCP Telecommunications with local loops for long-distance competition has obvious parallels with the refusal long ago of both telephone and telegraph companies to interconnect rivals. Bell Canada's recent threat to disconnect the Bank of Montreal if the latter utilizes a competitor's equipment replays the tactic of intimidation used by carriers in the early years, for example, Western Union to gain control of Montreal Telegraph Company. Corporate spin-offs such as Tele-Direct mirror previous ploys at manipulating corporate form (for example, the creation of Bell Canada's clandestine telephone subsidiary in Winnipeg, which in 1885 undercut both Bell and the true competition). Likewise, continuing vertical integration between Bell Canada and Northern Telecom parallels a historical integration of content and carriage in the telegraph industry that persisted until 1910; both are examples of extending a monopoly from one activity to another, with distinct advantages given the carrier. Finally, non-compensatory pricing in telecommunications today replays pricing practices in the early years of telephony and telegraphy. Such parallels having been explicitly made, the reader is now encouraged to extend the examples indefinitely while considering the material to follow.

Another factor belying the doctrine of natural monopoly is the government's historical and continuing function of structuring industries – by bestowing or withdrawing exclusive privileges; by empowering, condoning, or inhibiting restrictive and predatory business practices; and by simply but ineluctably establishing the 'rules of the game.' Initially charters, franchises, and governmental grants were pivotal in establishing monopoly; today, regulatory rulings and licensing often serve the purpose of preserving it.

It is not merely with respect to the creation and preservation of monopoly in Canadian telecommunications that one detects a rich and continuing pattern of business practice, but also with the convergences and divergences of industrial sectors. Although a superficially persuasive case is sometimes made that years ago the nature of the underlying industrial arts necessitated fundamentally diverse industrial structures and legal/policy frameworks (see table 1.1 for details), careful historical analysis reveals otherwise. Rather, industrial and governmental powerplays, not mere machines, were decisive in causing the initial divergences. These prototypical powerplays continue today, restructuring and converging markets. None the less, visionaries currently are declaring, erroneously, that it is 'technology' which is imposing a convergence (more accurately, a reconvergence) among publishing, telecommunications, and broadcasting.[42] In this regard, the inauguration of digital techniques for transmission is most frequently cited as being key to comprehending such developments. Digitalization means that all types of messages – voice, video, print, data, photograph – are electronically encoded into a series of on/off pulses for purposes of transmission. But although various forms of message origination now frequently share digitized transmission networks, this sharing (confluence) among previously separate industrial sectors and transmission pathways should not be ascribed to mere digitalization.

Upon its inception and for more than seventy years thereafter, telegraphy was closely integrated with the daily press because telegraph companies not merely relayed press despatches but composed them as well. Likewise, telephony and telegraphy were initially highly integrated, both mechanically and institutionally. Furthermore, telephony played such an important role in the development of broadcasting that for years the latter was known simply as radio telephony. These various markets and services, then, could *always* have made

TABLE 1.1
Classical characteristics of three sectors of the communications industry

	Publishing	Broadcasting	Telecommunications
'Technology'	Printing press	Transmitters	Wires, cables, switching centres
Competition and entry conditions	Easy entry, market forces	Limited entry, apportionment of frequencies through licences	Monopolistic; licences, franchises, and charters; high entry barriers
Vertical integration	Complete between carriage and content	Complete between carriage and content	Absent, a common carrier
Regulation and special legislation	Market forces, copyright law	Cultural regulation, licensing: Broadcasting Act, Radio Act	Public utility regulation of prices and profits: Railway Act charters
Services	Information distributed from central point to customers who pay directly, frequently financed also by advertising	Information radiated broadly to audiences who pay only indirectly (advertising or taxation)	Transport of messages originated by customers who pay directly
Nature of the communication	Point to mass, largely one-way communication	Point to mass, one-way communication	Point to point, two-way communication
Aims of public policy	Market-place of ideas; protection of authors' rights	Nation-building, social and cultural improvement, market-place of ideas	Just and reasonable access; low cost, efficient, universal service; common carriage
Current strains on industry structure and public policy	Unauthorized electronic duplication at locations decentralized from centre of original publication	Audience fragmentation, increasing market-place pressures	Erosion of common carriage through integration with computers; maintaining universality of service given increasing competition

use of common facilities and techniques. The services and companies purveying them in fact diverged simply by dint of corporate agreement to split markets to reduce competition always with government compliance, whether explicit or implicit.

If the divergences that took place in the past cannot accurately be attributed to the equipment used, then neither can the convergences today. Separation versus convergence of communication markets, services, and products is an issue that today should be understood as being quite independent of the state of the mechanical arts. This point too is developed at length in the text.

One thing that current convergence or reconvergence among publishing, telecommunications, and broadcasting *is* accomplishing, however, is a dismantling of legal/policy frameworks within which the three industries functioned for so long. This process is euphemistically termed 'deregulation.' Increasing competition within broadcasting, for example, fostered by a largely deregulated cable TV industry, satellites, VCRS, and so forth, is currently making less viable pursuit of administered non-market social and cultural goals, even while increasing the freedom of certain corporations to manoeuvre. Likewise, applications of computer technology are giving telecommunications firms characteristics and functions of publishers, all the while throwing into question the extent to which they can continue being treated as common carriers. The advent of new competition in telecommunications is challenging that industry's public utility status, and the merging of publishing and telecommunications techniques is making the legal framework suitable for publishing problematic. Exponents of such deregulation may find 'technological causation' useful to propagate as justification for these developments, but usefulness of a doctrine and its truthfulness are not necessarily coexistent.

A further goal of this book is to extricate 'Technology' from these trends and to pinpoint through historical account corporate power as the motivating force. Once accomplished, it is hoped that policy will no longer lag events but help direct them.

A FOURTH MYTH: EFFICACY OF REGULATION

Regulation of Canadian telecommunications exists to protect subscribers from abuses of unrestrained monopoly power, or so it is commonly contended. However, as eminent economist and former U.S. senator Paul H. Douglas observed long ago, 'Wherever government controls a business, it becomes inevitable that the business should try to control the government.'[43]

In brief, it is sometimes argued that regulatory agencies, far from protecting the public from the ravages of monopoly, perhaps invariably become captured by the very industries they 'regulate,' aiding continued monopolization. In the words of Adams and Brock, 'The regulatees [come] to recognize that the better part of wisdom [is] not to abolish regulation but to utilize it.'[44]

Fresh insight into this issue is attained through detailed scrutiny of Canadian telecommunications history. In summary, it is concluded that Canada's major telephone company has had quite an easy time of it, being subjected only sporadically to effective regulation, particularly between 1976 and 1983, at which time it cast off what it perceived to be unwarranted and obtrusive regulatory shackles by 'reorganizing.' This discussion is found at chapter 10 and following.

YET ANOTHER MYTH: GALES OF CREATIVE DESTRUCTION

In 1942 Joseph Schumpeter wrote a now classic treatise, *Capitalism, Socialism and Democracy*, wherein he propounded the theory of 'creative destruction.' Not to worry about private monopolies, Schumpeter assuaged, since 'long-run monopoly must be of the rarest occurrence.'[45] 'New technologies,' capitalistic innovation, and the entrepreneurial spirit are quite sufficient to protect the public because in combination they give rise to a 'perennial gale of creative destruction';[46] old monopolies, reliant upon old processes and equipment, wither away in the wake of the new.

In more recent years Schumpeter's thesis has been taken up and embellished by the so-called 'Chicago theorists,' of whom George Stigler is exemplary. To neoclassicists like Stigler 'it is virtually impossible to eliminate competition from economic life. If a firm buys up all of its rivals, new rivals will appear. If a firm secures a lucrative patent on some desired good, large investments will be made by rivals to find alternative products or processes to share the profits of the first firm. If the state gives away monopoly privileges (such as TV channels), there will emerge a strong competition in the political area for these plums.'[47] Hence, neoclassical economists like Stigler spend a great deal of time and effort ferreting out and analysing the 'pervasiveness' of competitive pressures, content that monopoly, if detected at all, must surely be of 'minor' and 'transitory' concern.[48]

The history of telecommunications in Canada puts the Schumpetarian/Chicago treatise to the acid test. We shall discover below that engineering innovations, although frequently disruptive to the established industrial power alignments, have most generally been absorbed within the prevailing structure of power. When government policy and agreements among incipient rivals not to compete did not do the job, the results were achieved through cut-throat practices and corporate take-overs. Technical innovation alone, then, is quite inadequate to disassemble monopoly structures. Interventionist regulatory policy is a co-requisite. This too is a recurring theme of the book.

OUTLINE

Following a brief chapter describing current industry structure and types of apparatus used in provisioning services, the story of telecommunications in Canada begins with the birth of the electric telegraph. It ends, sixteen chapters later, with the modern era of electronic publishing. Along the way, definite patterns emerge. The early integration of the telegraph with the daily press, subsequent and deliberate segregation, and reconvergence today with the onset of electronic publishing, videotex, and computer communications parallel phases of another story: the early integration of the telephone and the telegraph, subsequent and deliberate segregation, and current reconvergence with digital transmission techniques and computer communications. And these two histories parallel the early integration of broadcasting with telephones, their subsequent and deliberate segregation, and current reconvergence with cable TV and satellites. Throughout, emphasis is afforded corporate power plays, recurrent predatory and restrictive trade practices, and government policy in structuring, segregating, and converging industries. As well, we see that legal/policy frameworks most usually have arisen after the fact, to justify or cope with what industrial power had already consummated.

U.S. ownership and control over Canadian telecommunications is another strand woven in the historical account, as is the insufficiency of Canadian governmental responses. Both trends help to put into proper historical perspective the doctrine of technological nationalism.

As well our journey back in time places in relief numerous current issues in Canadian broadcasting, telecommunications, and publishing: for example, the pros and cons of yet further reintegrating responsibilities for content and carriage; the efficacy of regulatory techniques for preventing monopoly pricing; issues arising from competition in telecommunications; 'rate rebalancing' and the accompanying threat to continued universality of telephone service; interconnection; corporate restructurings as means of bypassing regulation; government subsidization of innovation and the perpetuation of power; government-apportioning privilege; and 'privatization' of communication sectors in Canada.

The concluding chapter parallels closely the current one, and readers may choose to peruse it concurrently with this introduction. That chapter too addresses a ubiquitous myth of our day, inevitability of an 'information revolution.'

Finally, it is hoped that the ensuing historical account constituting the heart of this book will cast fresh light upon the literature of the information revolution, which so often abstracts from the nitty-gritty of actual institutions, corporate and governmental powerplays, rivalries, and greed to proclaim a vision of an inevitable future grounded on and evolving through information 'technology.' By stressing the importance of government policy, of corporate behaviour, and of the flexibility of communication devices, the author hopes that we will perceive the future to be within our grasp and realize that *we* bear full responsibility for it. That, ultimately, is the purpose of the book.

2

Telecommunications Today

TELECOMMUNICATIONS DEFINED

Literally 'communicating over distance,' and in that broad sense encompassing also the transportation of messages fixated on tangible form, the term *telecommunications* is currently confined to the meaning: 'any transmission, emission or reception of signs, signals, writing, images, sounds or intelligence of any nature, by wire, radio, optical or other *electromagnetic* systems.'[1] 'Telecommunications,' therefore, in modern usage denotes the transmittal of messages by electromagnetic spectrum, as opposed to either human travel or the transporting of messages enscribed on a palpable medium.[2] Telecommunications encompasses visual semaphores (an ancient art) as well as the electric telegraph, the telephone, radio and television broadcasting, cable television, and newer media and activities such as communication satellites, computer communications (telematics), and electronic publishing. The present book touches on all of these, but for reasons noted now, central position is afforded the telephone.

SUPREMACY OF THE TELEPHONE

For seventeen years prior to 1968, when the claim passed to our southerly neighbours, Canadians held the distinction of being the most talkative people on earth, at least as far as using the telephone was concerned.[3] In 1987 Canadians engaged in some 37 billion telephone conversations, 1436 per person.[4]

Call volumes are contingent in part on service availability, and in this area Canadians lack little. Almost 99 per cent of Canadian

TABLE 2.1
Components of Canadian telecommunications carriage industry
(19 largest carriers)

Company	1987 operating revenues		1987 total assets	
	$ millions	% of total	$ millions	% of total
Telesat Canada	118	1.0	469	1.8
CNCP				
Telecommunications	317	2.7	451	1.7
Bell Canada	6,378	53.6	13,508	51.2
Other carriers	5,085	42.7	11,967	45.3
TOTAL*	11,898	100.0	26,395	100.0

* Includes 19 carriers, which together account for over 98 per cent of
telecommunications carriage in Canada. In addition to the major telephone
companies, Telesat Canada, CNCP, and Teleglobe Canada are included.
SOURCE: CRTC, *Annual Report, 1987–8*, 69

households have at least one telephone set (compared with 92 per
cent in the United States). Virtually all Canadian businesses avail
themselves of telephone service. In 1987 there were 11.2 million residential telephone instruments, and 13.4 million access lines (52.1 per
100 people).[5]

The telephone industry has certainly usurped the position of predominance once enjoyed by the telegraph. As the table 2.1 shows,
revenues in 1987 from electronic message transmissions (voice, data,
image, and record, but excluding broadcast transmissions to the home
and cable TV) totalled $11.9 billion; of which merely 2.7 per cent
accrued to CNCP Telecommunications,[6] remnant of the once powerful
telegraph industry. Even for CNCP the traditional telegram or public
record message service has dwindled to less than 10 per cent of corporate revenues. Telephone carriers, meanwhile, garnered $11.1 billion
from message-transmission operations.[7]

Among Canada's smaller telecommunications carriers, Telesat Canada is of particular interest. Established by statute in 1969 with a
mandate to own and operate all domestic commercial communication
satellite systems, Telesat is owned equally by major terrestrial common carriers and the federal government. It is also a member of
Telecom Canada, the consortium of telephone companies known

TABLE 2.2
Telcommunications industry revenues by sector, 1985:
telephone, radio, and television broadcasting; cable TV

	1985 revenues ($ billions)	% of total
Telphone industry	9.963	70.6
Private radio broadcasting	0.579	4.1
Private television broadcasting	0.961	6.8
CBC Radio Canada	1.067	7.6
Cable TV	0.672	4.8
Other telecommunication carriers†	0.874	6.2
TOTAL	14.116	100.0

* CBC receives parliamentary appropriations as well as revenues
  from operations. In the table CBCs revenues are calculated by
  adding revenues from operations to 'net cost of CBC operations.'
† Principally CNCP Telecommunications, Telesat Canada,
  Teleglobe Canada
SOURCE: Statistics Canada, *Telephone Statistics*, cat. no. 56–203;
Radio and Television Broadcasting, cat. no. 56–204; *Cable
Television*, cat. no. 56–205, CRTC, *Annual Report*, 1985–6

previously as the TransCanada Telephone System (TCTS). In 1987
Telesat's operating revenues were $118 million,[8] merely 1 per cent of
the revenues garnered by terrestrial telephone companies.

Also treated in this book are the radio and television broadcasting
industries and the cable television industry. Despite undisputed importance to the Canadian economy in terms of stimulating consumer
demand, importing culture, diffusing information, and filling so many
leisure hours of Canadians,[9] these broadcast-related sectors are dimin-
uitive alongside the telephone industry (see table 2.2); overall, telecommunications carriage revenues are more than four times greater
than broadcast/cable revenues combined. None the less, in terms of
penetration, television about equals that of the telephone, with 98 per
cent of Canadian households having at least one television set. In
1987, 65.5 per cent of households subscribed to cable TV.[10]

At the heart of the Canadian telecommunications system, then, is
the telephone industry. All other sectors and activities – telegraph,
broadcasting, cable TV, satellites, electronic publishing – touch closely

upon it, but are dwarfed by it. A more extended description of the configuration of the telephone industry is thus warranted at this point, while relevant aspects of the other sectors will be dealt with as the need arises.

FACILITIES CONFIGURATION

The telephone network is made up of five components: terminals, access facilities, local distribution, exchanges, and long lines. Brief descriptions of each follow.

Terminals These are devices for initiating and/or receiving messages. For much of the industry's history, the only terminals connected to the system were telephone sets, devices that electronically encode and decode voice messages. More recently a plethora of other instruments has been connected to the network (computers, facsimile machines, teletypewriters, and so on). Moreover, analogue or continuous transmissions are increasingly giving way to digital encoding and transmission, whereby information inputs in the form of waves are sampled, made discreet, assigned magnitudes, and thence encoded as bursts of electric current. Digital transmissions improve fidelity (not being subject to noise or interference) and are compatible with digital computers.[11]

Telephone companies in many developed countries are currently digitizing their networks with the aim of implementing a so-called Integrated Services Digital Network (ISDN), based on the dual principles of superabundant capacity and digital transmissions. With ISDN, any communicating device (telephone, television set, facsimile machine, computer and so on) can be plugged into this 'single integrated network.'

Access Facilities[12] Traditionally, telephone sets have been connected to central offices (exchanges) by pairs of twisted copper wire, ('local loops'), one loop being assigned each single-line telephone and partylines sharing loops. Because copper pair wires in the analogue mode are severely constrained in message-carrying capacity, they are being replaced by fibre optical cables, which when transporting digital messages become part of ISDN. Radio waves, as with cellular radio, are alternative means of interlinking telephone sets with switching centres.

An additional locally based distribution system, composed of coax-ial cable, is owned by cable television companies; it possesses transmis-sion capacity several hundred times that of analogue copper pair wire. Cable systems have been continuing irritants to the telephone industry, and the latter's movement into ISDN may be explained in part by its intent to remonopolize urban telecommunications.

Local Distribution In the past, 'local distribution' included what are today referred to as 'access facilities' as well as trunk cables connecting local exchanges. In present usage, 'local distribution' denotes only these latter, interexchange trunks.

Exchanges Local exchanges, or central offices (also known as switch-ing centres), make connections between terminals; that is, they route calls to desired destinations, often through a hierarchy of switches. The first exchanges were manual switchboards requiring operators to insert plugs. Beginning in the 1890s a series of mechanical exchanges (first 'step-by-step,' then 'crossbar') substituted for switchboard opera-tors. Today these mechanical switches are being replaced by digital computers.

Long Lines Intercommunity communication is provided by various devices ranging from coaxial cables and microwave systems to fibre optical cables and communication satellites. Currently, one of the most hotly contested policy issues concerns the extent to which long-distance transmission media owned by companies other than tele-phone companies should be allowed to interconnect with monopolized access facilities.

SERVICES CONFIGURATION

Telephone operations may also be decomposed along service lines. Service costing, which entails the ascribing of plant utilization to service classifications, has been the object of recent attention. Because services frequently make use of common facilities, however, there is no necessary, one-to-one correspondence between system components and services. Moreover, there are numerous alternative and sometimes mutually incompatible systems for categorizing services.

Traditionally, telephone companies have been viewed as providing but two classes of service: local exchange and long distance. Long

TABLE 2.3
Breakdown of Bell Canada revenues, 1983

	$ billions	% of total
Non-competitive		
local services	1.389	29.3
toll services	1.988	41.9
Competitive		
network	0.386	8.1
terminal	0.878	18.5
Common (unclassifiable)	0.099	2.1
TOTAL	4.740	100.0

distance is sometimes further broken down into public message toll versus private line, the latter generally providing unlimited or maximum call volumes of a specified nature to a given party for a flat fee. In 1987 the Canadian telephone industry received $4.1 billion in local revenues (36.7 per cent of total revenues), $6.1 billion in toll or long-distance revenues (55.2 per cent), and $0.9 billion from other offerings (directory advertising, for example).[13]

Sometimes distinctions are made between competitive and non-competitive services. For 1983 Bell Canada[14] subdivided its total revenues along the lines shown in table 2.3.

Another way of classifying telecommunication carrier services is by distinguishing voice from non-voice originations or transmissions. The telephone instrument was conceived in 1876 to provide the former (the word 'telephone' is derived from the Greek, meaning 'speech over distance'), whereas the telegraph for nearly forty years preceding had been providing the latter ('telegraph' meaning 'writing over distance'). As developed in subsequent chapters, the distinction between voice and non-voice transmissions, still important from a policy perspective, has never been inherent in the medium of transmission.

A more recent approach distinguishes 'basic' from 'enhanced' transmissions. Formulated originally by the u.s. Federal Communications Commission (FCC), basic services are defined as 'pure' transmissions of information while enhanced services add 'value' – by changing or acting on messages in some way. For voice communication, a simple long-distance call is a basic service; call storage and call forwarding are examples of enhanced services.[15]

DEFINITIONAL PROBLEMS

All classifactory schemes are at least somewhat arbitrary and subject to flux. Facilities are to a substantial degree substitutable, as illustrated by PBX (private branch exchange), which is at the same time a terminal and a switching device. Located on the customer's premises, it is called a terminal; when provided by the telephone company on its own premises, it is a 'centrex,' an exchange. Another example is packet switching, where transmission and switching are commingled; complete messages are broken into 'packets,' each addressed en route. Likewise, access facilities are substitutable for exchanges. The length of local loops can be decreased by building more switching centres, and conversely the number of central offices can be decreased by increasing the average length of loops. Therefore, when considering even the physical components of a telecommunications network, clear-cut distinctions are not always possible.

At the services level, problems in rigorous classification are even more pronounced because service classifications depend most often on either marketing decisions or regulatory rulings, both subject to sudden change. For instance, there is no inherent or technologically imposed distinction between a local and a long-distance call. Through extended area service (EAS) a program has been in effect for many years to treat as local certain calls previously defined for billing purposes as long distance or toll. Moreover, 'foreign exchanges' (FX) is a tariffed offering that allows a business with large call volumes from a distant city to attain listings in the distant telephone directory and have all calls placed through that number treated, for billing purposes, as local. In addition, in many areas of the United States 'local service' is priced per call according to time of day and duration ('usage sensitive rates'), the same billing principles used for long distance. Finally, satellites make transmission costs insensitive to distance, again belying clear distinctions between local and long distance. These situations thus imply that either call type can be easily reclassified if management (and the regulator) deem it appropriate.

Similarly, the distinction between non-competitive and competitive services is subject to flux, thanks largely to regulatory policy, which is of course subject to revision. Likewise, classifying services as either public or private hinges ultimately on marketing considerations because private or 'leased' lines are not usually physically separate from facilities used by the public switched service. Even application of the terms 'basic' and 'enhanced' to particular offerings has been fraught with difficulty and contention. (Is the partitioning of transmission pathways for resale, when coupled with call monitoring, an enhanced service?) [16]

To summarize, the telecommunications system is precisely that, a *system*, whose constituents (whether in terms of facilities or services) are overlapping, interdependent, and in flux. This plasticity has important repercussions on the vitality of entrants into selective telecommunication markets, and also on appropriate regulatory responses. As well it may mean that constituents, when classified in one manner, could lead analysts to certain policy conclusions or research findings, while alternative classifications could lead to contrary conclusions. In this regard the reader's attention is flagged to the alleged cross-subsidy of local service by long distance, a subject for analysis below. In any event it is always important to bear in mind the full system, even while concentrating on certain components.

TELEPHONE INDUSTRY STRUCTURE

The Canadian telephone industry (1987) is composed of 81 systems, of which merely 16 receive more than 98 per cent of industry revenues.

Bell Canada, by far the largest, accounts for more than 55 per cent of industry revenues. Federally regulated, it was formerly parent of the Bell Canada Group but in 1983, through a corporate reorganization, became a wholly owned subsidiary of BCE Inc. Bell Canada's service areas include most of Ontario and Quebec (about 62 per cent of the Canadian population) and the Northwest Territories. Subsidiaries or affiliates of Bell Canada include Tele-Direct (Publications) Inc., publisher of telephone directories and Yellow Pages; Bell Northern Research (30 per cent equity interest), an industrial research and development organization; Telesat Canada (24.6 per cent equity interest), providing satellite communication services; and Bell Canada Management Corporation (100 per cent), manager of investments of Bell Canada, including Bell Data Systems Inc., Bell Cellular Inc., and Computer Innovations Inc. [17]

BCE Inc., parent of Bell Canada, is a holding company that manages interests in telecommunications services, telecommunications equipment manufacturing, energy, financial services, printing, and real estate.[18] In addition to Bell Canada, BCE has interest in the following telephone companies: 31 per cent of Maritime Telegraph and Telephone Company, Limited, provincially regulated, principal provider of telephone service in Nova Scotia; 100 per cent of Télébec Ltée., a provincially regulated company servicing portions of Quebec, formed through Bell's purchase and consolidation or local, formerly independent, telephone companies; 53 per cent of NewTel Enterprises Limited, parent of Newfoundland Telephone Company Limited, provincially regulated, purveyor of telephone service in Newfoundland; 31 per cent of Bruncor Inc., parent of the New Brunswick Telephone Company, Limited, provincially regulated, exclusive supplier of telephone service in the province; and 99.8 per cent of Northern Telephone Limited, provincially regulated, serving portions of northern Ontario, principal exchanges being Timmins, Kirkland Lake, Kapuskasing, New Liskeard, Haileybury, and Cobalt.[19]

BCE has been the main beneficiary in the telecommunications field of the Mulroney government's policy of 'privatization.' In the spring of 1987 BCE acquired 30 per cent of Memotec Data Inc. for $196 million, following the latter's successful bid to acquire Teleglobe Canada, previously a Crown Corporation and exclusive supplier of overseas telecommunications links from Canada.[20] In the summer of 1988 BCE and affiliates spent a further $370 million to acquire Terra Nova Telecommunications and NorthwesTel, previously subsidiaries of Canadian National Railway Company, a Crown corporation. Terra Nova, acquired through Newtel Enterprises, serves 50,000 subscribers in Newfoundland, while NorthwesTel supplies service to 35,000 subscribers in portions of the Northwest Territories, Yukon, and northern regions of British Columbia.[21]

BCE is Canada's fourth-largest corporation in terms of sales and assets, and in 1985 it became the first domestic corporation to surpass $1 billion in profits.[22]

In eastern Canada the largest telephone company outside the BCE group is Québec-Téléphone, operating principally in the Lower St Lawrence River region, the Gaspé, and the north shore of the St Lawrence River as far east as Labrador; its service area incorporates 325 municipalities with population totalling 550,000, of which 227,000 are customers.[23] Québec-Téléphone is owned 50.6 per cent by Anglo-Canadian Telephone Company, a wholly owned subsidiary of General Telephone and Electronics Corp. of the United States. Québec-Télé-

phone is regulated by the province of Quebec. Other telephone companies in eastern and central Canada that are unaffiliated with Bell
Canada include Ontario Northland Communications (owned by the
Ontario government), providing long-distance connections to portions
of northern Ontario; and municipally owned systems in Thunder Bay,
Kenora, and Dryden. In all there are thirty-two independent telephone
companies in Ontario and eighteen in Quebec.

On the prairies there are no privately owned telephone companies;
all are regulated at the provincial level. In Manitoba the single entity
providing public voice service is the provincially owned Manitoba
Telephone System (MTS). In Saskatchewan the dominant carrier is
Saskatchewan Telecommunication (Sask Tel), owned by the provincial government and connecting with seventeen small, co-operatively
owned exchanges. In Alberta public telephone service is offered by
Alberta Government Telephones (AGT), provincially owned, and by
Edmonton Telephones, owned by the city.

In British Columbia there remain but three telephone companies: a
small, municipally owned system in Prince Rupert; NorthwesTel serving certain northern regions of the province; and the federally regulated British Columbia Telephone Company (BC Tel), owned 50.1 per
cent by Anglo-Canadian Telephone Company, a subsidiary of GTE
Corporation.[24]

Despite today's grandeur, the telephone industry had humble origins. Tracing through its development, and noting particularly the
spread of monopoly, segregation from the telegraph, vertical integration, and the practice of regulation, will cast light on current policy
issues and options. First, however, attention is focused on the telegraph, the initial mode of electronic telecommunications, which provides a fitting prologue to the story of the telephone.

PART II

The Telegraph

3

Onset of Electronic Communication

Although others anticipated electric telegraphy, some even giving practical demonstrations, it is generally to the English partnership of William Cooke and Charles Wheatstone, and to the American Samuel F.B. Morse, that credit for invention is given. Cooke and Wheatstone received their patent for England in June 1837 and in the following month successfully demonstrated a five-needle telegraph over a distance of $1\frac{1}{2}$ kilometres to directors of the London–Birmingham Railway. Their first permanent line was constructed the following year, alongside the Great Western Railway. None the less the public remained unimpressed until 1845, when sensational news coverage depicted the telegraph's role in capturing a murderer aboard a London-bound train. Informed by wire of the fugitive's destination, police were on hand as the train rolled into the station, a convincing demonstration that messages can travel quicker than people.[1]

In North America, homage is paid to Samuel F.B. Morse (1791–1872), artist and professor of fine art. Forty-one years of age in 1832, returning to New York City from three years of study abroad and possessing little knowledge of either electricity or electromagnetism, Morse seized upon the idea of transmitting intelligence electrically. The notion was sparked inadvertently in his imagination by a dinner conversation aboard ship, whereupon he is reputed to have exclaimed: 'If the presence of electricity can be made visible in any part of the circuit, I see no reason why intelligence may not be transmitted instantaneously by electricity.'[2]

From the outset Morse believed the electric telegraph would transform society. Anticipating McLuhan's vision of a global village by some 130 years, Morse likened telegraph lines to nerves diffusing 'knowledge of all that is occurring throughout the land ... with the speed of a thought.' The telegraph, he believed, would create 'one neighborhood of the whole country.'[3]

Private capital was hard to come by, however, and Morse had to lobby hard for six long years to wangle a $30,000 subsidy from the federal government to finance an experimental line between Washington, DC, and Baltimore, Maryland, about 40 miles. But finally the connection was completed, and on 24 May 1844 the first and still famous message was relayed: 'What hath God wrought?'

But interest *still* remained slack, so much so that the postmaster general rejected Morse's offer to sell patents to the government, remarking that he was 'not satisfied ... that under any rate of postage that could be adopted, its [the telegraph's] revenues could be made equal to expenditures.'[4] Therefore the government was quite happy to lease the Baltimore–Washington line back to Morse and his associates, and it was run thereafter as a private, commercial operation.[5]

Meanwhile, Morse and his backers formed America's first private telegraph company, the Magnetic, to connect New York and Philadelphia, subsequently joining the original Baltimore–Washington line. In addition to constructing lines through the Magnetic Telegraph Company, the Morse patent group also licensed others on a royalty basis.[6] Telegraphic construction soon became vigorous, and by 1846 all major cities in the eastern United States were connected, by which time lines approached the New York–Canadian border at Saratoga, Oswego, and Buffalo.[7]

PROVINCE OF CANADA

In Canada Samuel Morse was precluded from taking out a patent. Under legislation enacted in Lower Canada in 1823 and duplicated in Upper Canada in 1826, patents were granted only to British subjects and to residents.[8] This legislation continued in force after the two provinces united under one constitution in 1841 to form the single province of Canada, composed of Canada East (today Quebec) and Canada West (Ontario).

The legislation meant that the Canadian telegraph industry was inaugurated on somewhat different principles and under somewhat different incentives than the American. In the United States, the telegraph came to be promoted mostly by entrepreneurs intent on quick exploitation of the patent per se. Sloppy construction, patent infringements and litigation, disputes and shifting alliances among rival patent claimants, and cut-throat competition all characterized the early years of the u.s. industry.[9] By contrast, there could be no entrepreneurs in Canada intent merely on patent exploitation; there was no Canadian patent to exploit. Rather, the earliest pioneers of Canadian telegraphy were established businessmen whose primary interest lay in other fields but who recognized that the new invention could be applied advantageously to their affairs. In particular, newspaper owners, merchants, and soon the emerging railways took special interest in developing the Canadian telegraph. Some colonial governments encouraged its introduction, even giving direct financial assistance and exclusive charters, anticipating that the telegraph could stimulate commerce. None the less, with the onset of the 1850s, business practices in the two countries converged as the u.s. patent became devalued while the Canadian industry fell into the hands of industry 'captains,' particularly Hugh Allan's, beginning in 1851. Indeed, the Canadian experience during the 1850s and thereafter so closely parallels that of the United States that the former cannot be adequately understood except in the context of the latter.

In Canada the first practical demonstration of the telegraph was given on 24 July 1846 in Toronto's (then) Old City Hall by Mssrs Forbush and Humphreys,[10] whereupon the Toronto press became particularly excited and stepped up pressures for a Canadian telegraph, anxious as it was to establish connections with Buffalo. At the time European news was being funnelled to New York City and from there routed by telegraph to various inland cities, including Rochester and Buffalo; only thereafter was news forwarded to Toronto, and then only by Lake Ontario steamer – hardly a speedy final leg for the journey.

Approximately three months after the inaugural City Hall demonstration, the first Canadian telegraph company was organized – the Toronto, Hamilton & Niagara ElectroMagnetic Telegraph Company. Principal instigators were Clarke Gamble, a railway promoter and lawyer, who became president, and Thomas Denne Harris, a hardware merchant. Included on the initial board of directors were two more merchants, a wharf proprietor, and a bank cashier.[11] By December Toronto was connected to Hamilton and Queenston, the first message being relayed on 19 December between Hamilton and Toronto, about 40 miles.[12] In January 1847 the line was extended to Buffalo, and the Toronto papers were content at last.

In Canada East, or Quebec, harbinger of electronic communication was the Montreal & Toronto Magnetic Telegraph Company, organized on 29 December 1846 by the Montreal Board of Trade with the financial backing of local business leaders, including Andrew Shaw (its first president), James Dackers, MP, H.P. Dwight, and Hugh Allan (about whom more will be said soon). In July 1847 it attained a federal charter (Parliamentary Act of Incorporation) and became simply the Montreal Telegraph Company. Destined to dominate the Canadian industry for many years, Montreal Telegraph chose as its logo a mailed fist grasping lightning bolts, a familiar symbol for decades to come. By the end of its first year the company had opened twelve offices alongside its single line of wire connecting Trois Rivières and Toronto.[13]

A second company in Canada East received a federal charter in 1847 as well. This company was the British North American Telegraph Association, progeny of one Fred N. Gisborne (1824-92), unsung hero in the annals of Canadian telegraphy. Gisborne emigrated from England in 1845 and was hired by Montreal Telegraph in 1847 as operator for Montreal. Soon transferred to Quebec City when an office opened there,[14] Gisborne promptly resigned his post to organize the rival company with financial backing from local merchants. B.N.A. Telegraph's purpose was to connect Quebec with the Atlantic coast through New Brunswick and Nova Scotia. Lines were built as far east as Rivière du Loup (about 112 miles), but construction stopped abruptly when Gisborne failed to win from the New Brunswick government exclusive rights to build lines in that province.[15] Initial vision shattered, B.N.A. Telegraph languished for several years until its owners decided in 1851 to compete head-on with Montreal Telegraph, at which time construction was resumed in both directions to join Montreal in the west and Woodstock, N.B. Prices were cut (to $12\frac{1}{2}$ cents for ten words, exactly half Montreal Telegraph's rate), but the deep discounts were matched immediately by the larger rival, which had the luxury of cross-subsidizing losses on competitive routes through profits earned elsewhere. Therefore, B.N.A. Telegraph collapsed in 1856.[16]

NEW BRUNSWICK

Gisborne's company was probably doomed from the moment it was shut out of New Brunswick, but it must be realized that prior to Confederation (1867) commercial relations between the province of Canada and both New Brunswick and Nova Scotia were limited. Each jurisdiction imposed duties on goods entering from the other territories.[17] Consequently merchants of Saint John perceived their financial advantage to lie more in telegraphic connections with the u.s. seaboard than with Canada East; and they vigorously opposed Gisborne's application for an 'all red' route from Quebec to Halifax via Saint John. Instead, local support coalesced behind Lawson Darrow, u.s. agent for the Morse patentees, who proposed connecting Saint John with Calais, Maine, and Amherst, Nova Scotia. On 30 March 1848 the New Brunswick legislature acceded.[18] A further thirty years went by before Toronto and Montreal came to enjoy direct telegraphic links with New Brunswick and Nova Scotia.[19]

Even after incorporation of the New Brunswick Telegraph Company, construction stalled as capital remained in short supply. At this point the New York Associated Press, a co-operative news-gathering agency, stepped in, proposing to aid construction financially and further guaranteeing business volumes upon completion. In return it was to receive an exclusive right to use the line upon arrival of steamers from Europe for periods long enough to transmit dispatches of 3000 words, a concession ultimately important in establishing an Associated Press news monopoly in the United States.[20] Associated Press's chief interests, then, were reducing costs of news transmissions between Halifax and New York and gaining an upper hand on rivals. In January 1849 the provincial telegraph connecting Saint John and Calais (80 miles) was opened. A short-lived era of the pony express was about to expire, awaiting simply the completion of the Nova Scotia segment.

NOVA SCOTIA

Rebuffed in New Brunswick, Gisborne pressed on to Nova Scotia, there again applying for an exclusive charter. In this case the provincial government decided to reserve the prize for itself and created by legislative enactment Nova Scotia Government Telegraphs. None the less Gisborne was offered, and accepted, responsibility for building the government-owned line to connect Halifax and Amherst, about 125 miles. Upon completion in November 1849 Gisborne was named government telegraph director, a post he retained for two years until influential shipping magnate Samuel Cunard procured the facility at cost, renaming it the Nova Scotia Telegraph Company.[21] Gisborne's activity in pioneering Canadian telegraphy was far from finished, however, as we shall see.

THE TELEGRAPH AND INDUSTRIALIZATION

The birth of the Canadian telegraph coincided with the inauguration of both a daily press and rapid railroad construction. The three industries were in fact highly integrated from the outset, feeding upon and nourishing one another. In combination the emergence and rapid development of the telegraph, daily press, and railroad mirrored and helped propel Canadian industrialization, beginning about 1851.

When the telegraph came to British North America at the tail end of 1846, the province of Canada was still overwhelmingly rural, its economy extractive. Only a few commercial centres existed. Of the 1.1 million inhabitants (1841), about 40,000 lived in Montreal, the most populous and leading commercial centre, with a further 35,000 in Quebec City. The next largest town in Canada East was Trois Rivières, claiming a mere 3000 residents. In Canada West Toronto was the largest community, with 14,000 people, followed by Kingston with 6000.[22]

Moreover, the small, scattered rural communities of the new province were but loosely connected. Certainly, elaborate inland waterways were in place – the Welland and Rideau canals had been completed and the St Lawrence system of canals partially so[23] – but they were navigable only eight months of the year. For communities not adjoining navigable water routes, transportation and communication were slow and tortuous. Even in 1846 Canada East boasted but one short steam railroad (the Champlain and St Lawrence), while in Canada West the only analogous operation was a single horse-drawn railway.[24] Roads were not plentiful either, and those that did exist were 'mud pits in spring and fall, rutted tracks in summer.'[25] A trip from Montreal to Kingston took a day and a half by steamer and coach, even in the summer of 1847.[26]

None the less Montreal and to a lesser extent Toronto were thriving and bustling commercial centres. Being Canada's principal port, Montreal sustained

dealers in grain, barrel staves and potash, millers who ground American wheat into Canadian flour for export, forwarders and importers who dominated the Upper Canada trade. There were shipbuilders and shipowners with fleets of river vessels, bankers and insurance agents who financed and ministered to the export trades ... The city displayed a noisy, zestful variety of life: buoyant habitant farmers come to market in queues and *bonnet rouges*, uncertain new Scots immigrants in kilts and plaid, brisk Yankee traders, boisterous Irish labourers.[27]

THE PRESS CONNECTION

Although pioneer Canadian 'newssheets' had been published as early as 1752,[28] the modern conception of the newspaper, reporting the day's developments from across the country and around the globe for a mass audience, necessarily awaited the telegraph. Without its speed, press coverage of distant happenings lagged occurrence by days, even weeks. Meanwhile, telegraph companies were equally reliant on the burgeoning press to generate business volumes required to sustain the infant carriage industry; concessionary press rates resulted from and pointed to this latter dependence.[29]

But the interdependence of newspapers and telegraphs ran deeper still. 'From the day that poles and wires went up in Canada and the keys clicked in the operating rooms, telegraph companies collected and sold news to the newspapers and the newspapers were glad to get it.'[30] Indeed, apart from a few professional journalists in the largest cities the only non–locally based correspondents until 1910 *were* telegraph operators. Even as late as 1903 the Hamilton *Spectator* is depicted as spending merely $548 on 'correspondence' to employ four reporters, compared with $1719 on 'telegrams.'[31] Not until 1910 did responsibilities for news content become segregated from transmission – the principle of the common carrier. This divergence is described below.

THE RAILWAY CONNECTION

Industrialization entailed the conjunction of mass consumption and mass production. To this end newspapers were vital, being foremost a means for mass merchandising – for fanning consumerism.[32] Equally important, however, was improved transportation, principally the railroad, to deliver goods to market, and the 1850s was a period of intense railway construction. For example, the Great Western, joining Suspension Bridge to Windsor and providing important links to u.s. railroads, was completed in 1854. The Northern, running from Toronto to Collingwood, was finished in 1855, supplementing the more round-about water route from Lake Ontario to Georgian Bay. And in 1856 the Grand Trunk between Sarnia and Montreal was completed, with extensions in place by 1860 to Portland, Maine, and Rivière du Loup. Whereas in 1850 there had been merely 60 miles of railway line in Canada, a decade later there were more than 2000 miles of track.[33]

The telegraph, of course, was of immense importance in railway-building – for facilitating consultation with engineers, speeding progress reports to supervisors, aiding instruction of foremen, and ordering supplies. Moreover, after construction was completed, the telegraph remained essential for dispatching trains along the single-line tracks then predominant in North America.[34]

The railways, meanwhile, aided the monopolization of the telegraph industry by selling exclusive rights to construct telegraph line along railroad right-of-way. Such concessions proved especially useful to Montreal Telegraph Company, beginning in 1869.[35]

THE POSTAL SERVICE

A fourth element in this effervescent amalgam of emerging transportation and communication 'technologies' may be noted also: namely, inauguration of a 'mass' postal service, about 1851. Upgraded mail delivery had awaited improvements in transportation, particularly the railroad. Once begun, the mass postal service 'became an important element in the widespread dissemination of daily and weekly newspapers' as well as an important 'distribution device for retail goods.'[36]

ECONOMIC GROWTH

Industrialization during the 1850s was intense. The population of
Canada East and Canada West increased from 1.8 million in 1851 to
2.5 million in 1861,[37] becoming more urbanized in the process. Island
of Montreal residents increased from 78,331 to 118,015 in those years;
Toronto grew from 30,775 to 44,821; Quebec City from 42,052 to 59,990;
and Ottawa from 7760 to 14,669.[38] Railway-connected factory industries, notably in Toronto, Montreal, and Hamilton, proliferated in
response to demand generated by railway construction. And there
was a boom in the agricultural equipment industry, particularly in
Ontario. Indeed, the 7.3 per cent average annual rate of growth in GNP
during the 1850s exceeded that of any other decade of the nineteenth
century.[39]

The 1850s was also the time when 'captains of industry' came to
prominence in Canada, promoting railways, starting banks, commingling politics and commerce.[40] Hugh Allan was one of the most notable. Son of a shipmaster who traded for thirty years between Clyde,
Scotland, and Montreal, Hugh Allan became a towering figure in
nineteenth-century Canadian capitalism. Emigrating from Scotland
to Montreal in 1826, he first obtained employment through relatives
as a clerk in the merchandising field. About ten years later, with his
brother Andrew, he became established in shipping, acting as agent
for his father's Allan Line and extending the family's business by
purchasing additional ships. From that base he became president of the
Montreal Board of Trade in 1851 and president of Montreal Telegraph
Company (also in 1851), persuaded the Canadian government in 1853
to use mail contracts as a means of subsidizing steamships (including
his own) between Montreal and Britain, became founder (1861) and
subsequently president of the Merchant's Bank of Canada, and became
founder and president in 1872 of the Canadian Pacific Railway Company. It was in this last capacity that Allan contributed $400,000 to
John A. Macdonald's electoral fund, resulting in the Pacific scandal
and Macdonald's defeat at the polls in 1873. Allan also had interests
in textiles, shoes, coal-mines, iron and steel, tobacco, and paper. He
is said to have used 'his banking and insurance interests to secure
favourable press coverage through generous loans to editors.'[41]
Knighted by Queen Victoria in 1871, he died in 1882.

It was as president of Montreal Telegraph Company, an office he held until his death, that Allan put his mark on Canadian telegraphs, causing that company to embark on an aggressive program of acquisitions and expansion, whereby it soon came to dominate the Canadian industry and continued to do so for many years.

4

Cartelization

Montreal Telegraph Company
In 1850, the year prior to Hugh Allan's presidency, Montreal Telegraph operated merely 500 miles of line, all in the province of Canada. By decade's end, however, its operations stretched 1900 miles, dipping even into some northern states.[1] Although the emerging giant had been barred entry to the Maritimes on account of exclusive charters bestowed on others, its lines touched the New Brunswick border as early as 1856 through take-over of Gisborne's defunct B.N.A. Telegraph. Growth continued unabated through the next decade. By 1865 most towns and villages, harbours on the lakes, and the lumbering districts of the Ottawa River and Eastern Townships of Quebec were served. By 1870 Montreal Telegraph had amassed 12,400 miles of line.

Corporate acquisitions constituted one important means whereby Hugh Allan's company, always well connected with banking circles, attained its hegemony. In 1852, for example, it purchased the pioneer Toronto, Hamilton & Niagara ElectroMagnetic Telegraph Company. Other early acquisitions included the Montreal and Troy, the Vermont and Boston, and the Prescott Bytown and Montreal.[2] Territorial expansion served the practical purpose of enabling the dominant company to withstand incursions from smaller rivals by cross-subsidizing losses on competitive routes through profits earned on the remainder of its system. The Grand Trunk Telegraph Company (unaffiliated with the railroad) was one such ephemeral irritant; it collapsed two years after its 1853 inception, whereupon Montreal Telegraph assumed its facilities for a nominal sum.[3]

Acquisitions aside, Montreal Telegraph's dominance was pursued also through deals with railroads. Initially only non-exclusive rights to string telegraph lines along railroad rights of way were sought,[4] but when the Dominion Telegraph Company entered the fray as a major competitor in 1868, exclusive privileges were hastily procured. In 1869, for example, $30,000 was sufficient to make exclusive existing rights alongside the Grand Trunk,[5] placing Dominion Telegraph at a distinct disadvantage.[6]

Also aiding monopolization was membership in the North American Telegraph Association, a cartel formed in 1857 by six major u.s. telegraph companies including Western Union and American Telegraph Company. The association's prime purpose was to eliminate competition – both among members and from outsiders. Through careful territorial divisions members were to become, so far as possible, monopolists in their assigned territories. The American Telegraph Company, whose operations are treated in some detail at the close of this chapter, was allocated Newfoundland, Nova Scotia, New Brunswick, and most eastern seaboard states stretching south to Florida; Western Union was apportioned much of the American midwest;[7] and Montreal Telegraph was granted the Canadas and certain regions of some northern states. Where duplication of routes existed, revenues were to be carefully prorated, with no new competing lines to be constructed. Interconnections among companies were confined to signatories alone except in fulfilment of previous contracts. Disputes were to be arbitrated by the cartel's own court, empowered to hold hearings, examine evidence, and hand down binding decisions.[8] Thus by 1858, through both ownership and cartel, telegraphy in British North America had become firmly entrenched as a component of a continental industrial structure.

One minor blemish to the cartel's hegemony festered briefly between 1864 and 1866, when several non-aligned companies in the United States merged to form the United States Telegraph Company.[9] In Canada the Provincial Telegraph Company was spawned at the same time to provide u.s. Telegraph with northern connections. Although the Provincial entered a brief period of cut-throat competition with Montreal Telegraph, it was rendered redundant when Western Union acquired its American rival in 1866 in exchange for a fresh press run of stock certificates,[10] thereby enabling Montreal Telegraph to take the Provincial over for a nominal sum.[11]

Dominion Telegraph Company
Another of Montreal Telegraph's irritants, more enduring than the Provincial, was the Dominion Telegraph Company, established through stock subscriptions in 1868 by Selah Reeves, who promptly appointed his own construction company to build two thousand pole miles 'at the rate of $250 gold per mile.'[12] James D. Reid comments: 'The profits on such a contract ... would have amounted to about $300,000 ... a most potent incentive to enterprise.'[13] After a few hundred miles had been built, the contract received an airing at a shareholders' meeting, and Mr Reeves was relieved of further corporate duties.

One factor precipitating formation of the Dominion Telegraph was Montreal Telegraph's extraordinarily high profitability (it had never failed to pay a cash dividend under 8 per cent, and it frequently paid out stock dividends of 25 to 33 per cent as well).[14] But also important were industry shenanigans south of the border, to which we turn briefly.

In 1866 the Atlantic and Pacific Telegraph Company was formed, in competition with Western Union. Like the u.s. Telegraph Company before it, the Atlantic and Pacific was in need of Canadian connections – Montreal Telegraph's lines being of course unavailable – and formation of Dominion Telegraph Company in Canada served just that purpose.[15] The Atlantic and Pacific soon fell on hard times, however, and presented itself for take-over in 1873. This time the now water-logged Western Union declined; it had already absorbed at inflated prices so many rivals that the stock market was in panic, and wu prudently deemed yet a further press run of stock certificates to be unadvisable.[16] Leaping at the opportunity was Jay Gould, one of early u.s. capitalism's most infamous robber barons. Railroad promoter, stock market manipulator, press baron, banking tycoon, and rogue, Gould eventually wrung some of the water out of Western Union's stock.[17]

Under Gould's leadership the Atlantic and Pacific became a formidable competitor. By early 1877 it had put together a system 17,759 miles long, but even more to the point it was cutting prices. So effective indeed was its competition that Western Union's revenues dipped by

$2 million in a single year. Its stock started tumbling too,[18] and the more the stock fell the more Jay Gould acquired, thereby multiplying Western Union's woes. Indeed so frazzled did the bloated behemoth become that it passed up Alexander Graham Bell's offer to sell his telephone patents for $100,000! In late 1877 the collapsing colossus conceded the battle, paying Gould off with more than $900,000 in cash and with 12,500 crisp, new stock certificates,[19] thereby taking over its erstwhile rival. The u.s. telegraph industry thus entered a brief period of tranquillity, Western Union using the respite to mount a belated foray into the emerging telephone field in both the United States and Canada in an attempt to rectify its recent mistake.

In Canada also the initial years of competition, between the Dominion and Montreal Telegraph companies, were vigorous and brutal. But merger between Western Union and the Atlantic and Pacific was a severe – indeed, as it turned out, a mortal – blow to the Dominion, causing it to lose important u.s. connections[20] and making its continuance quite problematic. Rumours were rife of impending amalgamation, and it seemed but a matter of time until investors could hammer out a deal. At one point in 1878 the companies actually agreed in principle to share certain revenues and reciprocally to abandon duplicate offices, but the proposal fell through when the larger company rejected an arbiter's recommendation that revenue be prorated in the ratio of only 7 to 3 in favour of Montreal Telegraph.[21] For the next two years competition sputtered on, but with disastrous financial consequences: Dominion's revenues declined from $177,081 in 1877 to $169,837 in 1878 and Montreal's from $514,122 to $485,302.[22] Stock prices dwindled too, until mid-1879, at which time Jay Gould struck again.

On 15 May 1879, less than eighteen months after selling off the Atlantic and Pacific, being at the time one of Western Union's principal shareholders, Gould organized the American Union Telegraph Company,[23] again to harass the rich monopoly. Acquisitions of small telegraph companies were again made, prices cut, lines parallel to Western Union's constructed, and secret deals concocted with railways – all finally erupting in violence.[24] By year's end American Union claimed 2000 offices and 10,000 pole miles. Conflagrations continued through the next year until finally, on 15 February 1881, Western Union threw in the towel, merging the two companies under the title of Western Union but with Jay Gould in charge. As one contemporary report put it, 'The cormorant of the past has been swallowed up and the Western Union of today is only the Western Union in name, and the American Union in fact.'[25]

Inception of American Union for a time both justified and made necessary continuance of the Dominion Telegraph in Canada. Gould, however, took no chances, given the Dominion's rocky finances and its proclivity to strike a deal with Montreal Telegraph. He leased its lines, beginning in June 1879,[26] and used the facilities to step up the price war with Montreal Telegraph.[27] Competition continued until the 1881 amalgamation in the United States, which entailed also transmittal of the lease on the Dominion's lines to the 'new' Western Union, which promptly re-leased the same to a newly acquired Canadian subsidiary, the Great North Western Telegraph Company (GNWT).

Great North Western Telegraph Company
Organized in 1880 in Winnipeg by the provincial premier, members of his cabinet, and a few Ontario businessmen to connect with Ontario, the district of Keewatin, and British Columbia, GNWT in Western Union's hands became an instrument of telegraphic consolidation.[28] With Dominion Telegraph's lines firmly in tow, GNWT immediately cast its sights on Montreal Telegraph, staunch ally of the 'old' Western Union but protagonist to Gould's American Union.

Gould's man in Canada was Erastus Wiman (1834–1904), Canadian expatriate who had attained some renown in his youth as reporter with the Toronto *Globe*. From there Wiman went on to publish his own market and trade reviews. Emigrating to the United States in 1866, he amassed a fortune in canal, railway, and telegraph projects, becoming also outspoken proponent of continental free trade. But this meteoric rise was complemented by a tragic and dramatic fall. In 1893 Wiman was dragged off to jail, charged with embezzlement, and his fortunes dissipated almost overnight. Although ultimately exonerated of criminal wrongdoing, financially he never recovered his past glory.[29] But in 1881 his star was still ascending as Jay Gould tagged him to head up GNWT. His mandate was simple and straightforward: secure a monopoly over Canadian telegraphy for Western Union.

Two obstacles stood in the way. The first was obstinacy on the part of Montreal Telegraph's shareholders, many of whom did not want to sell out. Mincing few words, Gould's representative in Canada threatened recalcitrant shareholders with an all-out price war,[30] raising also the prospect of terminating Montreal Telegraph's international connections, then accounting for some 40 per cent of its business. Little was left to the imagination when Wiman described the dire consequences should Montreal Telegraph's shareholders refuse his offer:

If the offer now before the Montreal stockholders be rejected, it will follow, of course, that they must lose the entire American business, and that the cable business will also be concentrated in the Dominion Company. The consequence would, of course, be that the Montreal Company, deprived of probably $200,000 a year, could not pay dividends; and its stock would certainly fall in value to a point lower than it has ever done before. What the final result might be, it is hardly necessary to indicate.[31]

In these circumstances Montreal Telegraph's shareholders could hardly be faulted for jumping at the offer; they gave GNWT a ninety-seven-year lease on their lines on 17 August 1881.[32]

But the amalgamation was quite illegal, the second obstruction in Wiman's way, for Montreal Telegraph's charter precluded it from leasing its lines. Indeed Parliament just the year before had explicitly refused the company's petition to grant it the right to do that very thing.[33] Wiman went ahead anyway. The courts soon ruled against the transaction,[34] but the quintessential capitalist was equal to the occasion and talked an inebriated[35] Sir John A. Macdonald into retroactively ratifying the deal,[36] not the last time a powerful Canadian telecommunication company was to benefit from retroactive ratification of a corporate structure hitherto of at best dubious legality.[37]

By 1881, then, the 'new' Western Union, controlled by Jay Gould, held through its subsidiary, the Great North Western Telegraph Company, a virtual monopoly over telegraphy in Ontario and Quebec. As we shall see immediately, WU by this time had attained a monopoly also in the Atlantic provinces. Few could have imagined that its hegemony would be challenged a mere four years later – through inception of Canadian Pacific Telegraphs.

ATLANTIC REGION AND AMERICAN CONTROL

Even as the Nova Scotia government was busy 'privatizing' the provincial telegraph system in 1851, Fred Gisborne journeyed to Newfoundland to secure a charter for the Newfoundland Electric Telegraph Company. The colonial legislature acceded, giving the vagabond telegrapher an exclusive thirty-year right to construct lines in the colony.[38] Soon Gisborne joined St John's and Harbour Grace by way of Conception Bay.[39] Next, armed with a £500 government grant, he surveyed the 400 inland miles between St John's and Cape Ray, managing, however, to build but 30 pole miles along this route.

The problem was Gisborne's sense of vision; he could not limit his sights to Newfoundland. Even as the inland line was being constructed Gisborne became imbued with the prospect of joining Cape Ray to the mainland, believing that a cable connection could cut by forty-eight hours the time required for European news to reach North America. Impulsively he set up yet another company, secured financial backing from u.s. capitalists, and soon linked Newfoundland with Prince Edward Island and New Brunswick. It was all to no avail, for at this juncture his fortunes changed abruptly: the cable snapped in 1852, his u.s. investors panicked and refused to inject additional funds, and Gisborne had to sell off all he owned to pay some of the debt. For a time it looked like he too was going to jail.[40]

Bankrupt but unperturbed, the romantic adventurer used the enforced respite to concoct a yet wilder and more brilliant scheme – an Atlantic cable between Europe and North America! Attempting to drum up financial support in New York City, the following year he chanced upon one Cyrus W. Field (1819–92), an eminently successful business tycoon who had accumulated a million dollars by age thirty-five. Business life no longer posing a challenge, Field was both retired and restless. But Gisborne's proposal was intriguing – in fact it became Field's obsession for the next thirteen years. He quickly organized the New York, Newfoundland and London Electric Telegraph Company, bought up Gisborne's charter for Newfoundland, and hired Gisborne on as 'chief engineer,' a post possibly reflecting certain misgivings the u.s. capitalist may have had about Gisborne's business acumen. Disillusioned, Gisborne resigned in 1857, dropping out of Canadian telegraphy entirely for fifteen years until appointed general superintendent of the Dominion Government Telegraph Service in 1872.[41]

Next Field approached the Newfoundland legislature, where he lobbied hard, dispensing enthusiasm like contagium so successfully that he walked away with an exclusive fifty- year right to land cables along Newfoundland's coast plus a further £50,000 in subsidy to defray costs. He received also generous endowments of hitherto public lands.[42]

Prince Edward Island also proved co-operative, bestowing on Field an exclusive charter in return for re-establishing connections to the mainland.

Construction connecting Cape Ray with St John's through the dense Newfoundland forests was resumed, completed finally in 1856. All this building cost about $1 million. It was only a decade later that the wisdom of it all was demonstrated; nor was Field's company to be the ultimate beneficiary.

Perhaps recognizing that an Atlantic cable was fraught with difficulty, Field also applied his talents to a related, if somewhat more nefarious, task – monopolizing telegraphy on North America's east coast. To this end he organized in November 1855 the American Telegraph Company,[43] which leased the lines of the New Brunswick Electric Telegraph Company in 1856 and those of Cunard's floundering Nova Scotia enterprise in 1860.[44] Through the late 1850s many other telegraph companies, primarily in the eastern United States, came under Field's control. One of these was Samuel Morse's Magnetic Telegraph Company, and Morse became an immediate shareholder in the emerging giant. The American Telegraph Company soon came to dominate, albeit briefly, telegraphy on the east coast of North America. As a founding member of the North America Telegraph Association it also enjoyed exclusive connections with most other major telegraph companies in Canada and the United States. But despite its size, privileges, and exclusive dealings, it soon fell on hard times. Its lines, which stretched north and south, were ripped asunder by the Civil War (1861–5), the Confederate Telegraph Company expropriating the southern facilities in 1861. Equally damaging was the expense and lack of success in laying the Atlantic cable: two failures occurred in 1857–8, the project was suspended entirely for the duration of the Civil War, and then came a further failure in 1865.[45] The result was that even as the ocean cable was at last being laid successfully in June 1866, the American Telegraph Company expired, exchanging its share capital of $4 million for a new press run of Western Union stock, nominally valued at $12 million, and becoming thereby absorbed into a now heavily diluted colossus.[46] Leases on the telegraph lines in New Brunswick and Nova Scotia and telegraph companies in PEI and Newfoundland now fell to Western Union, inaugurating that company's dominance over telegraphy in Atlantic Canada, a reign lasting more than sixty years. Only in 1929 were land-line facilities in New Brunswick, Nova Scotia, and PEI returned to Canadian hands through acquisition by Canadian National Telegraph Company. Even through the 1960s, however, Western Union continued operating ocean cables at Canso, Nova Scotia,[47] its Canadian transatlantic cable operations being terminated only in 1972.[48]

The telegraph industry in the Atlantic region, therefore, followed a parallel course to that in central Canada, until the two converged under the common ownership of Western Union in 1881. In both cases the telegraph early-on was integrated with the u.s. industry – in central Canada through cartelization and exclusive interconnection agreements; in the Atlantic region directly by lease and ownership. In both regions monopolization was a characteristic feature: in central Canada through predatory pricing, refusal to interconnect, exclusive covenants with railways, and other restrictive trade practices; in the Atlantic region through grants of exclusive privilege by provincial and colonial governments, usually accompanied by direct subsidy. In both regions there was a close relationship with the press, continuing until 1910.

5

The Telegraph Coast-to-Coast

BRITISH COLUMBIA

Despite non-overlapping territories and common membership in the continental cartel, the American Telegraph Company and Western Union were in other respects great rivals between 1856 and 1866, each company striving to dominate telegraphy in North America and the rest of the world. Whereas the former was entangled laying faulty Atlantic cables, the latter became ensnared in an equally massive scheme – an overland telegraph to Europe from San Francisco, via the west coast of North America and across the Bering Strait to Russia,[1] a project in which the u.s. government took keen interest. Benefiting from generous congressional funding, Western Union completed a survey of British Columbia in 1861.[2] Then in 1864 it won permission from the czar to connect with 7000 miles of line projected to join Moscow and the Pacific. This stimulus was sufficient to start construction in British Columbia, first through a subsidiary, the California State Telegraph Company, to link Washington Territory with New Westminster and Victoria,[3] and then in 1865 through another subsidiary, the Collins Overland Telegraph Company, to join New Westminster with Russia. On 18 April the first message over the Overland's still incomplete facility sadly related news of the assassination of President Lincoln.[4]

By the summer the Overland line stretched north from New Westminster to almost the present site of Hazelton, BC, about 850 miles. The work, while frantic in pace, was precisely co-ordinated. One authority has noted that the whole expedition was 'carefully planned on a semi-military basis,'⁵ some of the leading personnel in fact being seconded from the u.s. military.

In August 1866, $3 million later,⁶ news arrived by wire that the Atlantic cable had at last been laid successfully. Construction on the Overland route stopped abruptly. Disappointment reigned supreme. At Fort Stager linemen draped telegraph poles in black to symbolize their grief at the wasted effort. Tons of wire and other materials were abandoned to rust or rot in the forests and mountains. Hundreds of miles of line lay idle, until finally purchased by the Dominion government beginning in 1871.⁷ Only between 1891 and 1901 were the northernmost lines reactivated, activity simulated by the Klondike gold rush. A further legacy of Western Union's foray into British Columbia was acquisition of Alaska by the u.s. government in 1867.⁸

PRAIRIES

The next notable westward thrust of the telegraph was in 1872, as response to smouldering apprehension of Canadian politicians that the United States wanted to annex the western prairies and British Columbia.⁹ Indeed a proposal as early as 1862 by the Grand Trunk Railway to construct a line from the province of Canada to the Pacific had been welcomed for that very reason, but opposition from the Hudson's Bay Company, at the time proprietor of Rupert's Land and diligently amassing fortunes in the fur trade (giving it a vested interest in keeping the area unsettled), scuttled the plan. Sale of the territory to the Dominion of Canada in 1869, however, made possible a new initiative, and between 1872 and 1879 the Canadian government built 1300 miles of telegraph across the vast expanse separating Fort William and Edmonton.¹⁰ In 1881 these facilities were consolidated with other government-funded lines, becoming known collectively as the Government Telegraph and Signal Service, administered by Fred N. Gisborne for the Department of Public Works.¹¹

The telegraph to Edmonton in and of itself, was insufficient to prevent u.s. annexation, of course, because the prairies of the 1870s were largely uninhabited, except for 'a few outposts of the Great Fur Company, ... warring Indian tribes, and the wild animals native to the wilderness.'¹² Therefore, the Dominion government also staked its claim by dispatching a battalion of North West Mounted Police, five hundred strong, in 1874. Indeed former Saskatchewan premier James

T. Anderson declared that 'two of the most important milestones in the history of the west were the coming of the Mounted Police and the building of the Government Telegraph line,'[13] a synergistic confluence if ever there was one, illustrating well Harold Innis's astute asseveration concerning the conjuncture of empire with control over media of communication.[14] The telegraph speeded instructions from the east, while the mounties ensured compliance in the west.

Retrospectively, this Innisian symbiosis between communications media and military might was given a noteworthy workout a decade later during the Riel rebellion of 1885, the telegraph shortening dramatically the duration of the uprising.[15] Surprisingly, Louis Riel and his lieutenant, Gabriel Dumont, did not apprehend the importance of a communication link to Her Majesty's forces and only in isolated instances (and then largely for symbolic reasons only) did they cut the lines, to their distinct disadvantage. The rebellion itself, meanwhile, was an immense boom to the emerging western telegraph, helping it establish a secure financial footing. Major dailies in eastern Canada – the Montreal *Star*, Montreal *Witness*, and Toronto *Mail* – all sent correspondents to the trouble spot. Reflecting on these early years, CNCP Telecommunications has pointed out that 'net revenues of $70,000 were reported by the Telegraph Department [of the Canadian Pacific Railway] in 1884 [but] the next year, due to heavy press coverage of the second Riel rebellion, revenues jumped to $145,000.'[16] So encouraging indeed were these financial returns that CPR opened a full commercial telegraph service between Superior and the Rockies that year.

Whereas Western Union remained uninterested in the Canadian west through 1870s (apart from lingering lines in New Westminster and Victoria), it attempted entry on a grand scale in the early 1880s. In 1882–3 through its subsidiary, the GNWT, it built land lines north of Superior to link Winnipeg and Ontario.[17] Also in 1882 it applied, unsuccessfully, to take over the government's facility to Edmonton, the rebuff most likely stemming from populist revulsion at GNWT's monopoly power, exploitative tactics, and Jay Gould's control. In fact calls for a government take-over of the despised GNWT were quite widespread at the time,[18] alleviated only by inception of competing telegraphic operations in the east by CPR in 1886. In the end CPR was appointed beneficiary for the privatized facilities, beginning in 1884,[19] gifts that were the first seeds in the dismantling of Western Union's telegraphic hegemony in the rest of Canada.[20]

CANADIAN PACIFIC TELEGRAPHS

From the outset the Canadian Pacific Railway Company benefited much from public subsidy, the forementioned telegraphic benefactions forming but a small portion of the largesse. Initially endowed with $25 million in cash and 25 million acres in land, CPR was also gifted with sections of the government's railroad running between Selkirk and Lake Superior and also from Kamloops to Port Moody, the tracks along being valued at $38 million.[21] These dispensations were generously supplemented as construction proceeded, so that by 1916 the Canadian government had footed 43 per cent of the total cost of the transcontinental railway.[22]

Among other privileges, CPR's charter gave it the right to carry on a commercial telegraph business in Canada, [23] enabling it to open on a commercial basis a service between Lake Superior and the Rockies in 1885.[24] No wonder GNWT was distressed and attempted early on, unsuccessfully as it turned out, to acquire the fledgling service.

Even as CPR's main rail line westward was being constructed its promoters began acquiring eastern railways – and with them rights to string telegraph wires alongside tracks – resulting soon in a strong telegraphic presence in Ontario.[25] Indeed a full commercial telegraph service connecting important Ontario towns was opened in September 1886, with connections to the United States through the Postal Telegraph Company and the Baltimore and Ohio Company.[26] CPR then pushed further eastward, and by 1890 had extended operations to Saint John, NB, and by 1916 to Nova Scotia.[27] Canadian Pacific Telegraphs thus was Canada's first nationwide telecommunications carrier.

SEPARATION OF CONTENT FROM CARRIAGE

Like its predecessors, Canadian Pacific Telegraphs entered the news collection and distribution businesses. For some thirty years prior to inception of the CPR, Canadian daily newspapers had been highly dependent on telegraph companies for editorial content. Apart from a few professional journalists the only news correspondents were telegraph operators disseminating local happenings across the network.

According to one commentary, 'the telegraph companies ... in their field of collecting and distributing news operated in complete freedom from any authority except their own. The newspapers were nothing more than receptacles for the news the telegraph companies delivered them.'[28]

News-gathering and distribution were powerful means whereby CP Telegraphs got a leg up on the competition, notably GNWT, especially after 1894 when it procured Canadian rights for the U.S. Associated Press newswire. For years thereafter virtually every daily in Canada as a practical matter had to subscribe to both Canadian Pacific's news and its transmission service, simply because the company bundled the two together under one flat price. In this way GNWT got squeezed out of much vital press business, always important for the financial vitality of telegraph companies, a setback from which it never fully recovered and which contributed ultimately to its near-bankruptcy and government take-over. So heavy-handed indeed was Canadian Pacific Telegraphs in these years that it cut off all press connections to a paper in Nelson, BC, which had deigned to publish stories critical of Canadian Pacific – explaining briefly but sardonically that 'Nothing seems to please you.'[29]

Such manifest abuses aside, vertical integration between carriage and content at the time seemed 'natural,' in the order of things, until in 1907 when three Winnipeg dailies formed a co-operative news agency, the Western Associated Press (W.A.P.), to counter a doubling in CPR Telegraphs' rates to Winnipeg. Cancelling CPR's news service, the papers affiliated with smaller U.S. rivals of the AP and attained telegraphic transmissions from GNWT and other small, railway-affiliated telegraph companies. W.A.P. even began selling dispatches in competition with CPR to papers between Port Arthur/Fort William and British Columbia, much to CPR's chagrin. The railway countered by withdrawing press rates entirely from Winnipeg;[30] at one point CPR's flat monthly rate to clients in Saskatoon for the combined news/transmission service from Montreal was $200, compared with $467 for the same wordage, transmission only, from Saskatoon to Winnipeg.[31]

Such abuses were finally terminated in 1910, when the Board of Railway Commissioners, granted jurisdiction in 1908 over pricing practices of telegraph companies,[32] ruled that Canadian Pacific Telegraphs' press rates had been unduly discriminatory and were hence unlawful.[33] Very quickly Canadian Pacific abandoned the news-gathering field, as did its arch-rival, The Great North Western Telegraph Company.

Vertical integration between publishing and telegraphs – between content and carriage – thus ended, the era of the telecommunications common carrier began.

CANADIAN NATIONAL TELEGRAPHS

At the turn of the century a single transcontinental railroad was deemed inadequate for the needs of the burgeoning prairie economy. Rapid expansions in both livestock and wheat farming were straining the resources of the existing railway.[34] Immigration too was booming: 50,000 immigrants to Canada in 1902, 100,000 in 1903, and 250,000 in 1908, mostly settling on the prairies.[35] Consequently *two* additional transcontinental railways were perceived essential to improve transportation for the west. The first was the Canadian Northern, begun in 1898 as an amalgamation of small Manitoba railways; it was empowered by a 1902 act of Parliament to build eastward to Montreal and westward to Edmonton, and by 1915 it extended from Quebec City to Vancouver.[36] The second, the Grand Trunk Pacific, begun in 1905 and completed in 1914, connected Winnipeg and Prince Rupert, joining the Grand Trunk and National Transcontinental (built by the government) for eastern connections.[37] However, even as construction of the two new railways was being finished, economic conditions reversed: the boom ended in the early part of 1914; war broke out that summer; immigration ceased almost overnight; British investment dried up; and the new railways – 'outward and visible signs of the belief in the Canadian millennium'[38] – were stranded without sufficient funds or traffic.

These became lean years for the telegraph industry as well. Both of the new transcontinental railways (as was customary) established telegraphic subsidiaries, thereby increasing competition. Indeed by 1914 there were four major competing telegraph operations in the country:[39] Canadian Pacific Telegraphs, which was now national in scope; Great North Western Telegraphs, which operated primarily in Ontario and Quebec and in Winnipeg, connecting with Western Union for both the United States and the Atlantic region; Canadian Northern Telegraphs, operating primarily in the west; and Grand Trunk Pacific Telegraphs, also primarily in the west.[40]

The first casualty from this influx of entrants was the venerable GNWT, which owing to its geographically confined territory, lack of railway affiliation,[41] and sparse press business teetered on bankruptcy.[42] On 1 January 1915 it was acquired for $294,000 by Canadian Northern Telegraphs,[43] thereby establishing a nation-wide competitor for Canadian Pacific. Exclusive connections with Western Union for both the United States and the Maritimes made for a seemingly auspicious debut for this amalgamated operation, but Canadian Northern Railway was itself financially weak, requiring a government guarantee for a $45-million bond issue in 1914 and federal loans of $75 million in 1916.[44] In 1917 it was itself taken over by the federal government, which attained thereby Canadian Northern's commercial telegraph operations. Then in November 1920 Grand Trunk Pacific too was nationalized, its telegraphic facilities being promptly merged into a system shortly to become known as Canadian National Telegraph Company.[45] As of 1920, then, there remained but two major competitors in Canada for long-distance record (telegraphic) communication.

In 1924 Canadian National Telegraph Company extended its system by purchasing Western Union's telegraph operations in British Columbia (Vancouver, Victoria, and New Westminster), and in 1929, as we have noted, it acquired Western Union's land-line business and property in New Brunswick, Nova Scotia, and PEI.[46]

CNCP TELECOMMUNICATIONS

The formation of Canadian National for a time invigorated competition in the Canadian telegraph industry. Canadian National and Canadian Pacific each upgraded facilities as the state of the art improved: Morse keys and sounders were replaced by teleprinters; advanced land-line transmission techniques were introduced; and by the 1930s, through multiplexing, dedicated circuits were leased competitively as private lines.[47] Gradually, however, the rivals found it more lucrative to co-operate than to compete. Three developments in particular help explain this transition from competition to co-operation.

Emerging competition from the telephone industry was one factor encouraging co-operation between CN and CP Telegraphs. Initially, owing to inherent signal loss in voice signals, telephone companies had been limited to providing a local and limited long-distance service. When amplification became practical, however, various telephone firms started leasing wires and rights-of-way from the telegraph companies to link distant points[48] and also began building their own lines for this purpose. As telephone company–controlled long-distance facil-

TABLE 5.1
Canadian telegraph industry development 1938–82

	(1)	(2)	(3)	(4)
Year	Telegrams sent	Revenues from message record, national and international business*† ($ millions)	Total telegraph ('telecommu- nications') industry revenues, excluding telephones† ($ millions)	Relative importance of traditional telegram market for 'telecommu- nication carriers' (excluding telephone companies)† (2) ÷ (3)
1935	9,585,719	6.3	9.7	64.9
1938	11,220,047	5.7	10.6	53.8
1942	13,660,987	9.3	14.8	62.8
1946	16,221,953	10.6	18.0	58.9
1948	16,970,011	11.3	19.4	58.2
1952	19,513,250	18.2	33.1	55.0
1954	17,763,221	19.0	38.2	49.7
1958	15,375,361	18.6	47.6	39.1
1962	12,834,273	17.2	71.4	24.1
1966	10,327,820	14.2	95.5	14.9
1970	6,905,695	11.7	136.9	4.8
1974	3,743,340	10.3	230.1	4.5
1978	2,225,486	12.6	348.3	3.6
1982	1,816,305	10.9	536.3	2.0

* Includes (a) public and government message; (b) press message; (c) money order message; and (d) news service
† Includes Telesat since 1972 and Canadian Overseas Telecommunications Corp., or Teleglobe Canada
SOURCE: Dominion Bureau of Statistics, *Telegraph and Cable Statistics* (annual) and Statistics Canada, *Telecommunications Statistics*, annual, cat. no. 56–201

ities proliferated, telegraphic dominance over long-distance communication eroded. In 1931–2, upon establishment of the TransCanada Telephone System (TCTS), the major telephone companies began offering nationally private lines in direct competition with the telegraph and in 1947 even began competing in the private-line telegraph business ('leased teletype').[49] This heightened competition made the telegraph companies apprehensive, and as a defence they began to coordinate operations.

A second factor was a 1943 merger in the United States between

Western Union and the Postal Telegraph Company, the former having provided CN's U.S. connections and the latter CP's. The U.S. merger meant that two Canadian companies were no longer required for full U.S./Canada interconnection. Rather than seizing the competitive advantage inhering in the demise of Postal Telegraphs, however, CN chose to offer leased wires in co-operation with CP,[50] the exigencies of wartime perhaps helping to explain this decision.

Finally, by the mid-1950s, demand for public message telegraph service was dwindling steadily (see table 5.1). By 1976 the traditional market for telegrams (public record service) had shrunk to about 4.4 per cent of the total Canadian telecommunications transmission market (then $3556 million)[51] and accounted for less than 15 per cent of even CN and CP's revenues[52] (the two telegraph companies by this time were providing an increasing array of other services).[53] In the face of this market erosion, the erstwhile rivals finally agreed to abandon some offices,[54] in order to efface the last vestige of competition between them.

Despite the relative diminution in traditional record services, CNCP Telecommunications (legally a partnership of the two railways between 1980 and 1988) has been able to tap new markets in the technologically dynamic telecommunications field, in some areas becoming an innovative if beleaguered competitor of the telephone industry. In the fall of 1988, however, it was announced that Canadian Pacific would acquire its partner's share in the troubled enterprise for $235 million; CNCP had lost $2.4 million on revenues of $316.5 million in 1987 and lost a further $7 million in 1988.[55] In April 1989 cable TV king Ted Rogers bought 40 per cent of CNCP from Canadian Pacific, and the new ownership alignment announced immediately its intention to apply to the CRTC to compete head-on with the telephone companies in long-distance voice communication.[56] As this book went to press, a corporate name change was imminent.

The relations between CNCP Telecommunications and the telephone industry are explored in some detail in the next part of this book.

PART III

The Telephone

6

Inception

The telephone and telegraph industries in Canada have striking parallels in their inception and early development. Not only were the two fields closely integrated in telephony's early years, but also charters were decisive in shaping industrial structures. Moreover, in each case, an 'industry captain' – Charles Fleetford Sise in telephony and Hugh Allan in telegraphy – arrived early on the scene to develop and implement monopolistic practices for the soon-dominant firms. The restrictive measures used were similar too: refusal to interconnect, mergers and acquisitions, collusive deals with the railroads, predatory pricing, political wheeling and dealing, and vertical integration. Finally, both industries emerged and took shape only under the shadow of u.s. domination and control.

The story of Canadian telephones begins not only with the inventor, Alexander Graham Bell, but as well with his father, Melville Bell, an eminent professor of elocution. Indeed it was the latter who inaugurated the Canadian industry.

TELEPHONE WARS

On 21 August 1877, for remuneration of one dollar, Alexander Graham Bell turned over to Melville Bell three-quarter interest in the telephone patent for Canada, the remaining quarter interest being transferred to Charles Williams of Boston in exchange for one thousand instruments assignable to M. Bell.[1] Thereby Melville Bell became, in a double sense, father of Canadian telephony.

Patent in hand the elder Bell entertained fleeting visions of himself organizing the still nascent Canadian industry, although one might suspect his training as elocutionist touched at best lightly upon the skills needed for such a hard-nosed vocation.[2] One of Melville's first decisions was to appoint as general manager his friend and confidant, Rev. Thomas Henderson. Together the clergyman and the professor proceeded to hire local and regional agents to solicit subscribers. By January 1879 they had more than twenty representatives nation-wide to promote telephone leases, some of course meeting with greater success than others.[3]

One of the more energetic and skilful of M. Bell's agents was Hugh C. Baker of Hamilton. Variously a banker, broker, and promoter, Baker had previously helped organize the Hamilton Street Railway Company, the Hamilton Real Estate Board, and the Canada Fire and Marine Insurance Company. On 29 August 1877, only eight days after Melville Bell had assumed headship of the incipient industry, Baker took out the country's first leases. The original four grew to forty by December 1878, whereupon Baker's Hamilton and District Telephone Company (now with an exclusive franchise for Hamilton and area) opened the first Canadian switchboard, consisting of eight lines.[4] Elsewhere at this time, local agencies were also started by other interests, notably in London, Toronto, Windsor, Winnipeg, and Victoria.[5]

Although in one sense the emerging field was unified through Melville Bell's tight control over the patent, in another it was fragmented and but loosely organized, with local agencies of disparate skills and interests having responsibility for promotion. A step towards consolidation was taken in February 1879 when Melville Bell granted Dominion Telegraph Company an exclusive five-year licence to work the Bell patent nationally, excluding only Toronto, Hamilton, and contiguous counties.[6] Evidently M. Bell's enthusiasm for the exigencies and challenges of business life was waning, and in any event he wanted to join his son in Washington, DC.

Entry into the telephone arena by Dominion Telegraph naturally did not escape notice by Montreal Telegraph. But to understand how Canada's telegraphic wars came also to encompass telephony, it is necessary to turn again to events unfolding in the United States.

By August 1877 Alexander Graham Bell's financiers for the United States, operating under the title of the Bell Telephone Company, were strapped for funds, to such an extent that they offered to sell the U.S. telephone patent to Western Union for a meagre $100,000. At the time, the beleaguered telegraphic leviathan was being sorely tested by Jay Gould's Atlantic and Pacific. Indeed so frazzled had the lumbering giant become that it unwisely rejected the offer, paving the way for a telephone take-over by William Forbes (son-in-law of Ralph Waldo Emerson) and his moneyed New England connections, who shortly reconstituted the fledgling organization as the National Bell Telephone Company. A year later, the Gould problem in abeyance and seemingly resolved, Western Union invaded the u.s. telephone industry with a vengeance, attempting to rectify its blunder by enlisting Thomas A. Edison, Elisha Gray, and others to invent around the Bell patent.[7] So successful indeed was this foray that by November 1879 wu was operating 56,000 telephones in fifty-five u.s. cities. However, facing unwanted and potentially costly litigation instituted by National Bell for patent infringements, and becoming harassed once more by Jay Gould (this time through his American Union Telegraph Company), Western Union decided to withdraw from the telephone field forthwith, transferring to the Bell interests all telephone plant, instruments, and patents and recognizing the validity of the Bell patents. National Bell for its part agreed not to enter the telegraph industry.[8]

For Canada, Edison's telephone patent was assigned first to the Canadian District Telegraph Company, a Montreal-based signal box messenger service that opened an exchange in May 1879. But Montreal Telegraph then bought the company, securing thereby both the Montreal telephone exchange and the Edison patent, and began extending telephone operations into other communities.[9] At first Montreal Telegraph viewed the telephone merely as an extension to its existing business – it made it easier for customers to get messages to the telegraph office – and as a competitive ploy the company began giving free telephone connections between its premises and those of its largest customers.[10]

Dominion Telegraph welcomed neither Montreal Telegraph's intrusion into telephones, a field it deemed rightfully its own, nor the free connections its aggressive rival was providing. Price wars already characterizing telegraphy soon spilled over into telephony, and free service became the unexceptional marketing strategy.

To be expected, free service took its toll on the income statements of the two pugilists: Dominion Telegraph received only $3000 from telephone operations in 1879 while Montreal Telegraph garnered even less.[11] Consequently, Dominion Telegraph was in no position to accept

Melville Bell's offer, proffered in August 1879,[12] for full title to the patent for $100,000; therefore, M. Bell looked elsewhere, soon locating an acceptable suitor in William Forbes, president of National Bell. By early 1880 a deal had been struck for $100,000, and Melville Bell joined his son in Washington.

THE CHARTER

Meanwhile, in late 1879, Hugh C. Baker initiated efforts to consolidate the fledgling industry. Drawing up a charter to incorporate a national company, he approached Melville Bell and others to be directors and in February 1880 petitioned Parliament to enact legislation to create the Bell Telephone Company of Canada.

Both houses acted swiftly. The petition required merely five days to pass through first reading in the Commons, which quickly defeated motions to restrict the proposed company's autonomy in digging up streets without local authorization.[13] In the Senate a plea from Senator Haythorne that 'there is nothing which this House ought to look after with greater jealousy than the establishment of large monopolies'[14] went unheeded. In the end, seven weeks were sufficient for the bill to pass both houses. It received royal assent on 29 April 1880.[15]

As enacted, the charter empowered the Bell Telephone Company of Canada to (1) manufacture telephone and telegraph equipment;[16] (2) construct, acquire, maintain, and operate telephone systems in Canada and elsewhere; (3) connect with other telephone and telegraph companies in Canada and elsewhere; (4) construct lines along any and all public rights-of-way, subject only to certain minor provisos;[17] and (5) amalgamate with or become a shareholder in companies owning telephone or telegraph lines or possessing power 'to use communication by means of the telephone.' Charters at once empower and constrain, and Bell's was no exception. Although granted substantial power to pursue telephone development, the new company was precluded from offering a telegraph service[18] and from engaging in other activities not expressly enumerated in the charter.[19] It also had to apply to Parliament for a revised act each time it desired increases in its authorized capitalization; that is, to issue stocks or bonds beyond limits prescribed by the legislation.

Bell Telephone held its first meeting on 1 June 1880, whereupon three executives from National Bell (recently renamed the American Bell Telephone Company) were elected to the board: William Forbes (president of American Bell), Theodore Vail (its general manager), and, most notably, C.F. Sise (its special agent).[20] Thereupon the new directors appointed as president Andrew Robertson, a Montreal dry goods merchant and chairman of the city's Harbour Board. C.F. Sise became vice-president and managing director. Rev. Thomas Henderson was soon hired on as 'storekeeper.'[21]

On 15 December 1880, Hugh C. Baker 'turned over' the valuable charter to C.F. Sise,[22] officially concluding the u.s. take-over of Canadian telephony.

A RIDDLE[23]

But matters were yet more intricate and recondite. It is apparent that Melville Bell's sale of patent to National Bell was not entirely unrelated to Baker's petition for incorporation. As early as 17 January 1880 National Bell was 'making arrangements for Canada,'[24] while on 8 March 1880 W.H. Forbes, president of National Bell, instructed his newly appointed special agent for Canada, C.F. Sise, to 'consult with Hugh C. Baker, who with his Associates, has applied for a charter *in our behalf* from the Parliament, to see what has been done, and to aid in every suitable way in securing a favourable charter.'[25]

By at least January 1880, therefore, if not before, Hugh C. Baker and his fellow incorporators had become mere figureheads or fronts for National Bell. However, in the debates of both houses of Parliament pertaining to the act incorporating Bell Telephone there is nary an allusion to National Bell, its special agent for Canada, or even to the possibility of a u.s. take-over. Politicians are not normally noted for their reticence, and so complete quiescence on the topic is somewhat baffling.

The enigma redoubles when the political debates are considered within their proper historical context, for in September 1878 John A. Macdonald won a smashing electoral victory on a campaign of economic nationalism. Indeed, for the three previous years as leader of the opposition the elder statesman and father of Confederation had staked his political life promoting economic protectionism, eventually rewinning the electors' hearts by so doing. Once back in office his government's first budget, handed down in March 1879, set in motion the National Policy of high tariffs, active government intervention, western settlement, and of course construction of the Canadian Pacific Railway. High tariffs, Macdonald claimed, would provide revenues needed to undertake national economic expansion, encourage trade between east and west, and permit domestic private enterprise to expand and diversify. They would also provide traffic for the transcontinental railroad that was about to be launched. In the following year, 1880, the Macdonald government concluded negotiations to build the CPR thereby holding forth the prospect of an all-red route with which to move settlers to the west and goods among the regions. In brief, as historian Donald Creighton has contended, there can be little question that by 1880 Canada had 'set out on a career of economic nationalism.'[26] And yet not one eyebrow in either house was raised at bestowing the Bell charter on agents for National Bell. Could it be that Parliament had been deceived, or at best simply not informed, that Baker and his cronies were mere stools for National Bell? Unfortunately we will never know for sure, its now being quite impossible to ascertain the extent to which the legislators were made privy to these contrivings.

CONSOLIDATION

National Bell's man in Canada was indeed Charles Fleetford Sise (1834–1918), son of an American general merchant and ship owner. At the age of twenty he was made sea captain, spending several nautical years aboard one of his father's ships, the *Annie Sise*. During the Civil War he was private secretary to Jefferson Davis, president of the Confederacy, and he helped the southern war effort by running Union blockades, bringing into port munitions and taking out cotton. Later he took charge of his father's affairs in Liverpool, England, where he entered also the insurance business, joining the Royal Insurance Company. His association with Royal Insurance ultimately led to connections with the directors of National Bell Telephone Company of Boston who appointed him, at forty-six years, their special agent for Canada. During his professional life, Captain Sise kept detailed 'logs,' exhaustively indexed, on major and minor matters. Those covering his years with the Bell Telephone Company of Canada are of particular interest, constituting a record of telephony's formative years.

On 8 March 1880 Captain Sise received his commission from William Forbes of National Bell: 'set sail' for Canada and (1) organize a new company, the Canadian Telephone Company, to hold patents and own all telephone instruments for lease back to the Bell Telephone

Company; (2) help guide through Parliament Hugh C. Baker's petition for an act incorporating Bell Telephone; (3) 'harmonize the conflicting interests in the telephone business,' appropriating so far as possible telephone operations of the Dominion and Montreal Telegraph companies; and (4) establish relations between National Bell's two Canadian subsidiaries, namely the Canadian and Bell telephone companies.[27] Captain Sise was remarkably successful in carrying out all these tasks, facing only minor turbulence along the way.

Within days of his 9 March debarkation in Montreal he contacted both Hugh Allan of Montreal Telegraph and Thomas Swinyard of Dominion Telegraph, initiating negotiations to take over their telephone operations.[28] Sise knew that the two rivals, ever suspicious of each other, would need assurances of National Bell's neutrality. He knew also that both companies were eager to dump their costly and unprofitable telephone operations. Assurances granted, Dominion sold its plant for $75,000 cash, and Montreal Telegraph accepted a like sum in shares (15 per cent of issued stock) in the newly organized Bell Telephone Company of Canada.[29]

Sise began purchasing other telephone properties and by 1881 had acquired on his employer's behalf 'all remaining telephone properties in Canada' – 3100 telephones in all, up from 2100 the previous year.[30]

Captain Sise initiated the peculiar intercorporate arrangements envisaged by National Bell for its Canadian subsidiaries, securing a charter for the Canadian Telephone Company. The latter promptly acquired all telephone instruments from Bell Telephone for lease back to Bell, then granted Bell an exclusive licence to work the telephone patent in Canada.[31] These dealings, strange as they may seem at first, paralleled National Bell's strategy for the United States, whereby local capital was enlisted for expansion but tight control retained over both patents and telephone instruments.[32] This arrangement permitted National Bell to appropriate revenues collected by local companies through lease payments and patent royalties prior to divvying up profits with local investors. Bell's annual fee to Canadian Telephone was four dollars per instrument – $18,136 for 1881.[33]

The innovative intercorporate arrangements broke down in 1882, however, when the Canadian Telephone Company launched legal action against its affiliate for patent infringement.[34] To conclude a settlement out of court, Bell Telephone bought up its sibling, securing thereby all patents and telephone instruments. The Canadian Telephone Company thereupon expired, turning over to American Bell its

TABLE 6.1
Bell Telephone Company of Canada, selected statistics 1880–4

	1880	1881	1882	1883	1884
Telephone subscribers	2,100	3,100	4,400	6,000	7,418
Revenue	$29,671	$101,050	$161,786	$217,624	$283,044
Net income	$11,053	$32,889	$69,590	$112,233	$118,951
Issued share capital	$377,600	$500,000	$1,000,000	$1,000,000	$1,000,000
Net income/share capital (%)	2.9%	6.6%	7.0%	11.2%	11.9%

SOURCE: Bell Telephone Company of Canada, *Annual Reports*

shares in the Bell Telephone Company of Canada.[35] After all was said and done, American Bell ended up with 46.8 per cent of the issued shares in the Bell Telephone Company of Canada.[36]

By 1882 Canadian Bell, firmly in American hands, appeared to have a clear field in telephony. It had a federal charter, entitling it to extend its works throughout the Dominion; its charter permitted it to lay wires and erect poles along all public rights-of-way without need of further permission from other jurisdictions; it had acquired all telephone plant in the country; and it possessed exclusive rights for Canada to all major telephone patents. But in 1885, as discussed in the following chapter, the monopoly burst; the original Bell patent was declared void.

Table 6.1 summarizes Bell Telephone's first five years of operations. By implication, the table also depicts the state of the Canadian telephone industry for this period.

SEGREGATION

In yet another way 1880 was a momentous year for Canadian telecommunications, for it was then that the telephone and telegraph industries became segregated through restrictive covenant. On 1 November the Canadian Telephone Company, the American Telephone Company (successor to National Bell), and Western Union all signed agreements whereby patents for the telephone in Canada (including Edison's) would pass to the Canadian Telephone Company. The two U.S.

companies would share jointly in the company's ownership, with Western Union's allotment being about one-third interest.[37] The Canadian government remained passive during these negotiations, implicitly giving support to the final arrangements by not stepping in to modify them.

7

Independent Telephones

In early 1885 one pillar undergirding the Bell Telephone monopoly crumbled. The Minister of Agriculture, Sir John Carling (the brewmaster), serving also as patent commissioner, noted that Bell was importing parts for its telephone instruments and was leasing, not selling, sets.[1] Carling declared the original Bell patent void on 24 January.[2] Adding insult to injury, another patent was negated in 1887.[3]

Recognizing at once the gravity of the commissioner's ruling, C.F. Sise, still vice-president of Bell, turned to Theodore N. Vail, general manager of American Bell, for help in devising strategies to shore up the flagging monopoly. Vail's advice was succinct: rapid construction of long-distance lines to connect all exchanges within three hundred miles of Montreal. (At the time, Bell's longest toll line barely exceeded twenty miles.) Vail was prescient in remarking that this construction, although expensive, 'will unify and save your business.'[4]

TACTICAL WITHDRAWALS

Facing the prospect of costly construction and anticipating heavy onslaughts of competition, Bell's managers soon decided to withdraw from the fringes of the company's vast territory to better protect monopoly from incursions in the heartland. The tiny province of Prince Edward Island was jettisoned in 1885. Bell accepted $1500 cash plus $1000 in stock for its rights and facilities there. As might be expected, the facilities were not extensive – eleven telephones in all, seven of which were concentrated in offices of the PEI Railway at Charlottetown. But on this modest scale, the Telephone Company of Prince Edward Island was born.[5]

In 1889 British Columbia too was ejected. Bell transferred to the Victoria and Esquimalt Telephone Company 310 instruments hitherto operated under agreement with local interests. In this case the break was clean and enduring; Bell re-entered the BC telephone industry only in 1988 by acquiring NorthwesTel, serving some remote regions of the province.[6]

Far less drastic surgery was contemplated for Nova Scotia and New Brunswick, where Bell planned initially to retain the larger exchanges and all toll lines, turning over to local companies merely the unprofitable rural territories – a way, it was hoped, of enlisting local capital while retaining effective control. By 1887 a number of such rural lines were operating in both provinces.[7]

But soon competition struck. The Nova Scotia Telephone Company, incorporated under provincial law in 1887, was set up to serve Halifax and region and 'as great an area of the rest of the province as was practicable.'[8] After a brief but bitter conflagration, a truce was called and Bell sold off its provincial facilities in 1888, attaining stock control over its erstwhile assailant.[9]

Bell's plans for New Brunswick likewise ran awry in 1887, when the Nova Scotia Telephone Company, territorially ambitious, solicited also subscribers in the neighbouring province. In 1988 Bell included its facilities in New Brunswick in its sale to the Nova Scotia Telephone Company[10] – a situation that provoked anguish in the New Brunswick legislature: a Montreal-controlled, Nova Scotia–based company monopolizing provincial telephones. To remedy this unfelicitous circumstance, provincial politicians incorporated the New Brunswick Telephone Company, complete with an exclusive ten-year franchise to erect poles and string lines among principal communities, ostensibly obviating any prospect of a Bell Telephone/Nova Scotia Telephone monopoly over provincial long distance.[11] Immediately the Nova Scotia Telephone Company attempted a tactical retreat. But it found Bell Telephone's grip to be too tight, and so in 1889 it sold its facilities in New Brunswick back to Bell Telephone. Bell in turn resold the same to New Brunswick Telephone. Thus, at the conclusion of these transactions, Bell wound up with a strong equity position in the company chartered for New Brunswick.[12]

QUEBEC

Notwithstanding nullification of the telephone patent, the independent telephone movement started quite slowly in both Quebec and Ontario. In Quebec it appears only four independents were operational between 1885 and 1891. One was the Dominion Telephone Company, centred in Sherbrooke. Organized in 1882 by a Mr Webster to promote the ideal of universal telephone service for farmers, this was the company that had petitioned the minister of agriculture to nullify Bell's patent. Surprisingly successful, it stepped up its cut-rate telephone service, slashing prices to $17 and $30 per year for residential and business telephones, respectively, a substantial saving compared with Bell's charges of $30 and $35. Deftly Bell countered, offering its former subscribers one year's free service on a three-year contract, largesse sufficient to drive the upstart into bankruptcy.[13] On 13 January 1886 Bell Telephone purchased the property of the bereft business, including patents and goodwill, on condition that its owners 'neither directly nor indirectly ... re-enter [the] telephone business in Canada.'[14]

The People's Telephone Company took up the same challenge somewhat more successfully two years later. Also centred in Sherbrooke, People's territory grew to encompass much of the Eastern Townships. Still operating in 1905 it claimed 400 miles of toll line and 900 subscribers, at which point its president, Charles Skinner, correctly proclaimed the People's to be 'the oldest company now competing against the Bell Telephone Company.'[15]

A third Quebec irritant, quite ephemeral, was the Federal Telephone Company, incorporated in 1887 to compete against Bell in Montreal, which even briefly entertained notions of expanding to Toronto.[16] Set up by members of the CPR syndicate[17] and granted rights in April 1888 to erect poles on Montreal's streets, Federal Telephone opened for business in 1889, setting its price for one instrument at $35, $15 below Bell's annual charge. When Bell countered by not merely matching the $35 rate but undercutting it by a further $10, the parvenu wisely avoided provoking further retaliation, freezing its price at $35 while Bell continued undercutting at $25. Given these price discrepancies the popularity achieved by the Federal is quite surprising: at one point it managed to attract some 1500 subscribers.[18] None the less, and understandably, it was not a financial success, incurring losses of $167,000 over its two brief years.[19] Winding the company down in October 1891 its chief executive officer remarked sadly: 'It is quite evident that the Public prefers one Company at a fair price, to two Companies at low rates.'[20] Bell took the Federal Telephone Company over in 1892 for a hefty $182,700 and immediately wrote down the shares in its books to $28,185, explaining laconically to shareholders that there had been a 'decreased valuation in stocks.'[21]

With the Federal Telephone Company out of the way Bell announced it was going to reinstate charges existing prior to the outbreak of competition,[22] much to the dismay of some local merchants, a number of whom were distraught in any event over Bell's refusal to serve them in French.[23] Consequently, in the following year a number banded together to form the fourth Quebec company considered here, the co-operatively owned Merchants' Telephone Company (Compagnie de Téléphone des Marchands de Montréal, Limitée), which had as its objectives:

To prevent a monopoly in Telephone service and to insure –
1st – A reasonable rate not exceeding $15 per annum per Telephone,
2nd – A perfect service with latest improved apparatus and methods,
3rd – A Co-operative Association with Telephone Users as stockholders.[24]

The Merchants' certainly had a rough start. A Bell informant, keeping tabs on its progress, wrote sceptically to Captain Sise on 28 February 1893: 'The company has not yet got into operation awaiting permission from the City to erect poles and as yet have [sic] not begun drawing the necessary materials from the woods ... giving cause to doubt whether it will succeed.'[25]

But by 4 August the Bell watchdog, albeit grudgingly, was forced to acknowledge some progress, reporting: 'The Company have been granted permission by the City Council to erect poles in the City ...' Then on a more positive note, the memo added: 'They have not begun construction work and, by some, confidence is not felt in the success of the Company.'[26]

Five weeks later, on 14 September 1893, the Bell spy, still filing surreptitious reports, announced lugubriously that Merchants' 'have given the contract to build their lines to Beauchemin & Co. ... and at present about three car loads have arrived in the City.' But again the report concluded on a more optimistic note: 'Entire confidence is not felt in the success of the Company and the endorsation of L.E. Beauchamp [the Treasurer] is suggested.'[27]

Certainly the informant's scepticism was not unwarranted. The record reveals clearly that by October 1894 Merchants' was in financial disarray. Three directors had resigned during the preceding three months; St Henri and St Cunegonde, suburbs of Montreal, had refused permission to put up poles; and the company's contractor was refusing to do any more work, holding 'everything he has got in his possession' until paid the $48,000 then owing. Summarizing discussions of its annual meeting, Merchants' annual report for the year stated candidly: 'All work has been suspended: and the Company is burst. It was resolved to open books for fresh subscriptions in stock.'[28]

Somehow Merchants' did recover, however, claiming 595 subscribers in December 1894, of which 350 subscribed also to Bell.[29] By 1897 its listing had grown to 889, of which 410 subscribed also to Bell.[30] By 1905 Merchants' had 1546 subscribers, 190 residential and the remainder businesses.[31] Merchants' rates were well below Bell's [32] but it lacked long-distance connections, unlike its more opulent opponent.[33] Nor had it yet turned a profit.[34] None the less, Merchants' Telephone Company persisted languidly until 1913, when in liquidation Bell purchased its plant. Even at its demise it still retained 1500 faithful subscribers.

ONTARIO

Less robust still was the early independent telephone movement in Ontario. Only about three competing companies were started prior to 1892,[35] and for good reason. In Peterborough the new arrival faced the ignomy of being used as an example for others who might contemplate entry. Slashing prices to woo customers it succeeded only in bringing down the wrath of Bell, which immediately inaugurated an all-out price war, declaring the town a 'free exchange.' Bell's special agent, W.C. Scott, explained to the local press his company's 'liberality':

It has been held that the Bell Telephone Company were not justified in declaring this a free exchange, but should have simply come down to the cut rate instituted by the opposition. This would be taken as an acknowledgement that the lower rate is a profitable one which we know it is not, and would simply offer a premium to similar opposition throughout Canada, to the utter ruin of the telephone business, a result that would be as unsatisfactory to people generally as to the stockholders of their company ... There was, therefore, no other course open but to declare war to the knife. So far as The Bell Telephone Company is concerned, it is their settled policy to allow opposition companies first to invest their capital and then fight it out, as they are doing here and as they will continue to do so as long as the opposition continues.[36]

Short-lived too was competition at the Lakehead, inaugurated by the Port Arthur Telephone Company.[37] But in both Peterborough and Port Arthur competition flared again after 1900, when new companies entered – once more in direct competition with Bell Telephone.

THE WEST

In the west Bell for a time followed construction of the CPR, pre-empting in large measure independent lines on the prairies. Already in Winnipeg in 1881, Bell actually started 'competing' with itself in 1885 to ward off real competition, surreptitiously setting up the People's Telephone Company to undercut both its own prices and those of its true rival; when the latter collapsed in early 1886, the People's Telephone Company also packed it in, 'leaving Bell Telephone in full command of the situation at the old rates.'[38]

Bell inaugurated telephone service in Brandon and Portage la Prairie in 1882,[39] in Regina in 1884,[40] and in Calgary and Lethbridge in 1887 and 1891, respectively.[41] Significantly, however, the first telephones in Alberta were installed in 1885 by independent agents in Edmonton. But generally, non-Bell telephones on the prairies remained few and far between prior to 1892.[42]

INDEPENDENT TELEPHONES IN THE UNITED STATES

The Canadian independent telephone movement thus languished until about 1893, at which time the birth of an independent industry in the United States gave Canadian independents new impetus and support. In 1893 the basic u.s. patent to the telephone hand-set expired,[43] and so competitive entry resulted in vigorous and rapid growth.[44] Whereas telephones in the United States had increased on average by only 6.3 per cent per year from 1885 to 1894, between 1895 and 1905 the average annual increase was 28 per cent. Expansion during this competitive era was both extensive and intensive. Extensively, independents entered the less densely populated areas hitherto neglected by the u.s. Bell System; intensively, direct competition in urban centres where Bell had previously been established caused prices to tumble, bringing telephones 'within the financial grasp of a larger consumer group.'[45] By 1913 there were 20,000 u.s. independents servicing 3.6 million telephones; the Bell System, meanwhile, counted 5.1 million telephone sets.[46]

One of the tactics used by u.s. Bell to stifle competition was refusal to sell instruments to independents.[47] The strategy backfired, however, when numerous unaffiliated equipment manufacturers were set up to fill the void.[48] Kellog Switchboard and Supply Company, Stromberg-Carlson Telephone Manufacturing Company, Automatic Electric Company, and other suppliers proved essential to the Canadian independent industry as well as the u.s., constituting an alternative and more accessible source of equipment.[49]

Furthermore, the onset and expansion of independent telephony in the United States fanned the fading sparks of telephone competition in Canada through the publicity and interest generated and by demonstrating that independents could indeed survive. A new resolve was infused into the hearts of Canadian rural residents and entrepreneurs alike to bring about extensions in telephone service for the less densely populated regions of our country.

RURAL LINES IN QUEBEC IN 1905

Like its u.s. parent, the Bell Telephone Company of Canada was not particularly solicitous about provisioning rural service. It simply did not make good business sense to do so, given upper limits to the company's resources. As then-president C.F. Sise explained candidly to members of Parliament in 1905, 'We certainly, and quite properly ... give the preference to the needs of a larger number rather than to a lot of farmers' lines. There is a much better return from the expenditure of money on that work than there will be from the expenditure of the same money on smaller lines.'[50]

Statistics highlight an enormous disparity between rural and urban telephone development. As late as 1904 the Bell Telephone Company of Canada supplied merely 2000 rural telephones out of the 66,160 instruments it then owned, resulting in one set for every 1247 rural residents. By contrast, it provided 51,080 instruments in cities and towns with populations of 7000 and greater, or one set for every 21.9 urban residents (see table 7.1).[51] Montreal and Toronto alone accounted for 27,709 telephones, or 42 per cent of the company's total supply, even though the two cities combined represented less than 14

TABLE 7.1
Urban/rural telephone service, Bell Telephone Company of Canada, provinces of
Quebec, Ontario, and Manitoba, 31 December 1904

| | Urban | | | |
	Towns and cities with 7000 and over population	Other urban communities*	Rural	Total
Population	1,118,008	575,085	2,493,471	4,186,564
Telephones	51,080	13,080	2,000	66,160
Telephones per 100 population	4.6	2.3	0.08	1.6
Inhabitants per telephone	21.9	44.0	1,247	63.3

* Population in 'Other urban communities' estimated by author following Bell's
methodology for: 'Towns and cities with 7000 and over population' (by taking
census data for 1901 and adding 10 per cent of the increase during the ten-year
census interval for each of the three years since the 1901 census, then subtracting
from this total the two population estimates supplied by Bell)
SOURCE: The Bell Telephone Company of Canada, data printed in House of
Commons, Select Committee on Telephone Systems, *Proceedings*, 810–11; Census
of Canada 1891, 2, 4

per cent of the population in Bell's principal service areas of Quebec,
Ontario, and Manitoba.[52]
   To help fill the rural gap, independent telephone companies proliferated. In Quebec the largest of these was the Bellechasse Telephone
Company (La Compagnie de Téléphone de Bellechasse), which
received a provincial charter in 1893. Initially, however, it certainly
did not make utmost use of the privilege, and by 1900 it could still
count only 50 miles of line and twenty-three subscribers. But a more
aggressive entrepreneur, Dr T.J. Demers, took it over that year and
expanded it into a major system. Dr Demers had entered the telephone
business a couple of years earlier by setting up a small system (the
Métis Telephone Company) as an adjunct to his medical practice.
Then, with a provincial charter in his pocket, he began taking the
telephone business seriously and by 1905 was able to claim 1500 subscribers along 1200 miles of pole line connecting Rimouski, Matane,
Montagamy, Levis, and Rivière du Loup. Over much of the territory

Dr Demers held a clear monopoly, but in Levis he competed head-on with the Bell Telephone Company of Canada.

Bell did not take lightly to Dr Demers's intrusion. As soon as Bellechasse began soliciting subscribers in Levis, the larger company published advertisements in local papers under the signature of C.F. Sise, threatening to prosecute the independent system's *subscribers* for patent infringement.[53] None the less the Bellechasse company persisted in its independent existence, and areas opened up by Dr Demers today constitute the nucleus of Québec-Téléphone.

One of Bellechasse's principal connections was with the Beauce Telephone Company, established in 1895. Within a decade the Beauce had 600 subscribers and 200 miles of pole running 'alongside the Bell Telephone Company, [reducing] to nearly nothing the number of subscribers of the Bell Telephone Company and [increasing] their own more than in proportion.'[54] One of the reasons for Beauce's popularity may well have been its proffering a free local service.[55]

Although Bell Telephone for several years refused to provide long-distance connections to either Bellechasse or Beauce, in 1904 it relented, in a way, offering the latter toll connections, provided: (1) Beauce would connect with no other company, directly or indirectly, without first securing Bell's permission; (2) Beauce would not compete with Bell or extend its lines to places then occupied by Bell; (3) Beauce would purchase telephone sets only from Bell; and (4) Bell would receive first option to purchase Beauce.[56]

Beauce rejected the offer.

As Dr Demers was later to testify, the proposal was designed 'to take the Bellechasse Telephone Company out of the field.'[57]

Today the territory originally developed by the Beauce Telephone Company is subsumed also within the operations of Québec-Téléphone.

By the end of 1904 there were some sixteen independent companies operating in Quebec, accounting for 5507 telephones. Bell Telephone at that time operated 22,636 phones in the province.[58]

RURAL LINES IN ONTARIO IN 1905

In Ontario about eighty-three independent telephone companies, many quite small, were established between 1892 and 1905 (see table 7.2). As noted by Thomas Grindlay, more than a few of Ontario's early rural systems were set up by doctors to keep in touch with patients

TABLE 7.2
Formation by year of independent telephone companies
in Ontario (1892–1905)

Year	Number of Systems	Year	Number of Systems
1892	1	1899	7
1893	1	1900	5
1894	1	1901	3
1895	5	1902	16
1896	1	1903	4
1897	1	1904	12
1898	2	1905	24

SOURCE: Compiled from Thomas Grindlay, *A History of the Independent Telephone Industry in Ontario*, 254–305

scattered over their districts. As well, several independents were founded by general storekeepers fulfilling requests from neighbouring farmers to connect onto lines running from the general store to the village from which the merchant attained supplies. Still others were started by Bell 'agents' who received commissions for installing pay telephones on their premises; when other residents were connected, local systems were born. In yet other cases rural lines were opened by lumbering, mining, and manufacturing companies to connect with the nearest Bell exchange; once nearby residents connected, the companies found themselves in the telephone business.[59]

One of the early companies started by a physician was the Beatty Telephone System. Begun in 1895 by Alexander Beatty of Garden Hill, ostensibly to keep him in touch with patients living within a ten-mile radius of the village, in the good doctor's hands the communication network became a device for relaxation and entertainment. Dr Beatty was an inveterate eavesdropper, frequently listening in on conversations while on switchboard duty. He was also, however, an indiscreet eavesdropper, with a penchant for argument and a somewhat willful disposition. Not infrequently did the physician interrupt 'private' conversations to give vent to his own opinions. This eccentricity evidently did not prove unduly disconcerting to his subscribers, however, inasmuch as the Beatty Telephone System in 1946, the year of the medic's death, still claimed 200 customers along its 100 miles of pole line.[60]

G.W. Jones of Newtonville was the pioneer of a nearby system in

Port Hope. In 1899 he purchased wire and poles to inaugurate an independent company, but before his first pole had been planted Bell got wind of the project, bought Jones out, and secured his promise never again to enter the telephone field. The vexatious Jones thus seemingly neutralized, Bell dallied for several years in constructing lines in the area. Impatient at the lack of service, and sensing opportunity, Jones re-entered the business in 1905, albeit under his brother's name, and by 1908 his operations sprawled over parts of Clarke and Hope townships, linking Newcastle and Port Hope, whereupon the Port Hope Telephone Company became an incorporated enterprise. For many years Bell Telephone refused to as much as acknowledge the existence of Jones's company, steadfastly denying it connections to the outside world. Although Jones's customers in Newcastle had to visit the local Bell office if they wanted to call long distance, his clients in Port Hope were a bit less discommoded, having available as a second option the local mortuary, where the funeral directors, possessing phones from both companies, amicably undertook to relay messages to the Bell long-distance operator.[61] The Port Hope Telephone Company became one of the principal instigators of the interconnection battles that raged before the Board of Railway Commissioners after 1906, and these proceedings are addressed below.

MUNICIPAL TELEPHONES

Prior to 1906 a few municipally owned systems also sprang up, most notably in Fort William and Port Arthur (today amalgamated as Thunder Bay). Thomas Grindlay reports that in 1877 Neil McDougall and a certain Mr Cooke received two of Melville Bell's instruments to initiate an experimental connection between Prince Arthur's Landing and Town Plot, six miles distant. Then in 1884 town council passed a by-law granting rights to the Port Arthur Telephone Company to install a system, but Bell Telephone immediately opened its own exchanges, proclaiming that it alone had exclusive rights to provide service there, as in the rest of Canada. The status of Port Arthur Telephone Company for the years immediately following is unclear, but in any event it had certainly expired by 1902,[62] by which time local residents had become so disaffected with Bell's high rates and poor service that plebiscites in both towns confirmed surging support for municipal ownership.

By October the two municipalities had their own, mutually interconnected, systems operating. Rates were cut,[63] and a protracted confrontation ensued. Bell at first merely matched the price reductions, but when the Fort William system lay incapacitated in 1903 (the handiwork of an unidentified arsonist), Bell seized the opportunity, offering free telephones 'to all and sundry,'[64] soon establishing a free listing of about seventy-five phones. Throughout 1904 Bell continued providing more than one hundred free telephones in Fort William out of its total subscriber listing of 157, while in Port Arthur 28 of its total listing of 73 were free telephones.[65] The mayor of Fort William, lamenting before a parliamentary inquiry, explained: 'You all know gentlemen, there are a few people in every town who are always glad to get something for nothing, no matter how little it is.'[66] Then, on a more positive note, he added: 'I must say though that the people of the two towns have been wonderfully loyal to their system.'[67]

And loyal they were. In Port Arthur 515 continued subscribing to the municipal system, despite Bell's liberality, and in Fort William 500 continued with the town's service.[68]

Bell's harassment did not stop at free phones, however. In 1904 Mr W.C. Scott, Bell's special agent, accompanied by a certain Captain Holmes, representing himself as a grain dealer, visited the Lakehead. Captain Holmes circulated a petition, under false pretenses as it turned out, demanding a government audit of the Fort William system's books, most of which had been consumed in the fire of 1903. On the train home, according to an official report prepared for the town council, Mssrs Scott and Holmes together hammered out an article, quite inaccurate and misleading but none the less published by newspapers in Toronto and Ottawa, alleging the municipalities to be teetering on the brink of bankruptcy. Both municipalities at the time were trying to float new issues of bonds.[69]

Hostilities continued for several years but ceased finally in 1909, when Bell sold its exchanges to the municipalities, albeit retaining an exclusive right to operate toll lines. From that point to this, local service has been operated by the local governments with Bell continuing to provide long-distance connections. In 1970, with the amalgamation of the twin cities, the telephone systems were merged,[70] and today the operation is known as Thunder Bay Telecommunications.

Agitation for municipal ownership bore less fruit in other communities – Brantford, the very birthplace of the telephone and Ottawa being prime examples. In Ottawa ratepayers actually voted in support of municipalization despite adverse publicity accorded the scheme by

Bell Telephone, but to no avail; legislation did not exist whereby facilities could be expropriated, nor were there provisions in law to compel long-distance connections.[71] Bell therefore has persisted in the nation's capital to the present.

In Brantford, even as town council was fractiously debating whether or not to renew Bell's exclusive franchise – or rather perhaps to install its own system – Bell published in the local press an open letter from C.F. Sise alleging city ownership in Glasgow, Scotland, to have been a costly failure; the implication was that ratepayers in Brantford too would end up subsidizing municipal telephones.[72] Inaccurate allegations concerning the financial status of the town-owned systems in Port Arthur and Fort William were also made, as we have just seen, and when members of the Brantford council journeyed to the Lakehead to ascertain the facts for themselves they were accompanied by none other than the ubiquitous Mr W.C. Scott. Heated discussions also took place during Brantford's town council meetings when local businessmen were informed that long-distance connections and telephone communication with CPR and Grand Trunk Railway stations would be cut off if a municipal system were established. In the end such threats proved sufficient to cause town council to rescind its by-law enabling municipal ownership. None the less, a franchise was awarded to the Canadian Machine Telephone Company in 1905,[73] which just a few months earlier had also secured a municipal franchise for Peterborough.[74]

Headquartered in Toronto, Canadian Machine Telephone Company owned Canadian manufacturing rights to the Lorimer automatic-switching system, a device invented in Canada, which required no operators at the central office to make connections.[75] To sell its switches, however, the company found it necessary to itself attain telephone franchises because Bell was buying most of its equipment from its own subsidiary, the Northern Electric and Manufacturing Company, Limited.[76] Within three weeks of attaining the Peterborough franchise Canadian Machine had enlisted 400 subscribers,[77] its success quite possibly being attributable to its promise to charge no rentals until it surpassed Bell's listing,[78] a feat it never accomplished. In this case Bell Telephone found it unnecessary to cut rates.[79] The Canadian Machine Telephone Company endured none the less until 1925, at which time its 1026 subscribers in Brantford, Peterborough, and Lindsay were transferred to Bell.[80]

THE PRAIRIES

Independent companies spurted up in the west too. In 1899 the Manitoba government began intervening in telephone matters by enacting an amendment to the Municipal Act which, despite Bell's presence in Winnipeg, Portage la Prairie, Brandon, and elsewhere, would permit municipal ownership of local exchanges.[82] First off the mark was Neepawa in 1900, followed soon by dozens of other communities.[83] As elsewhere, Bell refused to connect any of the new arrivals to its long-distance lines; in Neepawa, to cite one startling illustration, Bell retained only twelve subscribers compared with the municipal system's two hundred, but it was the twelve who had access to long distance.[84] The municipal movement in Manitoba surged ahead until 1905, at which point the provincial government announced it would henceforth deny all further applications for incorporation;[85] none the less, it also announced it was initiating studies into the feasibility and desirability of a provincial take-over of all telephones in the province.

In Saskatchewan by 1905 there were at least two independent telephone companies: the Telephone and Light Company, Ltd., of Moosomin and Wapella, with 150 subscribers; and the Yorkton North West Electric Company, established in 1900, with 152. Bell Telephone at the time operated 168 phones in Regina and 76 in Prince Albert.[86]

In Alberta the principal non-Bell exchange was in Edmonton, where the District Telephone Company had received an exclusive ten-year franchise in 1893. In 1904 Bell tried to buy up the system, having previously established exchanges in Calgary, Lethbridge, and Red Deer, but the town fathers, intent on keeping Bell at bay outside the municipal limits, made a counter-offer, acquiring the company for $14,000.[87] By 1905 Edmonton had about 460 telephones,[88] while Bell operated 752 telephones elsewhere in the province.[89]

RAILWAY CONTRACTS

In addition to Bell's refusing interconnections and its cutting prices, its public relations, and its 'politicking,' mention must also be made of exclusive privileges negotiated by Bell during this early period, again helping to thwart entry. Exclusionary agreements were of two types: those negotiated with the railways, and those attained from municipalities.

Beginning in 1891 Bell secured agreement from fourteen major railways for exclusive rights to place instruments in railway stations and to construct telephone lines along railroad rights of way.[90] A contract of 1 May 1902 between Bell and the Canadian Pacific Railway Company is typical. Here Bell agreed to: (1) offer free exchange service between all offices and stations of the CPR and Bell exchanges; (2) give free long-distance telephone service to CPR officials; and (3) provide free telephone exchange connections and maintain a local exchange at CPR's head-office (Windsor Station, Montreal), affording both internal and external telephone service. In return CPR agreed to: (1) give annual passes to telephone company officials and employees for both its railroad and telegraph lines; (2) give Bell the 'exclusive right of placing telephone instruments, apparatus and wires in the several stations, offices and premises of the Railway Company throughout the Dominion of Canada'; and (3) grant exclusive rights to Bell Telephone to construct telephone plant along CPR premises and rights-of-way. This last provision foreclosed Canadian Pacific Railway Telegraphs from entering the telephone business utilizing CPR rights-of-way.

Bell Telephone, through a wholly owned subsidiary, the North American Telegraph Company, possessed at this time a federal charter entitling it to offer telegraph service throughout Canada; and indeed it was taking advantage of this right in the Kingston, Ontario, region. The threat of Bell's entering into full-scale competition with CPR Telegraphs, coupled with the trying times experienced previously by the CPR syndicate with the Federal Telephone Company, and the emoluments noted above, were sufficient to persuade CPR against offering a public telephone service. For Bell's part, it never extended telegraph operations beyond the Kingston vicinity.

Restrictive contracts with the railways enfeebled competition on other fronts too. It is to be recognized that the railroad station at that time was the centre of commerce in most communities. To competing telephone companies it was a severe blow to be barred from the local railway station; merchants, for example, could not use independent telephones to enquire about the arrival of merchandise. But sometimes the railways themselves suffered. In Fort William, as one flagrant illustration, 'The Canadian Pacific Railway Company, owing to its agreement with the Bell Telephone Company, are not subscribers of the municipal system, and therefore, have no means of communicating with the police or fire department for the protection of their property and the convenience of their patrons.'[91]

Parliament attempted to abridge some of these restrictions in 1903 by giving authority to the newly created Board of Railway Commissioners to order railway companies to permit telephone apparatus in stations 'upon such terms as to compensation or otherwise as the Board deems just and expedient.'[92] But in its first ruling on the matter the board declared that the act required indemnification of *Bell* 'for the loss of the exclusive privilege of telephone connection with such stations,'[93] thereby abrogating Parliament's intent. In response, the legislature passed an act in 1906 directing the board to ignore any exclusive contract that might exist in awarding compensation,[94] and so in 1909 the People's Telephone Company and the Caledon Telephone Company finally received access to the stations of the CPR and Grand Trunk Railway.[95]

EXCLUSIVE FRANCHISES

Bell also bought exclusive franchises from numerous municipalities: thirty of them by 1905[96] and forty more between 1905 and 1910.[97] In return for a guarantee of a local monopoly Bell paid each municipality a franchise fee, frequently throwing in some free telephones. Bell promised also not to raise rates for a specified time. For a number of years this regulatory rate control was the only one Bell faced.

CONCLUSIONS

The foregoing historical account should aid in dispelling certain myths today enveloping Canadian telecommunications. First, it is to be concluded that Bell's predominance in Ontario and Quebec was certainly not 'thrust upon' it by characteristics inhering in plant and equipment; nor was it achieved by dint of superior service or operating efficiency. Rather, the imperium it attained and currently enjoys was an outcome both of government privilege and of aggressive and frequently predatory business practices.

Second, monopoly provided no guarantee of service universality; precisely the opposite was the case. Bell chose to concentrate on serving lucrative urban areas. Rural districts, in contrast, received service primarily through small independent companies.

Third, telephony has hardly been an instrument for national unity and sovereignty. Almost from its inception the industry resided predominantly under u.s. ownership and control, with corporate policies being set south of the border. Moreover, telephony has proved to be regionally divisive, a matter taken up below.

Myths of 'natural monopoly,' of 'service universality through system-wide cost averaging,' and of 'technological nationalism' each retain persuasive power today only because we have lost touch with history, with the 'soiling trace of origin or choice.' But citizens at the turn of the century held no such illusions; they were too close to events for that. On the contrary, there was a great hue and cry over monopolistic price-gouging, over predatory business practices, and over service deprivation in rural areas. Opposition to Bell's monopoly was so intense and the clamour for public control so strong in this century's initial decade that the federal government, albeit reluctantly, was goaded into acting. The inception of regulation is described in the following chapter.

8

The Politics of Government Control

PETITIONS

The first attempt by the federal government to assume a measure
of regulatory control over the Bell Telephone Company of Canada
occurred in 1892, with an amendment to the Bell charter providing
that 'existing rates shall not be increased without the consent of the
Governor-in-Council.'[1] This provision was deemed nugatory by the
minister of justice in 1897, however, when he opined that the amended
clause pertained only to contracts existing prior to the act's passage,
meaning that Bell could raise prices indiscriminately – certainly to
new subscribers, but also to existing ones upon changes in the equipment rented.[2] Therefore rounds of rate increases ensued, and Parliament was inundated with petitions – from 104 municipalities in 1901
and from another 98 in 1902[3] – all demanding control over Bell's prices.

As response the company's Act of Incorporation was amended again
in 1902, providing: 'The rates for telephone service in any municipality
may be increased or diminished by Order of the Governor-in-Council
upon the application of the Company or of any interested municipality, and thereafter the rates so ordered shall be the rates under this
Act until again similarly adjusted by the Governor-in-Council.'[4] If,
however, this latter revision was intended to placate the public and
relieve pressure on the government, it certainly failed.

COMMONS UPROAR

One of the country's unrelenting voices for greater public control was
William Findlay Maclean (1854–1929), 'stormy petrel of journalism

and Parliament,'[5] member from East York between 1892 and 1904 and thereafter representing South York until 1926. He was, according to the Boston *Transcript*, 'a man of bull-dog tenacity.'

Prior to 1880 Maclean had been reporter with the Toronto *Daily Globe*, but upon graduation from the University of Toronto he established and edited his own daily, the Toronto *World*, first of the Canadian penny presses and that city's 'independent conservative organ.'[6] Maclean was clearly more independent than Conservative, however; his 'radical' views caused him to be drummed out of the Conservative party in August 1905. Sitting for the next several years as an independent, he ran afoul of the party's establishment yet again in 1926, when he failed to win nomination. His causes, although sometimes quaint (Hudson Bay to be renamed the Canadian Sea), were almost always progressive and invariably founded on a strong Canadian nationalism, most uncommon at the time. With his father, John Maclean, W.F. is credited with first suggesting Sir John A. Macdonald's national policy of protective tariffs to encourage east-west trade. As well he promoted public ownership of electrical utilities (long before Sir Adam Beck took up the mantle), of railways, and of telegraph and telephone companies; he recommended that banks and insurance companies be made subject to stringent public control. He won antipathy from fellow Conservatives, however, by pressing for greater Canadian independence from Britain (an elected head-of-state; made-in-Canada constitution; treaties to be negotiated by Canadians), but fared no better with the Liberal continentalists either: 'No merger with the u.s. for Canada and Canadians,' said Billy Maclean, 'but on the contrary complete integrity for the Dominion on the continent of North America.' 'A journalist of rare talent,' he joined both the third and fourth estates to promote his independent views.[7]

In Parliament a milestone in the continuing telephone debate occurred on 26 June 1903, when Maclean pointed his finger at conflicts of interest within the government. He did so reluctantly and out of frustration. His private members' bill of 1902 to stop predatory pricing in the telephone industry and to initiate public regulation, 'with the option of public ownership at any time,'[8] had died on the order paper. His bill of the current session, to annul the agreement between Bell Telephone and CPR barring independent telephones from railway stations,[9] was meeting with no greater success. Nor, evidently, was Prime Minister Laurier about to make good on his promise of the previous session to legislate on telephone matters within the year.[10] So, on 26 June, Maclean set the Commons into an uproar. He began calmly and matter-of-factly reviewing the ban on municipal telephones from CPR stations at the Lakehead and elsewhere, adding: 'I say this is a shame. I know the people will rebel against it ... '[11]

Maclean then turned to the manner in which the government was opposing his amendment, in his view not on principle but rather through innuendo and character assassination. The minister of railways, Hon. A.G. Blair, had termed his proposal 'socialistic' and 'radical' and had accused Maclean of trying to 'disfigure' his bill.

Other members then arose to support Maclean. Mr Frank Oliver from Alberta, for example, complained that Bell's plans to install lines south from Edmonton through various towns, some of which already had municipally owned telephones, were designed to wipe out independent companies on the prairies.[12]

Buoyed by such affirmations Maclean pressed on, dropping his bombshell: A.G. Blair, minister of railways, was also president of the New Brunswick Telephone Company, controlled by Bell. Other directors of the New Brunswick Telephone Company included C.F. Sise and senators Mackay and Thompson, the last-named also its managing director. Maclean commented drily: 'I call the attention of the Prime Minister to this fact, that the Minister of Railways in his government is a member of this great Bell Telephone Company, now dominating this country; and when I proposed an amendment to his Bill that the public shall be fairly treated, he rises and accuses me of being a socialist, a radical, as one who wants to disfigure his Bill.'[13]

Maclean proceeded to sketch a dark history of the New Brunswick Telephone Company, relating how Hon. A.G. Blair, while premier of the province, along with relatives including his brother-in-law and son-in-law, Liberal senator F.P. Thompson, attained from the New Brunswick legislature a charter and exclusive privileges for the New Brunswick Telephone Company, in which they held substantial stock. Bell Telephone, as seen previously, soon took a large minority shareholding in the New Brunswick Telephone Company, sufficient for practical control, while Mr Blair continued to hold about one-sixth of the issued shares, even as federal minister of railways.[14] Maclean called for Blair's immediate resignation, commenting wryly; 'It is a peculiar thing that in some way there is an apparent connection between the kind of protection accorded to the Bell Telephone Company by the government, by the House, and by this committee so far; it is a peculiar thing, I say, that this company, in its monopolistic tendencies, should be specially guarded in every way.'[15]

Laurier's initial response was feeble:

I did not know that Mr. Mackay, when appointed a senator, was president of the Bell Telephone Company or that he was a member of it. That idea never entered into the consideration of the government in appointing him to the Senate. The same thing might be said in regard to Senator Thompson. It appears that Senator Thompson is a member of the telephone company, and my hon. friend says that my colleague, the Minister of Railways and Canals (Hon. Mr. Blair) is also a member of the telephone company. That is the first intimation I have had of it, but I do not know that it is a crime for anybody to hold the stock of such a company as that.[16]

Laurier went on to assert that the Railway bill was 'of general interest, not for the profit or benefit of any company whatever ... a general Bill for the regulation of trade and commerce on railways.'[17] Then having established his defence, such as it was, he went on the offensive: 'I accuse him [Maclean] formally, not of being a socialist, but of being a communist. I thought there was something in his Bill that smelt [sic] strongly of communism, because he has betrayed a tendency to commit depredations upon vested rights and the property of other people.'[18]

Whatever one may think of Laurier's defence, his minister of railways, A.G. Blair, did not survive the session, resigning his ministry shortly thereafter, ostensibly in opposition to Laurier's plans to build the Grand Trunk Pacific.[19] The telephone question, however, still smouldered.

In 1904 Maclean resumed his clarion call – 'Now is the time to nationalize the telephone and telegraphs of this country'[20] – but to no avail.

He was, however, gaining support outside Parliament. Early in 1905 Parliament received petitions from 195 municipalities and counties requesting that Bell Telephone be prevented from erecting poles and wires in any municipality without the consent of the local council. In addition the Union of Canadian Municipalities forwarded a petition urging that telephone systems be acquired by the government.[21] These entreaties were all in response to a ruling by the privy council in

London, England, confirming Bell's charter powers to place poles down any street in Canada without local governmental permission. A provincial law purporting to govern Bell Telephone in this matter had thereby been ruled ultra vires.[22] Likewise, the Dominion Grange Convention announced support for 'federal operation of trunk telephone lines to facilitate municipal control of telephones.'[23]

The government, facing the prospect of an election, could dally no longer. On 17 March 1905 Prime Minister Wilfrid Laurier constituted a Select Committee of the House of Commons, chaired by Postmaster General Sir William Mulock, to report upon the telephone situation and recommend what changes, if any, should be implemented.

It is apparent that the telephone industry in Canada had come a long way in the thirty years or so that had lapsed since Alexander Graham Bell's remarkable invention and the industry's somewhat comical and unbusinesslike inauguration in the hands of Melville Bell and Rev. Thomas Henderson. Indeed it had become a big, vital, but cut-throat business. According to the climate of the times, some degree of government control was overdue.

PARLIAMENTARY INQUIRY

'I shall not prejudge the subject myself,' intoned Sir William Mulock (1844–1944), 'although, perhaps, if I must confess to a bias as regards the telephone, that bias would be that I cannot see why it is not as much the duty of the state to take charge of the telephone as it is to conduct the postal service.'[24] These remarks in the House of Commons by Laurier's postmaster general inaugurated the investigation into telephones by the Select Committee of the House of Commons.

Previously, as vice-chancellor of the University of Toronto between 1881 and 1900, the chairman of the committee, Sir William Mulock had been the primary force in federating denominational and professional colleges into the expanded, co-operative university. First elected to Parliament in 1882 as member for North York, he organized the Department of Labour and became its first Minister, bringing William Lyon Mackenzie King into public life as deputy. Since 1896 he had served also as Laurier's postmaster general, in which capacity he had acquired interest in telephones.[25] Soon Sir William was to embark on a long and distinguished career on the bench, initially as chief justice of the exchequer division of the Supreme Court of Ontario and subsequently as chief justice of Ontario. He would serve also for twenty years as chancellor of the University of Toronto, until his death in 1944 at the ripe old age of one hundred.

In the early spring of 1905, however, it was the telephone question that was foremost in Mulock's mind, and indeed he had been considering the matter for some time, even engaging expert advice, and had formed some tentative conclusions. Addressing the select committee at its opening session on 20 March, Mulock reiterated his considered opinion, always subject to revision in light of contrary evidence, that the telephone problem should be met by a federal take-over of all long-distance lines and by municipalization of local facilities, albeit subject to co-ordination by the federal government.[26]

The *eminence grise* behind Mulock's proposition was Francis Dagger (1865–1945), hired into the postmaster general's office as telephone adviser in 1903. Before emigrating to Canada in 1899 Dagger had gained eight years' experience with privately owned telephone companies in England. It was said that he had been 'the first man to suggest the municipalization of the telephone in England.'[27] After a short stint with the Bell Telephone Company of Canada, Dagger, by 1900, was agitating for a municipal take-over of telephones in Toronto. Later Dagger became instrumental in the provincialization of telephones in Manitoba and Saskatchewan, helped draft telephone legislation in Ontario, and, between 1910 and his retirement in 1931, was supervisor of telephones for the Ontario Railway and Municipal Board.[28]

Mulock introduced his adviser to the select committee on its second sitting, 21 March, whereupon Dagger submitted a report prepared for Mulock and was promptly hired by the committee as its telephone expert. In oral testimony Dagger succinctly summarized his concerns:

Judged from the standpoint of the public good, there is no doubt that the telephone facilities of the Dominion are not satisfactory, the principal causes of complaint being:
1. High rates in large cities;
2. Disproportionately high rates in cities from 25,000 to 60,000 inhabitants;
3. High long-distance rates;
4. Lack of rural interconnection.[29]

'It is an indisputed fact,' Dagger continued, 'that the number of telephones in use in the Dominion of Canada is out of all proportion to the population, if we take the best telephoned countries in the world as a standard of perfection.'

As soon as his expert concluded these initial remarks, Sir William exclaimed: 'The rates for Canada and the United States are apparently the highest in the world. There is nothing to compare with them.'[30]

In the following days and weeks the select committee heard testimony from some fifty witnesses, including representatives of the Canadian independent telephone industry, retail merchants, municipal governments, the railroads, members of Parliament, telephone experts and administrators from abroad, and of course the Bell Telephone Company. Indeed C.F. Sise was before the committee for six days. In the end, more than one thousand pages of oral testimony and associated exhibits were published. A second volume, composed of letters to the committee and other submissions, made up an additional eight hundred pages of evidence. The committee studied and dutifully published restrictive contracts between Bell and the railroads and franchise agreements with municipalities. On several occasions it heard complaints by independent telephone companies regarding both the lack of interconnection to long-distance lines and predatory pricing. There were municipal representations respecting high rates and the inability to control installations along streets. Evidence concerning lack of rural service was compiled. Data on profits, capitalization, intercorporate ownership, and other financial matters were received. In brief, this inquiry into telephony was one of the most exhaustive ever to take place in Canada. But in the end it all came to naught the critical day being 30 May.

It was then announced unexpectedly that Sir William would be absent from the committee for 'three or four weeks' to attend to government business in England.[31] In his stead, Mr Zimmerman assumed the chair, and immediately there was a turning of the tide. In his opening remarks, Zimmerman enthused:

While on my feet I think it is only right that I should say that the Bell Telephone Company gave us a most delightful outing, which I think was enjoyed, not only by the members of the committee, but by the members of the House who were with us on Saturday. I know personally I enjoyed it very much. It was not only a source of pleasure, but also a source of very great information, more information I think than we could have received on that particular line here in a month, as far as any witness could give it to us. On behalf of the committee I think I can safely thank the Bell Telephone Company for the information and the very pleasant outing they gave us on Saturday.[32]

Then too Mr Zimmerman announced that he had now become sceptical over whether the committee could usefully make any recommendations whatsoever to Parliament in that session, so voluminous and complex was the evidence, an opinion to which W.F. Maclean took no uncertain umbrage: 'I certainly have a clear cut opinion in the matter,' he began. 'We now have before us ... enough evidence ... to justify ... recommending to parliament to pass a law compelling interchange of business on the part of telephone companies.'[33]

Maclean must have been momentarily stunned by Zimmerman's sudden announcement, for this most eloquent of parliamentary orators was for the moment scarcely coherent, inserting all sorts of extraneous phrases and clauses into his declaration. Then, regaining composure, he continued: 'In the second place we have sufficient evidence before us to have the Railway Act so amended, if it requires an amendment, to compel all railway companies to give access to their stations and other places. So, Mr. Chairman, while I agree with you that the question is a complex one and that we ought to get the fullest information and certainly expert testimony, it does appear to me that we have quite sufficient evidence at present to recommend to parliament to pass, at this session, an Act ...'[34]

Despite Maclean's rallying cry, the committee under its new chair ground to a halt. A further sitting was called for the next day, but then no more for a month. And when the proceedings were resumed at the end of June, only three more evidential sittings were held. Finally on Friday, 14 July 1905, the committee met for the last time, passing the following brief resolution as its final report to the House:

During the course of their inquiry, your Committee have held some forty-three sittings and have examined about fifty witnesses, and have had a large number of exhibits and other papers and documents laid before them. Owing, however, to the voluminous nature of the evidence submitted, and to the late period of the session, your Committee feel that it is impossible for them during the present session to come to any conclusions, or to make any recommendations to the House upon the subject referred to them, but they beg to submit herewith for the information of the House the minutes of their proceedings from March 20 last, together with all the evidence taken by them and the exhibits and other papers laid before them.

All which is respectfully submitted.[35]

Thereupon, the Select Committee on Telephone Systems expired.

IN LAURIER'S HANDS

A few days after the committee's final sitting Parliament was prorogued and an election called. As the campaign progressed Captain C.F. Sise, under instructions from President F.P. Fish of AT&T,[36] started formulating strategies for the upcoming session, foreseeing correctly the government's re-election. By 7 October Sise had determined there was 'little or no prospect of "Government ownership," '[37] but taking no chances he set about having friends appointed to a reconstituted committee for hearings expected to resume after the election. Hired as spy was former MP and ex-Liberal whip A.T. Thompson to ascertain 'if possible the intentions of the Government and personal views of members of Cabinet,' the arrangement, Sise cautioned in his diary, 'to be kept secret.'[38]

But the Bell president was more concerned than he needed to be, for on 7 October, the very day he was confiding these covert plans to his log book, Sir William retired from politics, citing 'ill-health,'[39] maintaining that he was still in 'entire political harmony with the government, on most friendly and intimate relations with each minister, and [remained] deeply attached to the constituency of North York.'[40]

Newspapers of course smelled a rat. Speculating that Mulock had been run out of cabinet by the telephone company for supporting government ownership, they questioned how a man in ill health could take on the duties of chief justice of the exchequer division of the Supreme Court of Ontario, the position to which Laurier posted him.[41]

Running in Mulock's stead as Liberal candidate in North York was A.B. Aylesworth, a lawyer who, in Laurier's laudatory words, had made 'great sacrifice ... in giving up the large and lucrative practice which he has built up for himself' to enter politics.[42]

Large and lucrative the legal practice certainly was. Among Aylesworth's more affluent and munificent clients was none other than the Bell Telephone Company of Canada, in whose employ the advocate resided at the time of Mulock's resignation[43] and whose interests he had so ably defended before the Select Committee on Telephone Systems just a few weeks before. In parliamentary committee Aylesworth had not been content merely to cross-examine witnesses but had himself proffered opinions and evidence. Here is a sampling:

Well, gentlemen, if I owned a good fat beast which was fit for the market and someone came and said he would like to have one of the hind quarters and that I had to give him one, I think the value of that beast would be pretty thoroughly destroyed if he were to take that hind quarter or just a part of it and leave me the rest. That is, I submit, a perfectly accurate analogy to the situation that is absolutely proposed here.

A municipal service is an unmitigated nuisance to the citizens and an unmitigated loss.

Mr. Sise ... will do the best he can for his patrons because he does the best he can for his share holders, and he will manage that company in the best way his business experience enables him to do in the interests of the general public.[44]

As it turned out both the government and Mr Aylesworth were successful in the November election, the latter after having promised the voters of North York that he would pursue Sir William's telephone policies.[45] And on that score Bell's former counsel certainly had ample opportunity to make good, appointed as he was postmaster general in the new House, Mulock's previous office. But, sad to say, election promises on occasion are broken, and despite his position of prominence Aylesworth remained aloof, at least publicly, from the telephone debate, an oversight that did not escape the watchful eye of William Findlay Maclean, returned now from the neighbouring riding of York South, who made caustic comment in a bitter, ironic, yet eloquent speech. The following is a short excerpt:

In the election of that new Postmaster General in North York some months ago the statement was made to the public that he would continue in the footsteps of his predecessor and the public were given to understand that legislation of a very important character in regard to telephones would be forthcoming at this session. True the public were some what surprised to see that the advocate of public ownership of telephones in this government was to have his place taken by a gentleman who had been the champion of the Bell Telephone Company before that very committee. But the public were told that no matter what the new Postmaster General had said before the committee in regard to telephones he had said it purely as a lawyer, he was speaking for a corporation, and the doctrine was set up that a man in public life in this country, who appears before a committee of this House or in the courts may express opinions altogether different from his own opinions; that he can be a double faced man, a Jekyll and Hyde, that he can profess to be in favour of public ownership as a public man and can go into the courts or before a committee and plead the case of a monopoly or a corporation. The new Postmaster General led the people of North York to believe that he would follow in the footsteps of his predecessor and we were told that we might look out for a new Paul, a Paul greater than the preceeding Paul; but instead of that we have a Saul who stoned the prophets, and stoned public ownership before that committee ...[46]

The leader of the opposition, Robert Borden, proposed that the evidence gathered by the Select Committee on Telephone Systems in the previous session be referred to a similar, reconstituted committee and that the inquiry continue, as otherwise 'the time of this House and the time of members of this committee [will] have been absolutely wasted to no purpose ...'[47] But Laurier, safely ensconced for yet another term, would have none of it. Rather, his government introduced and passed legislation to place telephone companies falling within federal jurisdiction under regulatory supervision of the Board of Railway Commissioners for Canada. The telephone industry in Ontario and Quebec thereby entered a new era.

9

Western Reaction

Laurier's 'compromise' did not sit well on the prairies where the three governments each bought Bell out between 1908 and 1909. Only in British Columbia did the telephone situation in the west continue unaltered, but there, after all, Bell had pulled out in 1889. This chapter recounts developments in Canada's four most westerly provinces.

MANITOBA

As early as 1899 Manitoba amended its Municipal Act to permit municipal ownership of local exchanges. Dozens of local companies thereafter arose, each of course prohibited from connecting with Bell's long-distance lines. In an effort to resolve this perplexing and unsatisfactory situation, the provincial premier, Sir Rodmond Roblin, announced in 1905 that the government would study the feasibility and desirability of a complete provincial take-over – to give 'a telephone system to all classes at cost.'[1] For the interim, he continued, the province would cease incorporating additional municipal systems.

Shortly after making this pronouncement, Roblin hired the zealous and unflagging apostle of public ownership, Francis Dagger, into his office as telephone expert. Next he sought permission from the federal government to expropriate Bell's provincial operations, a request rejected a year or so later.[2] Then he set up a commission headed by Attorney-General Colin Campbell, composed of members from both sides of the House and including the leader of the opposition, to study provincialization. Reporting in February 1906 Campbell's committee recommended unanimously in favour of government ownership, whereupon the report was sent to the legislature for debate. The assembly of elected representatives then gave its unanimous endorsation.[3]

Between 1906 and 1908 several bills were passed empowering the government to construct long-distance lines and install and manage local exchanges. Meanwhile, negotiations were instituted with Bell to acquire the latter's provincial facilities. To strengthen its hand the government even started constructing an exchange in Winnipeg in 1907,[4] pressure sufficient to induce Bell to sell out. On 15 January 1908 the provincial assets of the Bell Telephone company were acquired for $3.3 million. At the time Bell had been serving 17,000 of the province's 25,000 subscribers.[5]

Manitoba was now to experience a brief boom in telephony. During the first year of government ownership 6000 subscribers were added and 1500 additional pole miles built. In 1909 a further 5300 subscribers were connected. In April 1909 the government reduced rural telephone rates by up to 30 per cent, courting still further growth, and 8146 more people signed on in 1910. In less than three years both the value of plant and the number of subscribers increased by about 80 per cent.[6]

But sometimes the expansion was more fanciful than real. Just prior to the provincial election of 1910, for example, the government vowed to extend service to the Woodbridge district, sixty miles south of Winnipeg, if re-elected. To add apparent substance to its promise – 'in the interests of pure and undefiled politics and honest administration of public affairs,' quipped the Manitoba *Free Press* – carloads of telephone poles were shipped to Woodbridge during the course of the campaign ('fishing poles for voters,' derided the paper). Campaign in progress, numerous electors were engaged at the rate of six dollars a day for telephone line construction. But 'before a fortnight had elapsed after the votes were counted,' jeered the *Free Press*, 'a train of empty flat cars came along, gathered up the poles and brought them back to Winnipeg.'[7]

Telephone and politics were commingled in other ways too. By order-in-council the three member Manitoba Government Telephone Commission was required to pay all receipts directly to the provincial treasury and to draw on the treasury to meet all expenditures,[8] a procedure conducive to laxity in bookkeeping. Although the system's annual reports recorded operating surpluses to 1911, these surpluses were more products of 'hazy accounting methods'[9] than accurate depictions of true financial vitality: no charges had been deducted for either interest or depreciation, and some maintenance expenses had been charged to capital.

The system's crumbling financial foundation came to light abruptly in December 1914 when Chief Commissioner F.C. Paterson announced to a startled public that rates would be increased immediately to cover anticipated losses of $153,000. Paterson also proposed introducing 'measured rates' to Winnipeg, whereby subscribers would pay according to the number of local calls placed. Under the commissioner's proposal a business making as few as ten calls a day would have to pay seventy-five dollars a year for telephone service. Because Bell's subscribers in Ottawa and Hamilton (cities of comparable size) were at the time being charged flat annual rates of forty-five dollars for *unlimited* call volumes, the consternation that arose within the Winnipeg business community is easily understood.

'Simply robbery,' wrote one irate subscriber, contractor A.T. Davidson, in a letter to the Manitoba *Free Press*; 'I think that many of the private citizens of the city will have their phones taken out.' Ranted shoe merchant C.F. Rannard: 'Candidly, I consider the enactment of this increase an outrage for which the people will not stand.'[10]

So ended the heady days of profligate construction and euphoria over booting out Bell.

Beleaguered by public protests, Premier Roblin issued an order-in-council on 13 January 1912 establishing a commission of inquiry headed by county court judge Corbett Locke to appraise the system's management and its finances. Over the next three months the three-member board held public sessions throughout the province, inspected telephone systems in the American midwest, and examined 234 witnesses. On 14 June 1912, the commission's report was released for publication by the local press.

Respecting the system's management, Judge Locke was critical but moderate in tone: 'The system has generally been administered extravagantly and ... a very large saving could be made by economic management ... [Furthermore] there [has] not been a proper system of accounting and of keeping records in the various departments.'[11] Judge Locke was perhaps a master of understatement; transcripts of the hearings point to voucher padding in rural construction and overcharging by rural suppliers.[12]

Judge Locke also condemned the telephone company's plans for measured local rates. Acknowledging measured rates as being 'the most profitable thing in the world for a telephone company,' the judge added that the practice flew in the face of public service, surely the very purpose of publicly owned enterprise.

Under extreme pressure, within two weeks Mr Paterson and his fellow commissioners resigned their posts, whereupon opponents of the government charged that the officials had been turned into scape-goats and that the system's problems lay entirely with the government, not with the commissioners at all – a view sustained, incidentally, thirty years later in a governmental consulting report reviewing this early history.[13]

Perhaps attempting to depoliticize telephones in the midst of contro-versy, the Manitoba government next took the unusual step of delegat-ing responsibility for prices charged by its wholly owned operation to a newly constituted Public Utilities Board. Although all possibility of measured rates had been scuttled by the committee of inquiry, the new board in the following summer approved general rate increases throughout the province. In Winnipeg prices for business service rose to sixty dollars per year from fifty, and residential single-line rates rose to thirty dollars, the same price Bell had charged four and a half years before. In smaller towns and rural areas price increases were as high as 67 per cent.[14]

Furthermore, the government enacted amendments to the Manitoba Telephone Act, giving increased autonomy to the commissioner of telephones respecting 'the keeping of accounts, application of funds, control of employees and other matters involved in carrying out the purposes for which ... he is appointed,' all matters over which the government had taken very keen interest. Thereafter the system began running its own affairs (subject to review by the Public Utilities Board) in accordance with its own perception of the goals of a publicly owned utility.

Although the initial heady days of profligate expansion were never to be equalled, growth did continue, depreciation reserves started being set aside, and surpluses even began peeking through the financial debris. Nor did the government forget entirely the major reason for which it had acquired the system – the provisioning of rural service. The extensions, however, were slowed down to become more in keep-ing with the resources at the system's disposal.[15]

Since these early years, the Manitoba Telephone System on the whole has been an exemplary operation. Its rates consistently have been the lowest in Canada, service has been provided throughout the province, and the efficiency of its operations has been unmatched (see table 14.1).[16] None the less, in 1986 MTS became embroiled in controversy once again when a subsidiary, MTX Telecom Services Inc., was accused of kickbacks, cover-ups, lies, discriminatory hiring, and financial mismanagement.

MTX Telecom Services

MTX Telecom Services was formed in January 1982 as a wholly owned subsidiary of Manitoba Telephone System (MTS) to deal in foreign markets, including the Kingdom of Saudi Arabia. MTX soon entered into a 50-50 joint venture with Saudi sheikh Abdullah Abdel Aziz Al Bassom under the name Saudi Arabian Datacom Co. Ltd. (SADL).[17] From this point onward MTX started engaging in highly questionable financial tactics. SADL advanced the sheikh $1.5 million one day after he and MTX had each deposited $750,000 into trust accounts towards SADL's share capital, the loan violating SADL's articles of incorporation; this advance became ratified by SADL's board only five months later. Indeed eighteen months passed before the transaction became 'reconciled' in intercompany accounts.[18]

Although MTX continually lost money on its Saudi business, Al Bassom evidently did quite well.[19] One factor accounting for his success and MTX's failure lay in the fact that MTX was seldom paid for equipment continually shipped the sheikh for resale in Saudi Arabia, certainly shaving Al Bassom's expenses to rock bottom but doing little for MTX's bottom line. Although the provincial auditor, William Ziprick, warned MTS as early as 1984 that there was a good chance it would never recover the amounts owing,[20] MTX blithely continued shipping the sheikh more and more equipment, even into August 1986, by which time Al Bassom had run up some $20 million in debts.[21] Financial mismanagement had been hidden from public view, however, by disarray in MTX's books; in 1984 the provincial auditor had cautioned that it was impossible for him to complete a report, so disordered was MTX's system of accounts, but no remedial action was taken. At about the same time Ziprick informed both MTS's chairman and the minister of telephones of rumours that MTX was paying kickbacks to Saudi businessmen purchasing equipment from the sheikh,[23] allegations later substantiated by affidavits of two MTX employees,[24] but again to no avail.

In 1986, amidst sensational news coverage, the government referred charges of criminal wrongdoing to the RCMP and appointed an accounting firm to look into questions of administrative ineptitude. Upon receipt of the accounting firm's report in November 1986 Al Mackling, minister of telephones, announced that MTX was being wound down immediately, that MTS president Gordon Holland and executive vice-president Glover Anderson had resigned at his request, and that he had fired three other senior MTS executives. Then Mackling himself vacated his ministry. In all it was estimated that the débâcle had cost Manitoba's taxpayers $25 million.[25]

SASKATCHEWAN

In Saskatchewan, too, pressures mounted in 1905 for a government take-over of telephones. Early that year the Dominion Grange Convention voted for 'federal operation of trunk lines in order to facilitate municipal control of telephones,'[26] while the Regina City Council and Board of Trade both complained about the lack of long-distance service and the paucity of rural lines, concluding: 'The feeling in favour of government ownership and operation is very strong.'[27] Astutely reading the political climate, both political parties, organized early that year, adopted platforms favouring public ownership of public utilities.[28]

Liberal leader Walter Scott won the new province's first election (1905) and wasted little time appointing Francis Dagger as provincial telephone expert, commissioning the outspoken reformer to report on the provincial telephone situation. Dagger's findings and recommendations were received in April 1908 and, as one might have expected, urged provincial ownership of all long-distance lines and municipal operation of local exchanges.[29] Most of Mr Dagger's proposals were subsequently embodied in three bills. On 1 May 1909 the government purchased Bell Telephone's provincial plant, then serving 1600 subscribers, for $369,000. Two months later facilities of the independent Saskatchewan Telephone Company were purchased for a much lower price, $150,000.[30]

The Saskatchewan government approached the telephone question somewhat differently than did Manitoba, reserving for itself only larger municipal exchanges and all long-distance construction; here the government was content merely to assist rural settlers in building their own telephone systems, albeit providing them with free poles and advice. None the less, construction in the years immediately following the Bell take-over was intense. By 1912 exchanges had increased from 20 to 93, and province-wide subscribers had quadrupled from 3410 to 14,826. By this time 337 rural telephone companies, 5 municipal systems, and 15 independent systems built by private enterprise were in full swing, in addition to the government-owned system.[31]

But in Saskatchewan as in Manitoba, the lustre of government-in-the-telephone-business soon tarnished. In 1916 the Conservative opposition made wholesale allegations of government corruption and bribery,[32] telephone operations being central to the inquisition. A royal commission, chaired by Sir Frederick Hamilton, chief justice of Saskatchewan, was soon appointed to investigate the telephone system and other matters, including irregularities in building an insane asylum at North Battleford ('a combination that produced much predictable merriment,' writes Tony Cashman), but the inquiry was discontinued after twenty-one months, before a report had been made.

In 1919 the newly elected Conservative government hired O.J. Godfrey and Company, public accountants, to study the affairs of the Telephone Department. The accountants were frustrated in their evaluation, however, remarking caustically: 'There are no satisfactory records in the Department prior to 1913 ... In the past it has been impossible to ascertain whether profit was made or not from the public accounts.'[33] And even fifteen years later, in 1934, G.E. Britnell derided: 'It appears impossible to get any really adequate picture of the Saskatchewan Government Telephone System as an operating utility since the telephone accounts in addition to being more hopelessly confused and inadequate than those of Manitoba or Alberta have ever been have continued down to the present day to illustrate what Professor Mavor would have described as "a total lack of elementary principles of commercial accounting." '[34]

None the less, telephones in Saskatchewan continue to reside under provincial ownership, and, as with the governmental system in Manitoba, few have questioned its overall efficiency. Official forums for such questioning, however, have been severely limited. For years Sask Tel was the only major telephone system in the country to remain unregulated. Only briefly, between 1982 and 1987, were Sask Tel's affairs subject to systematic scrutiny by an independent agency. The story of the short-lived Saskatchewan Public Utilities Review Commission (SPURC) is worth recounting.

Saskatchewan Public Utilities Review Commission
Created in 1982, the prime function of SPURC was to set rates for
three of Saskatchewan's largest crown corporations: Saskatchewan
Government Insurance Corp., Sask Power, and Sask Tel. Shortly after
inception the new commission gave a foretaste of its independent
stance, stating a case to the Saskatchewan Court of Appeal to challenge a regulation handed down by the provincial cabinet to the
insurance corporation. SPURC contended that it alone had authority
in the matter. In this instance, the court ruled against SPURC. In 1985,
however, the commission again appealed to the Court of Appeal, this
time against an order-in-council (cabinet direction) issued to SPURC
itself, and the court on this occasion ruled in SPURC's favour, declaring
the cabinet order null and void. Going into 1986, then, the series was
tied one-to-one, and a rubber match was obviously called for. That
came soon.

On 30 April 1986 cabinet issued yet another direction to SPURC,
ordering the commission '*to approve rates and conditions ...* within
one month of an application by Sask Tel' in order to enable the telephone company to implement universal single-line telephone service
throughout the province. Significantly, during the provincial election
campaign immediately preceding the order-in-council, the Conservatives had promised to replace all multi-party lines with 'universal
individual line service,' likely contributing to their sweep of rural
seats but also helping shut the party out of all urban centres.

Sensing this latest cabinet direction might just possibly undermine
the commission's rate-making autonomy, SPURC again appealed to the
Saskatchewan Court of Appeal, contending once more an order-in-
council to be beyond cabinet's powers. And again the court agreed.
Choosing to hear argument only from counsel for the government on
27 March 1987, the court recessed briefly and returning, pronounced
orally its unanimous opinion in favour of SPURC.

The government was horrified. It decided quickly that Saskatchewan did not really need an independent regulatory commission super-
vising Crown corporations after all. On 12 May 1987 the minister
responsible for the commission announced that SPURC would be wound
down, citing 'fiscal restraint and the high costs of operation of SPURC'
as justification.[35] Today once again Sask Tel and the other provincial
crowns are unencumbered by public hearings, sworn testimony, and
regulatory oversight.

ALBERTA

In 1906 the legislature of the new Province of Alberta met for the first time, and among the first items of business was the telephone question. Soon passed was An Act Empowering Municipalities to Establish and Operate Telephone Systems. Then in July the government announced that it would construct long-distance lines in areas not served by Bell, and connections between Banff and Calgary were soon established. In 1907 several small, independent systems were purchased by the government, while the government's program of long-distance construction continued.[36]

At this point Bell hit upon a new plan. It proposed dividing the province into two parts, one for itself and one for the government. Bell suggested that it be apportioned the more densely populated south and that the government take over construction in the north.[37] Provincial politicians were not amused.

Bell then served notice on the Edmonton town council that it would there invoke its charter powers to establish a competing exchange.[38] Meanwhile in Calgary a municipal committee recommended that the town inaugurate its own telephone system in competition with Bell, a resolution subsequently ratified by ratepayers.[39] In 1908 new provincial legislation further empowering government construction and operation of telephones was enacted, and, cashing in its chips, Bell sold out for $1.9 million, turning over 1170 subscribers to Alberta Government Telephones.[40]

As in Manitoba and Saskatchewan the period immediately following the government take-over saw an apparent vitality in telephone development, thanks in part to zero-depreciation accounting.[41] Growth was certainly rapid. The total number of government subscribers increased by about ten thousand at the end of 1911. Between 1912 and 1913 plant and facilities almost doubled, from $3.7 million to $7 million,[42] but then construction stalled with the outbreak of war, and the system actually began losing customers. Perhaps anticipating a political débâcle as had already been experienced in Manitoba (and which to a lesser extent was soon to break out in Saskatchewan), the government in 1915 passed a Public Utilities Act similar to Manitoba's to regulate the affairs of Alberta Government Telephones.[43] The opposition, however, was not mollified, demanding the names of all persons who had ever done work for the telephone branch of the government, how much they had been paid, and what had actually been accomplished for the remuneration.[44] Political ammunition was gained from disclosure that 47,000 telephone poles were languishing in the system's storehouse.[45] Pressing the issue the opposition succeeded in getting AGT's financial and managerial affairs turned over to the Public Accounts Committee for investigation, but that committee was unable to turn up much more in the way of waste or patronage. Although in 1917 there was a further flurry in the House over alleged 'mismanagement,' 'over-capitalization,' and 'waste,' the government, firmly in control, soon doused the debate.[46]

In 1919 AGT overhauled its system of accounting, set up a depreciation reserve, and started making appropriations for plant replacement, all along lines prescribed for telephone companies in the United States by the Interstate Commerce Commission,[47] thereby eliminating much of the potential for political fireworks.

Contentious through the years, however, have been relations between AGT and the municipally owned Edmonton Telephones. In 1926 the general manager of AGT recommended amalgamating the two systems,[48] and in 1928 AGT offered to purchase the municipal system for undepreciated book value of assets plus $600,000 goodwill, an offer refused by the municipality.[49] AGT then tried imposing an annual connecting charge of $100,000, which Edmonton refused to pay.[50] Only recently has resolution appeared imminent.[51]

BRITISH COLUMBIA

Of Canada's four westerly provinces only British Columbia refrained from taking over telephones – perhaps because Bell had voluntarily abandoned the territory in the late 1880s. The predecessor of today's British Columbia Telephone Company was the Vernon and Nelson Telephone Company, Limited, incorporated in 1891 and chartered by the provincial legislature in 1903 to operate throughout the province. In 1904 this company acquired the assets of the New Westminster and Burrard Inlet Telephone Company (which by that time included also the assets of the pioneer Victoria and Esquimalt Telephone Company), and to reflect its new-found grandeur and province-wide aspirations its name was changed to British Columbia Telephone Company, Limited.[52]

Mulock's Select Committee on Telephone Systems had a mandate to review telephone operations in British Columbia as in the rest of Canada, and in fact it canvassed municipalities in that province for submissions. None the less the committee understandably gave BC Telephone short shrift, focusing rather on Bell, by far the larger and more immediate concern. As noted by Lindsay Allen, this omission was an unfortunate one 'because the Committee would have found every questionable tactic employed by Bell also being used by BC Telephone.' Like its larger associate to the east, Allen advises, 'BC Telephone engaged in predatory pricing, exclusive contracts with municipalities and railways, and denial of interconnection with competing independents.'[53]

For a number of years there was in British Columbia, as elsewhere, a smouldering campaign for provincialization and local control. As well Vancouver's city council and the telephone company had a running battle over the control of streets.[54] But the provincial government refrained from enacting legislation permitting municipalities to operate their own telephone systems. The battle shifted in 1912 or so from agitation for municipal ownership to inauguration of regulation, and by 1915 provincial regulation seemed to be in the wings. BC Telephone thus petitioned the federal government to incorporate a new company, the Western Canada Telephone Company, to which BC Telephone, Limited, was to transfer assets, adroitly bypassing provincial regulation. In 1916, however, Parliament unexpectedly enacted a clause subjecting the new company to regulation by the federal Board of Railway Commissioners.[55] As a counter-ploy, the newly chartered company delayed acquiring assets from its affiliate, merely leasing the latter's facilities and thereby astutely bypassing most regulatory authority at the federal level too. Confusion intensified when in 1919 the names of the two companies converged, the federally regulated Western Canada Telephone Company being renamed British Columbia Telephone Company (without the 'Limited').

This anomalous and perplexing situation persisted until 1923 when the two BC Tels were amalgamated, finally bringing most of the province's telephone operations unambiguously within federal jurisdiction, where they reside today. Elaine Bernard has speculated that in the end BC Telephone opted for federal regulation because 'a federal regulatory body [located in distant Ottawa] was not as susceptible to pressure from municipalities or the local population.'[56]

In the 1920s, owing to expansion within the province and the introduction of higher-grade equipment needed for the emerging trans-Canada and international long-distance markets, BC Tel, short on capital, was sold to an American, Theodore Gary, and his National

Telephone and Telegraph Corporation, today known as Anglo-Canadian Telephone Company. In 1955 Anglo-Canadian itself was acquired by General Telephone and Electronics Corp. of United States, under whose control BC Tel still resides.[57]

Regulatory policies devised by the Board of Railway Commissioners and successor bodies for Bell Telephone historically have been applied with little or no modification to BC Tel; these policies are reviewed in subsequent chapters. Over the years, BC Tel, like Bell Telephone, succeeded in acquiring numerous independents, its last major acquisition being the Okanagan Telephone Company in 1966. Today BC Tel operates all public telephone lines in the province except for those in the City of Prince Rupert and a few remote lines owned by NorthwesTel.[58]

The foregoing brief recapitulation of the telephone history in the west highlights some policy alternatives that could have been pursued in the east. In the following chapters attention is focused primarily on telephone development in Ontario and Quebec from 1906 to the present and, in that regard, to the role of public policy.

10

Local-Exchange Competition in Ontario and Quebec

A NOTE ON EXPOSITION

This chapter, which marks a transition in expository style, opens by recounting the development of the telephone industry in Ontario and Quebec between 1906 and 1925, the latter date marking the demise of direct telephonic competition at the local level. The discussion then continues with an analysis of Bell's shifting relations over the intervening years with the surviving (non-competing) independents. It concludes with a review of a current issue, 'reversed rate rebalancing,' which is of immense importance to surviving independents and, beyond that, has far-ranging repercussions on the viability of competition in long-distance service, on the sustainability of telephone universality, on the prospects of maintaining an independent cable TV industry, and on regulatory techniques and priorities. The telephone industry has grown too complex to allow us to combine all important issues in the context of continuous historical development. Therefore, this chapter and the ones that follow in Part III will each focus on specific current issues as they have unfolded historically.

THE NEW ACT

By revising the Railway Act in 1906 the Laurier government gave responsibility to the Board of Railway Commissioners for Canada to oversee specified activities of telephone companies falling within federal jurisdiction. At the time there was but one such company, Bell Telephone, and so its rates were to be subjected to the board's approval. As well, the commissioners were empowered to order connections between local companies and Bell's long-distance lines 'upon such terms as to compensation as the Board deems just and expedient.' (Interconnections between competing local exchanges were not covered by the act and remained beyond the board's purview.) Bell also was required to seek consent from municipalities before digging up streets; if permission could not be attained, the board was to arbitrate.

AN EARLY BOOM

Evidently confident that sparkling opportunities were about to unfold, the independent telephone industries of Ontario and Quebec entered a brief boom after 1906, but by 1920 the true nature of regulation had become painfully apparent. While it lasted, however, growth was indeed rapid and impressive. Whereas in 1905 independents accounted for only 1100 of the 40,300 telephones in Ontario (2.7 per cent),[1] by 1915 they boasted 79,000 (32 per cent) of the province's 166,000 telephones (see table 10.1). Although only 83 or so independents had dared enter the field in Ontario between 1892 and 1905,[2] some 770 independents tested the waters between 1906 and 1920 (see table 10.2). Bell's response was co-operation with some, hostility towards others, and a carefully contrived pricing plan overall to limit and indeed eliminate independents.

Co-operation with Some
To many independents Bell was co-operative, affording connections to its long-distance lines. It will be recalled that Bell itself had decided earlier to neglect less remunerative territories, encouraging farmers to build rural systems. Provided such facilities were 'non-competing' and did not connect to other lines without Bell's express approval, Bell afforded them long-distance connections. The major grievance of such privileged independents during the early years of regulation concerned the larger company's proscriptions on additional connections. In the wake of a dramatic ruling by the Ontario Railway and Municipal Board in 1911, however,[3] reaffirmed by the federal regulator,[4] connecting agreements proscribing additional connections were banned, and for several years thereafter the 'non-competing' contingent was largely content.

Hostility towards Others
Much more contentious was Bell's treatment of 'competing' indepen-

TABLE 10.1
Telephones in Ontario 1913–85*

| Year | Independents | | Bell Telephone | Independents as per cent of total telephones† |
	Number of systems	Number of telephones	Number of Telphones	
1913	450	66,000	144,077	31.4
1915	580	79,000	165,642	32.3
1920	660	100,000	266,978	27.2
1925	626	104,000	400,601	20.6
1930	608	115,000	516,098	18.2
1935	600	103,569	451,977	22.9
1940	572	117,687	544,346	17.8
1945	560	144,615	687,037	17.3
1950	514	169,878	1,091,614	13.5
1956	372	175,320	1,692,846	9.4
1960	277	193,408	2,131,467	8.3
1965	127	185,968	2,736,898	6.4
1970	57	190,682	3,655,029	5.0
1976	39	259,392	5,087,937	4.9
1985‡	30	178,527	4,329,120	4.0

* Table excludes provincially owned telephones for all years but 1956 and 1960; there were between 1000 and 1500 telephones owned by the government in these years.
† Bell Telephone operating subsidiaries are termed 'independents.' Northern Telephone and Teleontario accounted for 73,187 telephones in 1976. (Bell Canada *Statistical Report*, 1976)
‡ For 1985, network access lines replaces number of telephones.
SOURCES: Rural Telephone Committee, *Report to the Hydro-electric Power Commission of Ontario Concerning Rural Telephone Service in Ontario* (1953), Exhibit 2; Bell Canada, *Annual Charts*, March 1978, Section 521; Dominion Bureau of Statistics, *Telephone Statistics*, 1955, 1960, 1965; Statistics Canada, *Telephone Statistics*, 1970; Ontario Telephone Service Commission, *Annual Report*, 1986, 13

dents. They could attain connection only upon express order of the board. The Ingersoll Telephone Company, supported by the Port Hope Telephone Company and nine others, was the first to test the federal regulator on the issue. In May 1911 Chief Commissioner J.P. Mabee pronounced the board's judgement, admitting he was of two minds: one the one hand, Ingersoll Telephone had been duly established under provincial law and therefore he had no right to interfere with it; but

TABLE 10.2
Number of independent telephone companies started,
by year, Ontario 1906–20

Year	Number of companies	Year	Number of companies
1906	41	1913	55
1907	74	1914	39
1908	86	1915	40
1909	100	1916	18
1910	97	1917–20	66
1911	77		
1912	67		

SOURCE: Compiled from Thomas Grindlay, *A History of the Independent Telephone Industry in Ontario*, 254–305
NOTE: Some new companies are amalgamations and reorganizations of pre-existing operations.

on the other, 'competition in connection with telephones has never appealed to me.'[5]

Turning next to the delicate question of which company his board should favour, and to what extent, the chief commissioner noted that Ingersoll Telephone had been set up only 'many years' after Bell, adding: 'It is just as much the duty of this Board to protect as it is to see that the subscribers of the Ingersoll system get long distance communication.'[6]

Mabee was definitely sympathetic to Bell's plight. He viewed the Ingersoll company as 'gradually encroaching upon ... the preserve of the Bell Telephone Company,' capturing so many of the latter's subscribers that 'today there are in Ingersoll twice as many subscribers to the Ingersoll system as there are to the Bell System,' despite the fact the former lacked toll connections. To Mabee, exclusivity of the long-distance connection was Bell's 'sheet anchor,' without which it would probably lose what was left of its then severely shrunken local business. Therefore, as a 'just and expedient' resolution and following consistently with previous (albeit overturned) board rulings concerning access by independents to railway stations, he ordered that compensation be paid to Bell for any fall-off in its subscribers arising from long-distance interconnection by Ingersoll. Mabee thereby interpreted 'compensation' as denoting not merely recompense for expenses incurred in fulfilling board orders, but as requiring indemnity for business loss stemming from competition.

Taken aback, Port Hope Telephone Company petitioned the board in 1914 to declare it a 'non-competing company,' hoping thereby to obviate the necessity of indemnification.[7] Commissioner S.J. McLean (not to be confused with W.F. Maclean, outspoken parliamentarian and Bell watchdog) delivered the board's judgment, a remarkable one given Mabee's previous ruling, holding competing and non-competing to be words not 'of legal precision.' Rather, McLean explained, they had been used by the chief commissioner 'in a descriptive, not in a definite sense.' McLean ventured that 'there is nowhere in the Railway Act any definition of a competing company insofar as a telephone company is concerned';[8] therefore, he concluded, he was under no obligation either to define what the board had meant in using the words or to decide whether Port Hope Telephone Company was 'competing' or 'non-competing.'

These thorny questions resolved, it remained merely to determine the terms under which one company, unable on its own to secure connections with Bell's long-distance lines, should connect by order of the board, raising now the sensitive question of discrimination. But again the commissioner handled the problem deftly, writing: 'The provisions of the Railway Act are applicable only insofar as companies are concerned to companies within the legislative authority of the Parliament of Canada. It follows, therefore, that a telephone company not within such authority cannot invoke the power of the board on an allegation of discriminatory treatment on the part of a telephone company subject to the board's jurisdiction. That is to say, the Bell Telephone Company may make an agreement with one provincially chartered company, while it may refuse to make an agreement with another which is alleged to be similarly situated.'[9]

In another of McLean's judgments, the fee payable to Bell by an independent was increased.[10] When this precedent later became applied to other 'competing' connections through a general order, the new chief commissioner, H.L. Drayton, was appalled, writing in dissent: 'The Bell Telephone Company would appear bound to afford the subscribers of the Independents just as much as members of the general public that seek to go into a long distance station that the Bell Telephone Company at its own expense provides, all reasonable and proper facilities for the forwarding of telephonic messages – a service which must be performed without discrimination or preference.'[11]

But competing independents could take cold comfort in Drayton's 'support,' as he then went on to lament his very own findings, invoking the doctrine of natural monopoly: 'I much regret the result ... because I fully appreciate the evils of telephone duplication. With Government regulation this duplication is merely a waste of money ...'[12] And, of course, they had been anything but mollified by McLean's interpretation of 'just and expedient.' Consequently, the competing independents turned to the bench. By a three to two decision the Supreme Court declared the board's general order to be lawful, not because it was necessarily 'fair' or 'good,' considerations quite arguably beyond the jurisdiction of the Court in any event, but simply because 'large discretionary powers are given [the board] with regard to the compensation to be paid by the use of the words "just and expedient." '[13]

Rebuffed by regulator and judiciary alike, independents now petitioned Parliament. It was their last recourse, and one independent operator termed the struggle 'the battle for our life.'[14]

BACK IN PARLIAMENT

By 1917 Canadian railroad policy had become completely unhinged, so profligate had the Liberal government been in funnelling public funds into new lines. Between Winnipeg and Edmonton the Canadian Northern, the Grand Trunk Pacific, and the Canadian Pacific all ran functionally parallel tracks, while in the Maritimes the National Transcontinental duplicated the Intercolonial, adding yet a third rail to the eastern ports then served also by Canadian Pacific. In Ontario and Quebec too there was a multiplicity of routes. Moreover, rumours were rife of outrageous patronage in building the National Transcontinental, and the Canadian Northern and Grand Trunk Pacific were in constant need of cash transfusions from the public purse. 'In confusion and frustration,' writes James Marsh, 'Prime Minister Robert Borden appointed in 1916 a royal commission to inquire into railways and transportation in Canada.' This Drayton-Ackworth Commission, reporting in May 1917, recommended 'immediate nationalization of all railways of Canada, except for American lines and the CPR.'[15]

Meanwhile, in May 1917 a Commons special committee on the Railway Act was meeting with regularity and urgency to devise solutions to the railway crisis. The committee's mandate encompassed a review of the entire Railway Act, and so sections pertaining to telephones fell into its lap. Given the context, the attention afforded telephone matters by the committee was indeed remarkable; but then, the telephone problem had long remained unresolved.

In the proceedings Aime Geoffrion, counsel for Bell, informed the committee that there was *local* interchange with 675 independents (servicing 89,000 telephones in Ontario and Quebec), with Bell refusing local interchanges with only 74 'competing' systems (8000 telephones). Bell insisted it be allowed to retain power to deny local connections to 'competing systems' and that indemnification be continued for loss of local business resulting from forced toll connections.[16]

Next up was F.D. Mackay of the Canadian Independent Telephone Association. He recalled for the committee the origins of the independent telephone movement in Canada: '75 per cent of these men in the telephone business, the men representing these systems, were not ambitious to become telephone men. They were farmers or something else in a small country village. I may say that the doctor played an important part because he wanted to reach his patients by telephone and save long drives in the cold. They went into the business because it was the only way they could get telephone service.'[17]

The witness then turned quickly to his main concern, the 'club in the hands of the Bell Telephone Company.' Indemnity, he charged, allowed the giant utility not only to disadvantage competing companies but to control non-competing ones. For any system not wishing to accept the terms of connection proffered by Bell there remained but the dubious option of appealing to the board in full knowledge that indemnity would be ordered. He went on to ridicule the premise on which indemnity was based, alleging that long-distance connections increased, far from decreased, Bell's revenues. And even if such were not the case, he continued, ordering compensation for loss of business was 'a new and novel law that applies in no other business; if you are in any other line of business there is no talk about getting compensation for the business a competitor may take away from you.'[18] Mackay concluded: 'We are simply asking them to take our subscribers and trust them the same as if they went into a booth in a railway station and asked for a long distance call.'[19]

The committee was completely won over by the independent telephone industry. Reporting to Parliament it recommended that all reference to 'compensation' be struck from the revised Railway Act,[20] noting that such action would be sufficient to prevent the board from ever again awarding indemnity.[21] Surprisingly, perhaps, the Commons agreed. Although the contentious clause was debated at length in the House, Bell's allies there were unable to have the words 'as to compensation or otherwise' reinstated, and the amendment proposed by the committee passed third reading.[22] But the whole Railway Bill died in the Senate, such was Bell's strength in the 'other place.'

The following year the Senate sent its own revised Railway Bill to the Commons, complete with a clause calling for 'compensation or otherwise' to be paid to Bell, but this time it was the lower House that refused to comply.[23] With Canadian railway policy hanging in the balance, the two houses were deadlocked over a telephone clause.

In 1919 the Commons again sent to the Senate a revised Railway Bill from which all reference to 'compensation' had been struck, but again the Senate balked, refusing to approve the deletion.[24] Stalemated, a joint Commons-Senate committee was formed, finally recommending that the revised bill reinstate a clause concerning 'compensation' to expedite passage of the much-needed railway legislation. In the Commons, the minister of railways, pleading with the House to accept the joint committee's recommendation, promised he would soon introduce a separate bill once more deleting the offending clause.[25] The minister's word was sufficient for the Commons at long last to give its assent. As for the separate bill, however, it awaits to this very day.

'RATE REBALANCING' – PHASE I

A Strategy for the Time
'Competing' telephone companies, consequently, experienced an abrupt and early demise. By 1925 the last laggard had gone under,[26] enabling Bell to veer in a new direction, realigning its relations with the survivors – the so-called 'non-competing' companies. First up for adjustment was the connecting agreement. The new arrangement, known as the 'commission and prorate system,' was actually adopted by the board in 1923 upon publication of General Order no. 375.[27] It provided that Bell's long-distance charges only would be collected, out of which the originating company would receive a commission; the remaining revenue would be split in proportion to the airline miles the call traversed on each company's lines.[28] 'Service stations' (companies lacking their own local switching), however, were to

receive no commission, nor of course was there to be any prorating of revenues. Rather, service stations were to pay Bell a fee for each subscriber as well as its regular toll charges.[29]

At this point it is important to note a fundamental change in Bell's overall pricing strategy, ultimately serving to wipe out even most 'non-competing' independents. The company, it will be recalled, had inaugurated long distance on a major scale upon losing its patent in 1885. The plan had been to maintain high local rates, provide long distance at a loss, and refuse toll connections to competing companies. Loss-leadering long distance was foreseen as means for precluding rivalry in toll while also putting at a disadvantage local competitors lacking long-distance connections.[30]

Once direct competition at the local level was eliminated, however, this particular pricing strategy no longer made sense. Loss-leadering long distance meant that Bell was not only *cross-subsidizing* its own toll business through local revenues; it was also *subsidizing* connecting independents. The problem became more acute with General Order No. 375, which required Bell to share toll revenues (inadequate to cover costs in any event) with independents. The company's response to this predicament was sensible indeed: it rebalanced its rates.

The precise date on which 'phase one rate rebalancing' began cannot be pinpointed (it was a consequence not only of relative price changes in toll and local but of relative cost and equipment changes). But 'rebalanced' they most assuredly were, reversing the apparent cross-subsidy between local and toll and thereby reversing the subsidy between Bell and connecting independents.[31] Henceforth, independents were to subsidize Bell.

Devastation Results

A result of this initial round of 'rate rebalancing' was financial distress for independents possessing few or no long-distance lines. On the one hand, lacking extensive long lines of their own, they were to receive but minimal shares of increasingly lush toll revenues; but on the other, because Bell 'set the standard' for local rate levels,[31] the independents were inhibited by provincial regulator and public pressure from charging local rates that were compensatory.[32] Further, because independents generally were confined to smaller communities and rural territories where costs per telephone were greater, they had little opportunity to cross-subsidize. In brief, independents faced a cost/price squeeze. Losses mounted and service deteriorated.

The problems created by rate rebalancing did not receive much attention in officialdom until the early 1950s. At the federal level, the Depression and then the Second World War meant that the government had concerns far greater than simply restraining Bell Telephone. Regulation is inherently reactive in any event, and for its part Bell Telephone applied for no general rate increases between 1928 and 1949.

Provincial authorities too were quiescent until the conclusion of the war, but were finally jolted from hibernation by a marked erosion in the quality of rural service. A task force, appointed by the Ontario government to make recommendations for improvement, reported in 1953. Describing events leading to the unsatisfactory service existing in 1951 – at which time Bell operated 1.1 million Ontario telephones while 497 independents accounted for 164,000 phones (about 13 per cent of the provincial total) – the report advised: '... it is believed that taking an average of the whole province, service is no better than fair though gradual improvement is being effected. There is wide variation in quality between systems ... Many systems have not proceeded with necessary work due to lack of capital ... The [independent] telephone industry, due to the small size of systems and the fact that at best only modest returns can be expected, has never been attractive to investors.'[33]

Regulatory Complicity

Some measure of responsibility must be placed squarely at the door of the federal regulator, since Bell's connecting agreements were subject to board approval. Yet it appears the federal commissioners were unconcerned about independent telephones. In a 1951 ruling, for example, they diffidently denied having any 'responsibility for the revenue plight of companies not subject to our jurisdiction.'[34] Again in 1954 the board affirmed that it was 'not responsible for the financial welfare of such companies.'[35]

Ethical considerations aside, the board's reasoning was quite erroneous, for it justified withholding toll revenues from independents lacking toll lines through the so-called 'board-to-board' methodology of allocating costs. That method, banned by the u.s. Supreme Court as early as 1930,[36] presumes that local loops, local exchanges, and even telephone sets are not used in making long-distance telephone calls. Not only did the Transport Board in Canada rule that independents should receive no compensation for the use of such 'local' equipment; as well, long-distance billing expenses were decreed non-compensable.[37]

Take-overs
The board's posture, of course, coupled with 'phase one rate rebalancing,' resulted in decimation of the independent telephone industry. Between 1950 and 1959 Bell purchased about 160 Ontario independents, and between 1960 and 1975 it acquired an additional 218.[38] By 1976 independents had been reduced to less than 5 per cent of Ontario's telephones (table 10.1).

Far from magnanimous in sharing toll revenues, Bell none the less demonstrated considerable liberality in making acquisitions. Under cross-examination in 1977, Gordon E. Inns, executive vice-president of Bell, testified that in Bell's take-overs substantial 'acquisition premiums' were normally paid, despite low anticipated returns. He further agreed that local service rates charged by erstwhile independents would have to more than double to generate an attractive return if such companies were to remain unamalgamated with Bell; with amalgamation, internal cross-subsidies could sustain the operations at original local rates.[39]

Nor has the stratagem been laid to rest in recent years. Bell's 1988 acquisition price of $370 million for the 85,000 subscribers of Northwes-Tel and Terra Nova Telecommunications ($4353 per subscriber) raised eyebrows in both the press and the financial community. 'On a financial basis, this transaction cannot be justified,' commented Jonathan Cunningham, vice-president and director of Nesbitt Thomson Deacon Inc.[40] Responded Gordon Maxfield, general manager and secretary of the Canadian Independent Telephone Association: 'Obviously, they [BCE] were hungry to get those two companies and they just sort of put a price tag that was unreachable by anybody else.'[41]

LOCKING THE BARN-DOOR

In 1976 federal responsibility for regulating telecommunications passed to the Canadian Radio-television and Telecommunications Commission (CRTC). On 29 December of that year, the new federal regulator[42] received an application from the City of Prince Rupert, BC (the only surviving independent in that province), to arbitrate a dispute concerning the interchange of messages with BC Telephone Company. The review marked the CRTC's initial foray into clashes between connecting telephone systems within a province. The commission appointed a committee of representatives from federal and provincial regulatory boards to consider the case and make recommendations. Reporting in 1978 the committee recommended reversing several key regulatory precedents. These recommendations were later adopted by the CRTC,[43] and it is useful to review some of them while speculating on how the telephone industry would now be structured had they been in place thirty years before.

First, the board-to-board approach to revenue settlements inaugurated by the railway commissioners was termed simplistic; in the committee's opinion it created a severe financial drain on independents lacking toll lines. Second, the committee advised, the federal regulator should 'have regard to the interests of *both* bodies of subscribers and not just the subscribers of the company under its jurisdiction.' Third, the committee alleged that the Railway Act indeed prohibited 'unjust discrimination by a federally regulated telephone company in favour of its own subscribers as compared with the subscribers of a connecting company,' finally repudiating the outrageous 1914 ruling of the board of railway commissioners (Port Hope Telephone case). Finally, the committee concluded, once the CRTC had assurance that the connecting company's operations were efficient and construction plans prudent, terms of interconnection should permit the connecting company to earn a just and reasonable return on investment.

No matter how much one might be inclined to applaud the committee for its report and the CRTC for adopting it, the simple truth is that most of the independent telephone industry had long since passed into oblivion. In fact, by 1976 Bell claimed it was satiated – it had largely lost interest in acquiring additional territory in Ontario.[44]

'REVERSED RATE REBALANCING'

Facing the prospect of direct competition in long-distance voice (message toll service, or MTS) and warily eyeing reduced long-distance prices south of the border (raising the prospect of bypass[45]), Bell in the 1980s has been proposing a scheme of reversed rate rebalancing, whereby long-distance prices are to be slashed and local rates more than doubled. Although the proposal is addressed in greater detail in subsequent chapters, it is worth noting the consternation the plan has provoked in independent telephone industry circles.

For 1988 Bell's own studies have indicated that partial or interim rebalancing alone would reduce settled toll revenues between Bell and independents by \$4.2 million per year.[46] Québec-Téléphone, one of the largest independents, advised that these interim reductions would further diminish its revenues by \$2.4 million, contending Bell's previous reductions in long-distance prices had already cost the company \$6.2 million.[47] Other parties, such as the Consumers' Association of Canada, have predicted that reversed rate rebalancing could well increase pressure on independents to sell out to Bell or other independents.[48]

For its part Bell has promised to maintain settlement revenues at existing levels, provided independents do not lower their long-distance charges – cold comfort in the view of the Ontario Telephone Association which asserts that 'rates charged by Bell tend to be regarded by independents' subscribers as the norm.'[49]

Surprisingly, in light of the Prince Rupert decision, the CRTC recently has accepted wholeheartedly Bell's position on reversed rate rebalancing and also Bell's proposals for toll settlements with independents. In a ruling consonant with previous decisions of the Board of Railway Commissioners for Canada, the CRTC declared: 'The Commission considers that it would not be appropriate to leave an independent's settled revenues unchanged in cases where it adopts Bell's lower toll rates, since doing so would result in support for the independent's lower toll rates coming from Bell's subscribers.'[50]

This decision, of course, quite ignores the interdependencies and disparities of telephone companies in Canada, implicitly assuming that rural companies with 1500 subscribers are on equal footing with Bell.

One can perhaps anticipate a final shake-down of Ontario's and Quebec's now-lilliputian independent telephone industry, stemming from the current stratagem of reversed rate rebalancing and from the CRTC's new hard-nosed attitude. Indeed, by the summer of 1988 the shake-down was under way. Fresh from acquiring NorthwesTel and Terra Nova Telecommunications from Canadian National, Bell's president and CEO Raymond Cyr told the press that his company would 'welcome talks with smaller companies that may want to sell.' He added: 'We are not trying to get *all* of them at *any* price. But I would think we would always be on the lookout for potential acquisitions, particularly in Ontario and Quebec.'[51]

11

Long-Distance Competition and Reversed Rate Rebalancing

In addition to having a lethal effect on most local companies, the initial rounds of rate rebalancing undertaken between 1923 and the early 1970s also stirred up longings for rivalry in long distance, now the more lucrative field. One would-be entrant was Northern Telephone Limited. Founded in 1905 as the Temiskaming Telephone Co., Northern extended its territory to encompass vast reaches of northern Ontario, stretching from Chibougamou, Quebec, to the Manitoba border, and north from Cobalt, Sault Ste Marie, and Atikokan to Hudson Bay, embracing some 150 communities and settlements. In 1963 Northern applied for connection at Fort William for a proposed toll line to Kenora. Its application was supported by the Town of Kenora, which operated the municipal exchange.

In its brief to the board, Northern alleged that Bell for many years had neglected northern regions, noting that the dominant firm, merely leasing circuits from Canadian Pacific Telegraphs, had yet to establish its own long-distance facilities between Kenora and Fort William. Northern promised that the increased toll revenues its connection would generate would be applied to lowering local rates and upgrading service in its sparsely settled territory.

The Transport Board, however, was unimpressed. Its attention rather was riveted on a perceived erosion in Bell's revenues – of between $150,000 and $300,000 per annum – if the application were approved. On these grounds alone, it turned Northern down, stating sardonically: 'The fact that a competing carrier is prepared to offer more is not a ground for substituting it for the existing carrier.'[1]

Bell acquired Northern in 1966, plying its shareholders with hefty acquisition premiums and confident that 'the elimination of continuous friction' was well worth the extra costs.[2] Northern's operations in Quebec were spun off as a separate entity, Téléphone du Nord de Québec[3], and its Ontario territory shrunk.

CNCP INTERCONNECTION

Faring somewhat better was CNCP Telecommunications, albeit thirteen years later. On 14 June 1976 Canadian Pacific Limited applied to the CRTC for connections to Bell's switching centres and local loops. No longer was Bell to joust with the likes of Port Hope, Ingersoll, and Northern telephone companies. Rather, it was now locked in a battle of corporate titans. Although the division CP Telecommunications was dwarfed by Bell, the parent, Canadian Pacific Limited, certainly was not. Nor was its ally, Canadian National Railways, always among the fifteen largest Canadian companies. Canadian Pacific complained that it was unable to compete effectively with Bell Canada in data communications owing to the latter's interdiction proscribing connections between CNCP's long-lines transmission network and the telephone company's local switching facilities.

Background
Relations between Canada's two major telecommunications consortia, CNCP Telecommunications and TCTS, have ranged from co-operation to obstructionism. Between 1931 and about 1965, for example, CP leased long lines to members of TCTS to enable the latter to provide a nation-wide long-distance voice service,[4] although this co-operation was complemented by competition, particularly after 1947, in the providing of private lines, hook-ups for network broadcasting, and communication facilities for the Department of Defence.

In the early 1950s microwave began to replace land lines as the most efficient transmission medium for record as well as long-distance voice communication, at which point rivalry spilled over to encompass ownership of facilities as well as provisioning of services. In 1952, for instance, CBC asked both carrier groups for tenders on microwave hook-ups for a proposed national television network, whereupon the Department of Transport, at the time licensing authority for all users of radio frequencies, including microwave, tried in vain to have the two consortia undertake a joint project. Although the telegraph companies were amenable, Bell insisted that the telephone industry alone should own all microwave. Unenthused at the prospect of becoming mere leasees of emerging techniques, the telegraph companies declined. Cabinet stepped in to mediate, announcing its decision on 24 September 1953: 'The Cabinet agreed that no one person or corporation should receive monopoly to operate a microwave relay system ... [provided] the technical features of the applications submitted were satisfactory.' Thereafter microwave in Canada developed competitively. By 1958 TCTS had a coast-to-coast system in place while CN and CP concentrated facilities east of Manitoba.

Contentions arose again in 1962, when CNCP won a tender from the Canadian Overseas Telecommunications Corporation (COTC; today Teleglobe) to establish a second nation-wide microwave relay system. Bell again protested, charging that CNCP's projected system would give rise to undue overcapacity.[5] The telephone companies announced further that TCTS was planning to build soon its own additional coast-to-coast network in any event, making a CNCP system doubly redundant.[6] Once again cabinet stepped in to permit the telegraph companies to extend their system nation-wide.

Nor has microwave been the sole contentious facility over the years. Also in dispute have been access to the switched telephone distribution system, the subject of the CRTC's interconnection proceedings, and communication satellites to be discussed in chapter 18.

The CRTC's First Interconnect Decision
After much preliminary skirmishing, hearings were held in two phases in 1978. In the first phase evidence was presented by CNCP and interveners supporting its application. Testifying were the director of Combines Investigation as well as representatives from such heavyweights of the Canadian business establishment as IBM, Canadian Industrial Communications Assembly, Canadian Information Processing Society, Canadian Business Equipment Manufacturers Association, and Canadian Press.[8]

Phase two, lasting eleven days, gave expression to arguments in opposition. Bell Telephone called six witnesses. Also appearing were representatives of the telephone companies of the Atlantic and Prairie provinces and of the Atlantic provincial governments.

Witnesses in rebuttal consumed another two days. Altogether, including a prehearing conference, the formal proceedings required twenty-five days and resulted in 4375 pages of transcript.

Bell's final argument alone was 352 pages long, although its thrust is summarized easily: 'The public switched telephone network as it exists today constitutes a clear and workable boundary of the basic, natural monopoly of Bell Canada in telecommunications ... It is Bell Canada's view that any services *not* connected to the public switched telephone network should be ... tested in the marketplace [emphasis added].'[9] If CNCP were granted connections, Bell continued, 'there [would] no longer be a clear boundary between monopoly and competitive services ... [and] the slide down the slippery slope will have commenced.'[10]

Bell provided three basic supports for its position. First, it alleged that forced interconnection with a competitor amounted to 'expropriation' of Bell's 'greatest asset,' its switched network. Second, Bell claimed interconnection would erode its revenues by $235 million annually, requiring the company to raise local rates (the first intimation of reversed rate rebalancing). Third, interconnection would impose costs on society from inefficiencies because Bell would no longer be able to take full advantage of purported 'economies of scale, scope and technology'.[11]

After weighing the merits on both sides the CRTC departed significantly from positions established by the Canadian Transport Commission and its predecessors. Whereas the Board of Transport commissioners had denied responsibility for the financial welfare of companies not under its jurisdiction, the CRTC stated that it was indeed required to take a wide view of its obligations – that in particular it would consider indirect effects of granting the application upon telephone subscribers in the Atlantic provinces and on the prairies.[12] The commission also ruled that CNCP was required only to make a prima facie case that access to Bell's local loops would be useful to it, that duplication of the local distribution system would not be in the public interest, and that no unreasonable technical harm would result from interconnection. Once these minimal requirements were met, the CRTC continued, the onus fell on Bell to justify denials of access, thereby overriding the judgment of the Northern Telephone case.[13]

Next the CRTC rejected Bell's contention that compensation by CNCP should be 'on the basis of the expropriation of a proprietary right,' reference being clearly to precedential awards of indemnity by the Board of Railway Commissioners. Rather, the CRTC ruled, 'business loss arising from the introduction of fair competition is non-compensable.'[14] In any event, the CRTC chided, Bell had grossly overstated revenue erosion from interconnection: 'As an upper limit,' the commission reproved, the revenue loss to Bell in 1982 would be 'no more than $45.7 million, rather than $235.3 million as Bell had estimated.'[15] Finally, the CRTC admonished, 'Bell failed to provide adequate empirical evidence to support its contentions regarding the nature and extent of any economies of scale enjoyed by it.'[16]

Meanwhile, the commission did foresee substantial benefits from interconnection: 'The evidence in this case indicates that competition would be greatly enhanced with interconnection [and that] interconnection would provide significant benefits to users in terms of improved responsiveness, particularly on the part of the telephone company, in satisfying their telecommunications requirements.'[17]

And so in May 1979 the CRTC ordered Bell to provide CNCP with certain limited network connections. Two and a half years later BC Telephone Company also was ordered to provide similar connections.[18] Although these two decisions permitted CNCP to begin transmitting both private line voice and switched data over switched telephone lines in Ontario, Quebec, and British Columbia, it remained barred from offering these services elsewhere. CNCP was also prevented from providing a public long-distance voice service anywhere in Canada.

In the Federal Court

Having attained limited connections to the switched local loops of both Bell Canada and BC Tel by 1981, CNCP applied to the CRTC in September 1982 to order similar connections form Alberta Government Telephones (the third largest telephone company in Canada). The matter, CNCP claimed, fell within the jurisdictional competence of the federal board because AGT's lines connected with other provinces.[19] AGT in turn applied to the federal court, trial division, for a writ of prohibition to be directed against the CRTC and preventing the commission from proceeding with the application.[20] In its affidavit AGT argued that it was a 'local' undertaking, hence subject to provincial control; moreover, as a provincially owned corporation, it benefited from Crown immunity.[21]

The case came before the federal court, trial division, in May 1984, and on 26 October the Honourable Madame Justice Reed handed down a decision. Although finding AGT's operations not to be 'local' in nature she none the less accepted AGT's contention concerning Crown immunity.[22] CNCP promptly appealed the learned judge's ruling to the federal

Court of Appeal. In a judgment rendered on 4 December 1985 Mr Justice Pratte concurred with the trial judge that AGT was not a 'local' undertaking, but he reversed her finding regarding Crown immunity. On 14 August 1989, however, the Supreme Court affirmed the original judgment, declaring: 'AGT is an interprovincial undertaking ... and accordingly lies exclusively within federal jurisdiction. However, as a provincial Crown agent, AGT is entitled to claim Crown immunity.'[23] The federal government, then, is legally entitled to regulate all major telephone companies in Canada, owing to their provincial interconnectedness. Provincial governments, however, have been scrambling to reaffirm jurisdiction through ongoing negotiations.[24] On the bargaining table in March 1987 was a 'Proposal for an Agreement in Principle on Government Responsibilities and Joint Policy Development in Telecommunications' whereby the federal government would exercise jurisdiction over all interprovincial and international telecommunications, albeit subject to policy direction from the provinces. This proposal was followed in early 1988 by a policy paper from the federal Department of Communications, entitled 'Proposed Guidelines for Type 1 Telecommunication Carriers,' which is addressed at the close of this chapter.

The Second Interconnect Decision

Although by 1981 CNCP was interconnected to Bell and BC Tel for data and private line voice, it was still barred from switched public long-distance voice. On 23 October 1983 it applied to redress this omission, raising for the CRTC yet again the provocative question of 'whether, and if so to what extent, the long distance telecommunication market should be opened to ... competitive entry.'[25] Hearings were held in 1984, lasting thirty-six days and resulting in 7219 pages of transcripts. In the end the CRTC again found competition likely to 'increase productivity and reduce costs and that these savings would likely be reflected in lower MTS/WATS rates [which] would, in turn, have a positive impact on the performance of the Canadian economy as a whole.'[26] Moreover, the commission concluded, 'competition would likely result in increased innovation and flexibility with respect to the pricing and marketing of interexchange services ... the introduction of new services and new service features ... [and] more rapid introduction of improved switching and transmission facilities.'[27]

None the less, the commission rejected CNCP's application. In the commission's opinion, approval 'would not yield these anticipated benefits to a significant extent throughout the territories served by Bell and BC Tel. In particular, the Commission is not convinced that CNCP would be able to meet its commitment to provide universal service and to offer price discounts of the order of magnitude assumed in its business plan.'[28]

Although the CRTC's financial analysis was disputed by CNCP,[29] that particular controversy need not be reviewed here. Of greater relevance was Bell's response to the threat of long-distance competition. Bell used the proceeding as opportunity to publicize its proposal for 'reversed rate rebalancing (that is, to 'align' local and long-distance prices more closely with 'costs'). As noted by the CRTC, 'The principal element of the proposed rebalancing plan involved decreases in MTS/WATS rates of up to 70% and increases of as much as 150% in average rates for primary local service.'[30]

Bell insisted that its rates should be rebalanced irrespective of whether CNCP were allowed to compete in long-distance voice, but the company carefully added that in the event CNCP were allowed to compete, rates definitely needed to be rebalanced first.

In autumn 1987 the CRTC held a full-scale inquiry into Bell's proposal. Previously (Decision 86-17) it had permitted Bell to reduce its intra-toll rates by 20 per cent effective 1 January 1987. Bell now wanted to implement commensurate increases in local service prices of $1.25 per month per individual line.[31] Bell's costing studies had shown that only 30 per cent of access 'costs' was being recovered through local service revenues, compared with 70 per cent from monopoly toll,[32] and hence the company wanted to begin redressing this purported 'imbalance,' eventually recovering 100 per cent (!) of 'access' costs *from local service*.[33]

In its decision the CRTC endorsed in principle 'reversed rate rebalancing,' even while holding back local rate increases in this particular proceeding.[34] In the CRTC's opinion, rebalancing would (1) reduce telecommunications cost for Canadian business; (2) lessen the potential for a future diversion of traffic through the United States, where long-distance rates are lower than in Canada; (3) increase national 'understanding' through increased communication among the regions; and (4) 'create an environment better suited for competitive entry [!] in the MTS/WATS market should that, in the future, appear desirable.'[35] With regard to this last point it is to be noted that it is Bell's position that 'reversed rate rebalancing' is 'superior to [i.e., a substitute for] competition as a mechanism for efficiently reducing toll rates because all revenues from local increases are applied to toll rate reductions.'[36]

As with the CRTC's recent about-face on toll settlements with independent telephone companies (discussed in the preceding chapter), a dramatic shift in CRTC postures towards Bell, its rivals, and its customers is evident. Recent endorsements of 'reversed rate rebalancing' and the explicit denial of competitive entry into message toll contrast sharply with the commission's pro-competitive decisions of the late 1970s and early 1980s.

ADDITIONAL COMPLEXITIES

In March 1988 the federal Department of Communications (aka Communications Canada) issued a policy document which, if followed, would shore up monopoly in long-distance transmission. The discussion paper proposed that DOC itself assume licensing or authorization power 'for the construction and operation of *any* telecommunications transmission facility that crosses provincial or international boundaries, whether radio or non-radio technology is used.' That document also made clear that would-be competitors would face formidable barriers in attaining such authorization. On the one hand the onus was to be on them to pass stringent tests of 'public convenience and necessity.' On the other DOC admitted a strong predilection against competition in transmission, declaring: 'Open entry to the telecommunications markets of Type 1A and 1B carriers [could well] result in unnecessary duplication of costly facilities, threats to socially desirable cross-subsidies, and service disruptions resulting from the failure of new entrants.'[37]

Not only did DOC contemplate erecting high hurdles in front of newcomers desiring entry, but it was planning to freeze the present rivalry between Telecom Canada and CNCP. Telephone companies were being termed Type 1A carriers, while CNCP, Telesat Canada, Teleglobe Canada, and Cantel were declared to be Type 1B. Again, stringent tests of 'public convenience and necessity' would have to be met before any reclassification.

None the less, in the spring of 1989 CNCP, now owned jointly by Canadian Pacific and Ted Rogers, announced it would be filing yet another application with the CRTC to provide long-distance message toll service in competition with the telephone companies.[38] Given

Rogers's control of Cantel (a cellular telephone company with 127,000 subscribers) and his servicing of 25 per cent of Canadian cable television subscribers, CNCP's new proprietorship and imminent long-distance application spread shock waves through the telephone industry, so much so that BCE's feisty chairman, A.J. de Grandpré, told the press: 'What we're talking about is competing in Rogers' [cable TV] territory with a duplicate cable system. That's what he wants to do in long distance – duplicate the long-distance network.'[39] While acknowledging that Bell Canada itself was currently precluded from engaging directly in the cable industry, Bell president Raymond Cyr confided that 'appropriate steps' were being taken to amend the restricting legislation.[40] Less than a week later communications minister Marcel Masse confirmed Cyr's declaration, telling two thousand cable executives that his department was investigating the possibility of allowing open competition in both the cable TV and the long-distance telephone industries.[41]

RECAPITULATION

In historical perspective there has been a continuing oscillation between competition and monopoly in Canadian telecommunications. The brief inaugural period of local rivalry was squashed abruptly in 1880–1: through legislative enactment conferring charter privileges on the Bell Telephone Company of Canada, through patent pooling and agreement to split the telephone and telegraph fields, and through acquisitions by Bell and its affiliates of rival telephone systems. Nullification of a patent in 1885 restored the possibility of competition, but soon a well-honed panoply of restrictive and predatory trade practices was in place, helping eliminate the trickle of insurgents. Regulation, introduced in 1906, initially gave some encouragement to a newly burgeoning independent telephone industry, but rather quickly the federal regulator began favouring Bell in its interconnections, eliminating all direct competition by 1925. Thereafter Bell turned its sights to the non-competing segment, and by astutely rebalancing rates wreaked such financial havoc on the independent contingent that by 1975 it had been decimated. Rivalry between the telegraph companies on the one hand and major telephone companies (co-ordinating operations through the TransCanada Telephone System) on the other began to blossom in the 1930s and 1940s, growing to encompass switched data in 1979, but efforts to extend competition into long-distance voice were rebuffed by the federal regulator in 1985. Today, however, a renewed effort by a reinvigorated CNCP to enter the fray is planned.

As this manuscript went to press, the future direction of telecommunications policy was far from clear. On the one hand, consistent with its historical anti-competitive predilictions, DOC issued a discussion paper in 1988 that seemed to enshrine the doctrine of natural monopoly; on the other, in early 1989 the communications minister was musing publicly on the possibility of head-to-head competition among telephone companies, CNCP, and the cable television industry. Since the doctrine of natural monopoly will undoubtedly continue being invoked in the months and years ahead, it is important to appraise its validity, the topic of the next chapter.

12

Natural Monopoly:
Arguments and Evidence

'Personal interest,' John Kenneth Galbraith once observed poignantly, 'always wears the disguise of public purpose, and no one is more easily persuaded of the validity or righteousness of a public cause than persons who stand to gain personally therefrom.'[1] Galbraith's remarks enlighten perception when considering the doctrine of natural monopoly and examining its application to Canadian telecommunications.

'Natural monopoly,' coined in 1848 by John Stuart Mill,[2] denotes instances where competition is perceived as being unsustainable or undesirable. Early in this century the telephone industry began applying the appellation to itself, attaining thereby an aura of necessity, respectability, and even benevolence for an industrial structure that otherwise could have generated even more controversy. Today, in light of policy-makers' renewed resistance towards competition, careful historical analysis of the evidence and the claims underpinning telephony's status as 'natural' monopoly is essential.

In telephony, 'natural monopoly' historically has had three underpinnings; first, reputedly vast and inexhaustible economies of scale; second, the claim that 'service universality' (widespread availability of telephone service) can best be achieved through system-wide cost averaging and cross-subsidization; and third, the doctrine of 'systemic integrity' (maintenance of high service standards) through end-to-end control. Although in recent years these three props have grown weaker, concerted effort is being made to revive the credibility of 'natural monopoly.' This chapter reviews through historical account the current status of the three venerable underpinnings.

THE FIRST PROP: ECONOMIES OF SCALE

Although telephone companies' insistence of vast and barely tapped economies of scale in long-distance transmission served the industry long and well, the contention went both unchallenged and unsubstantiated for decades. In the 1970s, however, independent analysts launched a series of inquiries to confirm or disprove their existence and measure their magnitude. This independent research repeatedly failed to detect much in the way of economies of scale.[3] By the decade's end, therefore, the claims concerning inexhaustible scale economies were beginning to ring quite hollow.

None the less, in the 1978 CNCP interconnection case, Bell Canada, once more attempting to forestall competition, again boldly claimed 'economies of scale,' even alleging economies of 'scope and technology' too.[4] Usefulness of the doctrine seemingly died when in the ensuing decision the CRTC chided curtly: 'Bell Canada failed to provide adequate empirical evidence to support its contentions regarding the nature and extent of any economies of scale enjoyed by it.'[5]

The brevity of the regulator's rebuke should not be construed as signifying unimportance, for in those few words the CRTC shifted onto Bell the onus of proving economies of scale, and thereby relieving interveners and would-be competitors of the task of proving the contrary.

And Bell, of course, was quite unable to prove anything.

Consequently in 1984, even while mounting yet another defence to delay or preclude competitive entry by CNCP, this time into long-distance voice, neither Bell nor BC Tel invoked economies of scale. To the contrary, as noted by the CRTC, 'Both Bell Canada and BC Tel conceded that their toll markets are of sufficient size to sustain an additional supplier ... that more than one supplier could achieve economies of scale in the provision of interexchange service.'[6]

Despite this admission, the doctrine of economies of scale has recently been resuscitated by the Department of Communications. In an important policy document issued in 1988 the department averred that entry into telecommunications transmission would normally result in 'unnecessary duplication of costly facilities.'[7] The department declined, however, to cite evidence to support its claim.

THE SECOND PROP: SERVICE UNIVERSALITY THROUGH CROSS-
SUBSIDIZATION

The Bone of Contention
For years private as well as publicly owned telephone companies
claimed that, through cost-averaging and cross-subsidization, they
were extending service both geographically (to sparsely settled
regions) and demographically (to lower-income groups). *Cost-averaging* means that the entire operating territory is treated as one unit
from which revenues sufficient to cover company-wide expenses are
extracted, with little or no attempt to relate cost to price in any
specific service or locality. *Cross-subsidization* means practically the
same thing – that one region, service, or subscriber grouping subsidizes
another. The principle of ignoring or minimizing service costs when
setting rates is called *value of service pricing*. A principal form of
service cross-subsidy claimed to have taken place since the 1920s is
from lucrative long distance to costly local service, thereby enabling
virtually all citizens to avail themselves of basic telephone service.

Competition, it follows, undermines service universality because
entry centring on the most lucrative markets ('cream-skimming') will
invariably drive price towards cost there, leaving the telephone company insufficient funds with which to cross-subsidize high-cost regions
and disadvantaged subscriber groupings.[8] Entry to selective markets,
therefore, it is claimed, will serve the interests of the urban dweller
at the expense of the rural, the business user to the detriment of the
residential, and the rich while hurting the poor – mostly because
long distance, the largest money-maker, will become less profitable as
competition pushes prices down.

It must be emphasized that the existence of universal telephone
service in Canada at present is not in doubt: in 1986 almost 99 per cent
of households subscribed to some form of telephone service. Nor does
anyone seriously question that telephone companies do indeed engage
in one form or another of cross-subsidization and cost-averaging. But
what are service costs and which services benefit from cross-subsidization? These are the disputed issues. Historical analysis is valuable in
casting light on them and on the relevance of cross-subsidizations for
attaining and maintaining the laudatory goal of service universality.

Historical Evidence
The historical record belies claims to service universality through

cost-averaging and cross-subsidization by privately owned telephone companies. The independent telephone industries of both Canada and the United States were conceived because dominant, privately owned telephone companies were slow to extend service to sparsely settled regions. Provincialization of Bell Canada's operations on the prairies was a response in part to that company's reluctance to serve rural areas. Likewise, in the United States independents continued to serve some 52 per cent of that country's land mass even in the early 1970s, albeit accounting for just over 17 per cent of the nation's telephones,[9] indicating 'cream-skimming' of the first order by AT&T. Similarly, Ontario's independent telephone industry as recently as 1951 provided 50 per cent of rural telephones although accounting for only 13 per cent of telephones province-wide. Bell, of course, was then concentrating its Ontario operations in the lush, urban markets where 92 per cent of its telephones were located; in contrast, only 42 per cent of independent companies' telephones were located in urban markets.[10]

Nor has Bell Canada's sharing of toll revenue been conducive to service universality. As we have seen, its parsimony was responsible for a slow but unabated deterioration in rural service through the period 1940-70, helping Bell to acquire independents as bankruptcy set in or was knocking at the door.

Again, as will be discussed in chapter 14, it was rural service that received cutbacks when Bell failed to attain all the 'rate relief' requested from the Canadian Transport Commission during the first half of the 1970s. 'Competitive' services, meanwhile, continued to receive the full allotment of planned construction expenditures.

Current Evidence
Historical experience concerning the development of telecommunications in the south is paralleled by that in the north. Bell Canada has been at best a reluctant purveyor of telecommunications in the eastern Arctic, a portion of its territory. Indeed, so unreliable and scarce were telecommunications in the Northwest Territories even through the 1970s that the Department of Communications in 1978 instituted a Northern Communications Assistance Program (NCAP), earmarking $9 million over five years to subsidize Bell and its compatriot (and now subsidiary), NorthwesTel, to supply and upgrade service. As a first initiative under the program, Bell was awarded $822,000 to extend telephone service to Hall Beach and Whale Cove.[11]

By 1985 the northern assistance program was complete, and today all communities in the Northwest Territories with more than one hundred residents enjoy some form or other of telecommunications service. How long northern communities would have had to wait in the absence of direct government subsidy is unknown.

None the less, the service provided remains far from adequate. One of the principal grievances of northern residents is Bell's 'value of service' pricing, whereby intercommunity calls are billed according to distance. Given the small size of most isolated northern communities, residents there find the long-distance network to be at least as important as local exchanges are to southerners. But because the distances separating the communities are vast, 'value of service pricing' makes telephone communications in the north very expensive. In 1984, for example, for its full territory Bell Canada received only $291 in long-distance charges per main station, while in the eastern Arctic it received $917.16 per main station.[12] Given the substantially lower incomes of northern residents, high telecommunications charges take on even greater significance.

Nor is it clear that distance-related ('value of service') prices are in any sense justifiable from a costing perspective. After all, one of the virtues of satellites is to make costs independent of distance.

None the less, Bell has been adamant in the face of suggestions that it abandon distance-based prices for the north, contending: 'In an environment where rates for various telephone services are being driven more towards cost, the company does not believe that it should be expected to perform a social wealth redistribution role to benefit a group of subscribers in one section of its territory, at the expense of another. Such a role, if necessary, would appear more appropriately borne by the citizens at large.'[13]

Bell's declaration is highly ironic. Its acquisition price of $200 million for NorthwesTel's 35,000 subscribers ($5714 each) will cause 'cost of service' to skyrocket in the Arctic, and someone somewhere of course will have to pay.

Costing Evidence
In 1978 Bell Canada produced a study ('The Five Way Split') purporting to show that local service costs the company $1.32 for each dollar of revenue produced, while long-distance costs merely $0.31 for each dollar of revenue generated.[14] This purported cross-subsidy has received other expressions: in 1985, for example, Bell claimed that its

TABLE 12.1
Revenues, costs and profits by service category, Bell Canada, 1983
($ millions)

Service category	Revenues	Costs	Difference
Local	1389	868	521
Access	0	1762	−1762
Toll	1988	626	1362
Competitive network	386	317	69
Competitive terminal	878	834	44
Common	99	333	−234

SOURCE: CRTC, 'Interexchange Competition and Related Issues,' Telecom Decision CRTC 85–19, 29 August 1985, 53

subscribers in Ottawa were being charged a flat monthly fee of $9.35 for a local service costing the corporation $24.00 per month per subscriber;[15] again in 1987, in a circular to its subscribers, Bell claimed that it had been providing 'local service rates substantially below its underlying costs.'[16] These cross-subsidies, Bell continued, are no longer viable now that pressures are mounting for entry into the lucrative long-distance market.

In addressing the question of whether local service subsidizes or does not subsidize long distance, costs must be apportioned because both telecommunications services make use of common plant and equipment. Briefly stated, it is in a telephone company's interest to allocate as few usage-insensitive and common costs as possible to services threatened by entry in order to 'justify' lower prices to impede such competition.

In 1985 the CRTC published an analysis based on Bell's own data for 1983, depicting both local and long-distance services as immensely profitable (see table 12.1). Far from losing $0.31 on the dollar, Bell was there portrayed as earning a surplus of $521 million on local revenues of $1389 million.[17]

The CRTC's finding concerning the stupendous profitability of local service can be reconciled with Bell's contention concerning its gargantuan unprofitability only by focusing attention on access costs. In its five-way split, Bell allocated all access costs to local service and none to long distance; because access facilities constitute up to 50 per cent of telephone plant and equipment, large losses for local service emerged in Bell's calculations. The CRTC, however, declared that access facilities should be allocated neither to long distance nor to local service because both must use access facilities whose costs are insensitive to usage. Consequently, the CRTC found both local and long distance to be highly profitable in and of themselves, and both to be making 'contributions' to access costs, albeit long distance to be making the larger contribution.

Apart from other considerations cited in this section – the historical record on the spread of telephone service to rural areas, the provisioning of service to the north, toll settlements with independent companies, and so on – the Cost inquiry has demonstrated conclusively that the purported cross-subsidy between local and long distance is a consequence merely of arbitrary accounting allocations, throwing once more into doubt the telephone industry's venerable claim of being 'naturally' an end-to-end monopoly.

Other Indicators
Again looking ahead to ensuing discussions, it is indeed unlikely that Bell Canada would have juggled corporate forms, spun off lucrative profit centres, concentrated equipment purchases with its own unregulated subsidiary, and folded capital-intensive but unprofitable operations into itself had its main objective been cost-averaging and cross-subsidization to maintain service universality. The creation of BCE as the parent firm of Bell Canada again shows the company to be quite selective in the ways it is willing to carry out its cross-subsidies (see discussion in chapter 15).

THE THIRD PROP: SYSTEMIC INTEGRITY

A third decades-old claim undergirding 'natural monopoly' in Canadian telecommunications has been 'systemic integrity,' the notion that network performance can be maintained at high levels only through centralized administration of 'end-to-end' operations. By analogy to the weak link in a chain, telephone companies charged that subscribers, attaching their own terminal devices, would pollute the system with substandard, malfunctioning equipment. So persuasive indeed were the telcos in advancing this point of view that *Instant World*, a federal task force report on telecommunications, merely parroted the allegation in 1971: 'The telecommunications carriers ...

advance powerful technical arguments for complete control of the public networks, including terminal devices and attached equipment. To maintain a high quality of service to all users, they must be able to guard against technical pollution of the network from other signal sources.'[18]

In addition to barring 'foreign' terminal devices, this doctrine of 'systemic integrity' served admirably to advance telco interests in another way, namely as support for continued vertical integration between the (regulated) telephone-operating company and its (unregulated) subsidiary equipment supplier/manufacturer. It was argued that owning the supplier helped ensure system-wide compatibility of equipment.[19]

Critique

The credence afforded 'systemic integrity' through end-to-end control is hard to fathom, given that the industry's very structure for at least seventy years belied the claim. In the United States as far back as 1902 there were 3000 independent telephone companies supplying 44 per cent of that nation's telephones,[20] while by 1972 there remained 1758 U.S. independents fully interconnected to the American Bell System.[21] Likewise in Canada, as recently as 1972 there were 1170 telephone systems fully interconnected to constitute a national telephone grid.[22] Despite this profusion of participants, 'systemic integrity' was somehow maintained.

But old myths die hard, especially when continually propagated by a powerful industry lobby, and no regulatory board wanted an accusing finger pointed at it for creating a tower of babel. So, until the late 1960s, telephone companies in both the United States and Canada had free rein regarding what could and could not be plugged into 'their' system. Sometimes, as Manley Irwin has suggested, attempts at 'safeguarding' the network scaled absurd heights, as when plastic covers for telephone directories and shoulder rests for telephone sets were banned – in the name of 'systemic integrity.'[23] The key steps in a program of liberalized attachments are recounted below. Had telephone companies been correct in their dire prognostications, by now the whole network would be quite cacophonous.

A Revised Bell Charter

Although a program of liberalized attachments was begun in the United States as early as 1956,[24] in Canada the battle for terminal interconnection was joined only in 1967 when Dr H.S. Gellman of DCF Systems testified before a Commons committee on transport and communications, his main bone of contention being that 'Bell Canada has, on occasion, used its existing powers to restrict the development of advanced communications systems in Canada. In so doing it has prevented the establishment of a vigorous Canadian communications equipment and services industry, and it has denied Canada the economic benefit of such an industry.'[25]

After illustrating his allegations with numerous case studies, Dr Gellman recommended that Parliament revise Bell's charter 'to include a clause requiring Bell Canada to establish standards governing the use of non-Bell equipment on both private and switched communication circuits. These standards will be subject to the approval of the Department of Transport.'[26]

Parliament responded quickly to Dr Gellman's brief. It amended Bell's charter in 1968, authorizing the company itself to draw up such 'reasonable' attachment requirements as were needed to protect subscribers and the public whenever any equipment, apparatus, line circuit, or device not provided by the company was to be connected to the public telephone system. The revised charter also empowered the Canadian Transport Commission (CTC) to become final arbiter on the 'reasonableness' of Bell's requirements, and to substitute its own requirements, if need be, for those drawn up by Bell.[27] The amended act further provided that any person 'affected' by the requirements prescribed by the company could petition the CTC to make alterations. But as in the United States, so also in Canada: the regulator initially was quite reluctant to order terminal attachments.

The Case of Dr Morton Shulman

In 1975 Dr Morton Shulman, millionaire stock speculator, author, former coroner, and maverick Ontario MPP complained to the CTC that Bell had disconnected his phone in the provincial legislature. Dr Shulman acknowledged that he had not complied with a company order to detach his automatic dialler, known as 'Magicall,' from his telephone set. The device, owned by Dr Shulman, stored up to four hundred telephone numbers for automatic dialling.

In the ensuing hearings Bell countered that Dr Shulman had no right to attach his own 'Magicall' to the company's lines because the company had drawn up no 'requirements' for its use. Bell submitted, however, that Dr Shulman remained at liberty to lease the device from Bell, which was offering 'Magicall' on a lease-only basis. Bell claimed further that all terminal devices should be 'owned, installed and maintained by it,' rather than by customers, for reasons of systemic integrity, because 'such terminal equipment [constitutes] an integral part of [the] public switched network [and is] capable of controlling Central Office addressing equipment.'[28]

The CTC agreed, ruling that because Bell had published no 'requirement' for the attachment of customer-owned 'Magicalls' there was 'no such requirement before the Commission which the Commission could judge to be reasonable or not.' To the obvious question of whether a requirement not having been published was not in itself unreasonable, the CTC responded: 'The Company's decision not to establish such requirement is, in our view, completely within the discretion of the company.'[29]

Thereupon the CTC dismissed the application, maintaining 'we have no jurisdiction to grant the relief sought in this case.'

Harding Communications
At about the same time Dr Shulman was sallying forth unsuccessfully before the CTC, Harding Communications Limited, a distributor and manufacturer of communications equipment, chose wisely to prosecute a somewhat similar grievance in a different forum – the Quebec courts. Approached by the Bank of Montreal in 1974 to design and install a system whereby calls could be diverted to the bank's Master Charge authorization centre, Harding spent a good deal of time and money drawing up a system to meet the bank's specifications. Bell Telephone, however, refused to supply the couplers (interface devices) required by Bell's own tariff before the bank could legally have the system installed. Negotiations between Harding and the bank none the less continued – for a while – the latter apparently being on the verge of installing Harding's system without the couplers when Bell, becoming apprised of the bank's evident disdain for its rules, threatened to pull the plug – to disconnect the Bank of Montreal's entire telephone system – 'if it installed Plaintiff's equipment in any manner whatsoever.'[30]

Not wishing to leave a valued customer in the lurch, however, Bell made a counter-offer: it would install the exact same system on a lease-basis once it had acquired the requisite equipment from Harding's U.S. supplier. Although the bank turned Bell down flatly, it also broke off negotiations with Harding, evidently fearful lest it lose its vital communication links to the outside world.

So, in 1975, Harding sought a court injunction to stop harassment, claiming it had already lost $400,000 and been forced to lay off many employees. The court complied, whereupon Bell appealed, first to the Quebec Court of Appeals and, unsuccessful there, to the Supreme Court of Canada. While both higher courts sustained the lower court's order, the legal manoeuvering consumed three years of precious time and unquantified amounts of human resources.[31]

Challenge Communications Ltd.
Terminal attachments, as with other matters pertaining to Bell Canada and BC Tel, fell into the lap of the CRTC in 1976. The following year the new commission received a complaint from Challenge Communications Ltd., a company that leased mobile telephone apparatus in competition with Bell, charging that the telephone company had introduced a discriminatory tariff favouring itself in order to take Challenge out of the field.

Prior to April 1977 all mobile telephone calls required the assistance of an operator, and customers had the option of securing mobile service from either Bell or Challenge. In that month, however, Bell applied to the CRTC to approve tariffs for a new offering, 'Automatic Mobile Telephone Service' (AMTS), initially restricted to the Toronto/Hamilton and Montreal/Hawkesbury local calling areas. With AMTS, operator assistance was no longer required, and Bell announced that customers leasing automatic mobile telephones from companies other than Bell would not be connected to Bell's switched telephone network. Bell justified this new restriction, taken unilaterally, in these terms: 'We feel that it is necessary for the provision of guaranteed-quality service, and the protection of our network, that we install and maintain the complete system, including the mobile units. This approach is consistent with our policy towards all other network-addressing devices.'[32]

A second, less sublime but perhaps more authentic reason came to light during the course of public hearings when Bell's normally unflappable counsel, Ernie Saunders, unwisely blurted out: 'Having gone to the trouble to take the steps necessary to make this service available to the public, Bell Canada quite understandably desires to reap the benefits of this new offering.'[33]

The Commission, while perhaps marvelling at the candour, found Bell's desire to 'reap the benefits' insufficient ground on which to base exclusionary tariffs and declared that Bell's tariff was illegal, a ruling that has been termed 'a competitor's "Bill of Rights." '[34] This decision broadened the reach of section 321 of the Railway Act, which prohibits undue preference and unjust discrimination, so that it now encompasses actions whereby the telephone company gives *itself* unfair advantage. Previously the section had been used only to ban unjust favouritism by the company to selected clients. The CRTC's novel interpretation was later ratified, on appeal, by the Federal Court of Appeal.[35]

Liberalization
Rebuffed by the courts and regulator alike, Bell Canada took a different tack, filing an application in November 1979 requesting the CRTC to make a general ruling on the extent to which attachment of customer-owned, network-addressing equipment was in the public interest. Hearings were held between 17 November 1981 and 11 December 1981. In the proceeding, neither Bell nor BC Tel invoked the now outworn shibboleth of 'systemic integrity.' The doctrine, while serving the companies' interests for almost a century, had finally run its course; it was simply no longer believed. Only the Canadian Federation of Communications Workers, whose real concern one suspects was job displacement, trotted it out for one last but unsuccessful fling.[36] In fact both Bell and BC Tel agreed that henceforth provisioning of *all* terminals, network-addressing or not, be on a competitive basis,[37] so drastically had public perceptions changed in the brief span since Dr. Shulman's unsuccessful skirmish and Bell's heavy-handed treatment of Harding. Since that time Cantel, a cellular telephone company, has been licensed nationally to provide mobile telephone service in competition with members of Telecom Canada, while most restrictions on attachment of customer-owned devices have been eased by federally regulated companies.

None the less, provisioning of terminals continues to be controversial. In the initial Phase III Cost Inquiry results (discussed below), BC Tel itself calculated a deficit of $8.7 million in its competitive terminal multiline and data category;[38] moreover, the independent interconnect industry has recently filed an application to the CRTC for a proceeding to determine whether terminals are being cross-subsidized from monopoly revenues.[39]

CONCLUSIONS

Three historic pillars supporting the doctrine of 'natural monopoly' in Canadian telecommunications have grown frail. One of them, systemic integrity through end-to-end control, indeed appears to have crumbled completely in light of several years' experience with terminal attachments. The remaining two – economies of scale and service universality through cost-averaging and cross-subsidization – continue to be invoked but are operating at cross-purposes. On the one hand Bell now asserts that high long-distance prices must be slashed to avert 'uneconomic entry,' at least in the south; on the other, to compensate for the ensuing revenue loss, it presses for permission to double local rates. Slashing long-distance prices may well avert entry ('uneconomic' or otherwise) and thereby maintain the potential to realize purported economies of scale, but the concomitant escalation in local rates could prove deleterious to maintaining service universality. In fact Bell has itself estimated that 'full rate rebalancing' (whereby local service will cover 100 per cent of access costs) will result in 160,000 residential subscribers and 20,000 business subscribers ceasing to subscribe to telephone service.[40] These figures correspond to 'approximately 400,000 individuals losing direct access ... and the low income subscribers [will] be disproportionately represented among such individuals.'[41]

While policy-makers are currently trying to tread a fine line, allowing a degree of rate rebalancing to ward off 'uneconomic entry' and at the same time holding back 'full' rebalancing to prevent subscriber drop-off, the inconsistency of these dual underpinnings of 'natural monopoly' weakens them both.

13

Unnatural Monopoly: Predatory Pricing and the Cost Inquiry

A DOUBLE-EDGED SWORD

The contradiction discussed in the previous chapter – between the doctrine of economies of scale, and service universality through cost-averaging and cross-subsidization – is matched by yet a further contradiction, this time inhering in the latter proposition alone. On the one hand cost-averaging and cross-subsidization can indeed be practised in a manner conducive to service universality. On the other, cost-averaging and cross-subsidization can also be practised in a manner that erodes universality of telephone service, owing to the temptation telephone companies may experience to cross-subsidize competitive markets from revenues generated in monopoly markets, making competition less viable in the former while eroding universality in the latter. The present chapter explores evidence on this issue.

INKLINGS OF ABUSE

As we have seen, prior to the onset of regulation telephone companies routinely engaged in predatory pricing when beset by direct competition. Free service in those years was not an exceptional marketing strategy.

Even following inauguration of rate regulation, however, telephone companies retained considerable discretion in setting individual prices (the rate structure), regulators being largely content to supervise overall rate levels (revenue requirements). With the demise of direct competition (and the distain with which regulators held the same, in any event), the rate structure (i.e., the system of relative prices) was deemed unworthy of much regulatory attention.[1] In part this self-imposed regulatory limitation was justified; after all, undue profit-taking was not necessarily more likely in any one submarket than in any other when all were monopolized in any event.[2] All this changed, however, with the recent onset of competition in selected submarkets (terminals, private lines, mobile telephones, data), undermining the efficacy of maintaining these venerable regulatory blinders.

Perhaps the first rigorous investigation into the possibility of anti-competitive cross-subsidy and predatory pricing was the FCC's seven-way cost study of 1965, falling hard on price reductions by AT&T in 1961 of up to 85 per cent for bulk microwave circuits ('Telpak') then newly opened to competitive entry.[3] Under FCC order, AT&T estimated on a fully allocated cost basis percentage earnings by service category. The study's results were as follows:[4]

Monopoly services
Wide area telephone service (WATS)   10.1%
Long-distance message toll (MTS)   10.1%

Competitive services
Private-line telephone   4.7%
Teletype exchange (TWX)   2.9%
Private line telegraph   1.4%
Telpack   0.3%
Other   1.2%

Overall return   7.5%

At the time AT&T's permissible rate of return was 7.5 per cent, an approximation of its cost of capital (i.e., the cost of servicing debt and equity capital). Services earning substantially less than 7.5 per cent were therefore losing money (in the economic sense of opportunity cost) because AT&T needed to generate elsewhere (i.e., in monopolized markets) returns sufficient to pay bondholders and stockholders the going return for their investments. In brief, the monopolized services were cross-subsidizing competitive services, at least according to the system of cost allocations used in the study. These empirical results led directly to Docket 16258, inaugurated in October 1965, and the FCC's first overall investigation of AT&T since 1935, culminating ultimately in the breakup of AT&T through antitrust.

Policy-makers in Canada were not oblivious to regulatory initiatives in the United States. Once again it was Dr H.S. Gellman, president of DCF Systems Limited, who drove home the point in this country through case-study documentation. Testifying before the House of Commons Committee on Transport and Communications in 1967, Dr Gellman stated that his company, a consulting firm unaffiliated with any telecommunications carrier or equipment manufacturer, had no vested interest in appearing, except 'to make it easier for our clients and others to implement some of these advanced [communications] systems.'[6]

Dr Gellman's first case-study concerned a large petroleum company in Edmonton that required switched, high-speed data links to Ontario. CNCP's newly installed broadband exchange network matched perfectly the company's requirements; CNCP's published tariff was $200 per month plus $0.60 per minute of use. At the time TCTS had in place no comparable facilities; consequently, neither Bell nor AGT had filed tariffs with their regulatory boards for a switched, broadband service. None the less, on 29 November 1966, to the petroleum company's surprise, it received an unsolicited proposal from Alberta Government Telephone as sales agent for the TransCanada Telephone System to offer 'Data-line,' a private-line service said to be identical to CNCP's, at the same price as the rival's bid. Inasmuch as neither Bell Canada nor AGT at the time had any switched broadband facilities in place, Gellman surmised that the telephone companies were planning to use existing private lines, which normally would have been priced at $5500 per month, to provide the fictitious 'Data-line' for $200 per month plus $0.60 per minute of use. Bell and AGT, in other words, made the proposal as a stopgap measure, awaiting completion of their own switched broadband network, not scheduled for introduction until late 1968.

Dr Gellman's second case-study concerned a large Ontario paper manufacturer that needed switched broadband facilities to link the Maritimes and Winnipeg. Identical quotations were again received from CNCP and Bell. In this instance Bell was the successful bidder and the telephone company soon had a service installed. However, several months passed before the customer received its first bill. It turned out that Bell had in place neither the meters needed to measure usage, nor any of the high-speed switched data lines it was purportedly providing. Dr Gellman concluded: 'Bell Canada is using existing telephone leased circuits and charging privileged customer only for switched circuit utilization. In effect, clients across Canada who lease private telephone circuits from Bell Canada are subsidizing other clients who present Bell with a competitive threat.'[7]

Several other case-studies were presented as well, each involving pricing abuses relating to private lines. The government's response was uncharacteristically swift, bringing hitherto unregulated private lines of federally regulated telephone and telegraph companies under scrutiny of the Canadian Transport Commission,[8] accomplished by proclamation effective 1 August 1970. Following this step, and resulting therefrom, the CTC intitiated the cost inquiry, discussed below.

Subsequent to Dr Gellman's appearance before the Commons committee, other indicators of predatory pricing in the telephone industry have surfaced. In 1978, for example, CNCP Telecommunications filed evidence with the CRTC showing that price increases by Bell Canada in monopolized service categories far outstripped price increases in competitive (private-line) services.[9] The CRTC, too, in various rate increase decisions, has noted sceptically Bell's reluctance to apply for price increases in competitive services, although the commission also stated that in the absence of service-costing data and awaiting development of a service-costing methodology, it could reach no definitive conclusion on predatory pricing at that time.[10] Then again in 1986 CNCP filed with the federal regulator data comparing Bell's prices for Datapac with rates charged in the highly competitive U.S. packet-switching market, finding it 'remarkable' that rates of the American companies (Tymet and Telenet) were 98 to 363 per cent *higher* than Bell's rates. 'The inference to be drawn,' CNCP concluded, 'is that Bell's rates are non-compensatory.'[11]

CTC COST INQUIRY

'An Inquiry into Telecommunications Carriers' Costing and Accounting Procedures' was launched by the CTC in September 1972[12] to accomplish two tasks. First, it was to establish a general system of financial accounting for carriers under the commission's jurisdiction; second, it was to cast light on the extent to which telecommunications carriers were engaging in predatory (non-compensatory) pricing.[13] To monitor the work and vie for consensus, the CTC established a technical group made up of carriers and other interested parties to work with the commission's own consultants (Snavely, King, and Tucker, Inc.).

Little did the CTC at the time comprehend either the conflicts of interest inhering within the technical group or the difficulty of achieving consensus.

During 1973 and 1974 the consultants reported in nine volumes to the CTC. But from the outset, and understandably so, Bell Canada balked at any efforts at service costing,[14] with the result that little was achieved in this important area. As Snavely, King, and Tucker reported: 'There was no effort to examine the extent of discrimination, prejudice, preference, or advantage inherent in any of the carriers' existing rate schedules. Rather the Technical Group evaluated the principles and procedures which might govern the measurement of such discrimination.'[15]

However, even this latter and more limited task remained unresolved. While the consultants did manage to make their own recommendations on methods for developing a system of service costing, they noted that among the technical group itself there remained total disagreement.[16]

CRTC COST INQUIRY

Jurisdiction exercised by the CTC over federally regulated telecommunications carriers was, of course, transferred to the CRTC on 1 April 1976, and soon thereafter responsibility for the cost inquiry was transferred to it as well. New proceedings were initiated into such matters as depreciation, deferred income taxes, rate base, and the costing of new services. Then, on 15 December 1981, the CRTC issued a public notice,[17] inaugurating so-called Phase III, the costing of existing services. In its notice the commission stated emphatically: 'This focus on service costing is largely a consequence of concerns that carriers which operate in both monopoly and competitive markets may price their competitive services below cost, to the detriment of both their monopoly subscribers and their competitors.'[18]

To help resolve the Phase III issues the commission appointed Ken Wyman, then the commission's senior executive director of operations, as inquiry officer. Mr Wyman presided over a lengthy public hearing and submitted his report on 30 April 1984.

By the time of the Phase III inquiry, Bell Canada had altered fundamentally its stance towards service costing. In part owing to pro-competitive decisions taken by the CRTC in the late 1970s and early 1980s (the 1979 CNCP decision, the Challenge decision, the terminal attachment decision, and others), Bell now foresaw a great potential advantage to lie in service costing, provided the procedures were within its control; consequently, during the interim, Bell had pushed ahead developing its own 'five-way split' methodology, purporting to show tremendous cross-subsidies flowing from long distance (where pressures for competitive entry were increasing) to local service (still largely unchallenged in terms of monopoly). Such purported disparities in the profitability of the two services, the company began claiming, supported a need to 'rebalance' rates: local rates to be more than doubled, long-distance rates slashed. Therefore, rather than opposing service costing in principle, as had been the strategy of the early 1970s, for Phase III Bell reversed field, wisely endeavouring to ensure that costing was undertaken in a manner advantageous to it.

In its evidence for Phase III Bell Canada, supported by other TCTS members, presented several costing principles that, if adopted, would go a long way towards inhibiting entry, even while eroding service universality. Two of these principles are discussed here: computer-simulated models, and inclusion of local loops in local service costs.

Computer Simulations
Bell proposed that the commission adopt a costing methodology known as the 'five-way split.' That methodology, based on 'current costs,' entailed net present-value studies and incorporated notions of the opportunity cost of capital. 'Costs,' in other words, were not related to funds actually expended by the company but were based on projections of future streams of revenues and costs discounted back to the present, encompassing also theoretical apportionments.

The inquiry officer deemed the method, relying on computer simulations, unauditable.[19] Therefore, he recommended that the commission adopt the so-called revenue settlement plan (RSP) then used by members of the TransCanada Telephone System to share interprovincial toll revenues. Although Bell objected strenuously to its use for service costing, chief advantages of the RSP methodology were its auditability and the fact that it was then actually being used by the telephone companies.[20]

Access Costs Included in Local Service
Bell insisted that 'costs associated with network access should be assigned to local services alone.'[21] Network access, it is to be noted, includes all subscriber loops connecting telephone sets to local

TABLE 13.1
Investment and return by service category, Bell Canada and BC Telephone
Company, 1986 ($ millions)

Service category	Bell Canada		BC Tel	
	(1) Investment	(2) Surplus (shortfall)	(1) Investment	(2) Surplus (shortfall)
1. Access	4063.2	(2232.1)	900.1	(447.5)
2. Monopoly local	1585.1	528.4	508.5	47.8
3. Monopoly toll	1391.1	1811.1	264.7	446.7
4. Competitve network	795.3	43.8	148.2	1.6
5. Competitive terminal, Multiline, and data	721.6	30.7	138.6	(8.7)
6. Competitive terminals, other	149.1	59.2	37.6	15.7
7. Other	114.9	8.1	11.4	49.1
8. Common	68.4	(267.4)	33.6	(102.4)

SOURCE: Bell Canada, 'Cost Inquiry Phase III 1986 Study Report,' September 1987, 2, 3; British Columbia Telephone Company, 'Cost Inquiry Phase III 1986 Study Report,' September 1987, 2, 3

exchanges, drop and block wires and protective devices at the subscriber's premises, and the termination of the subscriber's loop into the main distribution frame at the central office.[22] Such access facilities account for up to 50 per cent of the telephone companies' plant and equipment.[23] They are shared in the provisioning of most telephone services and are quite insensitive to traffic volumes.[24]

The inquiry officer astutely rejected Bell's proposal to apportion all access costs to local service, recommending rather that a separate category for access costs be established.[25] His recommendations were largely accepted by the commission on 25 June 1985.[26]

In September 1987, pursuant to the commission's instructions, both Bell Canada and BC Tel filed with the commission investment and profit data for various broad service categories for 1986. The results are reproduced here as table 13.1. While the two carriers may take comfort that reported losses show up in only one competitive services category (BC Tel's Competitive Terminal, Multiline, and Data), the profitability of several other of these broad service categories is sufficiently minuscule to launch in the spring of 1988 yet a further proceeding on the issue.[27]

14

Rate Regulation

CONTEXT

Even in telephony's early years, apprehension existed that in selected markets prices were too low. From 1885 to at least 1905 Bell Canada, in the face of competition, routinely lowered rates for local service, sometimes to zero. In the modern era too, as we have just seen, concern has persisted that in selected markets telecommunications prices may be non-compensatory, designed to drive out rivals.

Such has not been the qualm preoccupying regulators' attention over the bulk of regulatory history, however. Rather, their major misgiving has been that telephone prices could be too *high*. Guarding against this possibility, which was a major reason for inaugurating regulation in the first place, continues to persist when attention is focused on monopolized markets.

The present chapter reviews regulatory procedures designed to inhibit monopolistic price-gouging, first in inter-provincial toll services and then in regard to intraterritory markets.

LEGISLATIVE AMBIGUITY

Railway Act revisions of 1906, subjecting tolls of telephone companies residing under federal jurisdiction to scrutiny and approval by the Board of Railway Commissioners, gave scant guidance on how the regulator was to construe its mandate. Legislative commands barring 'unjust discrimination' and 'undue preference' and requiring regulated utilities to afford 'reasonable and proper facilities' left ample room for widely divergent interpretations.[1]

Today the situation remains substantially unaltered. The key section of the current Railway Act specifies merely that 'All tolls shall be just and reasonable and shall always, under substantially similar circumstances and conditions ... be charged equally to all persons at the same rate.'[2]

It is apparent that Parliament left the regulator with the task of defining exactly what constitutes an *unjust* discrimination, an *undue* preference, *substantially* similar circumstances, and *just and reasonable* rates. It will be discovered that a major break occurred in 1976 when the CRTC, newly vested with telecommunications responsibilities, turned regulatory precedents on their heads through novel interpretations of 'just and reasonable.'

REGULATION OF INTERPROVINCIAL TOLL

Ambiguity aside, the Railway Act applied and applies only to companies residing under federal jurisdiction. Although recent court decisions[3] and some scholarly writings[4] indicate that *all* telecommunications carriers connecting interprovincially (that is, all major telephone companies) reside right there, historically such has been neither the interpretation nor the practice. Rather, federal jurisdiction has been applied only to companies incorporated federally while, conversely, provincial jurisdiction has held sway over companies incorporated provincially. But even this explanation is an over-simplification, for the federal regulator until recently has chosen not to regulate interprovincial telephone services when provided in part by a federally regulated undertaking. Likewise, provincial regulatory boards have eschewed supervision of interprovincial services provided in part by their carriers. There are two primary explanations for these important regulatory omissions: the 'local' nature of telephone operations, at least during the industry's infancy; and the 'informal' status of the TransCanada Telephone System, inaugurated in 1931.

A Local Service?
Initially, telephone communication was a local service only, completely lacking long-distance connections. From the perspective of the constitution, therefore, telephony bore characteristics of a local undertaking, placing it squarely within provincial authority.

But there was one complication: Bell Telephone had been created by act of Parliament, and indeed the federal government had endowed its creation with powers to construct telephone lines throughout Canada alongside all public rights-of-way, whether provincially controlled or not.

This benefaction did not go uncontested. Within a year of Bell's incorporation the municipal council of Quebec City took both the federal government and the Bell charter to court, claiming telephones to be local in nature and, hence, falling within provincial jurisdiction. In 1881 a Quebec court agreed, ruling that the federal government was without authority to empower Bell to enter public streets. Following hard on this ruling several provinces enacted legislation purporting to govern telephone installations within their boundaries.[5]

To reassert federal jurisdiction over Bell (then controlling all telephones in Canada), Parliament in 1882 declared the company's works to be 'for the general advantage of Canada'[6] pursuant to section 92(10)(c) of the British North America Act, squelching further provincial challenges until 1905. The federal government did not, however, attempt to claim authority over the trickle of independents springing up after 1885. To do so it would have had to declare their works also as being 'for the general advantage of Canada.'

In 1905, in *Toronto Corporation v. Bell Telephone Company of Canada*[7] ('the pre-eminent case relating to jurisdiction over telephone facilities and services,' according to a recent commentary[8]), the Judicial Committee of the Privy Council in London, England, held that Bell's local and long-distance operations were not divisible for purposes of regulation; consequently, inasmuch as the company's works had previously been declared 'for the general advantage of Canada,' Bell's *entire* operations, not merely long distance, fell to the feds. This ruling has never been reversed, and so federal jurisdiction over the corporate entity, Bell Canada, and all its operations has persisted to this date.

In 1906 the jurisdictional battle was joined once more when noted parliamentarian A.B. Aylesworth, then serving as postmaster general, invoked the forementioned charter amendment as ground to veto provincial plans to expropriate Bell's plant in Manitoba.[9] The federal government, however, chose not to intervene in ensuring negotiations between Bell and the prairie governments pertaining to provincial acquisitions, nor did it attempt to regulate provincially owned operations once the take-overs had been consummated.

In jurisdictions where provincial ownership was not introduced, legislation imposing provincial regulatory control over local companies was enacted to pre-empt further federal incursions. For example, upon incorporation in 1910, Maritime Telegraph and Telephone Company (MT&T) became subject to the supervisory powers of the Nova Scotia Board of Commissioners of Public Utilities. Likewise, independents in Quebec and Ontario were made answerable to provincial boards in 1909 and 1910, respectively.[10]

The result of these court decisions and legislative enactments has therefore been a system of bifurcated jurisdiction, with the federal government regulating federally incorporated undertakings in their intraterritory operations, provincial governments regulating provincially incorporated undertakings in their intraterritory operations, and both levels eschewing regulation of services provided jointly by carriers residing in different jurisdictions.

TCTS Telecom Canada

The foregoing regulatory gap was neither lamented nor contested by Canada's major carriers (although small independents frequently felt frustrated at bifurcated control over interconnections), and in 1931 the largest telephone companies took steps to cement this anomalous and perplexing situation, forming the TransCanada Telephone System for that purpose.

Study on the feasibility of an all-Canadian telephone network spanning the country had been undertaken as early as 1921,[11] and formulas for setting rates and splitting revenues had been agreed to at that time.[12] Ownership of facilities remained contentious, however, as the companies all wished to avert regulation of interprovincial communication. The dilemma was resolved in 1931 when seven signatories created an unincorporated association – the TransCanada Telephone System. Completely lacking assets and legal status and relying on CN and CP telegraphs for about 25 per cent of the transcontinental hook-up[13] and on member companies for the remainder and for facilities and all personnel, this will-o-'the-wisp, TCTS, commenced operations the following year.

Known today as Telecom Canada, TCTS has been a phantom from its inception. Although non-existent in law, it none the less has fulfilled an array of duties, including the following, as summarized by federal court judge Madame Reed: '[TCTS] engages in planning for the construction and operation of the overall [interprovincial] network which is comprised of each member's facilities; sets technical standards; establishes terms and conditions under which telecommunications services will be provided by the members; performs a joint marketing function; determines rates; acts as the pivotal entity for negotiating and implementing agreements for the provision of international services; [and] operates a system of revenue sharing through the TCTS Clearing House.'[15]

Despite such important and pervasive duties, TCTS's non-existence in law meant that neither federal nor provincial governments were able or at least willing to penetrate the affairs of this busy apparition. But as Madame Justice Reed has hinted, such regulatory refusal raises doubts concerning the effectiveness with which any and all other activities of major telephone companies have been regulated. She advised: 'It is because of the existence of this agreement [the TCTS Connecting Agreement] that I questioned, at the beginning of these reasons, the effectiveness of the Public Utilities Board of Alberta as a regulator of AGT. One can speculate that the Board's approval of AGT's activities is likely to be no more than pro forma in many instances ... '[16]

Regulatory Renewal

Only in 1978 was notice given that matters might change. In an oral rendering, the CRTC announced it was about to launch an inquiry into those aspects of TCTS affairs that impinged on the operations of Bell and BC Tel.[17] Soon thereafter the commission retained consultants to 'carry out an extensive study of TCTS settlement procedures and other matters.'[18] The commission also invited provincial regulatory participation to monitor the consultants' progress. Later in 1978, in a precendential ruling, the CRTC delayed rubber-stamping applications from Bell and BC Tel for increases in interprovincial rates, despite recognizing that, as was customary, 'the carriers were anxious to have the rate changes made effective for all TCTS members on the same date.'[19] Only after allowing time for written interventions, a first in the history of Canadian telecommunications, did the CRTC approve the two applications, and then only on an interim basis, subject to review at an ensuing formal inquiry.

The main hearings, delayed by much legal wrangling, began on 15 April 1980. The first major issue was raised by CNCP, which claimed that all members of TCTS were telegraph or telephone companies within the meaning of the British North America Act, inasmuch as each member's lines connected with lines in other provinces. Therefore, CNCP advised, all members of TCTS, with the exception of Bell and BC Tel, were 'in breach of [their] statutory duty ... to file ... tariffs for interprovincial services for the approval of the CRTC.'[20]

In rebuttal Bell's counsel, E.E. Saunders, scoffed: 'CNCP makes no legal argument to support this assertion and Bell Canada would simply note that there is much disagreement on this issue and it has never been decided by the court.'[21]

It is useful to pause and consider the extent to which Bell through the years benefited from its tactical and enforced withdrawals from Atlantic Canada and the prairies. Certainly in this 1980 proceeding it vigorously opposed extending federal regulatory scrutiny to interprovincial operations of its provincially regulated brethren. Likewise, BC Tel tried to block the CRTC from looking at the field.

To these protestations the CRTC responded: 'The Commission does not necessarily agree with the legal arguments raised by BC Tel. Indeed, it considers that a thorough review of the constitutional issue is overdue. Nevertheless, it accepts BC Tel's final point that no finding on the issue is necessary in order for the Commission to come to appropriate determinations on the matters before it in this proceeding.'[22]

The 'thorough review' in fact followed soon, instigated by CNCP and pointing to full and exclusive federal jurisdiction over all telephone companies connected interprovincially. Meanwhile, awaiting the Supreme Court affirmation, federal and provincial officials were busy negotiating an agreement to reapportion regulatory responsibilities. In November 1987 the communications minister, Flora MacDonald, announced that an 'historic agreement' with the provinces had been achieved, whereby 'for the first time, we will have a consistent set of rules from coast to coast on such matters as interconnection and the roles and responsibilities of the two levels of government.'[23] The proposals issuing from this agreement provide for two classes of carriers: Type I which own and operate facilities, and Type II, which merely lease facilities to provide services. For Type I carriers – telephone companies, CNCP, Telesat, Teleglobe, and Cantel – competition is to be restrained because their transmission facilities are deemed to afford 'great economies of scale and scope.'[24] For Type II carriers, providing 'value-added' or 'enhanced' services, competition will be encouraged. Federal jurisdiction will pertain to all interprovincial communication, whether utilizing radio frequencies or not. Possibly provincial governments will be afforded responsibility for intraprovince communications, even in Ontario, Quebec, and British Columbia.

What the telephone carriers may be losing in terms of hitherto ample discretion in interprovincial rate-setting they will be gaining through heightened if not impregnable barriers to entry into telecommunications transmission, as maintained by the ever-vigilant and protective eye of the federal DOC.

A Paper Tiger
Although interprovincial rates have been subject to regulatory scrutiny only recently, and then only in part, Bell's intraterritory rates have, at least in principle, been subject to regulatory oversight since 1906. The first of the federal telephone regulators, the Board of Railway Commissioners for Canada, put off making findings on the justness and reasonableness of Bell's rate level and rate structure for thirteen years, however, until confronted in 1919 by the company's application for general price increases.[25] (A seemingly innocuous clause in the 1906 legislation permitted rates existing prior to the onset of regulation to be retained for such further period 'as the Board allows.')

Upon donning fully its regulatory mantle, the board acted quickly and decisively, ruling that rates, once established and whenever and however, were by definition just and reasonable and hence in need of no further scrutiny. Thereby the regulator was able to bypass investigation into Bell's relative price structure and concentrate on the new rate level proposed.[26]

But if federal regulation at its inception was nominal, so also was it at its conclusion, at least as far as successive transportation tribunals were concerned. As late as 1975 the Canadian Transport Commission still apportioned but three person-years to telecommunications from its staff of five hundred, despite being called upon annually to pass judgment on more than four thousand telecommunications tariffs.[27] Understandably such modest resources were deemed insufficient by some. One outspoken vituperator, G.D. Zimmerman, president of Industrial Wire and Cable Company, volunteered the following to a Commons committee in 1967: 'We have dealt with this Board since 1961 or 1962 and I have failed, and our people have failed, to identify a single engineer, a utility expert, an electronic technician ... in short, any expertise to weigh the evidence that is presented to them ... Hear, listen and rubber stamp ... this is essentially what we have had so-called "in the public interest" to date.'[28]

Nor did the CTC escape criticism by the press. Noting that Bell routinely spent several times more on its rate increase applications than could be mustered by all interveners combined, columnist Alexander Ross termed the CTC's proceedings 'an elegant minuet,' a 'dance of the aged elephants,' and then, more prosaically, 'a distorted model of the adversary relationship that is supposed to prevail in court rooms.' Bell's deep pockets, Ross observed, permitted it to buy the top-priced lawyers, the most expensive consultants, and the experienced and skilled witnesses, leaving dross for interveners. Despite such lopsidedness the CTC, lacking resources of its own, assumed a posture of 'neutrality' – hearing arguments on both sides and in the end handing down quasi-judicial decisions 'which grant part, but not all of Bell's proposed rate increases.'[29]

Given the CTC's self-imposed posture of neutrality and its concomitant reliance upon interveners for critical appraisal of Bell's case, one might have expected the commission to welcome interventions and be supportive of experts testifying on behalf of those opposed to rate increases, but such was not the case. Note particularly the following opinion, penned in 1975 by commissioner John T. Gray while refusing to award costs to interveners:

When a public interest group appears before the CTC it usually retains the assistance of experts to assist it in the presentation of its views. The experts are usually either academics or consultants. The academics sometimes have no personal knowledge of or experience in the industry being regulated and tend to attempt to apply academic, economic or accounting principles to the affairs of the industry without making the reasonable adaptations or changes in the academic principles which the circumstances of the industry make necessary. The consultant, usually handicapped by the same lack of knowledge and experience, often earns the same criticism, and in addition probably feels obliged, to earn his pay, to make out some kind of case against the industry. For these reasons the views of such experts tend not to be helpful.'[30]

Gray then went on to complain how expert opinion, 'in addition to not being very helpful ... can do serious damage to a regulated industry and the regulatory system,' contending further that many experts had ulterior motives in testifying in regulatory proceedings, namely 'to gain as widespread publicity as possible for their opinions [and] ... to discredit not only the regulated industry but also the regulatory tribunal.'[31] He concluded his remarks with the following provocative conjecture:

It may be worthwhile to assume for the purpose of argument that the CTC is in fact under the control of the industries it regulates – what evils to the public may be expected to result? The answer is that the public can be expected to pay a modest percentage more for the service involved than would otherwise be the case, and the regulated industry would receive somewhat more in the way of profit than it deserved ... There would, however, be certain public benefits involved in that situation. The regulated industry would constitute an attractive investment and would be in a position to ensure that its capital plant would at all times be in a position to accommodate future increased demands so that the public would always be guaranteed of adequate service.[32]

There is yet a further indicator of the esteem with which the CTC held public participation. In 1974 it issued an order to index automatically telephone rates to 'uncontrollable costs.' The purpose of this order, the commission acknowledged, was to reduce or eliminate 'frequent, lengthy and expensive public hearings.'[33] Although the order was never implemented (the commission lost jurisdiction before all submissions had been evaluated),[34] it too highlights the manner in which the CTC was approaching its telecommunications responsibilities at the tail end of its jurisdiction.

Regulatory Limitations

Repeatedly and consistently through the years, the Canadian Transport Commission and its predecessors declined invitations from interveners to investigate questions of the utility's efficiency, emphasizing that its job was one of 'regulation,' not 'management,' and that, in the absence of conclusive proof to the contrary, there was to be a general presumption that the company was efficient and its decisions in the public interest.[35]

The transport boards' hesitancy to second-guess management led to occasional anomalies in reporting decisions. Several times the regulator expressed misgivings over managerial action but refused to impose its own judgment. In 1927, for example, perceiving waste and extravagance in Bell's capital expansion program, commissioner Frank Oliver remarked: 'It is difficult to appreciate the useful purpose of such large additions to or changes in the present plant and equipment ... That, however, is not a concern of the Board.'[36] A more recent example concerned Bell's two-phased application in 1975 for increased prices. Receiving only 50 per cent of its request in the first phase, the company selectively rolled back construction, awaiting a final determination.

As noted by the CTC, cut-backs took place 'at a point of great visibility and of patent disadvantage to the public, namely the point of installation of new telephones at the homes or places of business of would-be subscribers who have no telephone service.' The CTC continued that Bell 'has publicly placed firmly at the door of the Commission [the ensuing] distress of individuals and the dislocation of business.' It then termed Bell's recalcitrance 'something of a sideshow' making 'no positive contributions to the solution of the problems of the Company, the shareholders or the subscribers.' The commission went so far as to 'deplore' management's obduracy, disclosing that it 'was not impressed.' All the same, in its final decision it awarded Bell 100 per cent of requested 'rate relief.'[37]

Another concern receiving cursory attention from the CTC and its predecessors was service extension and quality. According to the board it possessed little if any jurisdiction.[38] In 1974 the CTC reversed field somewhat, entertaining evidence on Bell's lacklustre performance in non-urban areas and 'directing' the utility to expedite a survey, already being prepared by the company in any event, on how rural service could be improved. Demonstrating unusual audacity, the CTC went even further, expressing its 'belief' that expenditures on non-urban services could be increased by $30 million by reallocating funds from other non-compensatory offerings. The commission then added with uncharacteristic firmness that if such were not done, it 'will require an explanation.'[39] As it turned out, Bell's expenditures actually fell short of the CTC's suggestion by $60 million. Although the commissioners remained 'not convinced that these cutbacks were absolutely necessary,' they accepted the company's 'adjustments.'[40] Bell's private-line construction program, a competitive offering, proceeded on target, of course.[41]

Later in this chapter the regulatory methodology of constraining profits is addressed, and chapter 15 touches upon another hoary controversy, vertical integration. Discussions such as these could easily be extended to encompass other and more technical disputes as well, including depreciation rates and policies, magnitude and composition of the capital expansion program, and the capital structure.[42] However, the essential conclusion would remain unaltered: for seventy years the Bell Telephone Company of Canada was subjected to a loose form of regulation by a regulator which, it would appear, would rather have been doing something else. There were few mourners, therefore, when the CRTC took over in 1976.

CRTC Policies

The CRTC broadened significantly the factors deemed relevant to setting just and reasonable rates. Upon assuming jurisdiction, it was at pains to distance itself from its predecessor, stating: 'The principle of "just and reasonable" rates is neither a narrow nor a static concept. As our society has evolved, the idea of what is just and reasonable has also changed, and now takes into account many considerations that would have been thought irrelevant 70 years ago, when regulatory review was first instituted. Indeed, the Commission views this principle in the widest possible terms.'[43]

Subsequently the CRTC went on to reject the notion that there was a clear demarcation between the boundaries of regulation and management: 'In practice, virtually every decision of the Commission involves a review of certain managerial decisions ... While the Commission has no desire to "manage" the companies subject to its regulatory jurisdiction, it does not consider itself restricted by any purely conceptual dividing line in investigating and determining matters properly coming before it.'[44]

Again in contrast to its predecessor, the CRTC announced it would encourage widespread participation in its proceedings, adding, 'in very few of the cases can all the issues be decided solely on the basis of the interests of the parties before the Commission.'[45] This declaration found substance in a number of policies, including the awarding of costs to interveners,[46] greater financial disclosure,[47] and wider distribution of information on the public record.[48]

An area receiving significantly more attention from the CRTC than from the CTC has been service quality and availability. In 1977 the CRTC propounded the eminently defensible proposition that prices can be judged reasonable only if service quality and availability are adequate.[49] Therefore, it ordered companies subject to its jurisdiction to begin reporting annually on these matters, warning that in future proceedings service quality and availability would become central issues and that quality of service should be comparable in equivalent areas throughout Bell's territory,[50] a requirement flowing from the Railway Act's prohibition of unjust discrimination.

The CRTC has also demonstrated greater interest in the capital expansion programs of its telephone carriers. Noting in a 1978 decision the difficulty of assessing the propriety of Bell's construction program given the limited information provided, the CRTC ordered Bell to remedy its reporting deficiencies. It then also established a committee to review annually Bell Canada's five-year program.[51]

Telephone operations are complex, and no one is as atuned to the financial ramifications of the company's decisions as are its own managers. Therefore, broadening participation in regulatory proceedings and widening regulatory concerns are not guarantees that in the end regulation makes much difference. None the less, Bell Canada's reorganization, discussed in chapter 15, provides convincing evidence that regulation by the CRTC was indeed beginning to have an effect.

Earnings per Share

There remains, however, a basic flaw in the means whereby Bell (as well as BCTel) is regulated. In 1966, at Bell's behest, the Board of Transport Commissioners adopted a 'rate of return on rate base' formula for setting revenue levels, a method that had frequently been criticized in the United States for encouraging undue capital expansion and other wasteful and anticompetitive behaviour. Before enlarging on the policy problems and presenting some empirical evidence, however, the discussion turns first to the regulatory methodology existing prior to 1966, and the means whereby it had been circumvented.

Beginning in 1891, and occurring every year thereafter until the late 1950s (with the exception of the Depression years, 1932–7), Bell Telephone paid a two dollar per share dividend. In fact, soon after the railway commissioners began actively regulating the company's revenue requirements in 1919, the board judged historical precedent alone to have made such a dividend 'just and reasonable.' Therefore, the board ruled, the company should receive earnings sufficient to pay two dollars in dividends and to earn also a reasonable 'surplus' ('retained earnings') per share. Until 1966, therefore, controversies concerning returns to investors centred on the size of the 'surplus' per share.

Under the board's auspices the authorized surplus grew incrementally until 1950, at which point the board set it at forty-three cents per share (giving total permissible earnings per share of $2.43). In subsequent decisions the board affirmed and reaffirmed the justness of a surplus of forty-three cents per share, in 1958 even going so far as to announce that this surplus would be continued so long as Bell could raise as much equity capital as it wanted.[53]

It should be noted here that a constant dividend and constant surplus per share are recommended as regulatory means to restrain monopolistic profit-taking, *provided* certain safeguards are taken. Public utilities expert and consultant James Bonbright, in his classic text, has noted how the procedure eliminates the murky task of estimating the cost of equity capital (the return required by investors before buying new stock issues). According to Professor Bonbright, with constant earnings per share 'each new issue of stock could then be sold *at the highest price it would command in the current market*, and the resulting total annual "dividend requirements" could then be accepted as reflecting the Company's cost of equity capital.'[54]

Not that the methodology was unabused, for Bell (contrary to Bonbright's warning) astutely began selling shares at very low prices compared with market value. Issuing new shares to existing stockholders at deep discounts enabled the utility to pass monopoly profits back to shareholders (through capital gains) while simultaneously 'justifying' higher prices to the regulator (because stock dilutions made earning the authorized surplus per share impossible under existing rates). With laudable simplicity and clarity A.J. de Grandpré, in 1966 vice-president of law for Bell Telephone, explained to a startled Commons committee the means whereby his company had over the years circumvented earnings per share regulation:

Under the old basis of regulation, Mr. Lewis, the [board's] judgement of 1958 indicated that $2.43 per share was the maximum level of earnings per share that was authorized by the Board. Assuming that you [i.e., we] wanted $100 of new capital, you [i.e., we] could issue – to take simple figures – four shares at $25 or [we] could issue one share at $100. If [we] issued one share at $100 [we] would be entitled to only $2.43 on [our] investment because there was only one share. If [we] issued four shares, then [we] would be entitled to four times $2.43.[55]

Mr de Grandpré's 'confession,' it is to be noted, came two years *after* earnings per share regulation had been scrapped, and it was proffered in the context of trying to talk Parliament into stopping the board from overseeing future stock issues.

Certainly through the years Bell wasted few opportunities to water its stock, so bypassing in varying degrees profit control by the regulator. In 1927 it sold shareholders for twenty-five dollars new stock having a market value of $158.50.[56] So outrageous were the company's stock dilutions during the 1920s that even the board was shocked, urging Parliament to amend the charter to enable it thereafter to oversee terms and conditions of all future stock issues and dispositions. But although Parliament made this change in 1929, stock dilutions, albeit moderated in magnitude, persisted into the 1960s, regulatory oversight notwithstanding.[57]

In 1958, however, Bell became distraught when the board declared that permissible earnings per share were to be frozen (at $2.43 per share) until such time as the company could no longer raise all the equity capital it wanted.[58] Until then Bell had retained hopes of coaxing the regulator into ever-increasing earnings per share, in addition to taking advantage of regulatory laxity in the matter of stock dilutions. An important avenue of regulatory bypass seemingly cut-off, Bell started promoting a 'new and improved' method of rate control, namely rate of return on a rate base, inaugurated in 1966.

Rate of Return
Under rate of return a company is allowed to earn revenues sufficient to cover (prudently incurred) expenses plus a percentage return on investment (the rate base). Mathematically, the formula is

$$R = E + r.B$$

where R is 'revenue requirements'; E is operating expenses, including depreciation; r is the permissible percentage rate of return; and B is the rate base or total investment.

In the case of Bell Canada the rate base, B, has consisted of financial capital (debt, equity, and retained earnings), although it could as easily have been a net assets rate base.[59]

Although the new method of regulation was deemed to have certain (but in fact dubious) advantages, it most certainly entailed at least one major disadvantage. The inherent flaw was alluded to obliquely be Mr. de Grandpré in 1968: 'Under the new type of regulation that was instituted by the Board following the 1966 judgement, the number of shares became absolutely irrelevant. It was the total number of dollars invested in the business that became the yardstick, if you wish, to determine the level of earnings ... The pressure [is] on the company to obtain more than the maximum issue price for the stock because the number of shares [has] really nothing to do with the earnings that [are] authorized by the Board.'[60]

The greatest difficulty with rate of return regulation, then, hinges on built-in incentives for over-capitalization. Under the new method, profits (π) are given by the formula:

$$\pi = r.B$$

where π is profits, r is permissible percentage rate of return, and B is rate base. This equation means a company can increase profits by inflating B. After all, if r is fixed by the regulator and if $\pi = r.B$, then the only way for π to rise is by increasing B (Mr. de Grandpré's point). Increases in B can often be benign, but need not be so.[61] One undesirable way to increase B is through undue capital intensity; that is, substituting capital for labour to an extent greater than would occur in the absence of regulatory control. This ploy becomes particularly attractive if plant and equipment are purchased from an unregulated manufacturing affiliate. Bell Canada purchases 80 to 90 per cent of its equipment from Northern Telecom, its unregulated equipment supplier.

A second, equally nefarious, possibility is to engage in predatory pricing in competitive markets. If the regulated company serves several markets, some competitive and others monopolized, profits can be increased overall by offering service at a loss in the former (thereby expanding the rate base while driving out competitors) and cross-subsidizing that loss through high profit margins in the monopolized sectors. It was in light of just such possibilities that the CTC inaugurated an inquiry into carrier-costing in 1972 (the cost inquiry). Anti-competitive cross-subsidy and predatory pricing have been issues of continuing concern to the CRTC as well.

Appraisal
The foregoing theoretical concerns, while interesting, cry out for empirical support. Table 14.1 depicts rate increases implemented by five Canadian telephone companies between 1950 and 1967, and between 1950 and 1977. Two of the companies are investor-owned; they are regulated by the federal government, since 1966 on a rate of return basis. The other three are provincially owned; the subscribers and investors are largely the same, thereby alleviating pressure on management to harm the one group in order to benefit the other. It should be noted that over the period 1950–77 Bell Canada and BC Tel introduced rate increases which were orders of magnitude greater than increases needed by the three prairie systems.

Combining the foregoing data on rate increase revenues with data

TABLE 14.1

Percentage rate increases introduced by five Canadian telephone companies, 1950–67 and 1950–77

	1950–67		1950–77	
Company	Local rates	Intraterritory toll rates	Local rates	Intraterritory toll rates
Bell Canada	49.0	22.0	101.0	65.0
BC Tel	87.0	47.0	197.0	112.0
Manitoba Tel	17.6	18.0	45.0	46.0
Saskatchewan Tel	29.0	9.0	67.0	37.0
Alberta Gov't Tel	20.0	n.a.	62.0	n.a.

SOURCE: Robert E. Babe, 'Vertical Integration and Productivity: Canadian Telecommunications,' 10; based on Restrictive Trade Practices Commission Exhibit T–487C, table A-3, Telecommunications Equipment Inquiry (compiled by the author)

on inflationary costs, measures of gains in productivity have been derived. With 1967 as the base year, the present author has concluded:

Had Bell Canada been able to implement productivity increases equal to those of MTS [Manitoba Telephone System], it would have saved subscribers an additional $404.3 million in 1977, or approximately 25 percent of real output in 1977 ... The average productivity gains achieved by the nonintegrated companies [MTS, Sask Tel and AGT] are valued at about $1.6 billion (constant 1967 dollars) over and above the productivity improvements achieved by Bell Canada, for the period 1968–1977. This is about 14 percent of Bell's real output for the period and about 95 percent of the value of rate increases through the period. Compared to BC Tel, the nonintegrated companies achieved productivity gains valued at $315 million over and above that achieved by BC Tel for the full period (constant 1967 prices); the excess productivity on the part of the nonintegrated companies equals approximately 13 percent of BC Tel's real output for the period and 91 percent of the value of rate increases since 1967.[62]

This book is not the place to replicate a technical methodology for measuring productivity increases. None the less it is to be noted that the foregoing quantitative estimates of disparities in productivity gains were accepted by the Restrictive Trade Practices Commission as accurate after thirteen days of intensive cross-examination.[63] These findings were substantiated also in 1983 by Denny, de Fontenay, and Werner in their comparison of productivity gains of Bell, BC Tel, and AGT.[64]

15

Juggling Corporate Forms

Assessing regulation on the basis of such policies as rate base, rate of return, costing, and revenue requirements is, however, to miss the main point. There is no arguing the importance of such concerns. None the less, they bear about the same relationship to telephone company operations as do a few still-photos to a complete football season. The attention to detail hides what is taking place on the rest of the playing-field, in the dressing-room, and during the off-season.

Historically it has been within the telephone company's powers to determine *which* activities, investments, revenues, costs, prices, and profits will be brought under regulatory scrutiny. This rather astonishing state of affairs is a result of both the company's powers to organize corporate forms at will and the reluctance of the government to pierce the corporate veil.

PERSONA FICTA

More than fifty years ago Adolph Berle and Gardiner Means announced that corporations had ceased being 'merely legal devices through which private transactions of individuals may be carried on'[1] Their discovery, shocking no one today, was insightful at the time.

In the formative and developmental years of industrial capital, corporations were 'legal alter egos,'[2] nominal vehicles set up by industrialists or associations of individuals to represent investment, transactions, and activities of the incorporators. It was believed that the corporate form, conferring powers of organization incidental to the control of industrial activity, would help spur economic development.

None the less, even in the nineteenth century corporations were more than merely legal alter egos. They were also artificial persons (persona ficta), created by law and existing in their own right. Corporations were empowered by charter to carry on business under their own name; to sue and be sued on their own behalf; and to have perpetual succession – i.e., continuity as legal entities – even though the individuals comprising them changed and indeed passed into dust.[3] A corporation, John Davis has advised, 'is invisible, immortal, and rests only in intendment and consideration of the law.'[4]

In this century, as Berle and Means so clearly showed, the corporation's role as legal alter ego has diminished. The persons heading the largest corporations are but infrequently in the public eye, although BEC's recently retired CEO, A.J. de Grandpré, may have been an exception. Nor do industrial leaders retain appreciable shares in their enterprises. There has been, in other words, a 'separation of ownership and control ... through the multiplication of owners.'[5] Nor is incorporation any longer privilege, bestowed on the few by the state to pursue a particular public purpose. Rather, qualifying individuals and groups may avail themselves of general procedures for incorporation.

This distinction – between charter privilege and obligation on the one hand, and the modern ease of incorporation on the other – figured prominently in the controversy surrounding Bell Canada's spawning of a parent, BCE, a ploy to bypass both charter obligations and effective regulation. That story closes this chapter.

But if the corporation's status as legal alter ego has diminished, and if special obligations attendant with incorporation have declined, not so the corporation's status as persona ficta. For in law a corporation is still an artificial person, with its own legal existence, liabilities, and rights. Frequently the courts refuse to pierce the corporate veil, to attribute liability to the owners or those in control beyond the limited or proportional liability inhering in share ownership per se. Corporations then are even today, distinct, autonomous, individual entities whose rights and existence are legal fictions.

Over the years manipulation of corporate form has proven especially useful to Bell Canada as means for bypassing regulation. In this chapter we note merely three such examples among several: Northern Telecom, Tele-Direct and Bell Canada Enterprises.

NORTHERN TELECOM

Corporate History
Bell's charter of 1880, as amended in 1882, empowered the company 'to manufacture telephones ... and also such other electrical instruments and plant as the said company may deem advisable.'[6]

Bell began exercising this manufacturing privilege a year after its incorporation, setting up a small division (Bell Telephone Repair Shop).[7] In this activity it benefited much from an 1880 agreement with National Bell, an AT&T predecessor, whereby the Canadian company attained 'without further payment, all patents which the American Telephone and Telegraph Company might take out in Canada, ... a perpetual contract.'[8] As well AT&T provided its Canadian subsidiary with various services (handbooks, specifications, methods, traffic and plant circulars, and so forth),[9] initially free of charge. This co-operative arrangement subsequently became known as the Bell-AT&T Service Agreement.

In 1895 Bell spun off as a subsidiary, the Northern Electric and Manufacturing Company,[10] whereupon Northern began producing items previously manufactured by Bell under licence from AT&T, selling the same back to Bell.[11] Four years later Bell bought from the company president, C.F. Sise, Sr, the Wire and Cable Company. Acquiring it for a hefty $500,000,[12] Bell now had in its possession a second manufacturing subsidiary.

Over the next few years Western Electric, AT&T's wholly owned equipment manufacturer, bought up sizeable minority holdings in both the Northern Electric and Manufacturing Company and the Wire and Cable Company;[13] and when in 1914 Bell of Canada amalgamated its two manufacturing subsidiaries into a new Northern Electric Company, Western Electric acquired 43.6 per cent ownership, with Bell Telephone and its Canadian officers subscribing to the remaining 56.4 per cent.[14] Until as late as 1956, Western Electric continued to hold 43.6 per cent of Northern Electric.[15]

Upon its incorporation Northern, of course, began supplying Bell with virtually all its equipment. Bell's equipment engineer, Norman Knight, elucidated on the company's procurement practices in testimony of 1926: 'Of course we have no intention of getting equipment from other concerns; therefore, we do not ask them for a quotation.'[16]

In addition to supplying Bell with items of its own manufacture, Northern became Bell's purchasing agent and warehouse manager, providing its parent with a full range of equipment – even automobiles – for which it routinely tacked on a flat 9 per cent before turning the items over to the parent.

Moreover, Northern's manufacturing operations soon stretched well beyond the simple confines of the telephone industry, embracing also fire alarms and even sound recordings. At one time, company president, C.F. Sise, Jr, boasted that Northern 'manufactured all the gramophone records that were made in Canada.'[17] Northern also supplied hydroelectric companies with wires and cables as early as 1907 – the power utilities were then major distributors of 'white goods' (stoves and refrigerators) – and continued to do so until 1956.[18]

In 1922, its shareholdings in Bell having fallen to 33 per cent, AT&T informed Bell of Canada that it was no longer willing to provide patents and services free of charge. Indeed AT&T threatened to stop taking patents out in Canada entirely unless Bell began to pay. Not wishing to allow AT&T's inventions to be used by others in Canada, Bell in 1923 signed a new service agreement whereby it would retain exclusive rights. Under the revised contract the American company was to receive 1.5 per cent of the Canadian company's revenues; in return, AT&T promised it would continue taking out patents in Canada[19] which, as always, would be promptly turned over to Northern Electric. For the year 1926 alone, payments flowing to AT&T for previously free services amounted to $420,000.

Cosy corporate relations among AT&T, Western Electric, Bell Telephone Company of Canada, and Northern Electric continued along much the same lines until 1956, when AT&T signed an antitrust consent decree with the U.S. Department of Justice.[20] This consent decree became a factor in the eventual divestiture by AT&T and Western Electric of holdings in both Bell Telephone of Canada and Northern Electric; the two American companies henceforth were to be constrained to the domestic U.S. market alone. In 1962 Bell acquired the American companies' shares in Northern,[21] and in 1975 AT&T disposed of its lingering shareholding in Bell Telephone. Also in 1975 Bell's service agreement with AT&T was terminated.[22] A further fall-out from the consent decree was joint establishment by Northern and Bell in 1958 of their own research and development organization, Bell-Northern Research (BNR). While even into the early 1960s, by the companies' own admission, 'most of the designs and much of the technology employed by Northern Electric came from Western Electric,'[23] by the decade's end Northern was pioneering its own designs. In 1975 Bell and Northern proclaimed proudly that Northern had become 'largely self-sufficient in design and technology.'[24]

Today Northern Telecom, the new name for Northern Electric, is North America's second largest manufacturer of telecommunications equipment. Its manufacturing plants and subsidiaries are scattered about the globe, and it exports telecommunications equipment, systems, and components world-wide. But Northern remains Bell Canada's preferred supplier, accounting for 80 to 90 per cent of Bell's payments for telecommunications equipment, and Bell remains Northern's most important customer.[25]

Corporate Veil and Regulatory Refusal

In precedent-setting 1926 rate proceedings, counsel for Bell, Hon. F.H. Phippen, contended unabashedly: 'The Northern Electric Company has no connection with the Bell Telephone Company, except that the Bell Telephone Company is authorized to hold stock in third companies.'[26] Mr Phippen's declaration echoed a 1921 ruling wherein the board had decided that it was 'given no supervisory power in regard to intercorporate relations.'[27] The corporate veil, in other words, was sacrosanct.

None the less, over the years the railway board did attempt to ensure that prices paid by Bell to Northern for equipment had not been 'enhanced' by virtue of vertical integration. In 1927, for example, after scrutinizing a small sample of items, the board affirmed that Northern's prices to Bell 'were lower than those which the Bell Telephone Company would have been obliged to pay to other manufacturers' and 'were as low or lower than those charged to other customers.'[28] Only in dissent did one of the commissioners, Frank Oliver, a former member of Parliament from Alberta, take exception to Northern's very high profitability and low dividend payout, concluding that these returns and practices alone constituted evidence of Northern's prices to Bell had in fact been unreasonable.[29] Price comparisons have continued to the present as the standard regulatory test of the propriety of the Bell-Northern relationship, despite acknowledged inadequacies.[30]

The most convenient intercorporate arrangement, whereby the regulated entity, Bell Canada, buys the bulk of its equipment from its own unregulated subsidiary with but minimal regulatory scrutiny, has not been without snags. In 1963 Industrial Wire and Cable Company, competitor for Northern Electric in certain lines, contended in a proceeding before the board that Bell's ownership of Northern was, in fact, illegal. Citing the 1880 charter, Industrial noted that the telephone company had been authorized to hold shares only in companies processing as proprietor either a line of telephonic communication or power to use communication by means of the telephone. Since Northern did not appear to be a telephone company – indeed its letters patent specifically precluded it from carrying on such a business – Industrial argued that Bell should either fold the manufacturing operations back into itself as its charter provided or divest itself of them entirely.

In rebuttal R.C. Scrivener, then a Bell vice-president, testified that upon incorporation Northern Electric and Manufacturing Company purchased from Bell a single line of telephone wire running between its plant and Bell's headquarters in Montreal. Over the years the location of this line had been changed as both companies established new premises. Indeed the line itself had on several occasions been replaced. None the less, a line was maintained, which in 1964 stretched for 19,000 feet, connecting facilities on Shearer and Belmont streets in Montreal. Although it emitted messages in one direction only and was maintained by Bell, none the less it was owned by Northern. Hence, according to Mr Scrivener, Northern was 'proprietor' of a telephone line, and so qualified as subsidiary of Bell.[31] But, he added, Northern was not a telephone company because it offered no telephone service to the public, and hence, it was not in violation of its letters patent.

Mr. Scrivener's declaration was sufficient for the board. It declared: 'Northern is admittedly not doing business as a telephone company but the facts which have been developed indicate clearly that Northern owns a line as a proprietor; that it does not operate it; and that it makes no offering of service to the public.'[32]

Thereupon the case was dismissed, 19,000 thousand feet of one-way telephone line settling the issue.

The legal battle was on again a decade later when the Province of Quebec submitted that Northern Electric was in fact a 'telephone system' because it was exercising powers (namely the manufacture of telephone apparatus) originally vested with Bell and which Bell at one time exercised but later delegated to its subsidiary as a ploy to bypass regulation. Quebec further contended, now conversely, that if Northern were not a 'telephone system' subject to regulation by the board, then Bell's ownership was illegal by virtue of its charter proscribing the types of companies in which Bell was permitted to take an ownership interest. The Canadian Transport Commission summarized

Quebec's position in the following way, demonstrating that it at least understood the contention:

If Bell Canada, being a public utility company, were to pretend that it could hide behind the corporate veil of its subsidiary Northern Electric, by having any part of Bell's Parliamentary franchise carried out by Northern, such evasion would amount to unlawful delegation of authority. In other words, one may not do indirectly what one is prohibited from doing directly ... Bell Canada and Northern Electric cannot be disassociated [and] the Canadian Transport Commission, as the guardian of the public interest, has the clear jurisdiction ... to subject [Northern's operations] to its scrutiny ... Otherwise, the legality of the acquisition by Bell of any interest in Northern is open to question.[33]

In dismissing Quebec's allegations and legal arguments, the Transport commissioners once again invoked the doctrine of the corporate veil, ruling: 'We have no doubt that Northern, having its own charter and its own Board of Directors is a corporate entity separate from and distinct from Bell; further, *the mere fact* that Bell is a majority shareholder of Northern and has a close corporate relationship with it, does not in itself change the fact.'[34]

Simply because Bell had powers to manufacture but had chosen no longer to exercise them, the board continued, was not in itself reason for amalgamating Northern within Bell for regulatory purposes. 'Northern,' the commission ruled, 'manufactures such equipment pursuant to its own power under its own charter,' and therefore it had not been 'delegated' those powers by Bell.[35]

Thereupon, the case was dismissed.

The CRTC too has heard arguments that for policy reasons, as opposed to legal exigencies, Northern should be treated as a part of Bell for regulatory purposes. In rejecting the position the commission has stated flatly: 'In view of Northern Telecom's growing range of non-Bell customers, of its large minority shareholdings, and of the importance to Canada of an effective telecommunications equipment manufacturing company, the Commission does not believe Northern Telecom should be so treated.'[36]

RTPC Inquiry
None the less, despite consistent and helpful regulatory policy, vertical integration was kept under a cloud of uncertainly for seventeen years,

until early 1983, on account of an inquiry initiated by the director of investigation and research, Combines Investigation Act. For some years the director had received letters and accusations from competitors of both Bell and Northern complaining that vertical integration was stifling competition, and so in 1966 he launched an investigation, gathering documentation and even seizing records from the offices of two companies. The inquiry dragged on for ten years before finally, on 20 December 1976, submitting a 'green book' – 199 pages long – to the Restrictive Trade Practices Commission (RTPC), he recommended that Bell be divested of Northern.[37]

The director's submission first described and analysed the structure of the telecommunications industry in Canada and then assessed the conduct and performance of Northern Electric and Bell from the mid-sixties to the late seventies. Next it decried Northern's dominance of the equipment market in Canada (Northern had 70 per cent of Canadian sales) because, in the director's opinion, this market dominance was attributable to Bell's restrictive procurement policies and its appetite for acquiring independent telephone companies.

Following receipt of the director's report the Restrictive Trade Practices Commission initiated its own inquiry in 1977. It travelled back and forth, coast to coast, for three years, holding meetings in major centres. In the end it sat for 228 days, heard evidence which in transcript occupies 35,000 pages, listened to testimony of two hundred witnesses, and studied two thousand exhibits.[38] Between 1981 and 1983 it published three volumes of reports, the first dealing with terminal interconnection, the second with Bell Canada's reorganization, and the third with vertical integration.

In the end the inquiry came to naught, the RTPC's major conclusions being that 'competition in the telecommunication equipment market ... in much of the world ... is highly restricted;'[39] that the 'market security' afforded Northern through vertical integration with Bell 'provided it with some breathing space to engage in expensive product development';[40] and that 'there has never been any doubt of the benefit to an equipment supplier of having a more or less captive market.'[41] Although the RTPC did concede that 'vertical integration undoubtedly makes regulation more difficult and costly,'[42] it professed confidence in the ability of the CRTC to handle the problem. Therefore, it concluded: 'The evidence in this inquiry does not establish that, on balance, the separation of Bell and Northern would improve performance in the telecommunications equipment industry or in the delivery of telecommunication services by Bell and other carriers.'[43]

TELE-DIRECT

Analogous is the story of Tele-Direct. For nearly a hundred years Bell Canada undertook all aspects of telephone directory operations in-house, but in 1971 it spun off Tele-Direct to take over the business.[44] Bell chose not to own Tele-Direct directly, however, but rather through a provincially incorporated subsidiary, the Capital Telephone Company, which provided about 121 telephones to the tiny hamlet of Maberly, Ontario. The decision to own Tele-Direct indirectly through Capital Telephone Company was based on the contentious charter provision alluded to earlier whereby Bell was authorized to own shares only in companies 'possessing, as proprietor, any line of telephonic communication, or any power or right to use communication by means of the telephone ... or to become a shareholder in such corporation.' Whereas a directory publishing company did not qualify, the tiny Maberly telephone outfit did, and Bell held indirectly what its charter prohibited it from owning directly.

The spin-off was beneficial to Bell in so far as the lucrative directory revenues were thereby removed from Bell's regulated 'revenue requirements.' Meanwhile TeleDirect's spin-off, not being capital-intensive, had little deleterious impact on Bell's rate base, which, as Mr de Grandpré pointed out, the company wishes to keep as large as possible. As planned, for the period 1971–7 incomes earned by Tele-Direct were excluded from Bell's regulated 'revenue requirements' (apart from the dividends Tele-Direct paid back to Bell). Tele-Direct used some of its profits during the period to acquire additional companies, such as the Sanford Evans Group specializing in direct mail advertising, trade magazines, and commercial printing. Tele-Direct also set up a commercial leasing division whose assets included a Falcon jet leased to Execair Aviation Limited and four fishing trollers on the Atlantic coast.[45]

In 1977, however, in the CRTC's initial rate increase decision, the corporate veil was lifted for the first time in Canadian telecommunications history. For investments deemed 'integral' to Bell, including Tele-Direct, the commission announced that corporate form would henceforth be ignored. All of Tele-Direct's revenues, costs, and investments were to be folded back into Bell, in the very manner that interveners had so long argued should be done with Northern.[46]

The second regulatory joust at corporate manipulations came three years later when the commission announced that investments not 'integral' to telephone operations would thereafter be deemed to have paid a reasonable return, whether or not such returns were actually paid. Henceforth, Bell would be unable to carry investments in its regulated rate base for which it was not earning an adequate return. (Profitable subsidiaries, including Northern Telecom, were keeping most of their profits as retained earnings instead of flowing them back to Bell through dividends.) Prior to inception of the 'deemed rate of return,' Bell's telephone subscribers had been footing the difference in order to keep Bell's realized return on total investment at a 'just and reasonable' level.[47]

Bell Canada was appalled. The final straw! It began casting about for a way to get the commission off its back. And it finally succeeded – by birthing a parent.[48]

REORGANIZATION – BCE

Background
Even as early as 1966 the Bell Telephone Company of Canada had set its face towards diversification. Obstructing the way, however, was its own charter, which delimited the types of firms in which the company could make direct investments. Furthermore, the charter confined the company's own operations to provisioning 'telephone' service and to manufacturing electrical equipment.

An initial attempt at unshackling these fetters was made in 1967 when Bell petitioned Parliament to revise its Special Act. First, Bell requested that its 'objects' be redefined to embrace 'telecommunications,' not merely 'telephones.' Bell president, Marcel Vincent, assuaged members of Parliament by saying that this modest word change was 'merely using more up-to-date language,'[49] explicitly denying any intent on Bell's part 'to get into other fields or broaden our functions.'[50] Mr Vincent's pledge was echoed unflinchingly by Mr A.J. de Grandpré, then Bell's legal counsel and vice-president of law, who stated pointedly: 'We do not intend to be anything but excellent common carriers. That is what we intended to be; that is what we have said in the past and that is what we intend to do in the future.'[51]

Bell made a second entreaty as well, requesting authorization

ILLUSTRATIONS

Corporate Offices of Three Ontario Telephone Companies, 1987

Even into the 1950s Ontario was served by hundreds of independent telephone companies, of which a remnant survives to this day, pointing
either to an industry structure now obsolete or to one which, given
different regulatory policies, could even now exist. Here we see (top right)
the exchange and corporate offices of the Westport Telephone Company
Ltd., serving some 1700 subscribers north of Kingston; (bottom right)
the North Frontenac Telephone Company Ltd., serving Sharbot Lake and
region (in the photo, the author is inspecting the facilities); and
(above) Bell Canada, the particular office tower displayed here being
Place Bell Canada in Ottawa.

Organizers of Canadian Telegraphy

Canadian telegraphy had its share of heroes and antiheroes; represented
here are three of the most notable. From left to right: Frederick Newton
Gisborne (1824–82), pioneer of telegraphy in Atlantic Canada and one
of the first to envisage an Atlantic cable; Erastus Wiman (1834–1904),
whose acumen and clout succeeded in fulfilling Western Union's desires
for a telegraph monopoly in Canada; and Sir Hugh Allan (1810–82),
banking, shipping, and merchandising magnate who master-minded
Montreal Telegraph Company's dominance in Ontario and Quebec until
1880, and who helped integrate Canadian telegraphy into a continental
industrial structure.

Crisis in the Commons

Demand for public control of telephones escalated until 1905, when Prime
Minister Sir Wilfrid Laurier set up a select committee of the House of
Commons to investigate the industry and to make policy recommendations. Here are represented five of the main protagonists. From left to
right: (top) Sir William Mulock (1844–1944), then Postmaster-General
and chairman of the Select Committee (he could not see 'why it is not
as much the duty of the state to take charge of the telephone as it is to
conduct the postal service,' but his influence waned when he was suddenly
dispatched to England); Francis Dagger (1865–1945), telephone expert
and Mulock's chief adviser (after the demise of the select committee
Dagger moved on to help provincialize Bell's operations in Manitoba and
Saskatchewan); William Findlay Maclean (1854–1929), newspaper editor
and member of Parliament, whose frequent calls for nationalization of
telephones in Parliament and in his paper placed Bell on the defensive
for several years; (bottom) Charles Fleetford Sise (1834–1918), Bell's
second president, who oversaw the take-over of Canadian telephony by
American Bell and who ably represented his company's interests before
the Select Committee; and Allen B. Aylesworth, Bell's legal counsel before
the Select Committee and, after 1906, Postmaster-General.

Unsightly Overhead

At the turn of the century, profusion of overhead telephone wires
proved distressful to municipal government, which clamoured
for local control. This scene was not atypical.

A. Jean de Grandpré

If Charles Fleetford Sise Sr laid the tracks, A. Jean de Grandpré drove the engine. He was appointed Bell's chairman in 1976, after having served the company for only ten years. Through the next several years the company he headed embarked on a remarkable program of diversification, capped in 1983 by formation of BCE Inc., an international holding company whose interests now encompass such diverse fields as financial services, real estate, energy, printing, publishing, and international consulting. De Grandpré's legacy will continue on for years to come.

Mythologizing Technology

Technological imperative and technological determinism are intellectual doctrines positioning 'Technology' at the forefront of political, economic, and social change. Perhaps less subtly, but not infrequently none the less, mystification of artefacts is undertaken through visual representations. Here we see the 'Golden Boy,' corporate symbol of the American Telephone and Telegraph Company. Originally hoisted above AT&T's headquarters at 195 Broadway, New York City, in 1916, this 16-ton, 24-foot icon now welcomes visitors to the lobby of the corporation's main office at 550 Madison Avenue. Since the 1930s pictures of the statue have adorned the cover of many a telephone directory.

The Gandalf Hybrid™

Productivity through systems connectivity.

Getting improbable partners to work together for maximum productivity is what we do best.

It's what you'd expect from a company that spends over 12% of its revenues on research and development.

The result: The Gandalf Hybrid. A customized information processing and delivery system combining the best features of all your computing resources.

No matter how uncongenial your processing partners may appear, a Gandalf Hybrid makes them perform together as if they were born that way.

Which is why Gandalf networking systems are so efficient and so reliable.

The Gandalf Hybrid, one of a series.

Paul M. Breiden

One of a series of advertisements from a Canadian high-tech firm, not only illustrating the myth of technological evolution, but depicting as well man as the Nietzschean 'rope' between beasts and the divine.

through charter amendment 'to diversify our investments.'[52] On its face this second request appeared to some naive MPS to contradict denials proffered but moments before of not wishing 'to get into other fields,' but such was not the case, assured Mr de Grandpré. On the contrary, he attested, his company wished merely to gain authority to invest in debentures and bonds of companies (namely telephone and telegraph companies) for which it already had authority to acquire shares; in other words, to diversify its portfolio of financial instruments. For, Mr de Grandpré opined, Bell's charter confined it to holding shares in companies owning telegraph or telephone lines and in those having authority to establish communication. Bell, its counsel suggested, now merely wanted permission to acquire bonds and debentures in such companies too.[53] 'Since 1880,' he confided, 'we have never gone outside of telephone operations or of our Northern operation.' He concluded by affirming once again that his company had no intention of doing so now.[54]

Others were sceptical. Tilting for one last time at the Bell windmill, G.D. Zimmerman, president of Industrial Wire and Cable Company, warned: 'We have learned to approach Bell's public pronouncements with a sharp eye for pragmatic possibilities. We recognize the Bell as a master of public relations in the soft sell, also the sidewise drift into preselected positions from which they subsequently have approached Parliament over the years for authorization.'[55]

Industrial Wire and Cable's legal counsel, Mr J.G. Torrance, then advised that Bell's current charter in no way restricted its ability to invest in securities other than shares; 'so I submit that this in not the reason that they are asking for section 8,' he concluded. Rather, the real reason, Mr Torrance advised, was there for all to see, in the explanatory notes to the bill, namely: 'To broaden the Company's power to invest in other companies having objects in whole or in part similar to those of the Company and calculated to advance the objects of the Company.'[56]

In conclusion, Mssrs Zimmerman and Torrance submitted: 'What Bell is really asking for is that it be allowed to engage in a field far greater in scope than the telephone business, in fact one so fundamentally different that it seems highly inappropriate to describe the requested amendment as a "re-phasing" of its charter.'[57]

Bell in the end was only partially successful. On the one hand, it succeeded in having its powers to engage in 'telecommunications,' as opposed to mere 'telephones,' recognized officially by revisions to its

Special Act. On the other hand, the proscriptions of the 1880 charter regarding investment in other companies were retained verbatim, except as now qualified by express permission to own those research and development firms and telecommunications equipment manufacturing firms in which Bell held interest on 7 March 1968[58] – a provision affirming retroactively Bell's right to hold shares in Northern Electric, an investment of at best dubious legality to that point.

In other respects the committee members, newly enlightened on telephonic restrictive and predatory trade practices, ended up recommending that the utility's powers be phased back, certainly not enhanced. And their recommendations found fruition in the revised act. First, the revised charter now expressly prohibited Bell and its subsidiaries from applying for or becoming holders of broadcasting licences, including cable television licences. Second, the charter now declared: 'The Company shall, in the exercise of its power – act soley as a common carrier, and shall neither control the contents nor influence the meaning or purpose of the message emitted, transmitted or received.'[59]

Undaunted, Bell proceeded to undertake dramatic diversifications, always carefully ensuring that its non-telephonic acquisitions were held either through Northern Electric or through the intermediary of telephone operating subsidiaries. By 1976 a corporate empire was in place, consisting of seventy-four companies, with operations spanning the globe (figure 15.1).

But even so, Bell remained disconsolate over the now constraining charter. So, late in 1976, it approached the Senate to pass Bill s-2, An Act Respecting Bell Canada. Of the bill's several provisions, two stand out. First, section 16 of the Canada Corporations Act was to be brought into the charter. Mr de Grandpré, back once again on Parliament Hill, this time as Bell's chairman and chief executive officer, explained to the senators: 'By requesting to incorporate section 16 of the Canada Corporations Act into its charter ... the company would be allowed to invest in any other company having objects altogether or in part similar to those of the company.'[60]

Second, the bill also provided that Bell would become authorized to itself alter those very same objects and purposes – through letters patent to be tabled in Parliament. If within thirty days either house voted against the changes ('a negative resolution'), they would not come into force.[61] Mr de Grandpré modestly termed these revisions 'an updating of the company's powers.'[62]

Questioned about exactly what objects and powers his company might aspire to through alterations to letters patent, Mr de Grandpré responded: 'We may never use that clause ... There could very well be circumstances where we could operate for a period of 15 to 20 years without any change in our objects or powers. But there could be circumstances where different objects and powers would be needed.'[63]

The senators, seldom before noted for their celerity, acted with uncharacteristic haste. They passed Bell's bill the very next day, so convincing had been Mr de Grandpré's appearance.[64]

The proposed legislation was promptly sent to the House of Commons for ratification. The lower house, however, did not greet the bill with the same warmth and enthusiasm afforded only days before by the Senate. In fact some MP's were downright hostile. The New Democratic Party in particular, supported by the Créditistes, launched a filibuster, quite preventing Mr. de Grandpré's 'updating' from even reaching committee.[65] Certain of the honourable members contended that the company was quite out of control. Week after week, month after month, the filibuster continued; John Rodriguez and Cyril Symes in particular were always 'johnny-on-the-spot' to fill up the alotted time with verbiage sufficient to postpone a resolution.[66]

Finally Bell caved in. It requested a meeting to work out a compromise, at which the present author was a privileged attendee. Beginning with affected bravado, Bell's representatives asserted that politicians were dawdling while the company's opportunities for profitable acquisitions were dissipating. But Mr Rodriguez stood firm, and finally Bell capitulated, promising to delete the contentious 'updating' provisions if only Parliament would please authorize the much-sought-after increase in capitalization.

On 16 March 1978 the compromise was announced in the House of Commons by Bell's parliamentary representative, whereupon a jubilant Cyril Symes, MP from Sault Ste Marie, bounced to his feet, bursting out gleefully: 'I consider the amendment that will be moved a tremendous victory for my party and those in the Créditiste party, who assisted us in debating the bill for over a year ... I think it is a great achievement ... that Bell Canada has finally come around to our point of view and has agreed to drop the offending clauses from the bill.'[67]

Little did Mr Symes, or any other of the honourable members for that matter, know that Bell had another card up its sleeve.

Thereafter matters remained in abeyance until 1981, at which time the CRTC still invigorated in its pursuit of the public interest,

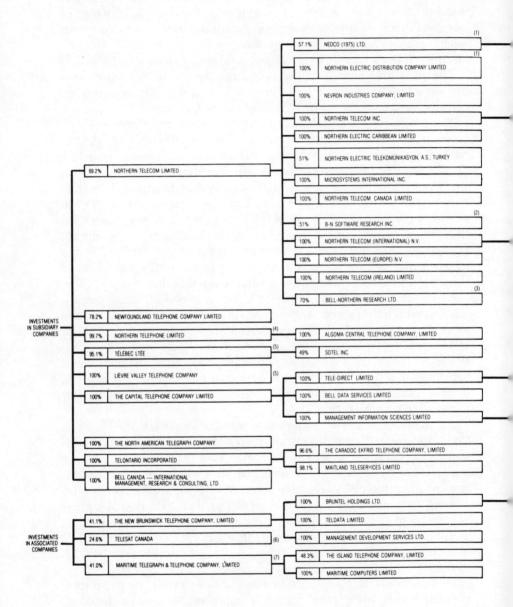

Figure 15.1
The Bell Canada Group
Investments in Subsidiary and Associated Companies

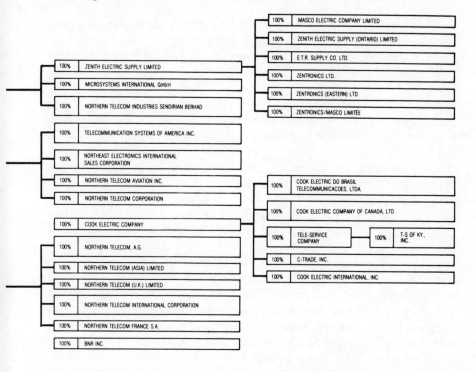

100%	MASCO ELECTRIC COMPANY LIMITED
100%	ZENITH ELECTRIC SUPPLY (ONTARIO) LIMITED
100%	E.T.R. SUPPLY CO. LTD.
100%	ZENTRONICS LTD.
100%	ZENTRONICS (EASTERN) LTD.
100%	ZENTRONICS/MASCO LIMITÉE

100%	ZENITH ELECTRIC SUPPLY LIMITED
100%	MICROSYSTEMS INTERNATIONAL GmbH
100%	NORTHERN TELECOM INDUSTRIES SENDIRIAN BERHAD

100%	TELECOMMUNICATION SYSTEMS OF AMERICA INC.
100%	NORTHEAST ELECTRONICS INTERNATIONAL SALES CORPORATION
100%	NORTHERN TELECOM AVIATION INC.
100%	NORTHERN TELECOM CORPORATION

100%	COOK ELECTRIC DO BRASIL TELECOMMUNICACOES, LTDA.
100%	COOK ELECTRIC COMPANY OF CANADA, LTD.
100%	TELE-SERVICE COMPANY — 100% T-S OF KY., INC.
100%	C-TRADE, INC.
100%	COOK ELECTRIC INTERNATIONAL, INC.

100%	COOK ELECTRIC COMPANY
100%	NORTHERN TELECOM, A.G.
100%	NORTHERN TELECOM (ASIA) LIMITED
100%	NORTHERN TELECOM (U.K.) LIMITED
100%	NORTHERN TELECOM INTERNATIONAL CORPORATION
100%	NORTHERN TELECOM FRANCE S.A.
100%	BNR INC.

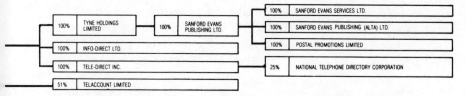

100%	TYNE HOLDINGS LIMITED — 100% SANFORD EVANS PUBLISHING LTD.
100%	INFO-DIRECT LTD.
100%	TELE-DIRECT INC.
51%	TELACCOUNT LIMITED

100%	SANFORD EVANS SERVICES LTD.
100%	SANFORD EVANS PUBLISHING (ALTA) LTD.
100%	POSTAL PROMOTIONS LIMITED
25%	NATIONAL TELEPHONE DIRECTORY CORPORATION

80%	DOBBIN SURVEYS LIMITED

(1) Northern Electric Distribution Company Limited owns 42.9% of common shares of Nedco (1975) Ltd.

(2) Bell Canada owns 49% of common shares of B-N Software Research Inc.

(3) Bell Canada owns 30% of common shares of Bell-Northern Research Ltd.

(4) Bell's percentage of all common and preferred voting shares is 89.5%.

(5) Lièvre Valley owns 4.9% of common shares of Télébec Ltée.

(6) Bell Canada owns 27.9% directly and indirectly of Telesat Canada.

(7) Including the common and preferred shares, Bell's ownership is 40.0%. Under Nova Scotia statute percentage of company voting stock is 0.04%.

*As of December 31, 1976

announced that Bell's investments in 'non integral' companies would henceforth be 'deemed' to have paid Bell through dividends a reasonable return. Bell was outraged. An intolerable ruling! It would not sit still. It reorganized.

Birthing a Parent

On 20 April 1982 Bell Canada unilaterally filed articles of continuance with the Department of Consumer and Corporate Affairs pursuant to the Canada Business Corporations Act, essentially annulling its charter and bringing the company under the same corporate law that applies to virtually all other federally incorporated businesses.[68] Then on 23 June it announced its proposed 'reorganization,' to be effected no later than 31 December 1982, whereby Bell Canada Enterprises (BCE) would become parent to the Bell Group, with Bell Canada reduced to mere subsidiary.

BCE had received its name only the day before, on 22 June, being until that time known affectionately as Tele-Direct Ltd. Indeed as recently as 11 June the company had been a subsidiary of the Capital Telephone Company, to which allusion has been made. Little could the good folks of the tiny hamlet of Maberly have foreseen the exalted role that had been cast for their diminutive telephone company in the grand game of Canadian telecommunications policy.

Bell Canada was pleased. It informed shareholders proudly: 'Under its charter, BCE is empowered to make any investment without being subject to restrictions or prohibitions.'[69] And it continued confidently: 'The proposed Reorganization is not subject to CRTC approval.'[70]

Whereupon it expanded on motives for reorganizing:

With the present corporate structure, the parent company of the Bell Group, Bell Canada is regulated by the Canadian Radio-television and Telecommunications Commission ('CRTC') and all the income of its investments in both regulated and non-regulated companies must pass through it before reaching the shareholders. With the non-regulated income co-mingled with the regulated income in this fashion, the proper sharing between subscribers and shareholders of the risks and rewards associated with these investments has become a major regulatory issue.[71]

It is important to pause in the recollection of these events to contemplate some of the regulatory implications of the reorganization. If Bell Canada had incentives to cross-subsidize and engage in predatory pricing before reorganizing, BCE certainly would have the same after. As noted by the U.S. comptroller general, corporate organization as such has no effect on the incentives of the parent company.[72] The big difference, however, now would be that the CRTC, to that point standing astride the corporate apex through its jurisdiction over Bell Canada, would henceforth be reduced to regulating a mere subsidiary of a much grander corporate complex. Far from being able to apply cost separations to the multitude of BCE subsidiaries doing business with Bell Canada in order to ensure transactions were reasonable and just, affiliates of BCE not controlled through Bell Canada (the great bulk of BCE's affiliates – figure 15.2) were being moved quite beyond regulatory oversight.

Moreover, and of even greater importance, since CRTC jurisdiction extended only to Bell Canada, the commission was about to lose jurisdiction over the management ultimately controlling Bell Canada. Indeed, as a point of law, the CRTC might well be losing jurisdiction over even Bell itself through that company's continuance under the Canada Business Corporations Act, in effect voiding its charter.

Returning to the sequence of events, on 22 October 1982, and evidently in the face of strident behind-the-scenes lobbying,[73] cabinet (much to the credit of Communications Minister Francis Fox) instructed the CRTC to make findings regarding the likely ramifications of the reorganization – on prices charged Bell's subscribers and on the ability of the commission to continue regulating Bell Canada effectively. As well the CRTC was instructed to give advice on what modifications to the proposed reorganization might be needed to eliminate or mitigate impairment to the commission's effectiveness as regulator, as well on the limitations that should be imposed on the range of activities undertaken by BCE and its subsidiaries.[74] In due course the commission announced that it would hold public hearings on these matters, to begin 1 February 1983.[75]

In preparation for the hearings the CRTC hired three consultants to advise it on the issues and to recommend appropriate responses: Walter Bolter, formerly of the U.S. Federal Communications Commission and then telecommunications consultant; William Stanbury, professor of business at the University of British Columbia, and Robert E. Babe, consultant. Three interim reports were duly submitted to the commission in January, and the three consultants, independently of one another, advised the commission to oppose the reorganization as it was then set out. All three contended that the reorganization was

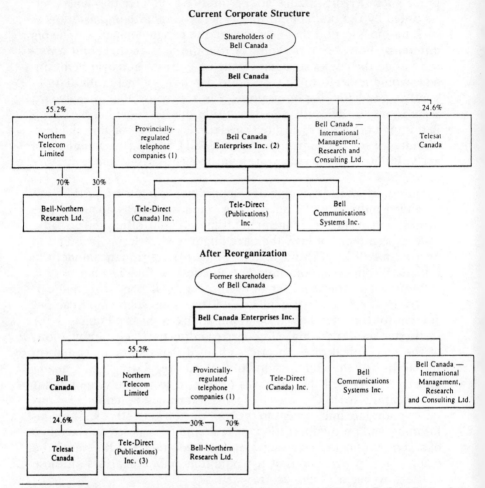

Current Corporate Structure

After Reorganization

(1) Newfoundland Telephone Company Limited, 63.5% owned; Northern Telephone Limited, 99.8% owned; The Capital Telephone Company Limited, 100% owned; Télébec Ltée, 100% owned; Maritime Telegraph and Telephone Company, Limited, 35.4% owned; The New Brunswick Telephone Company, Limited, 35.8% owned.

(2) Formerly named Tele-Direct Ltd. Tele-Direct Ltd., formerly a wholly-owned subsidiary of The Capital Telephone Company Limited, became a direct, wholly-owned subsidiary of Bell Canada on June 11, 1982. Tele-Direct Ltd. was renamed Bell Canada Enterprises Inc. on June 22, 1982 and a new company was created named Tele-Direct (Canada) Inc. to carry on printing, publishing and related businesses.

(3) It is intended that as soon as practicable after the Reorganization this corporation will be transferred by BCE to Bell Canada. The description reflects this eventual transfer.

Figure 15.2

devastating in its implications respecting the commission's ability to regulate.[76] But within a few days of receiving the interim reports, the CRTC relieved all three consultants of further duties in the matter, dismissing two of them entirely and reassigning the present author to other tasks. No final reports were prepared.

On 18 April 1983 the commission handed down its recommendations, which to the three consultants, at least, were by no means surprising. Replete with phraseology reminiscent of the bygone days of the Board of Railway Commissioners, this new, invigorated, reform-minded CRTC announced to one and all: 'The Commission has not been persuaded that the public interest requires it ... [to] second-guess managerial judgements about an optimal corporate structure ... In the Commission's view, managerial flexibility is particularly necessary ... at this stage in time. As Canada proceeds into *the information age*, its future as an industrialized state will depend heavily on high quality managerial, technical and research skills such as those found within the Bell group of companies.'[77]

The commission concluded: '*Provided the recommended legislative amendments are enacted* ... there would not be any negative impact on subscribers.'[78]

The reorganization was accomplished on 28 April 1983, but at least four years went by before any of the legal safeguards suggested by the CRTC had been put into law. Indeed in late 1985 Mr de Grandpré, as chairman and chief executive officer of BCE, was back once more before the parliamentary committee, soothing over apprehensions with declarations that no legislated safeguards whatsoever were needed.[79]

But although Mssrs Zimmerman, Shulman, and Gellman had long since passed from the telecommunications scene – as had Francis Dagger, William Mulock, and W.F. Maclean before them – in December 1985 the flickering torch of public interest was carried yet again into the parliamentary committee room, this time by A.J. Roman, executive director of the Public Interest Advocacy Centre. Although Mr Roman's lengthy testimony was erudite and makes interesting reading, for present purposes it can perhaps best be summarized by one pithy observation: 'With all due respect to all of our collective imaginations, we cannot today even begin to imagine the ways in which the kind of cash-cow that a regulated utility is can be milked.'[80]

A few of the various means of milking came to light almost immediately, however, as BCE began exercising its new freedom. Within eight months it had acquired 11.8 per cent of Trans-Canada PipeLines (TCPL), the largest single block of shares, for $167.5 million. BCE at the time offered a take-up of all other outstanding shares for the same price,[81] even while maintaining its acquisition should be construed simply as an 'investment,' certainly not a 'take-over.'[82] By 1986 BCE owned 48.5 per cent of TCPL,[83] and was casting about for yet other acquisitions in the oil patch. Its CEO, A.J. de Grandpré, candidly confided that his company had on hand a 'cash surplus' of $475 million.[84] In the spring of 1989 BCE entered the financial services industry in a big way acquiring 100 per cent of Montreal Trust Company for $875 million.[85]

By 1987 BCE could make the following claims: Canada's most profitable corporation; Canada's largest corporate employer; Canada's most widely-held corporation, owner of more assets than any other company in Canada; owner of the largest pipeline company in Canada; owner of the largest printing conglomerate in Canada; and of course owner of the biggest telephone utility in the country.[86]

Dubbed the 'Emperor of BCE,'[87] Mr de Grandpré, reflecting on his many years at the helm of Bell Canada and then of BCE, has confessed that the Bell reorganization was undoubtedly his most outstanding achievement. Between 1983 and 1987 BCE's assets grew to $26 billion from $15 billion, up roughly 70 per cent. Revenues rose to $14.6 billion from $8.9 billion (up 64 per cent). Profits swelled to $1.09 billion from a relatively paltry $830 million in 1983. 'The company I leave behind,' judged the BCE chairman with obvious satisfaction, 'will be completely different from the company I took up over twelve years ago.'[88] And the company was grateful, rewarding its founding chairman with $997,300 in salary for 1987.[89]

In May 1988, fresh from yet another dramatic victory at the political level,[90] de Grandpré retired as BCE's chief executive officer. Shareholders at BCE's annual meeting gave him a well-deserved standing ovation.[91]

A New Act
On 15 June 1987, just over four years from the date the reorganization had been consummated, the House of Commons gave third and final reading to Bill C-13, 'An Act Respecting the Reorganization of Bell Canada,'[92] an attempt to atone for and redress the regulatory slippage accomplished by Bell's reorganization. Some of the bill's provisions are simply silly. For example, the subsidiary company Bell Canada

and any of its subsidiaries are still precluded from holding broadcasting licences, but the door is left wide open for BCE and any of *its* subsidiaries (except Bell Canada and companies controlled by it) to enter broadcasting. Again, Bell Canada is forbidden to acquire shares, directly or indirectly, in telecommunications research and development companies and equipment-manufacturing companies, except those in which it owned shares on 7 March 1968. But once again the door is left wide open for BCE and any of *its* subsidiaries (except Bell Canada and companies controlled by it) to acquire such shares. Evidently the efficacy and sanctity of the corporate veil are still being upheld, the futility of forming public policy in that context being scarcely recognized.

Other provisions are more substantial, however. For one thing the CRTC is now entitled to demand information from BCE on its subsidiaries in the same manner and to the same extent as from Bell Canada. Moreover, the commission is empowered to fold unregulated telecommunications affiliates into Bell, lessening the likelihood of BCE's spinning off lucrative but monopolized profit centres out of Bell Canada into the unregulated sector. Furthermore, the CRTC is authorized to order Bell Canada to divest itself of competitive activities, perhaps folding them into another company, to avoid undue commingling of competitive and monopolized revenues.

Only time will tell how effective these provisions will be in coping with the regulatory burden created so suddenly by Bell Canada's reorganization.

PART IV

Broadcasting and New Technologies

16

Broadcasting

ROOTS IN TELEPHONY

'Broadcasting' via Telephone
At telephony's inception, point-to-point communication was hardly the only use of the telephone. The 16 November 1877 edition of the *Bobcaygeon Independent*, for example, reported that Mr Fowler, one of Melville Bell's local agents, held soirées 'almost every evening during the past week ... at which songs, duets and even glees have been so perfectly conveyed over the wire between here and Lindsay [about 20 miles] that the separate voices could be distinguished.'[1] Perfection not infrequently discloses imperfection, however, and the festivities in Bobcaygeon were no exception; according to one wag gifted with an especially acute ear, a distant vocalist sang 'flat.'[2]

Just as spirits of Bobcaygeoners were elevated by mellifluous intonations from far-off Lindsay, so too in Hamilton did the telephone company convey joyful tunes about town, having installed in Knox Church ten instruments for the purpose. Three hundred of the more curious and adventuresome lined up to 'see, hear and wonder' as musical offerings from a choir a half-mile distant were wafted to the church through telephone line.[3]

Nor were early 'broadcasting'-type experiments entirely musical. In 1881 devotional services from St James Street Methodist Church, Montreal, were transmitted with such clarity to Highgate, Vermont, a popular summer resort with Montrealers, that the *Star* reported vacationing members of the congregation to have taken part in the devotions 'as perfectly as if they were in church itself,' enjoying 'one of the pastor's most eloquent and impressive sermons.'[4]

Newsworthy as these point-to-'mass' experiments via the telephone in Canada may have been, domestic applications paled beside experimental uses in Europe. In Budapest, for example, a comprehensive news and entertainment package was inaugurated in 1883 for the city's 6000 telephone subscribers, complete with program guides listing 'concerts, lectures, dramatic readings, newspaper reviews, stock market reports, and direct transmissions by members of Parliament.'[5] The system was even equipped with emergency signalling to permit the 'station' to ring subscribers as special news broke. Back in North America, returns for the 1896 u.s. presidential election were reported 'live' over that country's telephone system. Thousands sat 'with their ears glued to the receiver the whole night long, hypnotized by the possibilities unfolded to them for the first time.'[6]

It is apparent, on the one hand, that there was no inherent reason why telephone systems could not have developed into 'broadcasting' or one-way, point-to-mass distribution systems. On the other hand, neither was there an inherent reason why radio apparatus should have been deployed the way it has been. Indeed, with one notable exception, broadcast-type uses of the wireless were scarcely conceived until 1919, a full twenty years after the first successful application of electromagnetic radiation for purposes of communicating.

The Wireless

As early as 1865 James Clerk-Maxwell (1831–79), the great Scottish physicist, began publishing papers on electromagnetism, maintaining that 'electrical action' in the form of invisible waves passes through space at the speed of light.[7] Later Heinrich Hertz (1857–94), after whom the invisible as well as visible radiations are sometimes named, gave proof of the former's existence through experiments involving oscillating circuits.[8] Upon these and other theoretical foundations and discoveries, Guglielmo Marconi (1874–1937) gave practical application, sending messages in Morse code a full mile and a quarter in 1895,[9] thereby launching a new industry. So obvious were the strategic implications of radio even then that the British admiralty and war office began beating paths to Marconi's door.[10]

Meanwhile, in 1901 a Canadian inventor, Reginald Fessenden (1866–1932), successfully concluded experiments in wireless telephony by transmitting for the first time the human voice through the ether.[11] But Fessenden was not merely father of the wireless telephone;

he also initiated the world's first 'broadcast,' on Christmas Eve, 1906. Alvin Harlow gives an account:

Early that evening, wireless operators on ships within a radius of several hundred miles [of New England] sprang to attention as they caught the call 'CQ, CQ' in Morse Code. Was it a ship in distress? They listened eagerly, and to their amazement, heard a human voice coming from their instruments – someone speaking! Then a woman's voice rose in song. It was uncanny! Many of them called to officers to come and listen; soon the wireless rooms were crowded. Next someone was heard reading a poem. Then there was a violin solo; then a man made a speech, and they could catch most of the words. Finally, everyone who heard the program was asked to write to R.A. Fessenden at Brant Rock, Massachusetts – and many of the operators did.'[12]

Only with the lapse of a further thirteen years, however, were programs inaugurated for public reception. During the interim it was to military applications of ship-to-shore communication that major companies devoted their energies.

Patent Deadlock

It is surprising that North America's major telephone companies initially remained aloof from experiments with wireless communication, but just as Western Union had scoffed at the telephone during its initial phase of development, so too did AT&T and its Canadian subsidiary, the Bell Telephone Company of Canada, believe that no practical applications could be forthcoming from wireless communication. The art of radio telephony continued to progress, however, and AT&T finally grew restive. By 1910 it had bought up many patents, the rights for Canada reverting of course to Bell of Canada, thanks to the Bell-AT&T service agreement.

When the war broke out the major equipment manufacturers (including General Electric, Westinghouse, and Marconi, as well as AT&T) pooled patents. But this co-operation created a deadlock when peace was restored, and no company was able to move without violating another's patents.[13] The armistice also caused a drying up of lucrative military markets, inducing leading firms to cast about for ways to re-establish sales volumes. It was then that Fessenden's 1906 Christmas Eve broadcast was recalled.

Divergence
To replace desiccated military markets for radio apparatus, Westinghouse Electric and Manufacturing Company inaugurated a daily program service out of Pittsburgh (KDKA), its first broadcast covering the November 1920 presidential election.[14] But KDKA was not, as is sometimes asserted, the first to transmit on a regular basis for general reception by the public. That honour goes to XWA, Montreal, owned by Canadian Marconi, also a manufacturer of radio-receiving equipment. Authorized to broadcast in May 1920 under the call letters CFCF, XWA actually began an 'unofficial' service in September 1919, becoming thereby both the world's first radio broadcaster and its first pirate station.[15] KDKA and CFCF were overnight successes,[16] and a new, burgeoning broadcasting industry was under way.[17]

The novel, potentially lucrative uses to which radio waves were now being put did not escape notice from North America's major telephone companies. Still controlling in 1922 some vital patents for radio, AT&T announced that it too would enter broadcasting, albeit on principles of common carriage. Just as one could enter a telephone booth, deposit a coin, and talk to a friend, so too could one soon address the general public by visiting an AT&T 'toll broadcasting station,' paying, of course, the appropriate fee. AT&T envisaged thirty eight such stations blanketing the United States, all linked by longlines to form a network. In August 1922 the first of these was opened, WEAF in New York City, followed in 1923 by WCAP in Washington, DC, which was connected to WEAF by wire.[17]

'Toll broadcasting,' the hiring of radio facilities by advertisers, blossomed under AT&T's control to become the basic model directing development of broadcasting in North America. As Daniel Czitrom has written, radio was becoming a 'latch key' by which advertisers could invade nearly every home.[18]

Nor was AT&T's Canadian subsidiary, the Bell Telephone Company of Canada, far off the mark, attaining in 1922 licences from the federal Department of Marine and Fisheries for CKCS, Montreal, and CFTC, Toronto.[19] Although it remains uncertain whether Bell of Canada actually offered a programming service over these stations,[20] the record does reveal that both one-year licences were allowed to lapse in 1923, when a patent pool was signed with Canadian subsidiaries of foreign manufacturing companies. Telephony, in Bell's territory at least, was thereafter to remain Bell's exclusive domain, with broadcasting to be undertaken only by the other signatories. Bell's annual report for 1923 described the deal this way:

An agreement has been concluded with the Canadian General Electric Company, The Marconi Wireless Telegraph Company, the Canadian Westinghouse Company and the International Western Electric Company, covering the use by all for radio purposes of the respective patents of each concern. Under the terms of the agreement, each of the companies agrees to the uses of its patents *within the natural field of such other company*. The Marconi Company will have the use of all the patents for wireless telegraph purposes; The Bell Telephone Company of Canada for the purposes of public telephone communication; and the manufacturing companies, including the Marconi Company, for the purposes of manufacture and sale. [emphasis added][21]

An Exception
Although the Bell Telephone Company of Canada retreated from broadcasting in 1923, Manitoba Government Telephones (MGT) persisted until 1948.

In 1922 the Winnipeg *Tribune* and *Free Press* each established stations in the provincial capital. Although both operations intitially lost money, neither owner wanted to abandon the new medium to its rival and so the two papers struck a deal and approached MGT to bail them out.[22] The provincial telco then turned to the federal government, securing a promise for a perpetual monopoly over radio broadcasting in Manitoba: no new stations were to be licensed without MGT's express permission. Federal commitment in hand, only then did MGT agree to buy the beleaguered stations. In March 1923, CKY, Winnipeg, went on-air and in 1928 provincial coverage was extended through a second station, CKX, Brandon, both owned and operated by Manitoba Government Telephones.

In MGT's annual report for 1923, commissioner John E. Lowry expounded on factors underlying his company's decision to enter broadcasting. First, Lowry contended, the limited Manitoba market could not be expected to sustain more than one commercial station, reason enough for government ownership. But in any event, Lowry continued, competition even if sustainable would lead inevitably to 'indifferent broadcasts' and would also likely cause interference. Furthermore, 'from a publicity viewpoint the identity of the province could be better preserved with the operation of one Manitoba station, than would be the case with several.'[23]

There was also an additional factor at work. Possessing none of AT&T's radio patents and excluded from Bell's patent pool, MGT was fretful over possibilities of competition. Management reasoned that a commitment from the federal government not to license additional broadcasters in the province would help preserve the telephone monopoly in the face of emerging techniques for communicating. This motive too was acknowledged in Commissioner Lowry's report:

That this move was justified as far as protection to the telephone plant was concerned is evidenced from the fact that at least two manufacturers were approached by one of our principal long distance users for a number of radio stations across the prairies, which, if practical, as undoubtedly it will be in the not too distant future, would have meant a considerable loss to our revenue ... It was, therefore, considered good business to spend a small sum and retain control of the art in Manitoba, than to probably lose an appreciable amount of toll revenue in the future.[24]

Despite the forementioned commital, the federal government in 1933, freshly invigorated by a jurisdictional victory in London before the Privy Council, unilaterally licensed James Richardson and Sons to operate a second station in Winnipeg.[25] From that time onward, Ottawa began developing a broadcasting policy excluding provincial participation. In 1944 applications by Alberta and Quebec to establish governmental broadcasting services were rejected, and in 1946 federal authorities refused to sanction the transfer of CHAB, Moose Jaw, to the Saskatchewan government. Curious eyes turned immediately to Manitoba, and questions about continued provincial ownership of CKY and CKX were raised in the House by John Diefenbaker in May 1946. C.D. Howe, as minister of reconstruction, affirmed that 'since broadcasting is the sole responsibility of the Dominion Government, broadcasting licences shall not be issued to other governments, or corporations owned by other governments. In regard to the two stations in Manitoba, discussions are taking place with the government of that province which we hope will lead to the purchase of these two stations by the Dominion Government.'[26] And so in 1948 the assets of CKY, Winnipeg, were sold to the CBC and the station became known as CBW. (The call letters CKY have since been reactivated for use by a private station.) CKX, Brandon, also was sold at that time, to Western Manitoba Broadcasters Ltd.[27]

The federal ban on provincial ownership of broadcasting persisted until 1972,[28] when an order-in-council reopened the door for provincial participation, albeit restricted to the field of educational broadcasting, resulting in the formation of TV Ontario and Radio-Quebec.

Recapitulation
It is therefore evident that in Canada segregation of broadcasting from telephony proceeded from collusive and restrictive covenant on the part of Canadian subsidiaries of foreign firms, certainly not from either a general principle that content should be separated from carriage or the premise that broadcasting and telephony used radically different types of apparatus. In fact, the opposite was the case: the two fields diverged through corporate agreement *because* the techniques are so substitutable! To the extent that the federal government played a role in segregating these industries, the burning issue was not whether telephone companies should engage in broadcasting; rather, it was how to squeeze the provinces out of an area of federal jurisdiction. None the less, the segregation persisted for fifty years. It is now being challenged, however, by cable systems, communications satellites, and 'deregulation,' a pot-pourri of devices and policies often summed up by the term 'new broadcasting environment.'

'NEW BROADCASTING ENVIRONMENT'

In the years subsequent to Bell's withdrawal, radio broadcasting began receiving continued attention from Canada's policy-makers. As articulated originally by Sir John Aird, chairman of this country's first royal commission on broadcasting, the field came to be perceived as having important social, cultural, and political consequences, in addition to the more obviously economic ones. Formation of the Canadian Radio Broadcasting Commission (CRBC) in 1932 marked the inaugural attempt to foster through legislation indigenous programming. The CRBC was replaced in 1936 by the Canadian Broadcasting Corporation (CBC) for like purpose. In 1958 the Conservative government of John Diefenbaker created the Board of Broadcast Governors (BBG) to regulate both the private and public sectors as 'a single system,' fixing thereby a certain equality between public and private agencies, but both, however, were still subject to overriding cultural obligations. In 1968 the BBG was superseded by the CRTC. Through all these years the broadcasting system has been expected to help 'safeguard, enrich and strengthen the cultural, political, social and economic fabric of Canada.' The system's success in achieving these laudable ends has been questioned on more than one occasion, of course.[30]

Since inception of the Board of the Broadcast Governors at least, the main dialectic in Canadian broadcasting has concerned the proportional strengths of the public and private sectors; the relative emphasis to be afforded ideals and profits; and Canadian nationalism vs. international information flows. These continuing philosophical tensions have been manifested at several levels: relative size and importance of the Canadian Broadcasting Corporation vs. the private sector; stringency or laxity with which Canadian content quotas have been formulated and enforced; and regulation and deregulation of cable television. In the 1980s, however, these central contradictions – between a broadcasting system that is to contribute to cultural sovereignty on the one hand and one that, on the other, is by and large erosive of the same – have been intensified by the emergence of the so-called 'new broadcasting environment.'

The 'new broadcasting environment' philosophy has received some of its most enthusiastic articulations from the federal Department of Communications. 'Broadcasting,' announced DOC in 1983, 'though very significant, is only one aspect of a larger whole.'[31] Hence, policies towards broadcasting, 'though very important, [can represent] only one aspect of a larger set of integrated policies now being developed by the federal government to meet the challenges and opportunities – cultural, economic and social – posed by the new technologies.'[32]

'New technologies,' then, are viewed as posing both challenge and opportunity. The challenge, in the view of DOC, is principally 'the globalization of the broadcasting environment,' particularly 'through satellite but also through VCR's, potentially destroy[ing] the infrastructure for program production in Canada.'[33] The opportunity in DOC's view, results from 'a continually growing and voracious demand [on a world scale] for new programming to fill the multiplicity of channels soon to be available.'[34] Because all of the developed world, DOC states, is participating in an information revolution, Canada too must be at the leading edge of 'technological advance,' not merely to foster export markets for home-grown telecommunications equipment but to ensure a domestic base for program material to be offered for sale in the emerging global-programming market-place.

Two thrusts of a so-called new broadcasting policy can be discerned. One is 'open skies' for program importation.[35] 'Open skies' liberate the 'new technologies,' thereby helping Canada's high-tech manufacturers garner a toe-hold in the international equipment market-place by writing off certain R&D expenses on domestic sales. Moreover, 'open skies,' it is asserted, will help make Canadian broadcasting 'more competitive'[36] by fostering increased 'quality' of productions as Canadian producers vie internationally for sales.[37]

The second thrust of the 'new broadcasting policy' is accelerated privatization,[38] albeit accompanied by tax incentives and public subsidy. On the one hand, DOC has inaugurated the Canadian Broadcast Program Development Fund 'to assist private production companies and independent producers.'[39] On the other, there has been a concerted effort to phase back, if not emasculate, the CBC.[40]

In the following chapters the growing interdependence of policies respecting broadcasting and telephony induced partly through the proliferation of cable TV, satellites, and other new technologies is explored in greater detail. For the present it is sufficient to note that this same interdependence has been an important factor in downgrading Sir John Aird's vision of a distinctly Canadian broadcasting system.

17

Cable Television

'I'm just the plumber who puts the pipes together,' quipped cable industry consultant Israel Switzer to a broadcasting conference in 1980. 'I don't care what people flush down them.'[1]

Switzer's perspective appears to have largely won the day. In the late 1980s Ottawa's paramount concern is promoting 'new technologies'; broadcasting content is increasingly perceived as a means towards that end. In speeding acceptance of this revisionary stance towards broadcasting, cable TV representatives have been not only loquacious but effective.

Introduced to Canada in London, Ontario, in 1952, cable for many years remained predominantly a six-channel rediffusion service, enhancing television reception primarily for rural communities. Even by 1964 only 215,000 homes (4 per cent of Canadian households) subscribed. But during the second half of the 1960s the industry's fortunes changed dramatically. Subscriptions rose from 516,484 in 1967 to 923,811 in 1969, a 79 per cent increase in two years,[2] by which time cable had begun its spread into metropolitan markets, primarily on account of its ability to alleviate ghosting caused by high-rise buildings, a problem especially acute with colour sets.

Anticipating yet further growth and anxious to affirm exclusive jurisdiction, the federal goverment in 1968 folded the budding industry into its new Broadcasting Act, designating cable systems as 'broadcasting receiving undertakings.' This careful if inelegant choice of words evidently substantiated federal claims to jurisdiction since, in the precedential Radio Reference case of 1932, Viscount Dunedin of the judicial committee of the Privy Council had written: 'Broadcasting as a system cannot exist without both a transmitter and a receiver. The receiver is indeed useless without a transmitter and can be reduced to a nonentity if the transmitter closes. The system cannot be divided into two parts, each independent of the other.'[3] Hence, 'broadcasting *receiving* undertaking.'

Until the inauguration of satellite-to-cable networking in the 1980s cable systems were essentially local – analogous to early telephone systems prior to construction of interprovincial long distance. Thus, had cable TV been deemed a *telecommunications carrier* instead of a broadcasting-receiving undertaking, federal authorities would probably have been powerless to legislate.

Even today cable resembles telephone operations in some important ways (see table 1.1). Both are capital intensive in plant and equipment; both deliver messages by wire to the home or office; neither radiates signals through 'ether' for general reception; and both can accommodate many message originators simultaneously. Like telephone companies, cable systems are increasingly interconnected to form a national grid.

Of course such similarities ought not to obscure marked differences. The cable 'house drop,' for example, has three hundred times the message-carrying capacity of the telephone 'local loop.' Cable systems most generally are treelike in configuration, with connections branching out from a head-end (antennae array) at the apex, whereas telephone systems are starlike, their connections emanating from a switching centre. Furthermore, telephone companies provide two-way, switched communications, while cable is unswitched and is still predominantly one-way. And finally, telephone companies most commonly distribute messages point-to-point while cable (like broadcasters) usually sends messages point-to-mass. Bearing characteristics of broadcasting and telephony but also departing in important ways from both, cable has therefore been termed a 'hybrid.'[4]

Inception of regulation of cable as a broadcasting-receiving undertaking in 1968 sent sparks flying: first from traditional broadcasters threatened by increased competition, second from levels of government squabbling over jurisdiction, and finally from telephone companies eyeing cable as a latent competitor. Some of the skirmishes are described below.

At present there is an uneasy truce, with cable none the worse for wear. Interlinked via satellite and carrying up to twenty-four channels, cable companies currently supply service to 66 per cent of Canadian homes, garnering (in 1985) $672 million in revenues by diffusing and rediffusing basic and tiered (or discretionary) programming and providing certain non-programming services.[5] And while cable continues to straddle broadcasting and telephony, converging and transforming both, it none the less remains subject only to provisions of the Broadcasting Act, still being perceived officially as merely 'broadcasting receiving undertaking.'

A CINDERELLA STORY: BLIGHT TO CHOSEN INSTRUMENT

Initially the CRTC was cool to cable, indeed viewing the nascent industry as a blight on broadcasting, potentially disrupting orderly custodianship over a system charged with public purpose. In the words of the commission's first chairman, the indomitable Pierre Juneau: 'Every time we talk about developing cable as if it were a utility, like telephone or hydro or water, what you are saying in fact is, "Let's make sure you get those four American networks into Canada as fast as we can ... We are not trying to find ways of subsidizing cable or cross-subsidizing cable in order to make the American channels available faster than they would otherwise be available ... Our mandate is not to wire up Canada as fast as possible for American television." '[6]

The chairman's apprehensions found formal expression in official policy statements of the late 1960s and early 1970s. In 1969, for example, the commission fretted that unmitigated cable growth, and accompanying increases in Canadian coverage by U.S. stations and networks, 'posed the most serious threat to Canadian broadcasting since 1932 before Parliament decided to vote the first Broadcasting Act.' In the commission's view, cable 'could disrupt the Canadian broadcasting system within a few years.'[7] Hence, it launched a two-pronged attack on cable. First, it attempted to prevent the industry from further extending its facilities into areas then unserved (the prairies, except Winnipeg; the Atlantic provinces; and northern regions of all remaining provinces) by refusing to authorize distant head-ends and microwave for the importation of signals. Second, it attempted to roll back subscriptions for systems then existing by restricting rediffusion of American signals to but one commercial and one non-commercial.[8]

The industry of course was up in arms, public hearings (particulary in British Columbia) became subject to disruption, and soon the commission ran for shelter, throwing its policies to the wind as it fled. None the less the CRTC remained wary of cable through the decade, twice refusing to license pay-TV and prohibiting cable program originations 'competitive' with over-the-air broadcasting.

By decade's end, however, it was becoming clear to all who cared to look[9] that the much-ballyhooed demise of over-the-air broadcasting had at least been postponed, if not put off entirely; television profits continued soaring at lofty levels despite the cable menace. Meanwhile policy-makers were becoming less sanguine about the willingness of private television station owners to help 'safeguard' the fabric of the country. These factors, combined with receptivity of rhetoric about the imminence of an information revolution, served to revolutionize policy postures towards cable. Suddenly cable became, of all things, a chosen instrument!

Ushering in this abrupt transformation was *The 1980s, a Decade of Diversity*, also known as the Therrien report after the CRTC commissioner who headed up the special inquiry. Noting that in 1980 some thirty-five non-network programming services were being transmitted on U.S. satellites, each capable of reception in Canada with backyard dish antennae, Therrien proclaimed that 'a new technological universe ... is already taking shape at a pace that is inexorable.'[10] Then, as if to illustrate poignantly the art of self-fulfilling prophecy, the report advised that cable systems should be authorized immediately to interconnect via satellite so that new pay-television and other satellite-to-cable services could be launched with all possible dispatch.

Twice previously the CRTC had given cold shoulder to pay-TV – on grounds of likely disruption to established broadcasting.[11] But this time out, under a new chairman, John Meisel, it acted swiftly and decisively, in one fell swoop licensing not just one but six pay services, all to be delivered by satellite to cable.

As it turned out several of the pay services were unable to survive a year's operations. The chief claim to fame of the most prosperous was to enter into a co-production agreement with a U.S. company to produce and diffuse 'adult' films – an ingenious means of complying with its Canadian content obligations.[12]

But in 1984, even as all initial pay channels were going belly-up or amalgamating, yet another flock of satellite-to-cable services were approved: the so-called specialty channels, funded by both subscriptions and advertising. Some had Canadian content quotas imposed on them, while others were allowed to remain 100 per cent American.

By the mid-1980s cable's about-face was complete. Like private broadcasting before it, cable was now held in such high esteem by Ottawa's mandarins that it too warranted special protection – from the even newer 'new technologies' of private dish antennae, VCRs, and apartment MATVs.[13] Had Ottawa become so totally besotted as to envisage remarkable cultural contributions from cable industry? To the contrary; in cultural terms cable was still regarded as a Trojan horse. But, more important, cable was now viewed as the cornerstone for an industry strategy that could sweep Canada into the information age. To quote the Department of Communications:

The [new] strategy calls for the entire range of new Canadian programming services and many foreign services to be made available over cable ... Cable operators [also] will ... be encouraged to provide the public with a range of new non-programming services, such as videotex, data bank services, intrusion alarms, meter reading, medic alert, etc. In short, cable will become a major vehicle for delivering the 'information revolution' to Canadian homes ... Canada has one of the most sophisticated and extensive cable systems in the world. The enormous amount of cable already in place in this country means that cable will be able to offer, at a much more economical price to Canadians than any other delivery medium, a far greater range of programming and non-programming services.

The department continued:

Canadian high technology industries should benefit directly as cable operators retool their plants to carry these new programming and non-programming services. Cable companies will require significant amounts of new capital equipment – such as earth stations, scrambling and descrambling equipment and a variety of other types of cable hardware. Canadian high technology industries manufacture much of this equipment and jobs should be created as a result.

These antipodal positions towards cable, whereby the despicably bad has been transformed in the eyes of policy-makers into the utterly good, give cause for much reflection on the state of policy-making in Canada.

FEDERAL-PROVINCIAL HIGHJINKS

If during the 1960s and 1970s the emerging cable television industry generated much heat and hostility from established television broadcasters and their regulator, it also helped reawaken provincial claims, long dormant, to the broadcasting field. Provincial prerogatives had seemingly been scuttled forever in 1932 by the Radio Reference case and ensuing federal policies, but the growth of cable TV, an apparently local, closed-circuit facility, rekindled these provincial aspirations.

First off the mark was Quebec in 1969. Just a few months after the federal government had claimed the industry as its own by enacting a new Broadcasting Act, Quebec too passed legislation dealing with cable, purporting to entrust provincial systems to its own Public Services Board (Régie des services publics).[15] Immediately the régie informed all provincial cable operators that they were now in need of provincial licences. For a while, then, Quebec's cable companies required two licences, one federal and one provincial.[16]

Next, Quebec's newly appointed minister of communications, Jean-Paul L'Allier, began courting other provincial leaders to establish a united front against federal hegemony. In this he was initially quite successful, finding ready allies on the prairies where governments were apprehensive lest federal incursions into cable TV disturb the comfortable monopolies so long enjoyed by provincially owned telephone systems.[17] Other provinces soon came aboard as well.

Thus buoyed, L'Allier escalated his demands – shortly to encompass not merely cable TV but all provincial radio and television broadcasting (save CBC/Radio Canada) and all other telecommunications (apart from Telesat Canada and Canadian Overseas Telecommunications Corporation, but including Bell Canada).[18]

Meanwhile, federal communications minister Gérard Pelletier developed a strategy of his own. Evidently believing the best defence to be a good offence, he started promulgating a need for enhanced federal jurisdiction, emphasizing a supposed 'national dimension' to telecommunications in Canada.[19]

The first show-down was a federal-provincial communications ministers' conference in September 1973. With lines sharply drawn, neither camp budged, and the conference ended with 'no agreement in sight.'[20] It was in this context that two of Quebec's small businessmen, François Dionne and Raymond d'Auteil, became ensnared in a Keystone Cops comedy/drama played on the grander field of federal-provincial 'diplomacy. Their story has been set out in full detail by Michel Guité[21] and is now summarized briefly.

In April 1974 Dionne, an accountant, received a federal licence to provide cable service to a large section of eastern Quebec, including Matane and Rimouski, operating territory of Québec Téléphone, a provincially regulated telephone company. Under Dionne's timetable, Rimouski was not to be wired for three years, much to the chagrin of the local citizenry. Seizing on a perceived advantage, the hitherto docile Quebec Public Services Board, to that point routinely duplicating CRTC licensing decisions, took the audacious step of awarding Rimouski to another party, Raymond d'Auteil (who was coincidentally the brother-in-law of the president of the Quebec board). According to the Montreal *Star*, 'provincial authorities had been waiting for years for a suitable test to challenge Ottawa's traditional authority.'[22] With federal financial backing Dionne promptly took the régie to court, at which point the Quebec government began to bankroll d'Auteil's defence.

Somewhat surprisingly the provincial court in November ruled in favour of d'Auteil and provincial jurisdiction. Not waiting for an appeals' court ruling, the rival licensees each negotiated with Québec-Téléphone to wire up Rimouski. Perhaps owing to provincial nudging, d'Auteil's system was ready first, and in August 1975, he opened his system for business. But no sooner were off-air signals being rediffused than the national police force rode into town and confiscated d'Auteil's 'illegal' head-end. Unperturbed, the provincial government generously forked over funds to replace the missing equipment, and service was soon restored. Whereupon the federal government sought a second court order, again to allow antennae seizure, but this time a technicality delayed the writs, giving d'Auteil precious time to dismantle the disputed hardware and hide it in the surrounding 'mosquito-ridden marshlands.'[23] Subscribers complaining about yet another disruption in service were told the antennae 'would be moved to high ground again as soon as federal Mounted Police agents called off their horses.'[24] Then, under the watchful eye of the Quebec Provincial Police – instructed to protect the antennae against federal 'vandalism' – d'Auteil's equipment was again restored to operating condition, at a new site.

The conflagration between police forces and levels of government was resolved only in 1978 when the Supreme Court affirmed federal jurisdiction over cable TV.[25] Provinces since that time have been relatively quiescent.

THE TELEPHONE CONNECTION

Cable has been at the centre of yet a further storm, one stirred up by the telephone industry. Since its inception in 1952 cable has been dependent on telephone companies for pole and duct space, and for twenty-five years the telcos made the most of this dependence. The reasons are obvious: the message-carrying capacity of coaxial cable as used in cable systems is more than three hundred times that of the copper pair wire used for telephone local loops. Unencumbered, cable systems could prove formidable competitors.

In Bell Canada's territory, cable systems were to be built by Bell alone, and cable companies were to pay Bell 80 per cent of building costs; yet the telephone company retained ownership of cables attached to telephone company poles. For an additional monthly fee Bell agreed to lease portions of the cable spectrum back to cable licensees ('lease-backs'), but cable companies were still precluded from transmitting certain types of communication: no limited-network or point-to-point messages were permitted, for example.

Although in the late 1960s the cable industry succeeded in getting some of the more debilitating restrictions lifted, even through the first half of the 1970s cable was still allowed only to transmit signals conveying television and/or radio programs. Signals not part of or ancillary to a broadcast or cablecast were precluded, as was 'inquiry-response communication.' Moreover, cable companies could not connect coaxial cables to any type of exchange or message-switching device; and they still could not own their own cables.[26]

The CRTC first heard of telephone company restrictions in one of its early public hearings (November 1968),[27] but because its jurisdiction was then confined to the broadcasting field, it could do little to rectify the situation. The most it could accomplish was to establish as general principle the requirement that licensed cable undertakings own at least head-ends, house drops, and amplifiers. The CRTC stated that such minimal ownership was necessary in order that cable companies 'exercise effective control ... to meet their regulatory obligations.'[28] The CRTC announced further that 'it would not be in the public interest to encourage common carriers to hold cable licences.'[29] (As we have seen, in 1968 Parliament had revised Bell Canada's charter, specifically prohibiting Bell from applying for or becoming a holder of a cable TV licence.)

But sometimes the law's intent is one thing and telephone company practices another. For several years Bell was in fact the cable-licensing authority in Ontario and Quebec. At a CRTC public hearing in February 1969, for example, it was disclosed that small cable firms, holding valid permits from the federal Department of Transport, could not persuade Bell to wire up their licensed territories, stymied as they were by a $5-million deal struck between Bell and five large cable firms. Even after the CRTC announced 1 August 1968 that cable companies should not extend territories until receiving CRTC approval, Bell continued to sign contracts and wire up new areas so that when the time came to receive CRTC licences, the territorial boundaries would be a fait accompli.[30]

Even after the commission began asserting a modicum of authority in 1969–70, negotiations and confrontations between the two industries continued unabated, albeit confined largely to the backrooms, until 1975. At this point, exasperated at their total lack of success, the Cable Association and several cable firms took their plight to Bell's federal regulator, the Canadian Transport Commission, charging that Bell had violated its charter by not permitting 'pole attachments' of cable company–owned cables. But with the same impeccable logic employed in the Morton Shulman case, the CTC ruled that since Bell itself owned the cables there was no 'requirement' governing the attachment of cables owned by cable companies which the CTC could rule to be reasonable or otherwise. Therefore, it dismissed the case.[31]

None the less, the CTC did recognize that a wrong was being done, for it continued: 'It appears to us that Bell's attitude and policy is [sic] influenced by the desire to assure itself of the control of the services which broad-band coaxial cable may be able to perform in the future ... A more liberal attitude on the part of Bell could have beneficial effects on the efficient development of communications services for the Canadian public.'[32]

The commission then took the most unusual step of inviting the applicants to resubmit grievances, but this time basing their appeal on a section of the Railway Act governing construction of telegraph, telephone, and power lines 'across or near such lines ... that are within the legislative authority of the Parliament of Canada.'[33]

And in 1975 just such an appeal was launched, by Transvision (Magog) Inc., a small Quebec cable concern that had suffered the ignominy of having its wires cut by Bell upon expiration of its 'partial system agreement.'[34]

Bell's defence in the ensuing hearings was quite technical and far removed from considerations of public interest. Its clever counsel, Ernie Saunders, argued that the CTC lacked authority to order pole attachments because the pertinent section of the Railway Act governed only wires 'near' or 'across' Bell's lines whereas Transvision in point of fact wanted to attach its cables 'upon' Bell's structures. To this legalistic legerdemain the commission responded: 'We have no difficulty with the proposition that "near" does not include "on" or "upon", but we think that it does not justify interpreting the application differently from what it purports to be, namely the proposed construction of a cable line "near" the telephone lines of Bell.'[35]

Next the CTC observed that for many years Bell had entered quite willingly into agreements with hydro companies for the joint use of poles, on which basis it reasoned that no technical harm would be inflicted by one more attachment. It then declared that there was a public interest in Bell's entering into a similar arrangement with the cable company. Therefore, it ordered Bell to afford Transvision (Magog) the right of attaching its own cables.[36] In 1977 a similar right was extended, by the CRTC, to all Quebec and Ontario cable companies within Bell's service area.[37]

Subsequent to these pole-attachment decisions the cable industry has begun offering pay television and an increasing array of non-programming services, all of which had been precluded by telco restrictions. Conceivably cable will become a competitor of telephone companies in fields such as electronic banking and home shopping. For these reasons, telephone companies have continued eyeing cable longingly.

Indeed as early as 1978 Mr de Grandpré was promoting publicly the concept of a single integrated network (SIN), in more recent years tactfully renamed ISDN (Integrated Services Digital Network), to be introduced sometime in the future through fibre optics. Mr de Grandpré elucidated: 'There is no doubt in my mind that fibre optics technology is rapidly developing to a point where we can expect it to become a replacement for copper wire in our local distribution facilities with the capacity to carry signals of a wide range of bandwidths over the local telephone network ... New technology is bound to remove any justification for separate [telephone and cable] facilities in the future.'[38]

Meanwhile Bell set to work behind-the-scenes to promote its position, particularly within the Department of Communications where it began circulating 'discussion papers,'[39] the essential purport of which is easily summarized: 'Bell Canada believes that the use of one integrated network for the transmission of all telecommunications services, including CATV, is the most practical and efficient method of bringing total telecommunication costs to the public at the lowest possible level.'[40] Moreover, Bell began actively intervening before the CRTC against cable applications to provide non-programming services.[41]

Nor has Bell in the 1980s abandoned plans to remonopolize urban telecommunications. In a 1985 presentation to the Caplan/Sauvageau Task Force on Broadcasting Policy, for example, the company again insisted that through fibre optics it would 'incorporate' bandwidth and technology 'for total service needs of business and residence subscribers,' foreseeing the 'carrying of CATV [cable television] on its future fibre optic distribution facilities as a natural extension of [its carriage] role' and contending finally that 'competition between service providers does not require their ownership of facilities.'[42]

In May 1989 de Grandpré changed his tune, however, declaring that BCE intended to offer cable services competitive with those offered by Ted Rogers by building duplicate cable systems. Added BCE president Raymond Cry, 'Our intention would be to have the best offering for the best price, not by buying another company [but rather] to develop gradually a better, more cost-effective franchise.'[43]

18

Communications Satellites

In 1945 Arthur C. Clarke, then chairman of the British Interplanetary
Space Society, was first to envisage artificial satellites in geosynchro-
nous orbit. Microwave and broadcasting signals, the futurologist and
science fiction writer advised, could be sent to and from geostationary
satellites, of which but three were required to overlie virtually the
entire surface of the earth.[1]

Whereas Clarke's extraterrestrial vision was peaceable, less so was
that of Wernher von Braun, best known of the German scientists who
emigrated to the United States upon the close of World War II and
who helped propel u.s. ascendency in the field of rocketry. Also writing
in 1945, von Braun predicted: 'The whole of the Earth's surface [will]
be continually observed from such a rocket [in earth orbit]. The crew
[will] be equipped with very powerful telescopes and be able to observe
even small objects, such as ships, icebergs, troop movements, construction work, etc.'[2] And thus was launched the u.s. military's enduring
fascination with satellites for purposes of potential combat and
defence.

Although for the next several years a relatively leisurely pace for
the u.s. space program was initially maintained, the successful launching by the Soviets of Sputnik in 1957 'galvanized the American
people into committing vast resources for the missile and space pro-
grammes.'[3] Quickly the fiscal floodgates were raised, and military
satellites, designed to accomplish a wide range of missions, began
being launched with increasing regularity. By 1984 more than two
thousand had been hoisted aloft by the United States and the ussr

alone. More recently the Reagan administration's instigation of 'Star Wars' has added once again to the military stakes in satellites.

TECHNOLOGICAL NATIONALISM AND THE CANADIAN SPACE PROGRAM

Although it is doubtful that satellites would have even gotten off the ground in the absence of immense military outlays, the devices can also be applied, as Clarke foresaw, to more peaceable missions. Compared with terrestrial systems of wire, cable, and microwave, satellites have a number of advantageous civil applications, particularly pronounced for sparsely populated countries like Canada[4] where the electronic birds quickly captured the imagination of our policy-making élite. In particular, satellites were foreseen as means of 'integrating' remote communities into the Canadian mainstream: through improved telephone, radio, and television services to the North;[5] through more rapid dissemination of medical information to help save lives; through increased accessibility to educational materials; and by facilitating lateral communication among remote communities.

Other factors too were at work: striving after 'national prestige;' lobbying by Canada's scientific/industrial élite; a desire by government to foster high-tech industry; perceived imminence of an information revolution; and finally, national unity through communication hardware, a recurring theme in Canadian public policy since the building of the Canadian Pacific Railway. Satellites, the government contended, would enable it 'to take major steps in protecting and strengthening Canada's cultural heritage,' adding 'a domestic satellite system is of vital importance for the growth, prosperity, and unity of Canada.'[6]

DESIRE AND LOATHING

By now it should be readily apparent that engineering innovations can be disruptive to existing industrial power alignments.[7] In this regard satellites have been no exception.

In terms of Canadian television, satellites substitute for terrestrial microwave as means for dispatching network programming across the land. Indeed, as we shall see, the first proposal for a commercial satellite system came from broadcasters themselves, interested in establishing a new national television network. But much less desirably from the broadcaster's point of view, the satellites multiply by many times transmission capacity for national networking, well beyond the capability of the domestic program production industry to keep up, and thus contribute to the diminishing status of traditional network broadcasting in this country.[8]

The cable television industry too has expressed mixed emotions. Like satellites, cable distribution systems are superabundant in capacity and hence in constant need for traffic (TV programs). To help satisfy this voracious appetite satellites have been just the answer, facilitating the rediffusion of new program services by cable systems scattered across the country. Meanwhile, cable's salute to satellites is dampened whenever wary eyes are cast upon the possibility of direct-to-home satellite broadcasting (DBS), since terrestrial facilities may be rendered quite redundant.

And finally, being potentially competitive with land-line telephone facilities, satellites (although employed in long-distance services) have given rise to machinations from that quarter as well. With their distance-insensitive costs, satellites can not merely complement but substitute for microwave and fibre optics, especially for communication to remote areas.

Little wonder then that broadcasters, cable systems, and telephone companies have eyed satellites with both longing and loathing.

PIES IN THE SKY

When Alouette I was launched by the u.s. National Aeronautical and Space Administration (NASA) on 29 September 1962, Canada became the third nation in space. Allouette I had been designed by the Canadian Defence Research and Telecommunications Establishment (later renamed the Communication Research Centre, or CRC), and for its exceptionally long life of eleven years was used exclusively for scientific experiments.[9] Within a decade three other Canadian-designed experimental satellites – Alouette II, ISIS I, and ISIS II – were launched, again for scientific research in the ionosphere.[10]

Then in April 1971 an agreement was signed between the federal Department of Communications and NASA to develop and deploy a Communications Technology Satellite (CTS): Canada was to design and build the spacecraft, and the United States was to provide some advanced components and perform the launch; experimentation time was to be shared equally by the two countries.[11] Forecast to cost $60 million in construction and with a two-year experimentation budget of $50 million,[12] CTS was to be used exclusively for experimental, non-commercial applications. But underlying these rather hefty expenditures was a desire to stimulate through 'make-work' an infant space industry – to incubate and nurture expertise, via open-ended contracts,[13] within firms like Spar Aerospace of Toronto and RCA's branch plant in Montreal. As well the $110 million was foreseen as benefiting Telesat Canada, created in 1969 as this country's commercial purveyor of satellite circuits. In brief, CTS meant an abrupt cash transfusion from the public purse to Canada's high-tech companies.

Since the 20 January 1976 successful launch of CTS from Cape Canaveral, Florida [14] the government's space expenditures have continued exploring exalted elevations. For the 1978–9 fiscal year for example the space budget stood at $95.7 million,[15] while more recently Brian Mulroney's government has pledged $476 million on satellite development to the year 2000, an amount attacked in some quarters as being quite inadequate.[16]

SATELLITE SEIZURE

None the less, despite the continued funding, as early as 1967 or 1968 emphasis in governmental circles began shifting from scientific to commercial applications.[17] Helping hasten the turn-around was a joint application to the Board of Broadcast Governors (BBG) in October 1966 by Power Corporation and Niagara Television Ltd. (the latter a licensee of independent television station CHCH Hamilton) to establish a Canadian satellite corporation (Cansat) to distribute programming nationally for a proposed new television network (NTV).[18] Cansat, to be publicly traded and shareholder-owned but controlled by Power Corporation, was to 'build, launch and utilize a Canadian space satellite system.'[19]

Although the BBG held a one-day hearing on the topic in March 1967,[20] it lacked authority either to approve or to deny the application, a responsibility then residing with the Department of Transport (DOT). Soon DOT was besieged by representations from Canada's land-based telecommunications carriers, and reminiscent of previous representations concerning the control of microwave, they claimed that existing terrestrial facilities were more than adequate to meet all present and emerging demand. In the wake of this pressure, approval for the satellite project was stalled.[21]

A report from the federal science secretariat, also in 1967, soon resuscitated the sence of urgency, however, for it claimed 'the need for communications satellites for domestic use is clearly established.' The report called for fast action, foreseeing 'a risk that ultimate control over the space segment may not reside in Canada'[22] owing to a perceived scarcity of suitable orbital slots. As response Canada's carriers astutely reversed field. An industry consortium (actually a consortium of consortia)[23] was assembled hastily, composed of hitherto arch-rivals TCTS and CNCP, a tactic the carriers hoped would enhance the likelihood of satellites tumbling into their hands. Far from reiterating previous contentions that existing land lines were adequate for present and foreseeable needs, the carriers now contended that satellites were critical for meeting projected demand, and so urged the government to proceed post-haste.[24] Lest undue hardship be imposed on the public through ownership and control by other parties, the carriers volunteered in the public interest to take complete control over the building, ownership, and operation of this as yet untried and risky commercial enterprise.[25]

In June yet another report – this one commissioned by the Department of Transport but prepared jointly by Northern Electric and Hughes Aircraft, hardly disinterested parties – provided further fuel, conjecturing that under certain circumstances a Canadian commercial satellite system could in fact be viable financially.[26] This report, however, was not released to the public at that time. Indeed it would appear that the government was not particularly anxious to direct public attention to financial/economic matters at all, perhaps being itself convinced that satellites, at least in the early years, would be something of an economic albatross. Thus to the charge proffered in Commons Committee a year or so later that financial aspects of the government's satellite strategy had been cloaked in secrecy, A.E. Gotlieb, deputy minister of communications, responded lamely: 'The government, in forming any policy, gets access to a great deal of information from a variety of sources, and I do not think it would be possible to bring forward some of this information from various sources with propriety, considering the nature, of the sources of the information.'[27]

Then in July 1967 the newly organized Science Council of Canada released yet a further document, *A Space Program for Canada*, urging creation of a central space agency in the form of a Crown corporation that would be required to pursue a 'buy-Canadian' policy, albeit 'subject to reasonable cost differentials.'[28] (In early 1989, twenty-two years later, the recommended space agency was created).

Meanwhile, as all this publishing, politicking, and aligning was going on at the federal level, Quebec was quietly negotiating an agreement with France covering installation of earth stations on provincial soil to receive programming from a proposed Franco-German symphonie satellite.[29] When Quebec made public these ongoing negotiations, however, federal officials had near apoplexy and soon short-circuited provincial prerogatives by issuing a white paper that declared 'a domestic satellite communications system is of vital importance for the growth, prosperity, and unity of Canada, and should be established as a matter of priority.'[30]

Effectively squeezed out by the white paper's proposals were both Power Corporation and the Quebec government, for the white paper recommended that the satellite system be owned jointly by the federal government and the common carriers, with ownership participation by the public at a future but unspecified date. The system was to operate exclusively under federal jurisdiction.

Still, the recommendations were not received with complete equanimity by the common carriers. After all, they wanted to control the system themselves. To the carriers, satellites were merely 'telephone poles in the sky,' and under their auspices 'wasteful duplication of facilities' could be avoided through an 'orderly' and 'integrated' introduction of the new system.[31] The carriers' proposal, however, was rejected forcefully by the white paper, for several reasons.

For one thing, it was not clear that the telcos, once ensconced comfortably in control, would be energetic in developing a field substitutable for their own investments in terrestrial cables and microwave. Indeed, just a few months after publication of the white paper, Bell's executive vice-president, A.G. Lester, in Commons Committee unwisely confirmed this suspicion, opining: 'I do not really think that the long term future of telephone facilities is via satellite. I think this lies more in some of these other directions of wave-guides and lasers.'[32]

Second, the government did not want to curtail entirely the possibility of competition between alternate media; thus the white paper stated that a separate corporate form would allow the satellite system to: 'sell its services efficiently to the common carriers and television systems, in order that it may compete effectively in those areas where competition is appropriate.'[33]

Thus rebuffed at efforts to gain total system control, the carriers turned next to the ground segment, suggesting they be given an exclusive right to own earth stations.[34] From their perspective this arrangement made more sense anyway. After all, owning ground stations would give them sway over access to the satellites while averting risks and expenses associated with the space segment. This scheme the government wisely rejected.

Then, as their final ploy, the carriers demanded that Telesat be prohibited from leasing channels to anyone other than themselves – that Telesat become in other words a 'carriers' carrier.' This ultimatum was backed up by threats to boycott the system entirely unless the government caved in. A strike against Telesat by Canada's common carriers would doom the system to financial disaster before even getting off the ground.

And so Eric Kierans, communications minister responsible for spearheading satellite legislation through Parliament, back against the wall, struck an 'informal deal,'[35] subsequently acknowledged in Parliament, whereby Telesat would lease capacity only to common carriers and to those non-carrier customers prepared to lease full transponders (equivalent to 960 telephone channels) on long-term (five-year) leases, with no resale to or sharing of channels by non-carrier lessees. For all practical purposes Telesat was indeed to become a carriers' carrier, the sole identifiable exception being the CBC, bankrolled as it was by the federal government.[36]

Its freedom to market facilities thus severely restrained, Telesat was soon to reel under the prospect of financial collapse. But the carriers were happy. They had won round one.

ROUND TWO

On 27 June 1969 the Telesat Canada Act[37] received royal assent, creating for the first time a private corporation on the pattern of tripartite ownership – the government, the carriers, and the public each to hold one-third of the shares.[38] (Even to this time, however, the public has not been invited to participate, the government and carriers owning 50 per cent each, with the decisive share voted by the corporation's president, appointed by the government.) However innovative the ownership arrangement envisaged for Telesat might have been, it did not escape the watchful and sceptical eyes of certain honourable members in Commons Committee. As one particularly alert and cantankerous MP observed: 'There is a great conflict of interest between the aims of the government, the aims of the common carriers, and the aims of the individual investors ...'[39] How right he was!

Between 1972 and 1976 Telesat launched three Anik 'A' satellites, with capacities of twelve TV channels each.[40] Although RCA Corp. of the United States briefly and unexpectedly took up some of the slack, for most of the period Telesat could manage to lease only eight of its thirty-six channels, so hamstrung had it been by Mr Kieran's informal deal. The CBC, a Crown corporation, subscribed for three of these channels at a cost to the public treasury of about $10 million a year, while Bell Canada, TCTS, and CNCP leased the other five.

Underutilization of Telesat's capacity was attributable not merely to Mr Kierans's agreement, however, for the carriers themselves had built-in incentives not to use satellites. As explained by Dr Melody: 'Telephone companies are regulated on the basis of their investment in landline plant and facilities. That means that every time Bell Canada spends a dollar [on] landline piece of investment, whether it's efficient or whether it isn't, they are allowed to earn the regulated going rate of return which is 10 or 12%. Everytime they lease a channel from Telesat, they are allowed to recover the cost of the lease, period!'[41]

And so, as one might have expected, Telesat's financial returns remained less than robust. None the less, by 1976 it found itself in the uncomfortable position of having to plan a new generation of replacement satellites[42] in the face of uncertain demand. At this point the telephone companies sallied forth once more in a renewed bid for total control. TCTS informed Telesat that if the satellite company did not join the telephone consortium as a full-fledged member, 'it would be very unlikely that TCTS would use the satellite service at all in the future.'[43]

Telesat was definitely in a bind, its largest customers threatening to jump ship, its existing capacity scheduled to disappear within a few years, and facing the immediate need to order equipment to maintain capacity for the future. Evidently deeming discretion the better part of valour, it fled into the open arms of TCTS. And what a sweetheart of a deal it was! Not only was Telesat to become a full-fledged member of TCTS, but more important the telcos promised to *guarantee* Telesat a high return on investment, whether its satellites were ever used or not.[44]

Of course there was a hitch. First, Telesat was to lose control over earth stations. Although it could continue *owning* them, it was no longer to *operate* them; nor to determine where they would be located; or to maintain support equipment. The telephone companies would look after all those details. Second, Telesat was now to be *officially* designated a 'carriers' carrier.' No longer could it lease directly to CBC or other non-carriers that might conceivably take a full TV channel for five years.

Although this marriage of convenience was endorsed with amazing alacrity by the Department of Communications (the Canadian government being a principal shareholder in the floundering enterprise), the CRTC obstinately insisted that a hearing be held, whereby the commission put itself in the unenviable position of having to pass judgment on an application already approved by cabinet. The ensuing decision was remarkable indeed, for the commission rejected the cabinet-approved agreement, declaring it contrary to the public interest.[45]

How embarassing! It did not take long for communications minister, Jeanne Sauvé, to annul the decision through order-in-council, her five-page press release declaring: 'The range of factors affecting these policy issues is far wider than that which the CRTC could reasonably have expected to consider. Many of these issues lie well beyond the purview of the Commission.'[46]

Thereafter crippled by an inability to market circuits and facing a clientele that did not really want to use satellites anyway, Telesat continued experiencing underutilization – so much so that in 1984, long before launch date, it even tried foisting off for $80 million one of its three projected Anik 'c' satellites on a third-world country[47] (but was unable to find a taker).[48] Again in 1987, Telesat began negotiating a sale – to a company controlled by the controversial arms dealer Adnan Khashoggi of Saudi Arabia, who had played the role of middleman in the White House–run scheme to trade u.s. arms to Iran for hostages in Lebanon, diverting profits to contra rebels in Nicaragua.[49]

But the telephone companies of Canada were pleased. They had won round two.

THE BATTLE CONTINUES

Since 1977, however, albeit cautiously and reluctantly, the federal government has edged in the direction of easing the restrictions that confined Telesat's independence and limited the uses made of satellite circuits. In 1979, for example, the Department of Communications announced that television stations and cable companies could begin owning receive-only ground stations (TVROS), even positioning them where they wished,[50] a liberalization extended subsequently to households.

Then in 1981 the CRTC, rashly flexing its regulatory muscles once again in contravention of Department of Communications' protective policy, ordered Telesat to open up its customer base to all potential clients and no longer to refuse leasing partial channels. Although the new communications minister, Francis Fox, like Madame Sauvé before him, threw out the CRTC's decision by order-in-council, none the less he agreed that broadcasters henceforth should be admitted into Telesat's select circle of clients and that 'approved' common carriers could henceforth lease partial channels.[51]

Again in 1984, in a decision for once not overturned by DOC, the CRTC ruled that Telesat must permit licensed broadcasting undertakings to resell excess capacity to other such undertakings for broadcasting purposes; [52] and in 1985 the commission opened the door for capacity resale by other carriers under its jurisdiction, so long as the capacity was not used for long-distance voice communication.[53]

And finally, in May 1986, a revised connecting agreement between Telesat and Telecom Canada was approved by the commission, whereby Telesat's customer base is no longer to be restricted to broadcasting undertakings and specified common carriers. Furthermore, subsidies from Telecom Canada to Telesat were no longer to exceed $20 million per year and were to stop entirely on 1 January 1988. Moreover, Telecom Canada guaranteed to lease at least four TV channels from Telesat until 31 December 1998, at a cost of more than $100 million,[54] business volume sufficient for Telesat to sign a contract with Arianespace (the consortium of European companies and banks that manages production of expendable launch vehicles developed by the European Space Agency) to hoist two more satellites in 1990, Anik 'E1' and 'E2,' at a total cost of about $300 million.[55] We might conclude with Jean McNulty that the new connecting agreement with Telecom Canada means that Telesat in the future will be less reliant upon the telephone industry as its primary user;[56] none the less, the terrestrial carriers continue owning 50 per cent of Telesat's shares.

And the amazing saga of satellite communications in Canada continues to unfold.

19

Electronic Publishing

If simultaneously funding and restricting satellite communication has been the number one priority of the Department of Communications over the years, promoting Telidon, has surely been the number two. Invented at the department's Communications Research Centre in the late 1970s, Telidon is at once an electronic device and a service.[1] Like Prestel in Great Britain and Teletel in France, Telidon is a means of digitally encoding/decoding graphic information in electronic transmission.[2]

Invention of Telidon in 1978 was heralded by the Department of Communications as a major Canadian breakthrough, and the annual report for that year waxed enthusiastic: 'Telidon, the world's most sophisticated videotex system, was introduced in August 1978, giving Canada a lead in what promises to be a major growth area in home and business communications in the 1980's and beyond.'[3]

In keeping with this euphoria the government announced in April 1979 a $9-million, four-year program to help industry set up field trials to refine Telidon's technical performance.[4] Then, in February 1981, acceptance by the public falling somewhat short of expectations, the department allocated Telidon a further $27.5 million 'to ensure the existence of a commercially viable videotex industry in Canada with a capability to compete in export markets.'[5]

In 1982–3 the department apportioned Telidon a further $23 million, 'to help the private sector develop the skills and resources to operate and market commercially viable videotex service.'[6] Whereas the department had optimistically predicted that 40,000 terminals would by that time be installed, in fact fewer than 5000 were then in operation;[7] hence, the 'need' for further cash transfusions.

Private industry too was inveigled into investing heavily in Telidon. Between 1979 and 1982 an estimated $130 million was spent by private sources, encouraged by the department.

By 1983, however, even the department's consultants were growing wary: 'While over $100 million has been invested in various Telidon programs to date, it would seem that successful and substantial revenues are not anticipated for at least another three to five years. It is likely that a five to ten year perspective is more realistic for achievement of the level of return most companies are expecting in order to support commercial ventures.'[8]

For 1984–5 the department parsimoniously limited its Telidon contributions to $7.5 million, tipping off seven years of governmental funding at about $80 million.[9] By this time fewer than one thousand homes had Telidon equipment.

'I don't think it has developed as fast as some people had hoped,' concluded departmental spokesman Colin Franklin sadly, 'but it's been developed.'[11]

CLOSING THE CIRCLE

In August 1985 experts from across the land gathered on the balmy shores of Point Grey, University of British Columbia, certainly to admire panoramic vistas but as well to attend this country's first conference on electronic publishing. Something of a milestone, the conference assembled in one large room educators, magazine and book publishers, cable and telecommunications industry exectutives, data base publishers, and government officials[12] to mull over an emerging field. Brain-child of David Godfrey, professor of creative writing at the University of Victoria and widely renowned for informed speculation on the future of publishing,[13] the conference confirmed Godfrey's main thesis at least, that many insiders perceived important changes to be taking place.

Of course, application of electronic telecommunications to publishing is not something new to the 1980s. As we have seen, for more than 140 years newspapers relied on telecommunications to gather news into editorial offices. What does distinguish this 'second era of electronic publishing,' rather, is the increasing use of telecommunications for distributing final editorial copy from publishing centres to widely dispersed printing plants and even to home video-display terminals.

Among North American newspapers the *Wall Street Journal* was pioneer. By the late 1970s it was 'broadcasting' text via satellite to printing plants around the globe where additional, more regionally focused material could be inserted before producing printed editions.[14] In Canada *The Globe and Mail* was first to mimic the procedure.[15]

Encoding text for diffusion by satellite ushered in a second innovation: the electronic storage of news stories in a computer, which makes them available for instant retrieval over telephone lines. In Canada *Info Globe* is a fine example. Computerizing news stories, Anthony Smith has told us, changes the role and importance of newspapers: 'The newspaper's computer contains what amounts to a mediated and filtered social memory of the affairs of an entire community ... In the past the newspaper ... regarded itself as a rapidly-made, throwaway product ... [but now] if it categorizes the material it has accumulated and then transfers the information into a computer, the newspaper creates a new asset which can be re-sold and re-used.'[16]

Simultaneous with electronic encoding and categorizing of news for storage and transmission has been a proliferation of computer terminals in newsrooms, thereby transforming editorial processes as well. The editor's function, Smith continues, increasingly becomes a kind of 'instant librarianship,' whereby 'research and writing become the input of a collectivized process of text-selection and text-manipulation.'[17] And David Godfrey adds that authors 'will drift back into anonymity; librarians will gain vast new powers and respect.'[18]

There is yet a third distinguishing characteristic of the modern era of electronic publishing, a commingling or reconvergence of carriage and content: the telecommunications carriers are increasingly making forays into text construction, editing, and storage. For present purposes, this trend is the most pertinent of the three.

TELEPHONE INCURSIONS

Telephone companies such as Bell Canada are entering the publishing business in three ways: first, by acquiring and owning publishing houses; second, by provisioning 'enhanced' telecommunications services; and third, by themselves assembling and maintaining data bases.

Owning Publishing Houses
In its annual report for 1984 Bell Canada Enterprises (now simply BCE) announced that its wholly owned subsidiary, Tele-Direct (Canada) Inc., had become one of North America's largest printers. Directly involved in sales of Yellow Pages' advertising in the United States and Australia, Tele-Direct (Canada) Inc. in 1984 controlled also a host of publishing and printing subsidiaries, including: Comac Communications Inc., Canada's largest publisher of controlled circulation magazines (*Homemaker's, City Woman, Western Living, Quest*); Ronalds-Federated, employing 4600 people in twenty-five plants in Canada and the United States for its printing, packaging, and custom cheque activities; and British American Bank Note Company Inc., engaged in the printing of securities (banknotes, bonds, treasury bills, postage stamps, lottery tickets, credit cards, travellers' cheques, and bank forms). In 1984 Tele-Direct (Canada) Inc. rang up $417 million in sales.[19]

In 1985 BCE's main publishing/printing arm changed its name to BCE Publi-Tech Inc. Revenues sky-rocketed to $602.3 million, despite the sale of Comac. Acquisitions during the year included Great Lakes Press Corp. and an electronic publisher in the United Kingdom.[20] By 1987 BCE Publi-Tech, controlling thirty-one subsidiaries, was Canada's biggest printing conglomerate. In June 1988 BCE announced acquisition of 21 per cent of Quebecor Inc., publisher of daily and weekly newspapers in Quebec. In exchange, Quebecor was to acquire from BCE Ronalds Printing and certain operations of British American Bank Note Company.[21]

Enhanced Service
Not only are telecommunications carriers engaging indirectly in publishing and printing through affiliates and subsidiaries, they are also directly providing publishing ('enhanced') services such as 'iNet 2000,' 'Envoy 100,' and 'Dialcom,' the first two being Telecom Canada offerings, the latter from CNCP. For such 'enhanced' services the carriers perform computer applications onto messages originated by others. In the case of 'Envoy 100,' messages are stored and forwarded using electronic-switching equipment located on the carriers' premises. In the case of 'iNet 2000,' the telcos provide both an electronic directory and a text-messaging service whereby customers may access a national electronic directory that lists information and services available from

'Information Service Providers;' customers may also exchange information among themselves.[22]

'Enhanced' services such as these constitute publishing in the sense that telecommunications carriers are engaged in the identification, storage, and/or extraction of data or text, as opposed to mere transmission. In the case of 'iNet 2000,' Bell and other Telecom Canada members provide 'gateways' to 1300 or more data bases maintained by others.

Assembling and Controlling Data Bases
Although 'Envoy 100' and 'iNet 2000' are electronic publishing services based loosely on the common carrier model, the telephone company itself not controlling in an editorial sense the contents of the data banks, that role is likely to expand. Particularly controversial is the possibility of a widely diffused electronic Yellow Pages. Telephone directories are out-of-date the day they are printed. It makes sense, therefore, to have an electronic telephone directory, always current, to replace printed versions. Telephone connections to video-display terminals in each home would make such directories possible. In France the government-owned telephone company has had a program in effect for a number of years whereby printed directories are being phased out and replaced by small computer terminals plugged into standard telephone outlets; the French terminal has been dubbed 'Minitel.' Not only can telephone listings be updated continuously with 'Minitel,' so can directory advertising. The North American newspaper industry has not been entirely oblivious to this possibility because electronic Yellow Pages means direct competition for classified ads and, more than likely, display ads as well. It is in this light that one should interpret Bell Canada's testing of four thousand 'ALEX' terminals in Montreal, beginning September 1988. 'ALEX,' a neologism in honour of the telephone industry's patriarch, is similar to 'Minitel' but uses a resurrected Telidon graphics, deemed much superior for display advertising.[23]

In the future, therefore, publishers may on the one hand rely increasingly on telecommunications carriers for gathering and diffusing information and on the other find themselves competing head-on with these same telephone companies in the publishing and display/classified advertising businesses. Problems seemingly alleviated forever by CP's withdrawal from the news gathering field may soon be evident again.

Transactions
Although videotex techniques like Telidon were initially hyped primarily as electronic publishing and information retrieval services, such are not their only capabilities. Increasingly they are now being viewed and marketed as 'transactional' media, integrating thereby the fields of retailing, banking, marketing, and consumer research.

Currently teleshopping is available in Canada through a specialty cable channel devoted exclusively to advertising. Using videotex instead of INWATS (1-800 telephone numbers) could further automate the ordering of goods from the home. Likewise, automated tellers, currently popular with consumers, could presage videotex terminals in the home to increase further the convenience and pervasiveness of electronic banking. Finally, since all transactions via videotex are in the digital mode, permanent computer-based profiles of individuals and households may prove invaluable to marketeers. We are entering, writes Kevin Wilson, a new era of 'cybernetic consumerism':

Every transaction which is executed, and every page of information or service which is delivered, will generate its own electronic (machine-readable) record ... This information will include the consumer's identity, the time and place of consumption (demographics), and product characteristics. This data, combined with other information, will generate an invaluable portrait of consumer activity for marketing purposes. These systems will create a truly cybernetic cycle of production and consumption, because every consumptive activity will generate information pertinent to the modification of future production.[24]

By all accounts the telephone industry intends to participate in the generation and sale of such transactional information; note, for example, BCE's acquisition of Montreal Trust Company and its forays into videotex. Hence, we come to the closing of the circle.

RECAPITULATION

Telegraph and telephone companies began reconverging in the 1930s as the two carrier industries started competing head-on in private lines. By the 1970s the competition embraced data, and in the 1980s long-distance voice had become the subject of contention, in regulatory proceedings at least.

Meanwhile, broadcasting has been reconverging with telecommunications through such hybrid media as cable TV and satellites. Today it seems reconvergence is so complete that concerns over Canada's position in international high-tech may have quite superseded the cultural questions historically moulding broadcasting policy.[25]

The rise of electronic publishing is now reconverging telecommunications with the daily press, encyclopedias, newsletters, and other types of text-centred activities. Telephone companies are selling computer 'space' to text originators and assuming the function of editors (middlemen between authors and reader). They may also undertake trials to try their hand at display advertising. In addition, publishing's convergence with broadcasting is not to be ruled out either, owing to teletext (transmission of alpha-numeric text via broadcasting transmitters).

It is tempting but misleading to attribute these reconvergences to 'Technology.' Although it is true that these various markets and services are increasingly using common and substitutable transmission paths, it is also a fact that the industries initially were highly integrated and their segregation came about only as a result of collusive deals and/or government policy, more generally the former; the equipment utilized demanded no such segregation.

If, however, segregation of content and carriage, irrespective of origins, is deemed desirable for the future, a position articulated forcefully by the Clyne Committee,[26] then it is government alone that can re-establish demarcations. After all, it is only within the legal framework of relative rights and obligations that economic insititutions become structured and economic activity takes place.[27]

We look briefly at present policy.

In 1984 and 1985 the CRTC ruled that Bell Canada's entry into the field of 'enhanced' services should be governed by several principles. First, Bell Canada may *not* exercise editorial control over content, nor may it create or distribute its own data bases, apart from electronic telephone directories and data bases for billing. Second, Bell *is*, however, permitted to offer store and forward services and electronic messaging, even though some non-editorial control is exercised over the information. Finally, the CRTC has initiated an inquiry into whether 'enhanced' services should be provided through a corporate entity separate from the telephone company.[28] Meanwhile, the Bell reorganization has permitted the parent firm, BCE, to engage in any and all publishing activities, electronic and otherwise, of its own choosing.

PART V
Conclusion

20

Political Economy

For introduction this book required two chapters – one to adumbrate certain mythic doctrines enveloping Canadian telecommunications, and a second, to describe current industry structure. Likewise for conclusion, two chapters again are called for. The present chapter recapitulates Canadian telecommunications policy issues in the context of historical development (political economy). The final chapter probes the existential meaning of communications 'technology' and the 'information revolution.'

MONOPOLY AND COMPETITION

For decades prior to the 1970s, telephony was regarded as a 'natural monopoly.' Grounded on a triumvirate of assumptions – *efficiency* through economies of scale, *systemic integrity* through end-to-end control, *service universality* through cost-averaging and cross-subsidization – monopoly in telecommunications was not merely entrenched, but seemed desirable too. Consequently, the policy debates, brief though they were, centred narrowly on how best to control this monolithic enterprise: whether through public ownership or through regulation of private enterprises.

Beginning in the mid-1970s, however, and lasting for a decade or so, the doctrine of 'natural monopoly' went into a seemingly irreversible decline. As in other countries, monopoly in Canada was opened up to competition in selective markets. Terminals, once the exclusive domain of telephone companies, were a major case in point (chapter

12). Likewise, restrictions on cable television, hitherto imposed unilaterally by the telephone industry, were eased through regulatory policy (chapter 17). Finally, competition in long-distance transmission (particularly data communications) was permitted and encouraged by the government through enforced albeit limited interconnections (chapter 11).

But old myths die hard, and just when it seemed the doctrine of natural monopoly was on its last legs it was suddenly revivified by the CRTC, which in 1985 forbade competitive entry to long-distance voice. More recently officials in the Department of Communications were predicting the disappearance of the independent cable television industry, to take place when ISDN (integrated services digital network) becomes operational.[1] In January 1988, the federal DOC even announced that severe tests of public convenience and necessity would have to be met before entry into telecommunications carriage would be permitted. DOC stated such entry normally would result in unnecessary duplication of costly facilities, threats to socially desirable cross-subsidies, and service disruptions resulting from the failure of new entrants.[2] None the less, as this book went to press, it was not clear that DOC had permanently shut the door on competition. Communications Minister Marcel Masse in the spring of 1989 announced he would consider allowing wide-open competition between cable TV companies and telephone companies in their hitherto monopolized markets,[3] making opportune a reconsideration of the doctrine of natural monopoly in Canadian telecommunications.

To anyone with a sense of history, the doctrine of natural monopoly in telecommunications should prove troublesome. After all, have not governmental awards of privilege (patents, charters, franchises, subsidies) had at least some role in establishing and maintaining monopoly? And did not a well-honed panoply of restrictive and frequently predatory business practices, astutely wielded by dominant telcos on tiny competitors, also help? Non-compensatory pricing, interconnection restrictions, acquisitions, legal battles, restrictive reciprocity agreements, collusive market divisions, intimidation, deception, lobbying, and public relations all are prime examples.

Apart from these historical considerations, the three pillars supporting the doctrine of natural monopoly can and should be viewed much more circumspectly than they have in fact been. Economies of scale, for example, repeatedly asserted, have been but seldom tested. It is interesting to note, however, that when in the 1970s analysts did begin probing economies of firm size and long distance transmission through empirical methods, they were scarcely visible to many. Meanwhile, the carriers are multiplying capacity many times through fibre optics, an attempt perhaps to turn illusion into fact.[4]

Systemic integrity through end-to-end control, the second girder of natural monopoly, has finally been laid to rest thanks to the fully satisfactory experience with terminal attachments. The same cannot be said, however, about service universality through system-wide cost-averaging and service cross-subsidization. That particular doctrine is now being articulated with renewed vigour and may well again win the day. Hence, a brief review is called for.

1. The independent telephone industry was spawned in the first place because the dominant company was reluctant to extend service to non-lucrative areas through cost-averaging and cross-subsidization. Likewise, the prairie provinces took over telephone operations in this century's first decade to alleviate nonfeasance by the dominant company. Service universality in Canada, then, came about *through*, not despite, rivalry in telecommunications, as well as through public ownership.

2. Analogous has been more recent experience concerning telephone service in the North. Bell Canada has required, and received, direct government subsidy to extend and upgrade service in its territory in the eastern Arctic.

3. Substantial evidence indicates that, through revenues generated in monopolized markets, the dominant firm historically has cross-subsidized markets infiltrated by competition. It is also to be emphasized that Bell itself has proposed eroding service universality by doubling local rates with the stated purpose of dissuading competitive entry into long distance.[5]

4. Although regulated since 1906, Bell Canada has spawned a corporate empire spanning the globe whose activities encompass a diverse array of activities ranging from pipelines to publishing. Indeed BCE today stands as Canada's most profitable corporation. Credulity is stretched beyond limits to contend that telephone subscribers in Ontario and Quebec have not helped foot the bill as unwitting and involuntary underwriters for this global corporate expansion.

5. Bell Canada and BC Telephone Company, Canada's largest and most profitable telecommunications carriers, are also among the least efficient. Studies by Bell and Alberta Government Telephones indicate that AGT's productivity gains were twice those of Bell between 1967

and 1975. Denny, de Fontenay, and Werner likewise have concluded that between 1967 and 1979 Bell and BC Tel remained stagnant respecting productivity while AGT made major gains. The present author arrived at similar conclusions.

It is in this context that we should consider current proposals for rate rebalancing and massive capital investments to inaugurate ISDN.

Telephone companies are currently deploying prodigious funds to construct a fibre optical ISDN whose capacity will be *ten thousand* times that of analogue copper wire. Given the enormous band width expected to ensue, the Department of Communications has contended that it will be possible, for example, to plug a television set, a burglar alarm, a computer and a telephone into the same socket and obtain service.[6] The department continues: 'All parts of the network – telephone transmission systems, computers, switches, and television sets – are merging into a *single unified machine*. The faster this development takes place in any particular country, the better its infrastructure will be, and the better it will be able to compete.'[7]

What DOC fails to address, of course, and which we with Nicholas Garnham must ask, is this: 'How is such a massive and socially strategic monopoly to be controlled?'[8]

Given the rather unsavoury history of predatory and restrictive business practices discolouring telecommunications for so long, is one not justified in speculating that telephone companies may be funding this investment primarily to remonopolize urban telecommunications? Is it entirely coincidental that Canada, which is said to be moving to full digitization of the national communications network [a prerequisite for ISDN] faster than any other industrialized country,[9] is also the most highly cabled country in the world, with penetration at about 66 per cent of households?

Once fibre optical ISDN is in place, 'natural monopoly' for urban communications will undoubtedly be asserted once again. Indeed, prospectively, the claim is already being made, for with ten times the capacity of coaxial cable and ten thousand times that of analogue copper pair wire, fibre optical ISDN will entail very low (short-run) incremental costs for transmitting additional messages. (Meanwhile, it most assuredly will entail very high access charges because the fixed investment is quite astronomical; hence, one cause for 'rate rebalancing' at this time.)

Fortunately, for the present, we are still able to view ISDN from this side of 'natural monopoly.' On the one hand we see cable systems not merely existing but prospering. On the other we see telephone companies mounting pressures to double local rates and deploying investment funds to expand local capacity in a massive way. From today's perspective, then, ISDN is merely one more engineering arte-fact, wielded by corporate strategists in a never-ending struggle for dominance in Canadian telecommunications.

CONVERGENCE

Today it is common to speak of convergence among hitherto separate communication activities. The integration of computers with tele-communications is one example of the crumbling of barriers that previously separated industries. As de Sola Pool has noted, IBM and AT&T, which once thought themselves giants of different industries, now compete; each can provide customers with the means of sending, storing, organizing and manipulating messages in text or voice.[10]

Another dimension of convergence is satellites, which decouple cost and distance on the one hand and, on the other substitute radiations over vast geographic expanse for guided transmission pathways. According to Simon Nora and Alain Minc, satellites offer the advan-tages of power, universality, accessibility and scope, making likely the gradual creation of worldwide 'telematics' [computer communica-tions] networks.[11] With many forms of electronic communications transformed into the digital mode, text, video, audio, and data will increasingly be broadcast via satellites.

A third trend, exacerbated particularly by fibre optics, is the expan-sion of transmission capacity in relation to information production. But as Nicholas Garnham again so perceptively has noted, expanded distribution capacity undermines domestic culture.[12] The pressure in Europe and in Canada alike has been to relax quotas on domestically produced material, remove restrictions on the importation of foreign (U.S.) programming, and generally increase reliance on advertising to fund television production. New devices, in other words, have been undermining nationally based communication and programming policies. This too is a convergence, of a sort, between media and messages.

Once again Canada's policy analysts and commentators are prone to describe such developments as 'natural,' as being 'technologically determined.' Again our Department of Communications leads the way:

These technological developments are blurring the boundaries that previously separated these different companies ...

The various networks are *now* able to handle traffic that was previously the monopoly preserve of others. So, for example, the telephone companies can carry telex record messages that were historically the exclusive preserve of the telegraph companies. For their part, the telegraph companies *now* have the ability to carry long-distance voice messages. The same has occurred between satellite and terrestrial services. Telesat – like CNCP – can offer long-distance voice, data and record message services in competition with both the telephone companies and CNCP.[13]

How unaware our policy-makers are of the historical record![14] As we have seen, transmission and text manipulation were highly integrated at the onset of electronic communications and remained so for seventy years as telegraph operators (analogues of today's digital computers) dispatched their own news stories. Similarly, telegraph companies, their facilities and services alike, were integrated with telephony upon the latter's inception; the same was true of broadcasting and telegraphy/telephony. The initial integration was definitely not technologically determined, nor was the subsequent divergence. In all these cases, divergence was the result of policy, whether governmental or corporate.

Certainly today's new technologies make possible the convergence noted by so many; but then so did the old devices. The old equipment required neither integration nor segregation; neither does the new.

What is at issue today, rather, is the underlying motivation of both corporate powerplayers and governments' response. Financial capital is still being deployed and industrial artefacts are still being introduced and wielded within a political/economic/legal context.

This brings us to the heart of the matter: the role of government in structuring and restructuring industries, in propping up and dismantling monopolies, in allowing activites to converge or encouraging them to diverge. In all these roles government is not, nor can it be, neutral. Of necessity government is present as an active participant, whether explicitly enacting policies to change industrial structures and trajectories or implicitly supporting current trends by refusing to alter the ground rules.[15]

Indeed government is in the business of awarding and withdrawing rights and freedoms, of imposing and relaxing duties and obligations. One might say this is its principal duty – setting the framework within which citizens and economic players interact – and thus government is not, nor can it be, neutral. Rights and privileges can and do collide, and government arbitrates. Bell Canada, for example, is allowed by the government to possess a monopoly, causing freedom of enterprise for others to be reduced. Eroding that monopoly by opening up possibilities for competition takes privileges away from Bell, but to the benefit of entrants. Likewise, since Bell's rates are regulated, the company's freedom (i.e. to set price) is circumscribed, but freedom for others (i.e. freedom from monopoly pricing) is enhanced. Rate rebalancing unquestionably will redistribute rights and freedoms among the telephone company, its competitors, and its customers; indeed customers will experience differential gains and losses – businesses and affluent householders will benefit at the expense of the poor. To summarize, there is yet to be a law passed or a regulation enacted that does not *simultaneously* enlarge relative rights for some while eroding relative rights for others.

DEREGULATION

The term 'deregulation,' then, is a misnomer, a myth. To be accurate, one should speak only of 'reregulation.' This latter term affords proper emphasis to government's role of apportioning and reapportioning relative rights and freedoms among contending interests. Reregulation highlights rather than obscures the central policy questions of who gains, who loses, and how the results are decided.

In our day the Canadian government is indeed obscuring its roles of apportioning privilege, structuring markets, aiding monopoly and converging industries. It is doing so by invoking the doctrines of technological imperative and technological determinism. 'Technology,' it is said, does all these things, and government's role is primarily to facilitate and sponsor transition to an information economy.

We can speculate on reasons why government expresses such a modest view of its function, and some thoughts on this topic are in fact entertained in the final chapter. But the essential point for now is that the area of telecommunications is today in transition.[16] Corporate powerplayers wielding new devices are attempting to firm up and re-establish monopoly in both long-distance transmission and intra-urban communications, even as others essay entry. The threat exists that, as previously separate information industries are 'converged,' monopoly's embrace will come to include a much wider range of activity than heretofore. The Canadian government needs to stop ringing its collective hands and muttering 'information revolution' and must instead acknowledge the active role it is playing in abetting these developments.

21

An Information Revolution?

If the 'information revolution' may be said to have had a father, surely it would be the late Fritz Machlup, formerly economics professor at Princeton. Machlup's 1962 book, *The Production and Distribution of Knowledge in the United States*, was the inaugural attempt to identify and explore the pervasive importance for the u.s. economy of information and knowledge production. That seminal work inspired two burgeoning literatures, most directly one on the information economy but another on the information society. The latter incorporates social, cultural, and political analyses and forecasts deemed attributable to the perceived exponential growth in information-related activity. Together these two literatures, one on economy and one on society, make up the conceptual underpinnning of the 'information revolution.'

It was Machlup's contention that in the United States since 1900 there has been a gradual but distinct shift in the occupational composition of the labour force, entailing 'a continuous increase in "knowledge producing" workers and a relative decline in what used to be called "productive labor."'[1]

Cumulatively these gradual shifts have been dramatic. By 1958, according to Machlup, the 'knowledge industry' accounted for roughly 29 per cent of u.s. gross national product.

Fifteen years later a monumental study encompassing nine volumes was completed under the auspices of the u.s. Department of Commerce. Attempting to quantify again the economic importance of information-related activity,[2] *The Information Economy* declared that the information sector in 1967 accounted for more than 46 per cent of u.s. GNP. Marc Porat, one of the principal authors, estimated information workers to have increased from 13 per cent of the u.s. labour force in 1900 to 25 per cent in 1940 and 46 per cent in 1974.[3] Hence, he summarized, 'we are now an information economy.'[4] Shortly thereafter Shirley Serafini and Michel Andrieu of our federal Department of Communications applied Porat's methodology to Canadian data, reporting that information workers had increased from 29 to 40 per cent of the Canadian labour force between 1951 and 1972, a trend generally replicated, according to the authors in all other developed economies. Most recently the federal DOC has informed us that information workers comprised 45 per cent of Canadian employment in 1986.[5]

While Machlup and Porat, at least initially, concentrated on economic aspects of the information revolution, it is to sociology professor Daniel Bell of Harvard that credit or responsibility must be granted for extending the revolution to culture and society. For Bell, history is composed of 'threes': three distinct infrastructures (transportation; electrification; and now, computer communications), three principal epochs (pre-industrial, based on agriculture and mining; industrial, or manufacturing; and now, post-industrial, that is, information-based), and three transforming resources (first, natural power; next, created energy; and now, information).[6] In other words Bell, like other post-industrial prophets, hypothesized a new centrality for information-related activities; and this centrality, he believes, represents a fundamental break with the industrial past.

TECHNIQUES

Although electronic techniques and devices for communicating are about 150 years old, the literature of the 'information revolution' emphasizes engineering developments since World War II – especially calling attention to dramatic increases in capacity, speed, and ubiquity and to equally dramatic reductions in cost and size. In this regard analogies and metaphors are both copious and imaginative. Alexander King, for example, has remarked that in three decades a whole roomful of vacuum tubes and other components has been reduced to the size of a cornflake.[7] Likewise, Christopher Evans compared developments in computing to a make-believe world of automobiles, writing:

Suppose for a moment that the automobile industry had developed at the same rate as computers and over the same period [about thirty years]: how much cheaper and more efficient would the current models be? If you have not already heard the analogy, the answer is shattering. Today you would be able to buy a Rolls Royce for £1.35; it would do three million miles to the gallon, and it would deliver enough power to drive the *Queen Elizabeth II*. And if you were interested in miniaturization, you could place half a dozen of them on a pinhead.[8]

Developments in computing have been paralleled by advances in transmission. Coaxial cable and now fibre optical cable have multiplied transmission capacity of the telephone network's original transmission medium (copper pair wire) by several hundreds of thousands, while satellites provide yet a further illustration: in 1965 the annual cost per telephone circuit on satellites was $22,000; in 1980, $800; and in 1985, $30.[9] During the past twenty years telecommunications costs, conceived broadly for all transmission media, have declined by 11 per cent per annum.[10]

Considered separately innovations in both computing and transmission have been impressive enough. Of still greater significance, however, has been the integration of these two industrial arts into 'telematics' or 'computer/communications.' On the one hand dramatic reductions in cost and size have allowed computing power to be distributed throughout telecommunications networks (distributed processing). On the other, telecommunications networks are being digitized – made capable of transmitting information in the same machine-readable form used in computing. Now any human-readable information (pictures, text, voice, data) can be coded into on/off bursts of energy, permitting texts to be instantaneously acted upon by computers (delayed or stored, edited, corrected, processed, combined in new ways) – even while in transit – prior to being retranslated at their destination into human-readable language (if in fact such retranslation takes place at all).[12]

POWER

Such devlopments bring us much closer to the essence of the information revolution. In describing the integration of computers and telecommunications, former communications minister Francis Fox noted sagely:

The important thing about information technology is not so much that it uses and processes information – which it does in abundance – but that it is fundamentally a *control* technology. This has led to a confusion about the nature of its impact, with much effort focused on the emergence of 'information economies', 'information societies', and such like. But in fact information stands in relation to the *the real agent of technological change* in much the same way as smoke to fire or dust to a sandstorm: it is an index, or superficial manifestation, of a deeper phenomenon. If we are to understand the nature of the new information technologies, it is necessary to focus less on their content and more on their function (i.e. regulation – in the cybernetic sense of the term – of systems, or in other words *control*).[12]

The 'revolution,' then, in the view of Francis Fox (albeit in an isolated and atypical extract), concerns the rapid development and application of new and increasingly powerful techniques of control and is to be contrasted with the Machlup-Bell-Porat paradigm that merely emphasizes an exponential growth in information-related activity in an idealized or depoliticized world. Mr Fox's statement invites us to reconsider communication devices in the real world of power struggle and powerplay. Such has been a purpose of this present book.

Unfortunately, much of the literature on the information revolution addresses what is happening and projects what will happen in an idealized world, far removed from the nitty-gritty of actual institutions, rivalries, corporate and governmental powerplays, greed, propaganda, and public relations. In the idealized world of the policy-maker and futurologist, engineered devices are mythologized as 'technology' and human agents become transformed into mere spectators, moulded by an ineluctably evolving technical environment. Re-establishing technology as industrial art, purposively deployed, is especially important today when persistent claims are made that Canada is being drawn inexorably into an information society and that Canadians must adapt meekly to the ensuing changes.

THE MYTH OF THE MACHINE

New Technologies, Old Idolatries
As may be readily apparent, the literature on the information revolution often encourages readers to stand in awe of 'new technologies.' Humanity in awe of its artefacts is nothing new to the information revolution, of course. Isaiah, for example, berated his countrymen for

worshipping the 'works of their hands, [bowing down] to what their own fingers have made.' He continued, 'So man is humbled and men are brought low.'[13]

And so it is in our day. Much of the literature on the information revolution attributes to information-related artefacts both inevitability and omnipotence in effects. In particular, two interrelated doctrines (or myths) are frequently propagated: technological determinism and the technological imperative. The former posits all important human phenomena to be attributable to or explainable by 'technology.' The later postulates 'technology' to be autonomous, having a 'life,' growth, and development of 'its' own; it is dependent perhaps on human agents for support but, in a more profound sense, is inevitable.[14]

Ubiquity

Mythologizing 'technology' is not limited to science fiction. Rather, the proclivity to mythologize can be detected in both non-fiction/ academic literatures on the 'information revolution' and government policy pronouncements. This section samples the former literatures to help establish ubiquity; extracts from Canadian policy documents have been presented in the introductory chapter and interspersed throughout the text.

Perhaps the most widely read exponent of an 'information revolution' has been Alvin Toffler, who developed the metaphor of the wave to describe (not explain) rapid innovation in the areas of electronics and computers, the space industry, oceanics, and biotechnology. Toffler's metaphor was intended not only to imply simultaneity of innovation across seemingly diverse fields but to connote the all-inclusive and unavoidable nature of the consequences. He wrote:

A powerful tide is surging across much of the world today, creating a new, often bizarre, environment in which to work, play, marry, raise children, or retire. In this bewildering context, businessmen swim against highly erratic economic currents; politicians see their ratings bob wildly up and down; universities, hospitals, and other institutions battle desperately against inflation. Value systems splinter and crash, while lifeboats of family, church and state are hurled madly about ... [However] many of today's changes are not independent of one another. Nor are they random ... They are, in fact, parts of a much larger phenomenon: the death of industrialism and the rise of a new civilization....

The grand metaphor of this work, as should already be apparent, is that of colliding waves of change.[15]

Throughout Toffler's book there are allusions to the inexorability of this 'third wave,' which transforms everything in sight. Nothing remains untouched, nor can anything stand in 'its' wake. This 'change,' while systematic and all-inclusive, 'itself' remains unexplained, is evidently uncaused, and is therefore unexplainable.

In like fashion, Daniel Bell pronounces:

'With the revolution in communications, all ... will change.'[16]

Why? Because information-related 'technologies' are pictured as proliferating (exponentially). Information is seen as growing in volume (again, exponentially); occurrences are deemd to be quite natural, evidently part of the 'order of things' – (despite Bell's conviction that traumatic cultural, social, and psychological consequences may result from our 'transition' to post-industrial society).

Marc Porat, too, after completing his quantitative studies on the information economy, succumbed to mythic explanations for an information revolution, maintaining 'technology' to be 'the big wheel that drives all the little wheels.' 'Little wheels' to Porat include economy, ideology, society, culture, and polity.[17] Even more unfortunately, from our perspective, Porat's conjecturing has been embraced uncritically by some Canadian policy analysts and academics pontificating on policy issues.[18]

An imaginative and possibly powerful twist to themes of technological omnipotence and inexorability was invented by Arthur C. Clarke, who merged the two mythologies of 'technology' and 'evolution.' 'Technological evolution,' Clarke rapturously announced, is transforming, if not utterly obliterating, humanity. He asks:

Can the synthesis of men and machine ever be stable, or will the purely organic component become such a hindrance [to whom?] that it *has* to be discarded? If this eventually happens – and I have ... good reasons for thinking that it *must* – we have nothing to regret and certainly nothing to fear. The Tool [his capital] we have invented is our successor. Biological evolution *has given way* to a far more rapid process – technological evolution ... No individual exists forever; why should we expect our species to be immortal?

Man, said Nietzsche, is a rope stretched across the abyss. That will be a noble purpose to have served.[20]

Clarke's theme was taken up, albeit in moderation, by Christopher Evans a decade and a half later. Reminiscent of Isaiah's countrymen Evans evidently deems human artefacts to be superior to their creators:

During the 1990's computers will increasingly serve as intellectual and emotional partners. We are about to embark on a massive programme to develop highly intelligent machines, a process by which we will lead computers by the hand until they reach our own intellectual level, after which they will proceed to surpass us ... When they *do* overtake us, computers will, in my view, become extremely interesting entities to have around. Their role as teachers and mentors, for example, will be unequalled. It will be like having, as private tutors, the wisest, most knowledgeable and most patient humans on earth: an Albert Einstein to teach physics ... a Sigmund Freud to discuss the principles of psyscho-analysis, and all available where and when they are wanted.[21]

Nor should the writings of Marshall McLuhan be ignored when considering influential myth-makers. That great guru of the electronic era interpreted media as prosthetic extensions, reorchestrating the senses and creating a new humanity:

To behold, use, or perceive any extension of ourselves in technological form is necessarily to embrace it. To listen to radio or to read the printed page is to accept these extensions of ourselves into our own personal system and to undergo the 'closure' or displacemnt that follows automatically ... By continually embracing technologies, we relate ourselves to them as servo-mechanisms. That is why we must, to use them at all, serve these objects, these extensions of ourselves, as gods or minor religions.[22]

Because humans are 'remade' by their manufactured extensions, and because humans serve them as well as use them, McLuhan believed that media transform virtually all aspects of culture and society; by comparison, uses made of media (the 'content') are 'ineffectual.'[23] As well, McLuhan refrained from addressing the topic of how, why, and by whom new media are introduced and diffused. In brief, all 'soiling trace of origin or choice' is absent from McLuhan's writings, at least in those of his period of celebrity.

DEMYTHOLOGIZING 'TECHNOLOGY'

One requirement for freedom, Jacques Ellul states, is to demythologize 'technology,' because 'Technique has come to represent both necessity and fate for modern man, and thus, the effort to recover our ethical identity is the equivalent of resuming the fight for freedom.'[24]

'Technology' as necessity and as fate, Ellul continues, has inculcated our hearts with an 'insidious ethics of adaptation,' resting on the notion that 'since technique is a fact, we should adapt ourselves to it;' 'anything that hinders technique ought to be eliminated, and thus adaptation itself becomes a moral criterion.'[25]

We cannot be free, Ellul insists, if technique is or becomes an end in itself, thereby reorienting the very values and criteria that should be used in making decisions concerning the development and implementation of our own artefacts. To *be* free, Ellul concludes, we must view our machines as mere tools, helping us to accomplish explictly articulated goals. Simply because something is possible to accomplish does not in itself make it desirable to do.

WHY MYTHOLOGY?

Three related suggestions are now offered to help explain the mythological allure of fabricated devices: the 'human conditon'; western culture; and purposeful propagation (the 'consciousness industry').

The 'Human Condition'
Innately, movement and change attract attention; constancy tends to be hidden. Alluding to McLuhan, Hugh Kenner once wrote that fish, always submerged, know nothing of water; while it is futile to explain water to them, they do understand swimming and will take particular note of how well one uses one's flippers. On the one hand, organisms must be sensitive to sudden environmental changes to survive. On the other, essentially unchanging or slow-to-change features of the environment tend not to be perceived – a defence against sensory overload. Gregory Bateson has wisely remarked that 'the unchanging is imperceptible unless *we* are willing to move relative to it.'[26] No wonder then that so much attention is today riveted on 'new technologies,' with underlying human traits and proclivities, such as the quest for dominance and power, becoming obscured in the process.

It is not merely attentiveness to change that is at work here, however; innate human frailty is surely a factor too. We are all born naked into the world, without power and vulnerable. And inventions provide an illusion at least of power and protection, seemingly equipping us to withstand better the vagaries of circumstance. To illustrate: with the onset of electric telegraphy in the nineteenth century, commentators not infrequently cited the following rhetorical question from the Book of Job to underscore heightened confidence in humanity's ability to control its destiny:[27] 'Canst thou send lightnings, that they may go and say unto thee, "Here we are?"' The supreme irony of course is not that we can now do what God said Job could not; rather, it is to be found in our increased vulnerability as we develop and deploy increasingly powerful techniques. Today the very survival of our species is at issue.

In this light the human propensity to mythologize 'technology' becomes more comprehensible. *We* don godlike powers as we 'put equipment on,' but we find ourselves yet more vulnerable as a result.

Western Culture
Apart from the human condition, we can also look briefly as well to historical development in western thought and culture. It is instructive to begin with Francis Bacon (1561–1626), author of *New Atlantis*, a utopian vision of a society ordered on scientific principles. Bacon is sometimes held to be father of technologism and scientism.[28] With him arose the idea that there is a kind of knowledge which grows incrementally and systematically, not as a result of hit-and-miss discovery but as the product of a deliberate activity of the mind. Bacon proposed that the inductive method (inference of general principles consistent with many particular observations) replace the a priorism of medieval scholasticism. Consequently Bacon's new 'will to know' left behind 'all philosophy and theology which end in passive meditation upon a cosmic order held to be fixed and unalterable.'[29] For Bacon the only true knowledge was practical knowledge, since 'truth and utility are here the very same things.'[30] Therefore knowledge for Bacon 'is that which yields a steady increase of human control over the environment ... and which is forthcoming upon deliberate exercise of the will to know.'[31]

While Bacon promulgated a 'will to know' to attain instrumental knowledge,[32] Friedrich Nietzsche (1844–1900) promoted its perhaps inevitable successor, the 'will to power.' For Nietzsche, all values, limitations, and beliefs are relative and man-made, exposed as such through environmental, institutional, and cultural changes wrought by applications of Bacon's instrumental knowledge.

But this belief creates an existential dilemma: more and more powerful means; less and less confidence in the ends, or purposes, for which they are deployed.[33] At the limit, George Grant has argued, our innovating and application of instrumental knowledge could become quite unencumbered of any intimations of what is good to will. Nietzsche's 'nihilists,' Grant tells us, are those who know nothing of what is good to will but none the less would 'rather will nothing than have nothing to will.'[34]

An example close to home may help illuminate this perplexity. To date in Canada the information revolution has been justified, in part, on the grounds of technological nationalism, which, as we have seen, is itself a fiction or myth. If government and business should finally perceive or acknowledge that communication devices, as hitherto deployed, erode rather than strengthen Canadian nationhood, then what will be the result? Concerted effort to restrain or redeploy new or alternative communciation media? Hardly. Far more likely is denial of the efficacy of the nation-state in a world made increasingly interdependent by communication media! The purpose for which communication devices are used becomes reversed, but faith in their ultimate benevolence remains.[35]

The proclivity to mythologize then becomes easily comprehensible in light of Nietzsche's insight. 'Technology' provides ever-more powerful means for accomplishing deeds, even while eroding criteria whereby the deeds, and hence the means, can be judged.[36]

Consciousness Industry

Finally, not to be neglected, is the consciousness industry, through which concerted effort is made to propagate technologism as inevitable, and hence as goodness and truth. Firms and industries producing hardware and software, nations and transnational corporations seeking to extend international influence and dominance, telecommunications carriers, and the scientific elite – all have vested interests in mythologizing 'technology.'[37]

How much easier it is, for example, for the government of Canada to proclaim that Canadians face an ineluctable information revolution – producing its own dramatic, unforeseen but inevitable effects – than to admit that information devices and their consequences are *variables* that get worked out only within a legal/policy framework of which the government is chief architect and for which the government bears ultimate responsibility!

How much more profitable is it for transnational high-tech firms to foster an aura of awe and inevitability respecting engineered artefacts than to acknowledge that emerging communication techniques are powerful devices wielded in a continuing battle for international influence and dominance!

How much more self-serving is it for a Bell Canada to plead 'natural monopoly' than to admit that massive investment funds are routinely spent to secure and expand market hegemony!

Mythologizing 'technology' serves well the interests of both government and industry. Mythologizing 'technology' transforms conscious acts (frequently entailing billions of investment dollars, tax write-offs, and subsidies) into the mythically 'inevitable' and 'natural' order of things. Moreover, mythologizing 'technology' obscures the locus of responsibility, no small advantage for those who deploy advanced techniques; after all, how can anyone be held responsible for the inevitable? Finally, mythologizing 'technology' sweeps aside debate concerning the distribution of power domestically and internationally and the utilization of communication media towards those ends.

Myths of communication 'technology' thus inform us that nothing is selected, nothing chosen. Rather, all one has to do is to possess these new devices from which all soiling trace of origin and choice has been effaced.

Hence, we find a third reason for the current pervasiveness of these myths: they are simply useful for some to propagate.

A FINAL WORD

This book has attempted to demythologize or desacralize 'technology' by reintroducing the soiling trace of origin and choice with a view to recovering our ethical identity and resuming the fight for freedom. It has highlighted how, for 150 years, emerging electronic communication media have been deployed as tactical weapons in ongoing struggles for wealth and power. Rather than contend that devices are inevitable and rigid, this book has demonstrated the inherent plasticity of communication techniques and shown how radically different industrial structures could have been accommodated. Rather than assuming that communication artefacts are necessarily benign, this book has glanced at the dark underside of facilities' deployment in the context of power struggle.

Most fundamentally this book has endeavoured to pinpoint responsibilities for outcomes. Power in the absence of responsibility is the essence of totalitarianism. The mythic doctrines of technological imperative and technological determinism, by denying human responsibility, are then most assuredly totalitarian ideologies, propagated by those who would relieve themselves of the burden of responsibility. To the extent that this book helps re-establish human responsibility in this Information Age, its purpose will have been fulfilled.

Notes

CHAPTER I

1 See generally David Lowenthal, *The Past Is a Foreign Country*, ch. 5.
2 The main exception is Christopher Armstrong and H.V. Nelles's merito-
   rious *Monopoly's Moment: The Organization and Regulation of
   Canadian Utilities, 1830–1930*. Although that book overlaps the present
   one in depicting the early development of the Canadian telephone
   industry, being also quite consistent in its treatment with the present
   work, the two books are written independently of each other. (The present
   author reviewed *Monopoly's Moment* only when preparing a late
   draft.)
3 For example, McLuhan's 'Preface' to *The Mechanical Bride* and Marshall McLuhan and Quentin Fiore, *The Medium Is the Massage*,
   150–1.
4 Roland Barthes, *Mythologies*, 151 (emphasis added).
5 Harry J. Boyle, 'The Canadian Broadcasting System,' speech to the
   Canadian section of the Association for Professional Broadcasting, Education Seminar, Washington, DC, 6 November 1970
6 Secretary of State, *1966 White Paper on Broadcasting*, 4
7 Minister of Communications, Gérard Pelletier, *Proposals for a Communications Policy for Canada*, 3
8 House of Commons, Standing Committee of Broadcasting, Films and
   Assistance to the Arts, *Minutes of Proceedings and Evidence*, 25
   April 1969
9 Department of Communications, *Communications for the Twenty-
   First Century: Media and Messages in the Information Age*, 5
10 Arthur Kroker, *Technology and the Canadian Mind: Innis/McLuhan/*

Grant, 12, 10. See also Maurice Charland, 'Technological Nationalism,' 196–220; also Robert S. Fortner, 'Communication and Regional/
Provincial Imperatives,' 32–46.

11 E.S. Hallman and H. Hindley, *Broadcasting in Canada* (Don Mills:
General Publishing, 1977), 55

12 Quoted in Harold A. Innis, *A History of the Canadian Pacific Railway*,
19. Nor was Macdonald's prognosis merely idle speculation. In
1866, for example, a bill was introduced to the u.s. House of Representatives providing for the annexation of the 'states of Nova Scotia,
New Brunswick, Canada East and Canada West, for the organization
of the territories of Selkirk, Saskatchewan, and Columbia.' To the
Americans this was their manifest destiny, and the doctrine gained
popular currency upon termination of the Civil War in 1865, lasting
well through the next decade. (See ibid.)

13 Ibid., 18–21, 35, 38–9. Also Telecommission, *Instant World*, 60

14 Royal Commission on Broadcasting, *Report*

15 The current movement towards 'free trade' with the United States may
be viewed as the latest important outworking of the integration
already made possible through communication media.

16 The current Broadcasting Act declares that the Canadian broadcasting
system should 'safeguard, enrich and strengthen the cultural, political, social and economic fabric of Canada.'

17 Mark Starowitcz, 'Slow Dissolve: How Canada Will Lose Its Broadcasting Sovereignty,' address to the Graduate Program in Communications,
University of Calgary, 27 November 1984. Also Department of Communications, *Vital Links: Canadian Cultural Industries*, 61–2

18 CRTC, Committee on Extension of Service to Northern and Remote
Committees (Therrien Committee), *The 1980s: A Decade of Diversity – Broadcasting Satellites and Pay-TV*, 2

19 Shirley Serafini and Michel Andrieu, *The Information Revolution and
Its Implications for Canada*, 27–42

20 Ibid., 13

21 Ibid.

22 Ibid., 96, 94. Although not addressed in this book, indications are that
computerization frequently *decreases* productivity in many sectors. See James R. Taylor, 'The New Communication Environment,'
ch. 1.

23 Shirley Serafini and Michel Andrieu, *The Information Revolution*, 8

24 Ibid., 104

25 Ibid., 27

26 Ibid.
27 Minister of Communications Francis Fox, *Culture and Communications: Key Elements of Canada's Economic Future*, 19
28 Department of Communications, *Communications for the Twenty-First Century*, 6, 8
29 James R. Taylor, 'The New Communication Environment,' 5, 117
30 See Armand Mattelart, *Multinational Corporations and the Control of Culture*. Mattelart reports that in 1974 twenty-four of the top twenty-five Defense Department contractors were electronics or aerospace firms (50).
31 Anthony Smith, *The Geopolitics of Information*
32 Department of Communications, *Communications for Twenty-First Century*, 99. For a wide-ranging critique, see James R. Taylor, 'The Twenty-First Century in the Rear View Mirror: A Critique of the DOC's 1987 Discussion Paper,' 63–85.
33 Science Council of Canada, *Planning Now for an Information Revolution: Tomorrow Is too Late*, 10 (emphasis added)
34 Telecommission, *Instant World*, 24–5
35 Department of Communications, *Communications for Twenty-First Century*, 6
36 Department of Communications, *Towards a New Broadcasting Policy*, 4
37 See also Arthur J. Cordell, *The Uneasy Eighties: Transition to an Information Society*, 66.
38 See particularly George Grant, *Time as History;* also Allan Bloom, *The Closing of the American Mind: How Higher Education Has Failed Democracy and Impoverished the Souls of Today's Students.*
39 Jacques Ellul, 'The Power of Technique and the Ethics of Non-Power.' 243
40 See Jean-Pierre Mongeau, CRTC commissioner and examination chairman, *Federal-Provincial Examination of Telecommunications Pricing and the Universal Availability of Affordable Telephone Service.*
41 Thus Manley Irwin, for example, writes: '*Technology* is dissolving industry boundary lines, assaulting geographic demarcations and softening global artifacts'; see his *Telecommunications America: Markets without Boundaries*, 3 (emphasis added). See also Arthur J. Cordell, *the Uneasy Eighties*, 50–72; and Ithiel de Sola Pool, *Technologies of Freedom.*
42 Manley Irwin, for example, writes: 'Technology engenders turbulence, disorder, competition and a pace of innovation bordering on the

frantic. Where regulation imposes ... neat, crisp industry boundary
lines, technology renders such demarcations irrelevant and mean-
ingless. Where regulation posits firm exclusivity technology breeds
endless substitutes, alternatives and options. Where regulation is content
with changes on the margin, technology welcomes quantum jumps.'
'Technology and Communications: A Policy Perspective for the
1980s.' Also Ithiel de Sola Pool, *Technologies of Freedom*; and Arthur
J. Cordell, *Uneasy Eighties*, 50–72
43 Paul H. Douglas, *Ethics in Government* (Cambridge: Harvard 1954),
33; quoted in Walter Adams and James Brock, *The Bigness Complex*, 215
44 Adams and Brock, *Bigness Complex*, See also Marver Bernstein, *Regulating Business by Independent Commission*
45 Joseph Schumpter, *Capitalism, Socialism and Democracy*, 99
46 Ibid., 87
47 George J. Stigler, *Memoirs of an Unregulated Economist*, 164
48 Ibid., 164

CHAPTER 2

1 International Telecommunication Union, *From Semaphore to Satellite*, 9 (emphasis added). This definition, adopted by the International Telecommunication Union, is also employed in Canadian law.
See Radio Act, R.S.C., C.233, S.2 (1).
2 James Carey notes that before the telegraph, 'communication' encompassed both transportation and message transmittal because apart
from semaphores, message transmittal necessarily entailed movement
by foot, horseback, or other mode of locomotion. (See his 'Technology and Ideology: The Case of the Telegraph,' 305.)
3 Robert Latham, 'The Telephone and Social Change,' 45
4 Statistics Canada, *Telephone Statistics 1987*, cat. no. 56–203
5 Ibid., 24, 18, 12
6 CRTC, *Annual Report*, 1987–8, 69. The data include operations of nine-
teen largest carriers only, which none the less together account for
more than 98 per cent of Canadian telecommunications activity.
7 Statistics Canada, *Telephone Statistics 1987*. 'Telephone industry' for
these purposes excludes Telesat and Teleglobe, considered by Statistics Canada to constitute non-telephone carriers.
8 CRTC, *Annual Report*, 1987–8, 69
9 Per capita radio listening per week in 1985 was 18.9 hours; per capita

TV viewing was 22.7 hours. Assuming 50 hours of sleep per week, broadcast media were utilized for 35 per cent of waking hours. CBC, TV and Radio: Figures That Count, 27, 13

10 Statistics Canada, *Cable Television 1987*, cat. no. 56–205, and CRTC *Annual Report*, 1987–7, 68

11 Analogue transmissions can be amplified to cover great distance but cannot be regenerated. Therefore, they are susceptible to transmission error and obstruction by noise or interference. By contrast, digital signals are regenerated en route. In 1985 some 52 per cent of Bell Canada's voice and data transmissions were digital. Within a decade, the company projects, 91 per cent of its transmissions will be digital. (See Bell Canada, 'Presentation to Task Force on Broadcasting Policy,' 18 November 1985, 13.)

12 Increasingly the term 'access facilities' is replacing the older 'local distribution' in the policy literature, on the one hand owing to regulatory-enforced interconnections ('access') for independent telecommunications firms and, on the other, in recognition that loops are used in long-distance as well as in local communication.

13 Statistics Canada, *Telephone Statistics 1987*, 14

14 Cited in CRTC, 'Interexchange Competition and Related Issues,' Telecom Decision 85–19, 29 August 1985, 53

15 CRTC 'Enhanced Services,' Telecom Decision CRTC 84–18, 12 July 1984

16 This was the point of dispute in 1988 concerning Call-Net's evidently illegal telecommunications service. It had been providing a discount long-distance service using Bell's lines, coupled with computerized billings until disconnected by Bell following a CRTC order. (See John Patridge, 'Call-Net Loses Another Appeal,' *Globe and Mail* 13 September 1988, B 10.)

17 Bell Canada, *Form 10-K, Annual Report Pursuant to Section 13 or 15(d) of the Securities Exchange Act of 1934*, 1985

18 BCE, *Annual Report on Form 10-K*, 31 December 1985

19 *Financial Post* card, *Northern Telephone Limited*

20 Teleglobe Canada is immensely profitable. In 1987 it earned net income of $174 million on revenues of $244 million, CRTC, *Annual Report*, 1987–8, 69

21 David Estok, 'Telephone Firms Answer BCE Call,' *Financial Post*, 3–5 September 1988, 1

22 *Financial Post 500*, 1985, 68

23 Quebec-Téléphone, *Annual Report*, 1988

24 In British Columbia both CNCP and BC Rail are authorized to connect

with BC Tel's access facilities to provide certain telecommunications services.

CHAPTER 3

1 C. Northcode Parkinson, *The Rise of Big Business: From the Eighteenth Century to the Present Day*, 86
2 Alvin Harlow, *Old Wires and New Waves*, 59. In subsequent years the originality of Morse's invention was contested hotly in the courts. One of the painter's chief protagonists was Dr Charles T. Jackson, the dining companion who had first broached the topic of electromagnetism en route home. Retrospectively, at least, Morse's idea was certainly simple: systematic openings and closings of an electric circuit in accordance with a code or system or signs substituting for the written language; at the receiving end was an electromagnet to deflect a pen, thereby recording the electrical flow. Be this as it may, Morse remains father of electrical telegraphy in North America, the artist's claim to invention having been upheld by the courts. (See Harlow, ibid., 68-9.)
3 From Morse's submission to Congress in application for a grant to construct an experimental line of telegraph; quoted in Daniel J. Czitrom, *Media and the American Mind: From Morse to McLuhan*, 11-12
4 N.L. Bethune, 'The Telegraph in Canada,' *Monetary Times*, vol. 26 (1892-3), no. 12, 73
5 *Old Wires and New Waves*, 107
6 Robert Luther Thompson, *Wiring a Continent: The History of the Telegraph in the United States*, 28
7 Ernest Green, 'Canada's First Electric Telegraph,' 6
8 Harold G. Fox, *The Canadian Law and Practice Relating to Letters Patent for Inventions*, 6
9 Competition was the result of disputes within the Morse patent group itself and also an outcome of the non-exclusive licenses issued to agents in the various territories by the patentees. Moreover, other inventors – principally Royal E. House and Alexander Bain – challenged the exclusivity of the Morse invention, and rival systems were soon constructed entirely outside the purview of the Morse group. Sloppy construction was attributable not only to undue haste, whereby rival entrepreneurs attempted to become established along given routes, but to vertical integration, as some builders flowed profits back to their own construction companies in lieu of sharing profits on tele-

graphic operations with patent holders. By the mid-1850s competition
was so vigorous and profits so low that many companies were
falling into debt, causing in 1853 the first of several attempts to 'stabi-
lize' the industry through formation of the American Telegraph
Confederation, a trust or trade association designed to eliminate direct
competition among members. (See Harlow, *Old Wires and New
Waves*, 155–34; and Thompson, *Wiring a Continent*, 186, 240.)

10 Ernest Green, 'Canada's First Electric Telegraphy,' 367
11 Ibid., 366; and James D. Reid, *The Telegraph in America: Its Founders,
Promoters and Noted Men*, 326
12 Robert Collins, *A Voice from Afar: The History of Telecommunications
in Canada*, 18–19
13 John Murray, *A Story of the Telegraph*, 108; and D.R. Richieson, 'The
Electric Telegraph in Canada, 1846–1902'
14 *Monetary Times*, vol. 25 (1891–2), 1558
15 Ibid., 1524; also Reid, *Telegraph in America*, 329–30
16 *Monetary Times*, vol. 25 (1891–2), 1524
17 Ibid., 1429
18 Reid, *Telegraph in America*, 342, 345
19 Joy Carroll, *Pioneer Days, 1840–1860*, 62
20 Thompson, *Wiring a Continent*, 227–37
21 Reid, *Telegraph in America*, 346, 348. The Nova Scotia Telegraph
Company, despite its enviable monopoly, began losing money
about 1855, leading to a take-over by the American Telegraph Company in 1860 (ibid).
22 J.M.S. Careless, *The Union of the Canadas: The Growth of Canadian
Institutions 1841–1857*, 21, 26
23 Duncan Alexander MacGibbon, *Railway Rates and the Canadian Railway Commission*, 8–13
24 Ernest Green, 'Canada's First Electric Telegraph,' 366
25 Careless, *Union of the Canadas*, 36
26 *Monetary Times*, vol. 25 (1891–92), 1558
27 Careless, *Union of the Canadas*, 23
28 W.H. Kesterton, *A History of Journalism in Canada*, 1–8. These early
news-sheets concentrated on official government proclamations
directed to a literate élite.
29 In 1881, for example, when the Great North Western Telegraph Company took over Montreal Telegraph, rates for news dispatches were
$0.25 per hundred words, compared with $0.25 for ten words for commercial dispatches.

30 M.E. Nichols, *(CP)*: *The Story of the Canadian Press*, 10
31 Paul Rutherford, *A Victorian Authority: The Daily Press in Late Nine-teenth Century Canada*, 95
32 See Gillian Dyer, *Advertising as Communication*, 15–54; and T.J. Lears, 'From Salvation to Self-Realization: Advertising and the Therapeu-tic Roots to Consumer Culture,' 3–38.
33 See Harold Innis, *A History of the Canadian Pacific Railway*, 69, note 2; Duncan Alexander MacGibbon, *Railway Rates and the Cana-dian Railway Commission*, 17–29; and D.G. Creighton, *British North America at Confederation*, 15.
34 *Monetary Times*, vol 26 (1892–3), 1040
35 A.B. Hopper and T. Kearney, Canadian National Railways, 'Synoptical History of Organization, Capital Stock, Funded Debt and Other General Information as of December 31, 1960,' 161
36 Briane Osborne and Robert Pike, 'Lowering "the Walls of Oblivion": The Revolution in Postal Communications in Central Canada, 1851–1911,' 221; see also William Smith, *The History of the Post Office in British North America 1639–1870*.
37 M.C. Urquart and K.A.H. Buckley, eds., *Historical Statistics of Can-ada*, 14
38 George A. Nader, *Cities of Canada*, 126, 198, 83, 166
39 William Marr and Donald Paterson, *Canada: An Economic History*, 19
40 See particularly Gustavus Myers, *A History of Canadian Wealth*, 168–217.
41 Margaret E. McCallum, 'Sir Hugh Allan,' *Canadian Encyclopedia*, 48

CHAPTER 4

1 *Monetary Times*, 20 September 1878, 371, 375–6. Montreal Telegraph operated in portions of New York, Vermont, New Hampshire, Michigan, and Massachusetts, as well as in Canada.
2 James D. Reid, *The Telegraph in America: Its Founders, Promoters, and Noted Men*, 330
3 John Murray, *A Story of the Telegraph*, 111–12; *Monetary Times*, vol. 25 (1891–2), 1398
4 Through contracts with the Grand Trunk in 1853–4, Montreal Tele-graph was enabled to connect Richmond, Quebec, and Portland, Maine, via Vermont and New Hampshire; by rights of way ceded by the Rome and Watertown Railroad it established 155 offices in New York State; a contract with the Great Western Railway, stretching 500

miles from Hamilton to Detroit through southwestern Ontario, drove out
of business the Great Western Telegraph, the initial telegraph occupant
of these routes, in 1855. (See A.B. Hopper and T. Kearney, 'Synoptical
History of Organization, Capital Stock, Funded Debt and other General
Information as of December 31, 1960,' 161; *Monetary Times*, vol. 25 (1891–
2), 1429, 1489, 1524.)

5 Hopper and Kearney, 'Synoptical History,' 161
6 *Monetary Times*, 21 December 1877, 728–9
7 Walter Luther Thompson, *Wiring a Continent: The History of the
Telegraph in the United States*, 306–17
8 Ibid., 329–30; and Reid, *Telegraph in America*, 427–32
9 Thompson, *Wiring a Continent*, 401; and Reid, *Telegraph in America*,
521
10 To finance acquisitions Western Union's share capital increased by
11,000 (sic) per cent between 1856 (the date of its inception) and
1867. In 1866 alone it printed $16 million in shares to absorb the United
States Telegraph Company and a further $12 million in shares to buy up
its friendly rival, the American Telegraph Company. (See Alvin Harlow, *Old Wires and New Waves*, 521.)
11 Murray, *A Story of the Telegraph*, 112; Thompson, *Wiring a Continent*,
401; and Reid, *Telegraph in America*, 521
12 Reid, *Telegraph in America*, 339
13 Ibid.
14 R. Southerland-Brown, 'A Bibliographic Review of the Canadian Telegraph Industry,' 47, note 5
15 Not only were Montreal Telegraph and Western Union members of the
same cartel, but Montreal Telegraph relied on its affiliate for equipment
and personnel. Hugh Allan was appointed to Western Union's board
of directors in 1869.
16 Alvin Harlow, *Old Wires and New Waves*, 324–5
17 See Matthew Josephson, *The Robber Barons: The Great American Capitalists, 1861–1901*.
18 Ibid., 205
19 Harlow, *Old Wires and New Waves*, 405–7; and Josephson, *Robber
Barons*, 205
20 *Monetary Times*, vol. 26 (1892–3), 381–2
21 Apparently Montreal Telegraph believed the 7:3 ratio did not adequately represent its grandeur relative to the Dominion. Certainly
Dominion Telegraph had grown rapidly through its brief history, but
even by 1880 it was still dwarfed by Montreal Telegraph. In that

year it claimed 400 offices and 4000 pole miles, connecting Halifax, St John, Quebec City, Montreal, Ottawa, Toronto, Buffalo, and Detroit; by comparison, Montreal Telegraph had more than 500 offices, and 12,000 pole miles, plus exclusive rights of way along the Grand Trunk, Intercolonial, and Great Western railways. (*Monetary Times*, 20 September 1878, 371, 375–6; Reid, *Telegraph in America*, 340; Ernest Green, 'Canada's First Electric Telegraph,' 372; and *Encyclopedia Canadiana*, vol. 10, 32)

22 *Monetary Times*, 16 January 1880, 840–1

23 Harlow, *Old Wires and New Waves*, 405–7; and Josephson, *Robber Barons*, 205

24 Harlow, *Old Wires and New Waves*, 409–14

25 Quoted in ibid., 414

26 The Dominion leased its lines for ninety-nine years at a fee of 5 per cent of paid-up capital or $52,000 per year, to increase to 6 per cent or $62,500 should American Union amalgamate or itself lease these lines. (Hopper and Kearney, 'Synoptical History,' 158; also Herbert Marshall, Frank Southard Jr., and Kenneth Taylor, *Canadian-American Industry: A Study in International Investment*, 125)

27 *Monetary Times*, vol. 26 (1892–93), 581–2

28 Western Union retained direct control of Dominion Telegraph plant in the Maritimes, however, consolidating it into facilities attained in 1866 when it took over the American Telegraph Company, to that point dominant in the region. (Hopper and Kearney, 'Synoptical History,' 448–9)

29 Wendy Cameron, 'Erastus Wiman,' *Canadian Encyclopedia*, 1947; and Robert Collins, *A Voice from Afar: The History of Telecommunications in Canada*, 84–95

30 Murray, *Story of the Telegraph*, 118

31 Erastus Wiman, 'The Union of Telegraph Interests in Canada: A Letter to the Shareholders of the Montreal Telegraph Company,' 1881, 5–6. The letter was signed 'Your obedient servant, Erastus Wiman.'

32 The annual rental of $165,000, or 8 per cent of capital, was guaranteed by Western Union. (See Hopper and Kearney, 'Synoptical History,' 118.)

33 House of Commons, *Debates*, 30 April 1880, 1894; and 43 Vic. c.64, Royal Assent, 7 May 1880

34 Eugene Forsey, 'The Telegraphers' Strike of 1883,' 257

35 Robert Collins, *Voice from Afar*, 92

36 45 Vic. c. 93, s.13; Royal Assent, 17 May 1882

37 See discussion of Northern Electric, chapter 15, below.
38 Harlow, *Old Wires and New Waves*, 222–3
39 Collins, *Voice from Afar*, 48–9
40 Reid, *Telegraph in America*, 339; Harlow, *Old Wires and New Waves*, 223; and Collins, *Voice from Afar*, 50
41 Collins, *Voice from Afar* 51–55; and J.S. Macdonald, *The Dominion Telegraph*, 30
42 Reid, *Telegraph in America*, 401; Harlow, *Old Wires and New Waves*, 224; and Thompson, *Wiring a Continent*, 300–2
43 Reid, *Telegraph in America*, 414–19
44 Ibid., 349
45 Corday MacKay, 'The Overland Telegraph,' 173
46 Reid, *Telegraph in America*, 422–7
47 Hopper and Kearney, 'Synoptical History,' 166
48 Dominion Bureau of Statistics, *Telegraph and Cable Statistics*, 1972, 5. On 31 January 1972 the operations of Western Union International Inc. were taken over by the Canadian Overseas Telecommunications Corporation (COTC), then a Crown corporation, today known as Teleglobe Canada, and recently 'privatized.'

CHAPTER 5

1 *Monetary Times*, 29 February 1884, 977. Nor did its plans stop with Europe and Russia; China and India also figured in Western Union's vision of a wired world (see Alvin Harlow, *Old Wires and New Waves*, 318).
2 *Monetary Times*, vol. 26 (1892–3), 1468
3 Harlow, *Old Wires and New Waves*, 319
4 Corday MacKay, 'The Overland Telegraph,' 174
5 Ibid.
6 James S. Reid, *The Telegraph in America: Its Founders, Promoters, and Noted Men*, 516
7 Through the Department of Pubic Works, the Dominion Government Telegraph Service continued operating the original Overland lines until the mid-1950s, when they were turned over to the provincial and commercial carriers (Telecommission, *Instant World*, 60).
8 See Dallas W. Smythe, *The Relevance of the United States Legislative-Regulatory Experience to the Canadian Telecommunications Situation*, 37.
9 Harold A. Innis, *A History of the Canadian Pacific Railway*, 35, 38–9

10 Telecommission, *Instant World*, 60; Allen Ronaghan, 'The Telegraph Line of Edmonton,' 15–16
11 J.S. Macdonald, *The Dominion Telegraph*, 30; and Jean-Guy Rens, 'La télégraphie,' 18
12 J.T.M. Anderson, 'Preface,' in J.S. Macdonald, *The Dominion Telegraph*, 12
13 Ibid.
14 Harold A. Innis, *Empire and Communications*
15 Desmond Morton and Reginald H. Roy, eds., *Telegrams of the North-West Campaign, 1885*
16 CNCP Telecommunications, 'Development of CNCP as a Telecommunication Carrier,' document supplied by CNCP to the author, n.d. 2
17 *Monetary Times*, 14 September 1883, 296, 1 December 1882, 505–6
18 Eugene Forsey, 'The Telegraphers' Strike of 1883,' 258
19 *Monetary Times*, 29 February 1884, 977
20 Although the government's main transcontinental telegraph lines were thus turned over to private enterprise, for many years the government continued to itself operate (through the Department of Public Works) lines in unprofitable areas. In 1947 the Dominion Government Telegraph Service operated 524 offices and 7457 miles of pole line in sparsely settled districts of Cape Breton, Grand Manon, Prince Edward Island, Magdalen Islands, Anticosti, Manitoulin Island, Vancouver Island, and settlements in the Yukon. Beginning in 1954, however, these facilities were transferred to other companies, and within three years the government's telegraph service consisted of merely 360 pole mile and 21 offices. (Dominion Bureau of Statistics, *Telegraph and Cable Statistics* [annual]; and *Encyclopedia Canadiana*, vol. 6, 120)
21 Innis, *History of Canadian Pacific Railway*, 98
22 J. Lukasiewicz, *The Railway Game*, 30. CPR received other benefits; for example, tax exemptions and remission of custom duties on construction supplies (see Duncan Alexander MacGibbon, *Railway Rates and the Canadian Railway Commission*, 48).
23 *Monetary Times*, vol. 26 (1892–3), 945–6
24 Innis, *History of Canadian Pacific Railway* 133–4
25 Initially the federal government's plan had been that the transcontinental railroad should terminate at Lake Nipissing, at which point connection to other lines serving Ontario and Quebec would be made; CPR insisted, however, that it control the complete transcontinental system of both railroads and telegraphs. Along with its railroad

purchases came exclusive telegraph privileges – for example, along-side the tracks of the Canada Central joining Pembroke, Ottawa, and Brockville; and also those of the Quebec, Montreal, Ottawa, and Occidental, giving it access to Lake Huron and southwestern Ontario. (See Innis, *History of Canadian Pacific Railway*, 112, note 3.)

26 Ibid., 133-4.
27 Lukasiewicz, *Railway Game*, 6; and MacGibbon, *Railway Rates*, 44
28 M.E. Nichols, *(CP): The Story of the Canadian Press*, 44
29 Ibid., 38
30 Ibid., 37
31 Ibid., 55
32 Prior to this time the major federal legislation pertaining to telegraph operations was the Telegraph Act (3 Edw. VII, c.58), which provided that messages were to be transmitted in the order received, forbidding also divulgence of information by telegraph employees (see Angus MacMurchy and J.S. Denison, *The Canadian Railway Act*, 320).
33 Ibid., 57, 69
34 G.P. de T. Glazebrook, *A History of Transportation in Canada*, 315
35 Ibid., 313
36 Lukasiewicz, *Railway Game*, 7
37 Glazebrook, *History of Transportation in Canada*, 333-7
38 Ibid., 341
39 CNCP Telecommunications, 'Development of CNCP as a Telecommunications Carrier,' 3
40 It will be recalled that the Grand Trunk Railway had ceded exclusive rights for commercial telegraphs along its tracks to Montreal Telegraph, these rights thereafter reverting the GNWT. Hence, the Grand Trunk Railway, confined to Ontario and Quebec, did not provide a commercial telegraph service.
41 In fact GNWT had lost exclusive privileges along several railroad rights-of-way when Canadian Pacific bought up eastern railways; upon acquisition CPR promptly opened its own telegraph service, utilizing these rights-of-way. So distraught was GNWT over this turn of events that it withheld partial rent payments due Montreal Telegraph on the grounds that this company was not enforcing exclusive rights it had acquired from these railways. In 1891, however, Montreal Telegraph won its suit, on appeal, and full restitution was made. (*Monetary Times*, 8 October 1886, 417; 31 January 1887; and 9 January 1891, 843)

42 Canada, Department of Communications, *A Review of the Public Message Telegraph Service in Canada*, 3
43 A.B. Hopper and T. Kearney, 'Synoptical History,' 159
44 MacGibbon, *Railway Rates*, 50
45 Hopper and Kearney, 'Synoptical History,' 166
46 Ibid., 164–6
47 CNCP Telecommunications, 'Development of CNCP as a Telecommunications Carrier,' 4
48 Ibid.
49 Ibid.
50 'Memorandum of Understanding between Canadian National Railway Company and Canadian Pacific Railway Company, 6 July 1943'
51 CNCP Telecommunications, 'Market Survey,' 1977
52 Canada, Telecommission, *Instant World*, 80
53 Department of Communications, *A Review of the Public Message Telegraph Service*, 1970, 8
54 J.G. Sutherland, 'Telecommunications in Canada,' in CNCP Telecommunications, *Statement of Evidence: Application for Interconnection to Bell Canada*, 15 February 1978, 15
55 Ken Romain, 'Canadian National Sells CNCP Stake for $235 million,' *Globe and Mail*, 1 December 1988, B1
56 John Partridge, 'Rogers Buying 40 Per Cent of CNCP, Planning to Tackle Phone Monopolies,' *Globe and Mail*, 20 April 1989, B1

CHAPTER 6

1 William Patten, *Pioneering the Telephone in Canada*, 59. While Samuel Morse had been unable to take out a patent on account of foreign citizenship and residence, Alexander Graham Bell was not likewise inhibited. The Patent Act of 1872 removed the requirement of residence in Canada. (See Harold G. Fox, *The Canadian Law and Practice Relating to Letters Patent for Inventions*, 7.)
2 Melville Bell was a professor of elocution at several universities, including Queen's College in Kingston, Ontario, and also the author of a famous textbook on the topic. So great was his renown that George Bernard Shaw's leading character in *Pygmalion* is modelled on M. Bell. (See H.M. Boettinger, *The Telephone Book: Bell, Watson, Vail and American Life, 1876–1976*, 44.)
3 See, for example, Elaine Bernard, *The Long Distance Feeling: A History*

of the Telecommunication Workers Union, 6–7; Lindsay Ross Allen, 'Factors in the Development of the British Columbia Telephone Industry 1877–1930,' 14ff; and Gilbert Muir, 'A History of the Telephone in Manitoba,' 69–70.

4 William Patten, *Pioneering the Telephone in Canada*, 24, 39–41

5 R.C. Fetherstonaugh, *Charles Fleetford Sise, 1834–1918*, 128–33; The Bell Telephone Company of Canada, *Annual Report*, 1880; and House of Commons, Select Committee on Telephone Systems, *Proceedings*, 471

6 William Patten, *Pioneering the Telephone*, 58

7 Federal Communications Commission, *Investigation of the Telephone Industry in the United States*, 76th Congress, 1st session, 4, 84; and Joseph C. Goulden, *Monopoly*, 31–5

8 John Brooks, *Telephone: The First Hundred Years*, 71; and Federal Communications Commission, *Investigation of Telephone Industry in United States*, 6

9 Patten, *Pioneering the Telephone*, 47–8

10 Fetherstonaugh, *Charles Fleetford Sise*, 115

11 Patten, *Pioneering the Telephone*, 53

12 Melville Bell courteously granted Dominion Telegraph first option to purchase. Not only was Dominion Telegraph his exclusive agent for most of Canada, it had also lent his son its lines to establish the inaugural long-distance call between Paris and Brantford in 1876. (See A. Roy Petrie, *Alexander Graham Bell*, 16–17.)

13 *Debates of the House of Commons*, 2d session, 4th Parliament, 12 March 1880, 624–5

14 *Debates of the Senate of Canada*, 2d session, 4th Parliament, 31 March 1880, 212–15; 8 April 1880, 267–72

15 43 Vic. c.67, 1880

16 An amendment in 1882 expanded Bell's powers of manufacture to encompass not only telegraph and telephone equipment but also 'such other electrical instruments and plant as the Company may deem desirable' (45 Vic. c.67, 1882).

17 Respecting height and straightness of poles, the painting of the same, and so forth

18 The incorporators had originally applied for this right, but lobbying by telegraph companies succeeded in having this provision stricken in committee. It is to be emphasized that the right to 'connect with' or 'become a shareholder in' telegraph companies is not the same as being

authorized to offer telegraph service; the distinction will become clearer below, in discussion regarding Bell's acquisition of the North American Telegraph Company.

19 See W.R. Lederman, 'Telecommunications and the Federal Constitution of Canada,' 350.

20 Patten, *Pioneering the Telephone*, 68

21 Ibid., 60

22 Fetherstonaugh, *Charles Fleetford Sise*, 113; and Patten, *Pioneering the Telephone*, 68

23 The author asked Bell Canada to help solve the riddle. Officials in the company's Telephone Historical Collection consulted internal documents and even queried the company's legal department, but they were unable to find an answer.

24 Fetherstonaugh, *Charles Fleetford Sise*, 112–13

25 Quoted in ibid. (emphasis added)

26 Donald Creighton, *Canada's First Century*, 27

27 Fetherstonaugh, *Charles Fleetford Sise*, 113

28 Ibid., 115; and Patten, *Pioneering the Telephone*, 67

29 Bell Telephone Company of Canada, *Annual Report*, 1880; and House of Commons, Select Committee on Telephone Systems, *Proceedings*, 471

30 Bell Telephone Company of Canada, *Annual Report*, 1881

31 The Canadian Telephone Company was incorporated on 29 June 1880 by Letters Patent granted under the Canadian Joint Stock Companies Act of 1877, and its first meeting of shareholders was on 10 August. No special legislation was required. Unlike in the chartering of the Bell Telephone Company of Canada, officials from National Bell were prominent as incorporators of the Canadian Telephone Company; included were W.H. Forbes, T.N. Vail, and C.F. Sise. President of the company was T.N. Vail; Sise was named vice-president. (Canadian Telephone Company, *Annual Report*, 1880)

32 Dallas W. Smythe, *The Relevance of the United States Legislative-Regulatory Experience to the Canadian Telecommunications Situation*, 46

33 In addition, Bell Telephone paid a flat fee of $167,000 to Canadian Telephone for its exclusive licence, plus annual dividends (amounting to $10,898 in 1881). (Canadian Telephone Company, *Annual Report*, 1881; and House of Commons, Select Committee on Telephone Systems, *Proceedings*, 121, 457–62)

34 *Monetary Times*, vol. 22, 7 December 1888, 648. Also Tom Naylor, *The History of Canadian Business 1867–1914*, vol. 2, 67, note 132
35 The Bell Telephone Company of Canada, *Annual Report*, 1882; House of Commons, Select Committee on Telephone Systems, *Proceedings*, 457, 467
36 House of Commons, Select Committee on Telephone Systems, *Proceedings*, 472; and Bell Telephone Company of Canada, *Annual Report*, 1883, 1884. Western Union also held shares, probably about 16 per cent of issued equity.
37 House of Commons, Select Committee on Telephone Systems, *Proceedings*, 469–72.

CHAPTER 7

1 By the Patent Act of 1872 (32 Vic., c.26), 'a patent was void if its subject-matter was imported into Canada after one year from its date or if the patented invention was not manufactured or worked in Canada within two years from its date' (Harold G. Fox, *The Canadian Law and Practice Relating to Letters Patent for Inventions*, 7).
2 The case is reported in vol. 2 of the *Exchequer Reports of Canada* at 495. See testimony of C.F. Sise before the Select Committee on Telephone System, *Proceedings*, 630.
3 William Patten, *Pioneering the Telephone in Canada*, 75. However, the Edison patent was affirmed in 1885. The Edison patent, of course, had been the subject of National Bell's infringement suit in the United States against Western Union in 1879 and, expecting to lose the case, Western Union turned this Patent over to National Bell. It is at least somewhat ironic that it was the Edison patent that withstood the test in Canada.
4 Ibid., 90
5 E.B. Ogle, *Long Distance Please: The Story of the TransCanada Telephone System*, 109
6 See generally Lindsay Ross Allen, 'Factors in the Development of the British Columbia Telephone Industry 1877–1930.'
7 *Montreal Daily Witness*, 28 January 1905, 2; and House of Commons, Select Committee on Telephone Systems, *Proceedings*, 803–4
8 TransCanada Telephone System, *History of Regulation and Current Regulatory Setting* (Report to the Telecommission) (Ottawa: Information Canada 1971), 14

9 House of Commons, Select Committee of Telephone Systems, *Proceedings*, 344–55; and vol. 2, Exhibit 309

10 Ibid., and TransCanada Telephone System, *History of Regulation*, 14

11 House of Commons, Select Committee on Telephone Systems, *Proceedings*, 299. This 'exclusive' provincial charter, of course, did not negate Bell's federal charter rights for that province.

12 Ogle, *Long Distance Please*, 113; and TransCanada Telephone System, *History of Regulation*, 14, 26

13 House of Commons, Select Committee on Telephone Systems, *Proceedings*, 159–61, 806

14 William Patten, *Pioneering the Telephone*, 74, as quoted from the C.F. Sise log book

15 House of Commons, Select Committee on Telephone Systems, *Proceedings*, 160

16 Bell Canada Telephone Historical Collection, memorandum, 'The Federal Telephone Company, 1887–1891,' October 1985

17 Christopher Armstrong and H.V. Nelles, *Monopoly's Moment: The Organization and Regulation of Canadian Utilities 1830–1930*, 11

18 Letter from W.A. Haskell, secretary treasurer of Federal Telephone Company, to Charles H. Ware, 24 October 1891; Bell Canada Telephone Historical Collection, cat. doc. 1952 85x2

19 Bell Canada Historical Collection, 'The Federal Telephone Company'

20 Letter from W.A. Haskell

21 Bell Telephone Company of Canada, *Annual Report*, 1892; also House of Commons, Select Committee on Telephone Systems, *Proceedings*, 159–61, 483, 556; and R.C. Fetherstonaugh, *Charles Fleetford Sise, 1834–1918*, 174

22 *The Shareholder and Insurance Gazette*, Montreal, 11 September 1891; Bell Canada Telephone Historical Collection, cat. doc. 12016

23 See Robert S. Fortner, 'Communication and Regional/Provincial Imperatives,' 39–42

24 The Merchants' Telephone Company (Limited), *Prospectus*, Bell Canada Telephone Historical Collection, cat. doc. 6444

25 Bell Canada Historical Collection, cat. doc. 17636

26 Ibid.

27 Ibid.

28 Merchants' Telephone Company, 'Report of Proceedings of the Annual Meeting,' Montreal, 2 October 1894; Bell Canada Telephone Historical Collection, cat. doc. 17636

29 Memo to C.F. Sise from W.C. Scott, 25 January 1895; Bell Canada Telephone Historical Collection, cat. doc. 27636

30 Bell Canada Telephone Historical Collection, memorandum, 'The Merchants' Telephone Company of Montreal,' October 1985
31 House of Commons, Select Committee on Telephone Systems, *Proceedings*, 257, 263
32 Ibid., 258
33 Ibid., 260, 263
34 Bell Canada Telephone Historical Collection, memorandum, 'The Merchants' Telephone Company of Montreal,' October 1985
35 One of these may have been the North American Telegraph Company, alluded to earlier. Incorporated in 1886 by the Rathbun family of Deseronto, it began offering telephone as well as telegraph service in the Kingston, Ontario, region. Inasmuch as this company was acquired by Bell Telephone in about 1900, it is not clear whether its telephone operations pre-dated Bell's acquisition. (See House of Commons, Select Committee on Telephone Systems, *Proceedings*, 251–3, 549–51; and vol. 2, Exhibit 309.)
36 'The Telephone War,' *Peterborough Review*, 11 December 1890; Bell Canada Telephone Historical Collection, cat. doc. 12016
37 Thomas Grindlay, *A History of the Independent Telephone Industry in Ontario*, 238
38 Armstrong and Nelles, *Monopoly's Moment*, 108
39 James Mavor, *Government Telephones: The Experience of Manitoba, Canada*
40 Dallas W. Smythe, 'A Study of Saskatchewan Telecommunications,' 5
41 Tony Cashman, *Singing Wires: The Telephone in Alberta*, 38–43, 58
42 Even by 1889 there were only about sixty telephones in all of Alberta, twelve of which were operated independently in Edmonton (ibid., 55).
43 In 1894 a second basic patent expired also.
44 Richard Gabel, 'The Early Competitive Era in Telephone Communication, 1893–1920,' 341
45 Ibid., 345
46 Kurt Borchardt, *Structure and Performance of the U.S. Communications Industry*, 29
47 Gabel, 'The Early Competitive Era in Telephone Communication,' 349
48 Ibid., 350
49 House of Commons, Select Committee on Telephone Systems, vol. 2, Exhibit 309
50 House of Commons, Select Committee on Telephone Systems, 1905 *Proceedings*, 622
51 The Bell Telephone Company of Canada data, printed in ibid., 810–11

52 Ibid., 810. Note that the foregoing data overstate Bell's telephone availability in so far as Alberta and Saskatchewan (then part of the Northwest Territories) are omitted entirely.

53 Testimony of Dr T.J. Demers, Bellechasse Telephone Company, House of Commons, Select Committee on Telephone Systems, *Proceedings*, 277–8

54 House of Commons, Select Committee on Telephone Systems, *Proceedings*, 218

55 House of Commons, Select Committee on Telephone Systems, vol. 2, Exhibit 309

56 The proposed agreement is printed at 238–41 and 501–4 of ibid.

57 Ibid.

58 Ibid., 666–74, and vol. 2 of Select Committee on Telephone Systems, Exhibit 309

59 Thomas Grindlay, *A History of the Independent Telephone Industry in Ontario*, 18–19

60 Ibid., 74. Eavesdropping was a common practice on the early party-lines, sometimes with serious implications. Among the stories handed down in telephone lore is that of Almond Strowger's invention of the automatic exchange (1899). An undertaker in Kansas City by profession, Strowger was so convinced that exchange operators were tipping off his rivals that he invented a device to eliminate them entirely. (See Alvin Harlow, *Old Wires and New Waves*, 521.)

61 Grindlay, *History of Independent Telephone Industry in Ontario*, 223

62 Ibid, 238

63 House of Commons, Select Committee on Telephone Systems, *Proceedings*, 271

64 Testimony of Joshua Dyke, major of Fort William, ibid., 77–83

65 Ibid., 77–83

66 Ibid., 78

67 Ibid.

68 Ibid., 71

69 Ibid., 78–87

70 Grindlay, *History of Independent Telephone Industry in Ontario*, 238

71 House of Commons, *Debates*, 1904, 3017

72 Testimony of W. Norman Andrews, alderman, Town of Brantford, in House of Commons, Select Committee on Telephone Systems, *Proceedings*, 116–19

73 Ibid., 131

74 The Peterborough franchise is printed in the House of Commons, Select Committee on Telephone Systems, vol. 2, 24–6. See also *Proceedings*, 116–20.
75 Canadian Independent Telephone Association, *Official Report of the Proceedings of the First Annual Convention*, 43
76 House of Commons, Select Committee on Telephone Systems, *Proceedings*, 472–3, 483, 543, 552
77 Ibid., 138
78 R.C. Fetherstonaugh, *Charles Fleetford Sise*, 174
79 Ibid., 175
80 Bell Canada, *The First Century of Service*, 11. Also Grindlay, *History of Independent Telephone Industry in Ontario*, 261; Fetherstonaugh, 175
81 Manitoba Telephone System, *People of Service*, 13
82 Statutes of Manitoba, 62–63 Vic., 1899, c.25
83 Ibid., 4
84 House of Commons, Select Committee on Telephone Systems, *Proceedings*, 64
85 Gilbert A. Muir, 'A History of the Telephone in Manitoba,' 74
86 House of Commons, Select Committee on Telephone Systems, *Proceedings*, 666–74; and vol. 2, Exhibit 298
87 Cashman, *Singing Wires*, 121
88 House of Commons, Select Committee on Telephone Systems, vol. 2, Exhibit 309
89 Ibid., Exhibit 298
90 Contracts are printed at 179–209 of House of Commons, Select Committee on Telephone Systems, *Proceedings*.
91 Testimony of Joshua Dyke, mayor of Fort William, House of Commons, Select Committee on Telephone Systems, *Proceedings*, 93–4
92 s.c. 3 Edw. VII, c.58
93 3 Can. Ry. Cas. 205 and 4 Can. Ry. Cas. 279
94 s.c 6 Edw. VII, c.42
95 9 Can. Ry. Cas. 161; reported also in A.H. O'Brien, *A Digest of Canadian Cases Relating to Railway, Telegraph, Telephone and Express Companies*, 729; also Angus MacMurchy and J. Shirley Denison, *The Canadian Railway Act*, 321–3
96 Testimony of C.F. Sise, House of Commons, Select Committee on Telephone Systems, *Proceedings*, 660
97 Fetherstonaugh, *Sise*, 175

CHAPTER 8

1 s.c. 55-56 Vic. c.67. Bell had petitioned Parliament to authorize an increase in its capital stock, a procedure necessitated by its chartered status. The foregoing amendment had been added by the Senate.
2 Senate of Canada, *Debates*, 1902, 131–2
3 *Journals of the House of Commons*, 1900–2
4 s.c. 2 Edw. VII c.41, 1902. Once again the charter had gone before Parliament for revision upon Bell's Petition to have authorized an increase in capital stock. Parliament again used the opportunity to include regulatory provisions in the revised charter.
5 'Newspaperman, Parliamentarian, W.F. Maclean Dies,' Toronto *Globe*, 9 December 1929, 1, 15
6 Maclean was actually a journalistic pioneer. The *World* was first of Canada's penny presses, providing four daily pages of brightly condensed news. According to the *Globe*, Maclean 'was something of a genius in the making of a paper, with a flair for finding the unusual, and for spicy discussion of airy nothings.' After being elected to Parliament in 1892, Maclean did not disdain casting aside news of the day, no matter how significant, to make room for verbatim reports of his own speeches in the house. Unfortunately, Maclean's skills at editing and writing did not extend to business management. Even in its palmiest days his paper struggled along hand-to-mouth for weeks at a time. One Christmas, so the story went, Maclean literally emptied the till, bestowing Yuletide compensation to employees in nickels, dimes, and quarters. On other occasions the *World's* presses whirled only by dint of generous loans of newsprint from rival John Ross Robertson, proprietor of the *Telegram*. C.F. Sise, president of the Bell Telephone Company of Canada, was one of Maclean's less congenial creditors, as his log-book entry for 19 May 1906 informs us: 'Wrote Dunstan in reply to request from Maclean via Smallpiece, that as we do not propose to subject ourselves to the charge of attempting to "chloroform" the "World" to do nothing whatever until Maclean pays us in full all he owes us.' The *World* continued trumpeting Maclean's causes until 1921, at which time it merged with the *Mail and Empire*. (See 'Newspaperman, Parliamentarian, W.F. Maclean Dies' and 'The Passing of W.F. Maclean,' Toronto *Globe*, 9 December 1929, 1, 15, 4. See also Henry James Morgan, ed., *The Canadian Men and Women of the Time*, 709–10.)

7 Toronto *News*, 10 May 1906, quoted in Morgan, ed., *Canadian Men and Women of the Time*, 709–10
8 House of Commons, *Debates*, 1902, 66
9 Ibid., 1903, 700
10 Ibid., 1902, 734; 1903, 700, 5515
11 Ibid., 1903, 5515–6
12 Ibid., 5523
13 Ibid., 5528
14 Ibid.
15 Ibid., 5531
16 Ibid., 5532
17 Ibid.
18 Ibid., 5533; Macleans's amendment read: 'the [railway] company shall, subject to the approval of the Board, grant equal telephone entrance to its station to all individuals or telephone companies asking therefore.'
19 Della Stanley, 'Andrew George Blair,' *Canadian Encyclopedia*, 193
20 House of Commons, *Debates*, 1904, 3019
21 *Journals of the House of Commons* 1905
22 *Toronto v. Bell Telephone Company in the Privy Council* [1905], A.C.
23 G.E. Britnell, 'Public Ownership of Telephones in the Prairie Provinces,' 11
24 House of Commons, *Debates*, 17 March 1905, 2600
25 W.J. Loudon, *Sir William Mulock: A Short Biography*
26 House of Commons, Select Committee on Telephone Systems, *Proceedings*, 2
27 Morgan, *Canadian Men and Women*
28 Ibid.; and House of Commons, Select Committee on Telephone Systems, *Proceedings*, x, 5–7
29 House of Commons, Select Committee on Telephone Systems, *Proceedings*, 5, 7–8
30 Ibid., 39. Not that the accuracy of Dagger's report went uncontested. Testifying on behalf of the Bell Telephone Company, H.L. Webb, a consultant from England, stated: 'It [Dagger's report] seems to be a compilation from various sources, the names of which are not given, and many of them must be considerably out of date. A great many of the statements are rather vague, there are no reasons given for the statements, and a good many of the figures are really inaccurate.' (Ibid., 842)
31 Ibid., 873

32 Ibid., 874
33 Ibid., 873
34 Ibid.
35 Ibid., xivi; Mr. Maclean, of course was aghast, while others also dissented, but the motion was carried on a split vote.
36 C.F. Sise's log book is replete with accounts of journeys to Boston to meet 'Mr Fish' and of instructions received.
37 Sise, *Private Log Book* no. 10, 7 October 1905
38 Ibid.
39 House of Commons, *Debates*, 16 March 1906, 254
40 Ibid.
41 Britnell, *Public Ownership of Telephones*, 20
42 Laurier's introduction in Parliament of his new minister. House of Commons, *Debates*, 1906, 256
43 Sise, *Private Log Book*, no. 10, entry of 7 October 1905
44 House of Commons, Select Committee on Telephone Systems, *Proceedings*, 764–90
45 House of Commons, *Debates*, 1906, 264
46 Ibid., 752
47 Ibid., 259

CHAPTER 9

1 Speech of 23 November 1905 of Sir Rodmon Roblin, premier, quoted in James Mavor, *Government Telephones*, 17. Mavor's book, a distinguished political scientist's (University of Toronto) vitriolic attack upon public ownership of telephones was commissioned by American Telephone and Telegraph Company and distributed as a product of independent scholarship at a time when pressures were mounting for a government take-over of telephones in the United States (see N.R. Danielian, *AT&T: The Story of Industrial Conquest*, 291–4, 243).
2 House of Commons, *Debates*, 1906, 7808–9
3 Speech of Hon. C.H. Campbell, printed in Canadian Independent Telephone Association, *Official Report of the Proceedings of the First Annual Convention of the Canadian Independent Telephone Association*, 8, 9
4 Mavor, *Government Telephones*, 26
5 Manitoba Telephone System, *A People of Service*, 4
6 Richard Starr, 'A History of the Manitoba Telephone System,' 9–10
7 Manitoba *Free Press*, 8 October 1910, quoted in ibid., 16

8 Starr, 'History of Manitoba Telephone System,' 10–11
9 Ibid.
10 Manitoba *Free Press*, 14 December 1911, cited in ibid., 12–13
11 Winnipeg *Telegram*, 14 June 1912, quoted in ibid
12 Starr, 'History of Manitoba Telephone System,' 14.
13 Carl Goldenberg, *Government Commercial Enterprises Survey*, 121
14 Starr, 'History of Manitoba Telephone System,' 15
15 Manitoba Government Telephone, *Annual Report*, 1922
16 Robert E. Babe, 'Vertical Integration and Productivity: Canadian Tele-communications,' 1–31. See also Woodrow and Woodside, 'Players, Stakes and Politics in the Future of Telecommunications Policy and Regulation in Canada,' 151–4.
17 Radha Krishnan Thompi, 'Sheik "Offset" Loan,' Winnipeg *Free Press*, 5 September 1986, 1
18 Ibid.
19 Thompi, 'MTX Reported Shipping to Sheik,' Winnipeg *Free Press*, 2 September 1986, 1
20 Catherine Mitchell, 'Kickback Issue Raised with Auditor in 1984,' Winnipeg *Free Press*, 9 September 1986, 1
21 Thompi, 'MTX,' 1
22 Mitchell, 'Kickback Issue,' 1
23 Mitchell, 'Kickback Issue'; and 'Timing of Claim Disputed,' Winnipeg *Free Press*, 10 September 1986, 1
24 Mitchell, 'Kickback Issue'; 'Timing of Claim'
25 'Heads Roll in Manitoba's Phone Firm,' Ottawa *Citizen*, 22 November 1986, A18
26 *Canadian Annual Review of Public Affairs*, 1905, 139; cited in G.E. Britnell, *Public Ownership of Telephones in the Prairie Provinces*, 11
27 House of Commons, Select Committee on Telephone Systems, vol. 2, appendix A, 96–7
28 Dallas W. Smythe, 'A Study of Saskatchewan Telecommunications,' 11, 14
29 Britnell, *Public Ownership of Telephones in Prairie Provinces*, 28–9
30 Ibid., 83–5
31 Smythe, 'Study of Saskatchewan Telecommunications,' 28
32 Britnell, *Public Ownership of the Telephones in Prairie Provinces*, 100
33 O.J. Godfrey and Company, *Interim Report*, 6 November 1919; quoted in Smythe, 'Study of Saskatchewan Telecommunications,' 47
34 Britnell, *Public Ownership of Telephones in Prairie Provinces*, 90

35 Hank Intven, 'Some Recent Court Decisions Related to the Functions and Operations of Canadian Regulatory Tribunals,' 12

36 Britnell, *Public Ownership of Telephones in Prairie Provinces*, 142

37 Tony Cashman, *Singing Wires: The Telephone in Alberta*, 137

38 Ibid., 142

39 Ibid., 143

40 Ibid., 164

41 Ibid., 185

42 Britnell, *Public Ownership of Telephones in Prairie Provinces*, 127

43 Cashman, *Singing Wires*, 248

44 Ibid.

45 Ibid., 249

46 Britnell, *Government Ownership of Telephones in Prairie Provinces*, 133–4

47 Ibid., 137

48 Ibid., 149

49 Ibid., 152

50 Ibid.; also Cashman, *Singing Wires*, 330–8, 470ff.

51 The conflict was referred to an arbitration committee in 1986.

52 Board of Transport Commissioners for Canada, *JORR*, file no. 32560.52, 4 May 1966, 370; and TransCanada Telephone System, *History of Regulation and Current Regulatory Setting*, 61

53 Lindsay Ross Allen, 'Factors in the Development of the British Columbia Telephone Industry 1877–1930,' 155

54 Elaine Bernard, *The Long Distance Feeling: A History of the Telecommunications Workers Union*, 75

55 Board of Railway Commissioners for Canada, *JORR*, file no. 32560.52, 4 May 1966, 370

56 Bernard, *Long Distance Feeling*, 77

57 Ibid., 72–3; and *Financial Post Card*, 'British Columbia Telephone Company'.

58 However, CNCP Telecommunications, and more recently BC Rail, compete with BC Tel for certain data and private-line voice services.

CHAPTER 10

1 Computed from data collected by House of Commons Select Committee on Telephone Systems, *Proceedings*, 666, 674, and vol. 2, Exhibit 309. The 694 telephones operated by the North American Telegraph Company are treated here as Bell telephones.

2 Thomas Grindlay, *A History of the Independent Telephone Industry in Ontario*, 254–305
3 Ontario Railway and Municipal Board, *Annual Report*, 1912, 109
4 *People's Telephone Company v. Bell and Canadian Telephone Companies*, 1911
5 *Rural Telephone Cos. v. Bell Telephone Co.*, 12 Can. Ry. Cas. 319; reported also in Board of railway Commissioners for Canada, *Annual Report*, 1912, 289–93
6 Ibid.
7 Board of Railway Commissioners for Canada, *Annual Report*, 1915, General Order 149, 431
8 17 Can. Ry. Cas. 343; reprinted in Board of Railway Commissioners for Canada, *Annual Report*, 1915, 122–3
9 Ibid.
10 *Independent Telephone Co. v. Bell Telephone Co.* (1914), 17 Can. Ry. Cas. 256; reported also in Board of Railway Commissioners for Canada, *Annual Report*, 1915, 179–81
11 Ibid.
12 Ibid.
13 513 Can. s.c.r. 503; judgment of Sir Charles Fitzpatrick, Chief Justice, reported in vol. LIII Supreme Court of Canada, 1916, 589–90
14 Letter from George Tait, the Welland County Telephone Company, Limited, 11 May 1917, printed in House of Commons, Special Committee on the Railway Act, *Minutes of Proceedings and Evidence*, 29 May 1917, 468–9
15 James Marsh, 'Railway History,' *Canadian Encyclopedia*, 1542; also J. Lukasiewicz, *The Railway Game*, 41–51
16 House of Commons, Special Committee on the Railway Act, *Minutes of Proceedings and Evidence*, 16 May 1917
17 Ibid., 268
18 Ibid., 270. Another witness made the point that Bell had termed his company 'competing' even though there was a distance of eight to ten miles between his company's lines and those of Bell. 'As I understood it, we come under the head of a competing company simply because the Bell Telephone Company's long distance lines were built through that district first.'
19 Ibid.
20 Ibid., 481, 491
21 Ibid., 470
22 House of Commons, *Debates*, 3542–9

23 *Journals of the House of Commons*, 1918, 218, 233
24 Ibid., 1919, 48–9, 115, 346, 351, 368, 379, 455, 464, 473, 508
25 House of Commons, *Debates*, 1919 4166–70
26 Committee of Inquiry, CRTC, City of Prince Rupert, Connecting Agreement with B.C. Telephone Company Report, 22 December 1978, 16; and Grindlay, *Independent Telephone Industry in Ontario*, 261
27 13 *JORR* 5
28 Committee of Inquiry, CRTC, City of Prince Rupert *Report*, 16
29 Ibid.
30 Commissioner McLean in a 1914 judgment made specific reference to the local-to-toll cross-subsidy, while the Supreme Court affirmed its existence in 1916. (See Board of Railway Commissioners, *Annual Report*, 1915, 180; and Supreme Court of Canada, vol. LIII, 1916, 591: 'Ingersoll Telephone Company and Others, Appelants and the Bell Telephone Company of Canada, Respondent.')
31 At this point the complex question of cost allocations intrudes. The analysis here assumes all 'local distribution' facilities are apportioned to local service, as undoubtedly Bell, the regulator, and the Supreme Court had at least implicity done. More recently 'local distribution' has been renamed 'access' in recognition that both long-distance and local exchange services require these facilities. When 'access facilities' are factored out of local service and made to stand alone as a separate cost category, the existence of a long-distance subsidy to local service becomes problematic (see discussion in chapter 12). None the less, 'access' facilities have to be paid for somehow, and in 1923 or thereabouts Bell decided it would be advantageous to have long distance make the large contribution.
32 See Grindlay, *Telephone Industry in Ontario*, 47; and Committee of Inquiry, 'City of Prince Rupert, Connecting Agreement,' 31
33 Rural Telephone Committee, *Report* to the Hydro-Electric Power Commission of Ontario, 12 At this time 92 per cent of Bell's telephones were in urban areas and 8 per cent in rural, while 42 per cent of independent telephones were in urban areas and 58 per cent in rural (ibid., 1–5).
34 Board of Transport Commissioners for Canada, 'Telephone Traffic Agreements for Joint Service and Tolls between the Bell Telephone Company of Canada and Connecting Telephone Systems,' file case no. 538, *JORR*, vol. XLI, no. 15, 1 November 1951
35 'Union Telephone Company Case,' *JORR*, vol. XLIV, no. 9, 1 August 1954

36 The U.S. Supreme Court ruled: While the difficulty in making an exact apportionment of the property is apparent ... it is quite another matter to ignore altogether the actual uses to which the property is put. It is obvious that, unless an apportionment is made, [local service] will bear an undue burden ...' Smith v. *Illinois Bell Telephone Co.* PURI931A I (1930) 282 U.S. 133; quoted in Jill Hills, *Deregulating Telecoms: Competition and Control in the United States, Japan and Britain,* 56

37 'Union Telephone Company case,' *JORR,* vol. XLIV, no. 9, 1 August 1954

38 Testimony of R. Barnard, Aylmer and Malahide Telephone Company, before Ontario Telephone Service Commission; *Transcripts,* 3 August 1977, 186

39 Ibid., 16, 37–49, 65–7, 112

40 David Estok, 'Telephone Firms Answer BCE Call,' *Financial Post,* 3–5 September 1988, 1

41 Ibid.

42 Between 1968 and 1976 the CRTC (then known as the Canadian Radio-Television Commission) regulated broadcasting and cable television only. With the added responsibilities, a new commission was created; the initials however, were maintained.

43 Committee of Inquiry, CRTC, 'City of Prince Rupert, Connecting Agreement'; and CRTC, 'City of Prince Rupert, Connecting Agreement with B.C. Telephone Company,' 9 November 1979

44 Bell Canada 'Summary of Discussion at Meeting of O.T.A. Directors with Mr. G.E. Inns, Executive Vice-President, Bell Canada, November 1976,' 3

45 See Jean-Pierre Mongeau, examination chairman, *Federal-Provincial Examination of Telecommunications Pricing and the Universal Availability of Affordable Telephone Service,* 1986.

46 CRTC, 'Bell Canada – 1988 Revenue Requirement, Rate Rebalancing and Revenue Settlement Issues' (Telecom Decision CRTC 88-4, 17 March 1988, 127)

47 Ibid., 133

48 Ibid.

49 Ibid., 135

50 Ibid., 141

51 Estok, 'Telephone Firms Answer Call,' 1

CHAPTER 11

1 Board of Transport Commissioners for Canada, *JORR*, 3 June 1964, 437ff
2 In an internal memo, Robert Scrivener, then director of business development, Bell Canada, wrote: 'A purchase price of $8 and $10 per
  share would be double the indicated price-earning ratio. The resulting
  over-capitalization could be justified however by the elimination
  of continuous friction that could prove very costly to our long-term
  and far greater interests in Ontario and Quebec.' (Memorandum
  quoted in Director of Investigation and Research, Combines Investigation Act, *The Effects of Vertical Integration on the Telecommunications Equipment Market in Canada*, 86)
3 John Gregory, 'Telephone Regulation in Quebec: A Study of the Quebec
  Public Service Board,' 42; and Thomas Grindlay, *A History of the
  Independent Telephone Industry in Ontario*, 187–93
4 Upon formation of the TransCanada Telephone System in 1931 approximately 25 per cent of the original 4263-mile system was leased from
  CP. Until 1952 all long-distance calls between Fort William and Winnipeg were carried over CP lines leased by Bell Telephone and Manitoba Telephone System. And until 1964 all traffic between Kenora and
  Fort William was carried on CP's lines. (Board of Transport Commissioners for Canada, *Northern Telephone case*, judgment, 438–9;
  CRTC, 'CNCP Telecommunications: Interconnection with Bell Canada,' 8–9)
5 In its 1962 brief to the government calling on the minister of transport
  to prohibit CN and CP from constructing the proposed nation-wide
  microwave network, TCTS claimed that '[our own] microwave system
  now carries between 250 and 1,000 telephone circuits ... It is the
  considered view of the members of the TransCanada Telephone System
  that it would represent flagrant economic waste because both present and *future* long-haul communications needs of this country are
  well provided by the *existing* TransCanada Microwave System.'
  (TCTS, 'Trans-Canada Telephone System Brief to the Department of
  Transport and the Government of Canada,' 1962)
6 Department of Communications, unpublished internal memorandum
  ('Intercarrier Competition'), undated
7 The foregoing sketch based on an unpublished Department of Communications memorandum, ('Intercarrier Competition'), undated.
  The history gives cause to reflect on the ramifications of BCE's recent

seizure of Teleglobe, acquiring the largest share block in that company's 'privatized' owner, Memotec Data Inc. (See Matthew Horsman, 'BCE Moved Fast to Beat Ottawa on Teleglobe,' *Financial Post*, 18 May 1987, 19.)

8 Reluctantly testifying also were three nervous Royal Bank executives who previously had filed written intervention with the CRTC. When Bell's feisty CEO, A. Jean de Grandpré, got wind of that, he cajoled the bank into pulling those executives out of the proceeding. Although forced to testify through a CRTC subpoena, the previously enthused executives became quite uncommunicative by the time the public hearings rolled around. See Michael Salter, 'The Power and the Profit,' *Report on Business Magazine*, vol. 4, no. 10 (April 1988), 35.

9 Bell Canada, *Final Argument*, 29 May 1979, Part II, Section 4 (Tab 87), 6–7

10 Ibid., 23.

11 Ibid., Part II, Section 5 (Tab 8,), 2; and Part I, Section 4 (Tab 7), 7–8

12 CRTC, CNCP Telecommunications: Interconnection with Bell Canada, *Report*, 102–5

13 Ibid., 251–2

14 Ibid.

15 Ibid., 186, 240

16 Ibid., 241

17 Ibid., 241–2

18 CRTC, 'CNCP Telecommunications: Interconnection with the British Columbia Telephone Company'; Telecom Decision CRTC 81-24, 24 November 1981

19 The British North America Act reserved to the federal government exclusive authority to enact legislation 'regarding lines of steam or other ships, railways, canals, *telegraphs* and other works and undertakings *connecting the province with any other* or others of the provinces, or *extending beyond the limits of the province*' (emphasis added). The courts have held consistently that this provision, which specifies telegraphs, is extendable to telephones, broadcasting, and other systems of telecommunications. (See, for example, W.R. Lederman, 'Telecommunications and the Federal Constitution of Canada,' 340–87.)

20 Federal Court of Canada, Trial Division, 'Originating Notice of Motion under Section 18 of the Federal Court Act, between Alberta Government Telephones, Applicant and Canadian Radio-Television and Tele-

communications Commission, Respondent, 18 October 1982. In the Matter of the Application, against Alberta Government Telephones, as Respondent, before the Canadian Radio-Television and Telecommunications Commission, Dated the 17th day of September, 1982'

21 Federal Court of Canada, Trial Division, '"Affidavit," between Alberta Government Telephones, Applicant and Canadian Radio-Television and Telecommunications Commission, Respondent, in the Matter of Application of CNCP Telecommunications, as Applicant, against Alberta Government Telephones, as Respondent, before the Canadian Radio-Television and Telecommunications Commission, Dated the 17th Day of September, 1982'

22 Federal Court of Canada, Trial Division, T-8340-82, Order 26 October 1984

23 The Supreme Court added, however, 'Had the *Railway Act* been expressly made to bind the Crown ... AGT would have been subject to its provisions as a constitutional matter.'

24 Kenneth G. Engelhart, 'High Tech Is a Tangle Ottawa Must Straighten,'' *Globe and Mail*, March 1987

25 CRTC, Telecom Decision CRTC 85–19, 'Interchange Competition and Related Issues,' 29 August 1985, 5

26 Ibid., 44

27 Ibid.

28 Ibid, 44–5

29 CNCP Telecommunications, 'Applications for Review of Telecom Decision CRTC 85–19,' 19 December 1985. The application for review was denied. See CRTC Telecom Decision CRTC 86–18, 31 October 1986.

30 CRTC, Telecom Decision CRTC 85–19, 50

31 CRTC 'Bell Canada – 1988 Revenue Requirement, Rate Rebalancing and Revenue Settlement Issues,' Telecom Decision CRTC 88–4, 17 March 1988, 91

32 Ibid., 93

33 Ibid., 118; and W.T. Stanbury, 'Evidence'

34 Ibid., 90

35 Ibid., 90

36 Ibid., 113

37 Communications Canada, 'Proposed Guidelines for Type 1 Telecommunications Carriers,' January 1988, 7

38 John Patridge, 'Rogers Buying 40 Per Cent of CNCP, Planning to Tackle Phone Monopolies,' *Globe and Mail*, 20 April 1989, B-1

39 Patrick Lush, 'BCE Chief Assails Curbs; Plans Thrust into Cable TV,' *Globe and Mail*, 3 May 1989, B-1
40 Ibid.
41 Canadian Press, 'Masse Considers Allowing Cable, Phone Competition,' Ottawa *Citizen*, 9 May 1989

CHAPTER 12

1 J.K. Galbraith, *The Age of Uncertainty*, 232
2 John Stuart Mill, *Principles of Political Economy*, cited in Paul J. Garfield and Wallace P. Lovejoy, *Public Utility Economics*, 15
3 For example Jack Carr, 'Demand and Cost: An Empirical Study of Bell Canada'; Rodney Dobell, et al., 'Telephone Communications in Canada: Demand, Production and Investment Decisions': Leroy Mantell, 'Some Estimates of Returns to Scale in the Telephone Industry'; Leonard Waverman, 'The Regulation of Intercity Telecommunications'; Institute of Applied Economic Research, *A Study of the Productive Factor and Financial Characteristics of Telephone Carriers.* By way of contrast Bell's own economic researchers in 1983 detected 'a robust indication of substantial overall economies of scale,' but such findings have been the exception. (See F. Kiss, et al., 'Economies of Scale and Scope in Bell Canada,' 78.)
4 Bell Canada, *Final Argument*, Part 1, Section 4, (Tab 4), 7–8
5 CRTC, *CNCP Telecommunications: Interconnection with Bell Canada*, 241
6 CRTC, *Interexchange Competition and Related Issues*, Telecom Decision CRTC 85-19, 29 August 1985, 30
7 Department of Communications, 'Proposed Guidelines for Type 1 Telecommunications Carriers,' 7
8 See, for example, Telecommission, *Instant World*, 189.
9 Kenneth Cox, 'Material Relating to the Testimony of Kenneth A. Cox,' in U.S. Subcommittee on Antitrust and Monopoly of the Committee on the Judiciary of the United States Senate on Bill S.1167, *Hearings*, 538
10 Rural Telephone Committee, *Report to the Hydro-Electric Power Commission of Ontario*, 1–5
11 Ursel Koebberling, 'The Application of Communication Technologies in Canada's Inuit Communities,' 109
12 Ibid., 133

13 Bell Canada, 'Report on the Economic Evaluation of Interexchange Calling Plan Proposals for the Remote Northern Areas,' 29 March 1982, 35; quoted in ibid., 136

14 See CRTC, *CNCP Telecommunications: Interconnection with Bell Canada*, Telecom Decision CRTC 79–11, 19 May 1979, 216.

15 Frances Phillips, 'Pace Stepping up in Long Distance Battle,' *Financial Post*, 18 May 1985, 5

16 Bell Canada, *Rebalancing Telecommunications Rates*, subscriber circular 87-0761 BE, 1987

17 CRTC, *Interexchange Competition and Related Issues*, Telecom Decision CRTC 85-19, 29 August 1985, 53

18 Telecommission, *Instant World*, 156

19 See, for example, H.W. Bode, *Synergy: Technical Integration and Technological Innovation in the Bell System*, 59.

20 Federal Communications Commission, *Investigation of the Telephone Industry in the United States*, 126–7

21 Kenneth A. Cox, 'Statement Submitted to the Subcommittee on Antitrust and Monopoly of the Senate Committee of the Judiciary,' 30 July 1973, printed in *Hearings on S.1167*, Part II: *The Communications Industry*, 30 and 31 July and 1 and 2 August 1973, 538

22 Statistics Canada, *Telephone Statistics 1972*, 12

23 Manley Irwin, *The Telecommunications Industry: Integration versus Competition*, 73

24 See Manley Irwin, *Telecommunications America: Markets without Boundaries*, 31–2.

25 Testimony of Dr H.S. Gellman, president, DCF Systems, Ltd., before House of Commons, Standing Committee on Transport and Communications, *Minutes of Proceedings and Evidence*, 30 November 1967, 324

26 Ibid., 336

27 16-77 Elizabeth II c.48, ss.5(4), (5)

28 Telecommunication Committee, Canadian Transport Commission, file no. 49645-26, *Decision*, 14 April 1975

29 Ibid.

30 'Plaintiff's Declaration,' 5 June 1975, 3

31 The case is reported in [1979] S.C.R., 395.

32 Quoted in CRTC, '*Challenge Communications Ltd. v. Bell Canada*, Telecom Decision CRTC 77-16, 23 December 1977, 8

33 Transcripts, 229, quoted in ibid., 15

34 Gordon Kaiser, 'Competition in Telecommunications: Refusal to Supply Facilities by Regulated Common Carriers,' 97
35 86 D.L.R. (ed), 351
36 CRTC, 'Attachment of Subscriber-Provided Terminal Equipment,' Telecom Decision CRTC 82-14, 23 November 1982, 22
37 Ibid., 31
38 British Columbia Telephone Company, 'Cost Inquiry Phase III 1986 Study Report,' Telecom Order 86-516, September 1987
39 Association of Competitive Telecommunications Suppliers, 'Application,' before the Canadian Radio-Television and Telecommunications Commission, Association of Competitive Telecommunications Suppliers, Applicants, and British Columbia Telephone Company and Bell Canada, Respondents, 7 April 1988
40 CRTC, 'Interexchange Competition and Related Issues,' Telecom Decision 85-19, 29 August 1985, 62
41 Ibid.

CHAPTER 13

1 See CRTC, *Report of the Inquiry Officer with Respect to the Inquiry into Telecommunications Carriers' Costing and Accounting Procedures; Phase II: Costing and Existing Services*, 30 April 1984, 11.
2 This statement needs to be qualified by recognizing that 'elasticity of demand,' that is, the sensitivity of demand volumes to price changes, provides varying degrees of freedom in price setting. However, elasticity depends in part on the substitutes available, so in a totally monopolized situation we can generalize that opportunities for undue profit exploitation would exist in all telecommunications markets in the absence of regulation.
3 Kenneth Cox, 'Material Relating to the Testimony of Kenneth A. Cox,' 540–2
4 From ibid., 542
5 See, for example, Harry M. Shooshan, ed., *Disconnecting Bell: The Impact of the AT&T Divestiture*; Jill Hills, *Deregulating Telecoms: Competition and Control in the United States, Japan and Britain*; and Carol L. Weinhaus and Anthony G. Oettinger, *Behind the Telephone Debates*.
6 Testimony of Dr. H.S. Gellman, president of DCF Systems, Ltd., before House of Commons Standing Committee of Transport and Commu-

nications, *Minutes of Proceedings and Evidence*, 30 November 1967, 324, 359–60

7 Ibid.

8 See Snavely, King, and Tucker, Inc., *Telecommunications Cost Inquiry, Report of the Consultants to the Canadian Transport Commission*, vol. 2: *Conduct of the Inquiry*, October 1974, 1. An additional factor expediting the inclusion of private lines in the regulatory mandate was acquisition in 1969 by CN and CP of Computer Sciences (Canada) Limited, a multi-subscriber computer time-sharing firm. The government was concerned that unregulated entry by telecommunications companies into computer processing could lead to discrimination by the carriers in favour of their own computer interests and to the detriment of their other customers, including competing computer service companies. (Letter of A.E. Gotlieb, deputy minister of communications, to D.S. Maxwell, deputy attorney-general of Canada, 4 May 1969)

9 See CNCP Telecommunications, 'Exhibit CNCP 14: Competitive Services vs. Non-Competitive Services, Cumulative % Increases in Rates, 1970–77, and Proposed for 1978'; CNCP Application for Interconnection, 1978.

10 CRTC 'Bell Canada, Increase in Rates,' Telecom Decision CRTC 77, 1 June 1977, 41–2; 'Bell Canada Increases in Rates,' Telecom Decision CRTC 78-7, 10 August 1978, 86; and 'Bell Canada, General Increase in Rates,' Telecom Decision CRTC 80-14, 12 August 1980, 91–9

11 CNCP Telecommunications, 'Datapac Rates; before CRTC, Bell Canada Review of Revenue Requirements for 1985, 1986 and 1987,' 25 June 1986, 1–2

12 Canadian Transport Commission, Telecommunication Committee, *Decision*, file no. 49645-1, 21 September 1972

13 Ibid., Appendix 1

14 Snavely, King, and Tucker, Inc., 33

15 Ibid., 40

16 Ibid., 40

17 CRTC, Telecom Public Notice 1981-41, 15 December 1981

18 Ibid.

19 CRTC, *Report of the Inquiry Officer with Respect to the Inquiry into Telecommunications Carriers' Costing and Accounting Procedures: Phase III Costing of Existing Services*, 11

20 Ibid., 145

21 Ibid., 86

22 Ibid., 93
23 See Bell Canada, 'Cost Inquiry Phase III Study Report,' 2.
24 CRTC, *Report of the Inquiry Officer*, 87
25 Ibid., 91
26 CRTC, 'Inquiry into Telecommunications Carriers' Costing and Accounting Procedures; Phase III: Costing of Existing Services,' Telecom Decision CRTC 85-10, 25 June 1985
27 CNCP Telecommunications, Application in the Matter of Bell Canada's Rates for Competitive Network Services and British Columbia Telephone Company's Rates for Competitive Network Services and Competitive Terminals before the Canadian Radio-television and Telecommunications Commission, 23 March 1988.

CHAPTER 14

1 The board was merely instructed to apply ss. 252 and 253, as contained in the 1903 Railway Act, to telephone rates (see 5 Edw. VII, c.42, s.30).
2 Railway Act, R.S.C 1970, c.234, s.321. Further subsections reiterate proscriptions against 'unjust discrimination,' 'undue or unreasonable preference,' and 'undue or unreasonable prejudice or disadvantage.'
3 Federal Court of Appeal, between CNCP Telecommunications, Appellant, and Alberta Government Telephones and Canadian Radio-Television and Telecommunications Commission, Respondents, and Attorney General of Canada, Intervenor, Judgement, 4 December 1985; and while this book was in press, the Supreme Court's decision on the appeal of that case
4 See, for example, A. John Beke, 'Government Regulation of Broadcasting in Canada'; W.R. Lederman, 'Telecommunications and the Federal Constitution of Canada' Robert J. Buchan, et al., *Telecommunications Regulation and the Constitution*; Charles Dalfen, 'Constitutional Jurisdiction over Interprovincial Telephone Rates.'
5 R.C. Fetherstonaugh, *Charles Fleetford Sise*, 154–5
6 45 Vic. c.67, 1882
7 [1905] A.C. 52 (P.C.)
8 Robert J. Buchan and C. Christopher Johnston, 'Telecommunication Regulation and the Constitution: A Lawyer's Perspective,' 118
9 House of Commons, *Debates*, 1906, 7098
10 See John Gregory, 'Telephone Regulation in Quebec,' 8; and Ontario Telephone Act, 10 Edw. VII c.84.

11 N.M. Lasch, 'Progress Report of the Study on a TransCanada Telephone Line,' 37
12 C.W. Blackford, 'A Plan for the Settlement of Tolls Interchanged over the Proposed All-Canadian Transcontinental Telephone Line,' 65
13 Board of Transport Commissioners for Canada, *Northern Telephone case*, file no. 3839-1054, *JORR*, 3 June 1964
14 See John C. McManus, 'Federal Regulation of Telecommunications in Canada,' 420; McManus writes: 'The TCTS is a contractual arrangement and not a legal entity.' In 1981 the Supreme Court of Ontario, however, found TCTS to be a partnership and hence a distinct legal entity. This finding was made after fifty years of operations! (See *Canadian Pacific Limited v. Telesat Canada* [Supreme Court of Ontario, 1981, unreported], cited in CRTC, Telecom Decision 81-13, 26.)
15 Federal Court of Canada, Trial Division, Order T-8340-82, 29 October 1984, 'In the Matter of the Application of CNCP Telecommunications, as Applicant, against Alberta Government Telephones, as Respondent, before the Canadian Radio-television and Telecommunications Commission, Dated the 17th Day of September, 1982'
16 Ibid
17 Cited in CRTC, 'Bell Canada, British Columbia Telephone Company and Telesat Canada: Increases and Decreases in Rates and Facilities Furnished on a Canada-wide Basis by Members of the TransCanada Telephone System and Related Matters,' Telecom Decision CRTC 81-13, 7 July 1981, 4
18 Ibid., 4
19 Ibid., 6
20 Quoted in CRTC Telecom Decision 81-13, 23
21 Ibid.
22 Ibid.
23 Hon. Flora MacDonald, Notes for a speech at the Information Technology Association of Canada, Ottawa, 6 November 1987, 5
24 Ibid
25 A few decisions were handed down before 1919 in response to petitions from particular municipalities. For example, 'Application of the City of Montreal re Bell Telephone Company Rates,' a 1912 decision printed in Board of Railway Commissioners for Canada, *Annual Report*, 1913, 19–35. In 1907 the board had actually held an inquiry into Bell's charges, but when the chief commissioner (A.S. Killam), who was responsible for writing the decision, died suddenly, Bell's proposed rates were allowed to stand. (See Christopher Armstrong and M.V. Nelles, *Monopoly's*

Moment: The Organization and Regulation of Canadian Utilities 1830–1930, 201–2.)

26 Board of Railway Commissioners for Canada, 'Re Bell Telephone Company's Application for Increase in Rates,' case 955, *JORR*, vol. IX, no. 5, 1919, 79

27 Frank Howard, 'The Bureaucrats,' *Ottawa Citizen*, 12 October 1975; Canadian Transport Commission, *Annual Report*, 1972, 26

28 Testimony of G.D. Zimmerman, president of Industrial Wire and Cable Company, before House of Commons Standing Committee on Transport and Communications, *Minutes of Proceedings and Evidence*, no. 4, 31 October 1967, 137

29 Alexander Ross, 'Fat Attaché Cases Show High Stakes at Bell Hearing,' Toronto *Star*, 11 January 1973, 26

30 Canadian Transport Commission, 'In the Matter of Whether the Canadian Transport Commission Should Award Costs to Parties That Appear before It and More Particularly to Some Intervenors under Certain Circumstances,' *Report*, 19 August 1975, 65, 69. (The full commission adopted Mr Gray's recommendation.)

31 Ibid., 70

32 Ibid

33 Telecommunications Committee Canadian Transport Commission, Order no. T-474, 'Rates Adjustment Formula Procedure for Telecommunication Carriers under the Jurisdiction of the Canadian Transport Commission,' 15 August 1974, 1

34 Disposing quickly of the CTC's order, the CRTC stated: 'The substantive weakness was a matter of general principle; namely, the Commission considers that carriers under its jurisdiction must continue to be accountable through public hearings for all general rate increases. In the Commission's view the automatic formula procedure is inconsistent with this approach.' (CRTC 'Public Announcement: Rate Adjustment Formula: Cost Inquiry and Other Pending Proceedings,' 7 September 1976, 3

35 Board of Transport Commissioners for Canada, 'In the Matter of the Application of the Bell Telephone Company of Canada for an Order under Section 375,' case no. 955-170, *Judgment*, Ottawa, 1950

36 Board of Railway Commissioners for Canada, 'Application of the Bell Telephone Company for Local Exchange Services,' C.R.C. no. 6057, *Annual Report*, 1927, 55

37 Telecommunications Committee, Canadian Transport Commission, Decision, 22 December 1975

38 Board of Transport Commissioners for Canada, *Judgment*, case no. 953-170, 15 November 1950

39 Telecommunications Committee, Canadian Transport Commission, 'In the Matter of Amended Application "B" of Bell Canada for an Order under Section 320 of the Railway Act and all Other Relevant Sections of Said Act approving, to be effective January 1, 1974, Revisions to Bell Canada's Tariffs of Rates for Service, Equipment and Facilities,' file no. C.955.182.1, *Decision*, 15 August 1974, 24–6

40 Telecommuinications Committee, Canadian Transport Commission *Decision*, case C-955.183.1, Ottawa, 22 December 1975, 15

41 On Bell's rural service during this period, see Thomas Pawlick, 'Ma Bell: Exacting the Country Toll,' 31–45.

42 An extensive analysis of telephone regulation prior to 1976 is provided in Robert E. Babe, *Performance Analysis of Selected Common Carriers*, research report to the Department of Communications, May 1976.

43 CRTC 'Telecommunications Regulation – Procedures and Practices: Statement of the CRTC in Preparation for a Public Hearing at the Château Laurier Hotel in Ottawa commencing September 17, 1976,' Ottawa 20 July 1976, 3

44 CRTC, *CRTC Procedures and Practices in Telecommunications Regulation*, Telecom Decision CRTC 78-4, 23 May 1978, 5. See also C.M. Dalfen, vice-chairman, CRTC, 'Telecommunications and Regulation,' 11–16.

45 Ibid., 8–9

46 CRTC, 'Bell Canada, Increase in Rates,' Telecom Decision CRTC 78-7, 10 August 1978, 107

47 CRTC, 'Bell Canada, Confidentiality and Other Preliminary Matters Concerning Support Structures Tariff Proceedings,' Telecom Decision CRTC 76-2, 31 December 1976

48 CRTC, *CRTC Procedures and Practices in Telecommunications Regulation*, 12–33. By registering as 'an interested party,' for example, any person or association can automatically receive complete copies of all applications in which they have expressed an interest.

49 CRTC 'Bell Canada: Increase in Rates,' Telecom Decision CRTC 77-7, 1 June 1977, 9

50 Ibid., 10

51 CRTC 'Committee to Annually Review Bell Canada's Construction Program,' Telecom Public Notice 1979-27, 12 June 1979

52 Board of Transport Commission for Canada, *Judgement*, case no. 955-170, 1950, 34

53 See Board of Transport Commissioners for Canada, case 955-172, *JORR*, vol. XLVII, no. 24, 15 March 1958, 401

54 James Bonbright, *Principles of Public Utility Rates*, 247 (emphasis added; the italicized words are of extreme importance, as the ensuing discussion will show).

55 Testimony of A.J. de Grandpré, vice-president of law, Bell Telephone Company of Canada, before House of Commons, Standing Committee on Transport and Communications, *Minutes of Proceedings and Evidence*, 1 February 1968, 463. In the quoted extract, the bracketed first person plural has been substituted for the second person pronoun in the original statement.

56 Board of Railway Commissioners for Canada, *Judgement*, C.R.C. no. 6057, 21 February 1927; printed in *Annual Report*, 1927, 54

57 In 1966 the board made special note of 'the heavy stock dilution resulting from rights' issues and sales of shares to employees at prices far below market prices.' New stock issues, made available only to existing shareholders and employees, were priced at about 75 per cent of market value.

58 Ibid., 401

59 See Bonbright, *Principles of Public Utility*; also Snavely, King, and Tucker, *Report of the Consultants to Canadian Transport Commission Cost Inquiry*, vol. 3.

60 Testimony of A.J. de Grandpré, vice president of law, Bell Telephone Company of Canada, before House of Commons Standing Committee on Transport and Communications, 1 February 1968, 462 (emphasis added)

61 See in particular Alfred Kahn, *The Economics of Regulation*, vol. 2: *Institutional Issues*, 47–59.

62 Robert E. Babe, 'Vertical Integration and Productivity: Canadian Telecommunications,' 19; article based on Exhibit T-487C in proceedings before the Restrictive Trade Practices Commission concerning the effects of vertical integration in telecommunications upon Canadian industrial performance.

63 Restrictive Trade Practices Commission, *Telecommunications in Canada*, Part III, 208

64 M. Denny, A. de Fontenay, and M. Werner, 'Comparing the Efficiency of Firms: Canadian Telecommunications Companies,' 122–3

CHAPTER 15

1 Adolph Berle and Gardiner C. Means, *The Modern Corporation and Private Property*, 3
2 Ibid., 5, 120
3 Ibid., 120
4 John P. Davis, *Corporations*, 214
5 Berle and Means, *Modern Corporation*, 5
6 45 Vic. c.95, 1882
7 Board of Transport Commissioners for Canada, *Judgement*, 955-176, 4 May 1966, 560
8 Testimony of Charles Fleetford Sise, Jr., president, Bell Telephone Company of Canada, case 955-71, vol. 455, 20 April 1926, 2854
9 Ibid., vol. 476, 24 September 1926, 12, 825
10 Board of Transport Commissioners for Canada, *Judgement*, case 955-176, 4 May 1966, 560
11 Testimony of C.F. Sise, Jr., before Board of Railway Commissioners for Canada, case 955-71, vol. 476, 28 September 1926, 12916
12 Ibid., 12925; and Testimony of L.B. McFarlane, before Board of Railway Commissioners, case 955-17, vol. 479, 13 October 1926, 14183
13 Statement by Hon. Mr Phippen, before Board of Railway Commissioners for Canada, 13 October 1926, 14104
14 Statement of Hon. Mr Phippen, before Board of Railway Commissioners for Canada, vol. 476, 24 September 1926, 12925–30
15 Bell Telephone Company of Canada, *Annual Report*, 1926, 15
16 Transcripts, case 955-71, before Board of Railway Commissioners for Canada, vol. 457, 30 April 1926, 3909
17 Testimony of C.F. Sise, Jr, before Board of Railway Commissioners for Canada, 19 April 1926, 2886
18 Testimony of V.O. Marquez, president, Northern Electric Company, before House of Commons, Standing Committee on Transport and Communications, *Minutes of Proceedings and Evidence*, 21 November 1967, 257
19 Testimony of C.F. Sise, Jr., before Board of Railway Commissioners for Canada, vol. 455, 20 April 1926, 2872–80, and of L.B. McFarlane, chairman of the board of Bell Telephone, vol. 479, October 1926, 13958ff
20 Final Judgement, United States District Court of the District of New Jersey, Civil Action no. 17-49, 24 January 1956
21 Bell Telephone Company of Canada, *Annual Report*, 1962, 15

22 Northern Electric Company and Bell Canada, *Prospectus* 7 October 1975, 30
23 Ibid. See also Arthur J. Cordell, *The Multinational Firm, Foreign Direct Investment, and Canadian Science Policy*, 49–54.
24 Northern Electric and Bell Canada, *Prospectus*, 7 October 1975, 30
25 Restrictive Trade Practices Commission, *Telecommunications in Canada*, Part III, 95
26 Board of Railway Commissioners for Canada, transcripts, case 955-71, vol. 476, 29 September 1926, 13084
27 Board of Railway Commissioners for Canada, *JORR*, vol. XI, no. 2, 15 April 1921, 47
28 Board of Railway Commissioners for Canada, *Annual Report*, 1927, 39
29 Ibid., 51–2
30 The inadequacies are summarized succinctly in documentation seized from Bell Canada's offices and subsequently published by the director of investigation and research, Combines Investigation Act. In a 1965 memo W.C. MacPherson, vice-president of Bell Canada, wrote: 'Present criteria with respect to N.E. Co. prices to Bell are not effective. The most favoured customer policy doesn't necessarily prove that Bell is getting the best possible price. It is possible that Bell might do better from someone else or that N.E. price might not be as low as it could be.' (Director of Investigation and Research, Combines Investigation Act, *The Effects of Vertical Integration on the Telecommunication Equipment Market in Canada*, 100)
31 Board of Transport Commissioners for Canada, *Judgement*, file no. 36730-4, 13 January 1964, 49–50
32 Ibid., 256
33 Telecommunications Committee, Canadian Transport Commission, *Decision*, 15 August 1974, Appendix G, 12
34 Telecommunications Committee, Canadian Transport Commission, *Decision*, 15 August 1974, Appendix G, 7 (emphasis added)
35 Ibid., 27–9
36 CRTC, 'Bell Canada Increase in Rates,' Telecom Decision CRTC 78-7, 10 August 1978, 71–4
37 Director of Investigation and Research, Combines Investigation Act, *The Effects of Vertical Integration on the Telecommunication Equipment Market in Canada*, 11
38 Restrictive Trade Practices Commission, *Telecommunications in Canada*, Phase I, 1

39 Restrictive Trade Practices Commission, *Telecommunications in Canada*, Part III, 199
40 Ibid., 201
41 Ibid., 202
42 Ibid., 204
43 Ibid., 207
44 See J. Patrick Boyer, 'Should the Regulators Do Some Walking through the "Yellow Pages": An Inquiry into the Unregulated Aspects of a Public Utility.'
45 Ibid., 34
46 CRTC, 'Bell Canada, Increase in Rates,' Telecom Decision CRTC 78-7, 10 August 1977, 56–7
47 CRTC, 'Bell Canada General Increase in Rates,' Telecom Decision CRTC 81-15, 28 September 1981, 31–2
48 Bell Canada, '*Evidence*,' 15 November 1982, 5–6
49 Testimony of Mr M. Vincent, president, Bell Telephone Company of Canada, before House of Commons Standing Committee on Transport and Communications, *Minutes of Proceedings and Evidence*, 19 October 1967, 71
50 Ibid.
51 Testimony of A.J. de Grandpré, ibid., 72
52 Ibid., 70
53 Ibid.
54 Ibid.
55 Testimony of G.D. Zimmerman, ibid., 31 October 1967, 117
56 Testimony of J.G. Torrance, ibid., 134
57 Ibid., 149
58 16–17 Eliz. II, 1967–8, c.48, s.7
59 Ibid., s.6
60 Standing Committee, Transport and Communications, Senate of Canada, *Minutes of Proceedings and Evidence*, 14 December 1976, 1:10
61 Ibid., 1:11
62 Ibid.
63 Ibid., 1:19
64 House of Commons, *Debates*, 16 March 1978, 3847
65 Ibid
66 Ibid
67 Ibid
68 Until 1978 telephone and telegraph companies had been expressly prohibited by policies implemented by the Department of Consumer and

Corporate Affairs from applying for continuance under the Canada Business Corporations Act, at which time the restriction was repealed. Exactly what role Bell played in persuading Consumer and Corporate Affairs to repeal these provisions remains unclear. (See CRTC, 'Bell Canada: Articles of Continuance and Proposed Corporate Reorganization,' CRTC Telecom Public Notice 1982-31, 12 August 1982, 1.)

69 Ibid., 9
70 Ibid., 12
71 Ibid., 7
72 Comptroller General of the United States, *Legislative and Regulatory Actions Needed to Deal with a Changing Domestic Telecommunications Industry*, 106–7
73 Interview with Ken Wyman, senior director of operations, CRTC, October 1982. Note Mr de Grandpré's own recollection of events: 'I told him [Francis Fox] "you're playing a political game, so you're playing the votes game. I'll play the votes games. I control about a million and a half votes [i.e., the number of Bell's shareholders], and you don't control anywhere close to that. And I'm going public [by urging shareholders to write Fox supporting the reorganization]."' (Quoted in Michael Salter, 'The Power and the Profit,' *Report on Business Magazine*, vol. 4, no. 10 [April 1988], 39)
74 P.C. 1982-3253, 22 October 1982
75 CRTC, Public Notice 1982-49, 2 November 1982
76 Walter Bolter, 'Bell Canada's Proposed Reorganization: Comparisons with U.S. Experience'; William Stanbury, 'Comments on the Proposed Reorganization of Bell Canada'; and Robert E. Babe, 'Bell Canada Reorganization: Non-Financial Studies'
77 CRTC *Report of the Canadian Radio-Television and Telecommunications Commission on the Proposed Reorganization of Bell Canada*, 18 April 1983, 2 (emphasis added)
78 Ibid., 3 (emphasis added)
79 House of Commons, Standing Committee on Communications and Culture, *Minutes of Proceedings and Evidence*, 17 December 1985
80 Testimony of A.J. Roman, in ibid.
81 Karen Benzing, 'Bell Enterprises Enters Pipeline Field,' Ottawa *Citizen*, 6 December 1983, 13
82 In the words of Dale Orr, BCE's direction of corporate relations: 'We are not characterizing it as a takeover. I can see that somebody might see it as that since we've offered all other shareholders the same

price. But its our view not all shareholders will want to take advantage of it.' (Ibid.)

83 Bell Canada Enterprises, *Annual Report* 1986, 7

84 Lawrence Surtees, 'BCE Is Looking for Acquisitions In the Oil Patch,' *Globe and Mail*, 2 May 1986, 1

85 'BCE Buyout,' *Globe and Mail*, 21 April 1989, B-1, 4

86 Michael Salter, 'Power and Profit,' 32

87 Ibid.

88 Dennis Bueckert, 'Bell Rings $1 Billion Profit with de Grandpré,' Ottawa *Citizen*, 18 November 1985, A15

89 Sheila Arnott, 'What Our Top Executives Are Earning,' *Financial Post*, 13 April 1987, 16

90 Cabinet set aside a CRTC decision specifying payments Bell Canada was to receive when employees were transferred to other BCE subsidiaries, particularly to Bell Canada International (BCI), whose operations in Saudi Arabia, critics had maintained, were being subsidized by Bell Canada's subscribers (Gord McIntosh, 'CRTC Ruling on Bell, BCE Is Rejected,' *Globe and Mail*, 25 April 1988, B8). Subsequently the cabinet order was quashed by the federal court which found parties to the CRTC's proceedings to have been 'deprived by the Governor-in-Council of a fair hearing in accordance with the principles of fundamental justice.' (See Federal Court of Canada, Trial Division, Judgement, case T-845-88, 27 June 1988.)

91 'Man who Built BCE Resigns as Chief Exec,' Ottawa *Citizen*, 4 May 1988, D7

92 35–36 Eliz. II, 1986–7

CHAPTER 16

1 Bobcaygeon *Independent*, 16 November 1877, Bell Canada Telephone Historical Collection, cat. doc. 12015

2 Ibid.

3 Hamilton *Evening Journal*, 30 November 1877; Bell Canada Telephone Historical Collection, cat. doc. 12015

4 Montreal *Daily Star*, 26 July 1881; Bell Canada Telephone Historical Collection, cat. doc. 12015. St. James Street Methodist had also the distinction of originating Canada's first church service for radio broadcast; this event took place on 1 April 1923 over CHYC, then owned by Northern Electric Company (Clarence D. Schnebly, 'History of Northern Electric').

5 Stephen Kern, *The Culture of Time and Space 1880–1919*, 69. Also Asa Briggs, 'The Pleasure Telephone: A Chapter in the Prehistory of the Media,' 40–65.
6 'The Telephone and Election Returns,' *Electronic Review*, 16 December 1896, 298; quoted in Kern, *Culture of Time and Space*, 70
7 Alvin Harlow, *Old Wires and New Waves*, 435–6
8 Ibid., 437–8
9 Ibid., 438–9
10 Marconi himself had pointed out that wireless telegraphy could be used to explode gunpowder and the magazines of ships from a distance. Others noted prospects of exploding forts, firing mines, and steering torpedos. (See Daniel J. Czitrom, *Media and the American Mind*, 67.)
11 Alvin Harlow, *Old Wires and New Waves*, 452
12 Ibid., 455–6
13 N.R. Danielian, *AT&T: The Story of Industrial Conquest*, 103–7
14 Erik Barnouw, *The Sponsor: Notes on a Modern Potentate*, 9
15 T.J. Allard, *The C.A.B. Story: Private Broadcasting in Canada*, 1
16 By March 1923, 556 stations had been licensed for the United States and 34 for Canada (see Frank Peers, *The Politics of Canadian Broadcasting 1920–1951*, 6).
17 Erik Barnouw, *The Sponsor*, 14–20
18 Czitrom, *Media and the American Mind*, 77
19 Emmanuel K. Mankumah, 'An Investigation into Bell Canada's Incursions in Pioneer Radio Broadcasting in the 1920s'
20 Letter to author from Professor Frank Peers, 25 November 1986. The Bell Telephone Historical Collection claims it possesses no documentation on Bell Telephone's early incursion into radio broadcasting.
21 Bell Telephone Company of Canada, *Annual Report*, 1923, 8. In this regard Bell of Canada led its American parent. AT&T did not leave radio broadcasting until 1926, when it signed a similar agreement, obliging it to sell off its radio stations to RCA, never to re-enter the field. For their part, RCA, GE, and Westinghouse promised to stay clear of telephony. (See Danielian, *AT&T*, 108–37.)
22 Richard Starr, 'A History of the Manitoba Telephone System,' 26
23 Manitoba Government Telephones, *Annual Report*, 1923, 25; quoted in ibid., 27
24 Ibid.
25 T.J. Allard, *Straight Up: Private Broadcasting in Canada, 1918–1958*, and Richard Starr, 'History of Manitoba Telephone System,' 18

26 House of Commons, *Debates*, 3 May 1946, 1167
27 See Manitoba, Department of Consumer, Corporate and Internal Services, *Broadcasting and Cable Television: A Manitoba Perspective*, 79, note 96.
28 See ibid., 28.
29 P.C. 1972-1569
30 See, particularly, Task Force on Broadcasting Policy (Caplan/Sauvageau), *Report*; Robert E. Babe, *Canadian Television Broadcasting Structure, Performance and Regulation*; and Herschel Hardin, *Closed Circuits: The Sellout of Canadian Television*.
31 Department of Communications, *Towards a New National Broadcasting Policy*, 1983, 3
32 Ibid
33 Ibid.
34 Ibid., 7
35 DOC affirms: 'Canadians are entitled to as much choice in programming as technical, contractual and international arrangements enable them to receive' (ibid., 3).
36 Ibid., 3
37 Ibid., 16
38 Ibid., 14
39 Ibid., 7
40 Robert E. Babe, 'Copyright and Culture,' 26–9. See also Dan Westell, 'Outcry Forecast over Cuts Facing CBC,' *Globe and Mail*, 28 April 1989, A13.

CHAPTER 17

1 Israel Switzer, 'How I Learned to Love the Satellite,' 177
2 Statistics Canada, *Cable Television*, annual, cat. no. 56-205; publication formerly known as *Community Antenna Television*
3 *Re Regulation and Control of Radio Communication* (1932), A.C. 304 at 313
4 CRTC, *A Review of Certain Cable Television Programming Issues*, Public Announcement, 26 March 1979, 7–10. See also Ithiel de Sola Pool, *Technologies of Freedom*, 151–88.
5 Statistics Canada, *Cable Television*, 1985, 10
6 Quoted in Manitoba, Department of Consumer, Corporate and Internal Services, *Broadcasting and Cable Television: A Manitoba Perspective*, 34
7 CRTC, 'Public Announcement: The Improvement of Canadian Broad-

casting and the Extension of U.S. Television Coverage in Canada
by CATV,' 3 December 1969

8 See CRTC, 'Guidelines for Applicants Regarding Licences to Carry on
CATV Undertakings,' Public Announcement, 10 April 1970; 'The
Improvement and Development of Canadian Broadcasting and the
Extension of U.S. Television in Canada by CATV,' Public Announce-
ment, 3 December 1969; and 'Policy Statement on Cable Television:
Canadian Broadcasting, "A Single System,"' 16 July 1971.

9 For example, CRTC, *Canadian Broadcasting and Telecommunications:
Past Experience Future Options;* and Robert E. Babe, *Canadian
Television Broadcasting Structure, Performance and Regulation*

10 CRTC, Committee on Extension of Service to Northern and Remote
Communities, *The 1980s: A Decade of Diversity – Broadcasting
Satellites and Pay-TV,* 2

11 R. Brian Woodrow and Kenneth B. Woodside, eds., *The Introduction
of Pay-TV in Canada*

12 See John Meisel, 'An Audible Squeak: Broadcast Regulation in Canada,' 129–37.

13 Department of Communications, *Towards a New National Broadcasting Policy,* 6–7

14 Ibid., 6, 7

15 L.Q. 1969, c.56

16 Michel Guité, 'Requiem for Rabbit Ears: Cable Television Policy in
Canada,' 22

17 R. Brian Woodrow, et al., *Conflict over Communications Policy;* also
Manitoba, Department of Consumer, Corporate and Internal Services, *Broadcasting and Cable Television: A Manitoba Perspective*

18 Quebec, *Quebec: Master Craftsman of Its Own Communications Policy*

19 Hon. Gérard Pelletier, minister of communications, *Proposals for a
Communications Policy for Canada,* 7, 23

20 Michel Guité, 'Requiem for Rabbit Ears,' 31

21 Ibid., 18–22 See also *Câblodistribution de l'Est Inc. v. J.R.Y. Pelletier,
Inspécteur de Radio, Ministère Fédérale des Communications et
al.,* Quebec Superior Court Docket 100-38-000-002-75, Rimouski, Que-
bec, 16 July 1975; and *Yvon Pelletier v. Câblodistribution de l'Est
Inc., et. al.,* Quebec Supreme Court, Docket 100-33-0003-75, Rimouski,
Quebec, 20 August 1975.

22 Montreal *Star,* 24 September 1975

23 Michel Guité, 'Requiem for Rabbit Ears, 180

24 Ibid.

25 *Public Service Board* v. *Dionne*, 1978, 2 RCS 191
26 CRTC 'Bell Canada, Tariff for the Use of Support Structures by Cable Television Licensees,' Telecom Decision CRTC 77-6; 27 May 1977, 8–9
27 CRTC *Transcripts*, vol. 1, November 1968
28 CRTC 'Bell Canada: Tariff for the Use of Support Structures,' 13
29 Ibid., 9
30 CRTC *Transcripts*, 1969, 97–104, as discussed more fully in Robert E. Babe, *Cable Television and Telecommunications in Canada: An Economic Analysis*, 120–1
31 Telecommunications Committee, Canadian Transport Commission, Decision, file no. 49616, 19 November 1973, 15–16
32 Ibid., 18–19
33 Ibid., 20–2
34 Telecommunications Committee, Canadian Transport Commission, Decision, file no. 49616.2, 15 October 1975, 5–7
35 Ibid., 15
36 ibid., 24–6
37 CRTC, 'Bell Canada, Tariff for the Use of Support Structures,' Telecom Decision CRTC 77–6, 27 May 1977. Subsequently a similar decision was issued respecting BC Tel; see CRTC, 'British Columbia Telephone Company, Support Structure Agreement with Cable Television Licensees,' Telecom Decision CRTC 79-22, 16 November 1979. The situation is somewhat different in Manitoba and Saskatchewan, however. On 10 November 1976 the minister of communications, quite possibly intent in dismembering the provincial alliance formed by Jean-Paul L'Allier, entered into an agreement whereby the Manitoba Telephone System would retain ownership of all cable, housedrops, and amplifiers used by federally licensed cable television undertakings in the province, quite repudiating the CRTC's established position regarding minimal degrees of hardware ownership. A similar deal was subsequently struck with Saskatchewan. (CRTC, *Annual Report*, 1976–7, 10–11; R. Brian Woodrow, et al., *Conflict over Communications Policy*, 44–5; and Task Force on Broadcasting Policy, *Report*, 53)
38 A.J. de Grandpré, 'Remarks at the Fibre Optics Demonstration in Toronto,' 12 December 1978
39 Bell Canada, 'Integrated Telecommunications Plant,' 21 February 1977; and 'Memorandum on the Technological and Cost Aspects of Integrated Distribution Plant,' March 1978

40 Bell Canada, 'Integrated Telecommunications Plant,' addendum, 2
41 For example, Bell Canada, 'Intervention in the Matter of an Application by Canadian Cablesystems (Ontario) Limited ... to Provide a Communications Service of a Non-programming Nature, Namely a Teletext Service,' 1 November 1978
42 Bell Canada, 'Bell Canada's Presentation to Task Force on Broadcasting Policy,' 18 November 1985
43 Patricia Lush, 'BCE Chief Assails Curbs; Plans Thrust into Cable TV,' *Globe and Mail*, 3 May 1989, B1, 4

CHAPTER 18

1 Arthur C. Clarke,'v2 for Ionosphere Research?' in Letters to the Editor, *Wireless World*, February 1945, 58
2 Quoted in Paul B. Stores, *The Militarization of Space: U.S. Policy, 1945–84*, 24
3 Ibid., 39
4 William H. Melody, 'Summary and Future Prospects,' 262; and John Chapman, 'Why Satellite Communications in Canada?' 10–12
5 From another perspective, however, these benefits could be turned on their heads. Rosemarie Kuptana, president of the Inuit Broadcasting Corporation, has likened the invasion of the North by southern media to a neutron bomb, writing: 'We might liken the onslaught of southern television to the neutron bomb. This is a bomb that kills the people, but leaves the buildings standing. Neutron bomb television is the kind of television that destroys the soul of a people, but leaves the shell of a people walking around. This is television in which the traditions, the skills, the culture, the language, count for nothing.' (Rosemarie Kuptana, 'Neutron Bomb Television,' 12). See also Ursel Koebberling, 'The Application of Communication Technologies in Canada's Inuit Communities'; and Jean McNulty, 'Satellite Broadcasting in Northern Canada,' 281–99.
6 Department of Industry, *White Paper on a Domestic Satellite Communication System for Canada*, 36, 8
7 See Joseph A. Schumpeter, *Capitalism, Socialism and Democracy*, 81–100.
8 William H. Melody, 'Direct Broadcast Satellites: The Canadian Experience,' 3
9 William H. Melody, 'Satellite Communications,' *Canadian Encyclopedia*, 1645; and *Ontario Technologist*, April 1975, 8

10 Department of Communications, *Direct-to-Home Satellite Broadcast-ing for Canada*, 13; *Ontario Technologist*, April 1975, 8; and Department of Communications, *Spacebound*, 48–102. The ISIS satellites (International Satellites for Ionospheric Studies) represented collaboration between Canada and the United States.

11 Department of Communications, *Spacebound*, 104–70; also 'Communications Technology Satellite,' *Canadian Electronic Engineering*, December 1974, 23–5

12 Don Sellar, 'Canada's $100 Million Gamble,' Ottawa *Citizen*, 17 October 1974, 90; and Patrick Finn, 'Year of Exciting Ventures and Key Decisions,' Montreal *Star*, 15 February 1975

13 Jeff Carruthers, 'CTS Technology May Aid Industry,' Ottawa *Journal*, 12 November 1974, 11. The article is based on an interview with Dr John Chapman (the 'father' of Canada's space program), then assistant deputy minister of communications. See also Department of Communications, *The Canadian Space Program: Five-Year Plan*, 7, 17.

14 'Satellite Fired to Fixed Position,' Montreal *Star*, 21 January 1976

15 Department of Communications, *Canadian Space Program*, 8

16 Stephen Straus, 'Tories Pledge $476 Million to Space Plan,' *Globe and Mail*, 13 May 1986, A1–2; and Andrew McIntosh, 'Space Station Budget too Low, Ottawa Told,' *Globe and Mail*, 23 June 1987, A4

17 Department of Communications, *Direct-to-Home Satellite Broadcast-ing for Canada*, 13

18 Niagara Television Ltd. and Power Corporation of Canada Ltd., 'Proposal for a Canadian TV Network and a Domestic Satellite Distribution System,' October 1966

19 Ibid.

20 Liora Salter and Debra Slaco, *Public Inquiries in Canada*, 136

21 Michel Guité, 'Requiem for Rabbit Ears,' 24

22 John Chapman, *Upper Atmosphere and Space Programs in Canada*

23 James Brothers, 'Telesat Canada – Pegasus or Trojan Horse?' 107

24 Guité, 'Requiem for Rabbit Ears,' 24

25 TransCanada Telephone System and CNCP Telecommunications, 'Canadian Communications Satellite System,' May 1967

26 Department of Transport, 'Satellite Communications in Canada'; cited in Brothers, 'Telesat Canada,' 32–3

27 House of Commons, Standing Committee on Broadcasting, Films and Assistance to the Arts, *Minutes of Proceedings and Evidence*, 25 April 1969, 1605

28 Science Council of Canada, *A Space Program for Canada*, 10

29 Guité, 'Requiem for Rabbit Ears,' 24
30 Department of Industry, Trade and Commerce, *White Paper on a Domestic Satellite Communication System for Canada*, 8
31 See Charles M. Dalfen, 'The Telesat Canada Domestic Communications Satellite System,' 199–200.
32 House of Commons, Standing Committee on Broadcasting, Films and Assistance to the Arts, *Minutes of Proceedings and Evidence*, 1969, 1912; quoted in ibid., 186
33 Department of Industry, *White Paper on Domestic Satellite Communications System*, 46
34 Dalfen, 'Telesat Canada Domestic Communications Satellite System,' 183
35 See David A. Golden, 'Anik-Experience with a Domestic Communications Satellite Serving the Public,' speech to the American Institute of Aeronautics and Astronautics, Washington, DC, 29 January 1974.
36 As Mr. Kierans put it in Parliament: 'Except in the instance of the C.B.C. and of certain possible purchasers of a complete undivided television channel on a sustaining basis, the sole customers of the corporation will be the common carriers.' (House of Commons, *Debates*, 14 April 1969, 7496; cited in Barry Milavsky, 'An Assessment of Telesat Canada and Its Canadian Domestic Satellite System with Respect to Canada's National Objectives,' 27)
37 S.C. 17–18 Eliz. II., c.51
38 House of Commons, *Debates*, 1968–9, 7495; statement by Hon. Eric Kierans
39 House of Commons, Standing Committee on Broadcasting, Films and Assistance to the Arts, Proceeding no. 41, 1968–9, 2127; quoted in Brothers, 'Telesat Canada,' 110–11
40 The Anik 'A' series had been developed by Hughes Aircraft of the United States for the Intelsat IV program, but Spar Aerospace and Northern Telecom were subcontractors. See Melody, 'Satellite Communications,' 1645.
41 Verbatim record of discussion, printed in Royal Society of Canada, *Hermes (The Communications Technology Satellite): Its Performance and Applications*, vol. 3, 276
42 The forecast operating life of its Anik 'A' series was five to seven years.
43 Gordon Hutchinson, 'Telesat's Decision to Join Phone System a Golden One?' *Financial Post*, 28 May 1977, 10
44 CRTC, 'Telesat Canada, Proposed Agreement with TransCanada Telephone System,' Telecom Decision CRTC 77-10, 24 August 1977

45 And for a number of reasons, including: (1) a perceived reduction in the Commission's ability to ensure Telesat's rates were just and reasonable; (2) a perceived likelihood that difficult to detect discrimination against non-carriers would be introduced; (3) the lessening in Telesat's autonomy; and (4) a lessening of competition.

46 Department of Communications news release, 'Statement by Minister of Communications Jeanne Sauvé in Respect of an Order-in-Council to Vary CRTC Decision 77-10 and to Approve a Proposed Agreement for Membership by Telesat Canada in the Trans-Canada Telephone System,' 3 November 1977, 2

47 'Telesat Puts $80 Million Satellites on Auction Block,' Montreal *Gazette*, 12 October 1984, F3

48 Laurence Surtees, 'Telesat, Khashoggi-Linked Firm Discuss Possible Deal Involving Space Satellite,' *Globe and Mail*, 14 May 1987, 87

49 Ibid.

50 Barbra Keddy, 'Cable Firms to Buy 130 Earth Stations for Satellite TV,' *Globe and Mail*, 14 February 1979, 4

51 See CRTC, 'Increases and Decreases in Rates for Service and Facilities Furnished on a Canada-Wide Basis by Members of the TransCanada Telephone System and Related Matters,' Telecom Decision CRTC 81-13, 7 July 1981, 193–5; and Francis Fox, Minister of Communications, 'Statement in Respect of an Order-in-Council to Further Vary Telecom Decision 81-13,' 10 December 1981.

52 CRTC, 'Telesat Canada – Final Rates for 14/12 GHz Satellite Service and General Review of Revenue Requirements,' Telecom Decision CRTC 84–9, 20 February 1984

53 CRTC, 'Interexchange Competition and Related Issues,' Telecom Decision CRTC 85-19, 29 August 1985, 87

54 CRTC, 'Telesat Canada and Bell Canada – Amendments to Connecting Agreement between Telesat Canada and Telecom Canada,' Telecom Decision CRTC 86-9, 8 May 1986

55 Andrew McIntosh, 'Telesat Canada Picks Arianspace to Launch Two Satellites,' *Globe and Mail*, 11 April 1987, B15

56 Jean McNulty, 'The Political Economy of Canadian Satellite Broadcasting,' 9

CHAPTER 19

1 Department of Communications, *Telidon Trials and Services*, i

2 Royal Commission on Newspapers, *Report*, 191; and John C. Madden, *Videotex in Canada*

3 Department of Communications, *Annual Report*, 1978–9, 6

4 Department of Communications *Annual Report*, 1979–80, 13

5 Department of Communications *Annual Report*, 1980–1, 10

6 Department of Communications, *Annual Report*, 1982–3, 4

7 Peter Booth and Russel Wills, 'Telidon Synthesis Study: Regulatory Industrial, Marketing and Social Issues,' 71

8 Ibid., 43

9 Communications Canada, 1983–4, Estimates, Part III, Expenditure Plan, 5

10 Dan Leger, 'Telidon Still Struggling as Federal Funding about to End,' Ottawa *Citizen*, 12 March 1985, 6

11 Ibid

12 Dave Godfrey, 'Preface,' in Canadian Conference on Electronic Publishing, *Selected Proceedings*, 3

13 See, for example, Dave Godfrey, 'Introduction to Gutenberg Two: All Information in All Places at All Times,' 1–11.

14 See Anthony Smith, *Goodbye Gutenberg: The Newspaper Revolution of the 1980s*, 153.

15 But even the uniqueness of the *Wall Street Journal's* venture into electronic distribution can be overstated. After all, for more than a century the major wire services, such as Associated Press, had been diffusing news stories from their centralized editorial headquarters to newspapers scattered around the globe.

16 Anthony Smith, 'The Future of the Newspaper: The Waning of the Fourth Estate,' 21

17 Ibid., 24

18 Dave Godfrey, 'Introduction to Gutenberg Two,' 2

19 BCE, *Annual Report*, 1984, 14

20 BCE, *Annual Report*, 1985, 18

21 John Partridge, 'BCE Deals for Stake in Quebecor,' *Globe and Mail*, 23 June 1988, B1

22 See Greg Barr, 'Telecom Canada Network Provides Access to Wide Range of Databases,' Ottawa *Citizen*, 16 December 1985, B9; and David Wolk, 'CNCP: Myriad Ways to Put Messages Out,' *Financial Post*, 5 October 1987, S4. It is reported that 'Telecom's Envoy 100 is the largest subscriber network in Canada with 72,000 users – about 65,000 more than its nearest competitor CNCP.' (See Brian McKenna, 'Electronic

Mail Sparks Change in Corporate Culture,' *Financial Post*, 5 October 1987, S5.)

23 Stuart Logie, 'Bell Battles French Service for Videotext Market,' *Financial Post*, 5 October 1987, 14

24 Kevin G. Wilson, *Technologies of Control: The New Interactive Media for the Home*, 35. See also Kevin Robins and Frank Webster, 'Cybernetic Capitalism: Information, Technology, Everyday Life,' 44–75.

25 Gertrude J. Robinson, 'Prologue: Canadian Communication Studies: A Discipline in Transition?' 3; Peter Lyman, *Canada's Video Revolution*; and Stephen Globerman, *Cultural Regulation in Canada*

26 Consultative Committee on the Implications of Telecommunications for Canadian Sovereignty, *Telecommunications and Canada*, 19

27 See particularly Warren J. Samuels, 'Interrelations between Legal and Economic Processes,' 43–50; Walter Lippmann, *The Public Philosophy*; and Robert E. Babe and Conrad Winn, *Broadcasting Policy and Copyright Law: An Analysis of a Cable Rediffusion Right*, 16–17.

28 CRTC 'Identification of Enhanced Services,' Telecom Decision CRTC 85–17, 13 August 1985; and CRTC, 'Enhanced Services,' Telecom Decision CRTC 84–18, 12 July 1984

CHAPTER 20

1 Department of Communications, *Communications for the Twenty-First Century*; and 'address by Donald Maclean, assistant deputy minister of communications' to the Innis Conference on 'The Strategy of Canadian Culture in the 21st Century,' Toronto 5 March 1988. See also 'Cable TV and Telephone Firms Heading for Clash,' *Financial Post*, 11 April 1988, 43.

2 Department of Communications (Communications Canada), 'Proposed Guidelines for Type 1 Telecommunications Carriers,' January 1988, 7

3 'Masse Considers Allowing Cable, Phone Competition,' Ottawa *Citizen*, 9 May 1989, B6

4 Department of Communications, *Communications for the Twenty-First Century*, 49. In the late 1980s both Telecom Canada members and CNCP Telecommunications were laying fibre-optical trunk cables between major cities, at an anticipated cost of more than $1 billion. It has been forecast that one-quarter of Telecom Canada transmissions

will be via fibre optics by 1990. (See Michael Wang, 'Cable TV and Telephone Firms Heading for Clash,' *Financial Post*, 11 April 1988, 43.)

5 Bell Canada, 'Memorandum on Rate Rebalancing,' updated 17 March 1987, 3

6 Department of Communications, *Communications for Twenty-First Century*, 50

7 Ibid., 48 (emphasis added)

8 Nicholas Garnham, 'Communications Technology and Policy,' 66

9 Department of Communications, *Communications for Twenty-First Century*, 49

10 Ithiel de Sola Pool, *Technologies of Freedom*, 27

11 Simon Nora and Alain Minc, *The Computerization of Society: A Report to the President of France*, 23. See also John Strick, 'Socio-economic Influences of Satellite Communications Technology,' 263–81.

12 Garnham, 'Communication Technology and Policy,' 68

13 Department of Communications, *Communications for Twenty-First Century*, 48 (emphasis added)

14 But then, how much can we expect from a government department which, in its single most important discussion paper in a half-decade, declares: 'Perhaps the greatest contribution by a Canadian to telecommunications was made by Alexander Graham Bell who invented the telephone in Brantford, Ontario in 1884'? (Ibid., 44)

15 See in particular Warren J. Samuels, 'Interrelations between Legal and Economic Processes.'

16 Subcommittee on Telecommunications, Consumer Protection and Finance, U.S. House of Representatives, Committee on Energy and Commerce, *Telecommunications in Transition: The Status of Competition in the Telecommunications Industry*

CHAPTER 21

1 Fritz Machlup, *The Production and Distribution of Knowledge in the United States*; quoted in Machlup, *Knowledge: Its Creation, Distribution and Economic Significance*, vol. 1, 14

2 Other studies were published in the interim. Burck, for example, calculated the information sector to stand at 33 per cent of GNP in 1963, while Marschak predicted the sector would account for 40 per cent of GNP by the 1970s. (Gilbert Burck, 'Knowledge: The Biggest Growth

Industry of Them All,' *Fortune*, November 1964, 128–31; and Jacob Marschak, 'Economics of Inquiring, Communicating and Deciding,' *American Economic Review*, vol. 58, 2 [1968], 1–8)

3 Marc U. Porat, *Definition and Measurement*, vol. 1 of *The Information Economy*; also Michael Rubin, ed., *Information Economics and Policy in the United States*, 20–4

4 Porat, *Information Economy*, 1

5 Department of Communications, *Communications for the Twenty-First Century*, 13

6 See particularly Daniel Bell's 'The Social Framework of the Information Society' and 'Teletext and Technology,' the latter in the *The Winding Passage*, 34–65.

7 Alexander King, 'A New Industrial Revolution or Just Another Technology?' 4

8 Christopher Evans, *The Mighty Micro: The Impact of the Computer Revolution*, 76

9 Thomas Ronald Ide, 'The Technology,' 52–9

10 Manley Irwin, *Telecommunications America: Markets without Boundaries*, 48

11 Joseph Pelton reports that twenty-first century space platforms will be capable of handling 100 billions bits of information per second, that 'two such platforms would be capable of handling in a day the entire U.S. population's thoughts and writings for a decade.' Pelton, therefore, continues: 'Such advanced telecommunications systems are thus oriented toward machine-to-machine communications.' (Pelton, 'Life in the Information Society,' 59–61)

12 Minister of Communications, Francis Fox, *Culture and Communications: Key Elements of Canada's Economic Future*, 4 (emphasis added). See also Kevin Wilson, *Technologies of Control: The New Interactive Media for the Home*; Raymond Williams, *The Year 2000*, 130ff; and J.R. Beniger, *The Control Revolution*.

13 Isaiah 2:8–9

14 See generally Langdon Winner, *Autonomous Technology: Technics-out-of-control as a Theme in Political Thought*.

15 Alvin Toffler, *Third Wave*, 1–5. Similar in tone and perspective is the bestseller by John Naisbitt, *Megatrends: Ten New Directions Transforming Our Lives*; see also Zbigniew Brzezinski, *Between Two Ages: America's Role in the Technotronic Era*.

16 Daniel Bell, 'Social Framework of Information Society,' 188

17 Marc Porat, 'Communications Policy in an Information Society,' 19–25
18 R. Brian Woodrow and Kenneth B. Woodside, 'Players, Stakes and Politics in the Future of Telecommunications Policy and Regulation and Canada,' 105–22
19 Evolution is here termed a mythic doctrine, not to deny that change (include biological change) is evidently an essential quality of our universe, but rather (a) to dispute the common interpretation that the term connotes *explanation* for the changes (its being rather merely a synonym for change); and (b) to contest the belief, again connoted by the term, that changes need to be progressive or benign. On these two points see, inter alia, Arthur Koestler, *Janus: A Summing Up*, 165–226; and Konrad Lorenz, *The Waning of Humaneness*.
20 Arthur C. Clarke, *Profiles of the Future*, 212–27; quoted in Winner, *Autonomous Technology*, 59. Of course, scientific knowledge *is* being applied to biology, giving rise to a new industry, 'biotechnology.' New life forms are being invented and patented, while human reproduction is increasingly 'technologized.' What can be disputed, however, is whether these developments are part of the cosmic game plan, as Clarke seems to contend.
21 Christopher Evans, *The Mighty Micro: The Impact of the Computer Revolution*, 229
22 Marshall McLuhan, *Understanding Media: The Extensions of Man*, 55
23 Ibid., 24
24 Jacques Ellul, 'The Power of Technique and the Ethics of Non-Power,' 246
25 Ibid., 243. This insight, following logically from the doctrine of the technological imperative, was acknowledged also by Marc Porat in writing: 'Two options emerge: either adapt institutionally, or suffer a traumatic demise as the wave of technology washes away the previously impregnable industrial bulwark ... Adaptation is the single solution.' (Porat, 'Communications Policy in an Information Society,' 13)
26 Gregory Bateson continues: 'Notoriously it is very difficult to detect gradual change because along with our high sensitivity to rapid change goes also the phenomenon of accommodation. Organisms become habituated.' (Bateson, *Mind and Nature: A Necessary Unity*, 97)
27 See Daniel J. Czitrom, *Media and the American Mind*, 8–10.

28 For example, Theodore Roszak, *Where the Wasteland Ends*

29 Ibid., 138

30 Quoted in ibid., 138

31 Ibid.

32 'Instrumental knowledge' is knowledge developed for the purpose of exercising power, i.e., manipulating objects. It is to be distinguished from 'communicative/interpretative' knowledge, which is intersubjective; this latter type of knowledge (philosophy, theology, music, poetry, aesthetics) is held to be valuable in and of itself. (See Joseph Weizenbaum, *Computer Power and Human Reason*, 258–80.)

33 Archibald MacLeish once wrote, exemplifying this dilemma: 'After Hiroshima it was obvious that the loyalty of science was not to humanity but to truth – its own truth – and that the law of science was not the law of the good – but the law of the possible ... What it is possible for technology to do, technology will have done.' (*Saturday Review*, 23 July 1968; quoted in Marshall McLuhan, *Culture Is Our Business*, 258)

34 George Grant, *Time as History*, 34

35 Cf James Carey and John Quirk, 'The Mythos of the Electronic Revolution,' 219–41, 395–434; and Joseph Weizenbaum, 'Once More: The Computer Revolution,' 439–458.

36 Or, in Jacques Ellul's terms, means or methods or *La Technique*, because of their enormity, take precedence over ends; goals are lost sight of in the face of ever more powerful means (see his *Perspectives on Our Age*). See also Lewis Mumford, *The Myth of the Machine: The Pentagon of Power*, 3–50. This view seems implicit in Toffler, who writes: 'Life may indeed be absurd in some large cosmic sense. But this hardly proves that there is no pattern in today's events. In fact, there is a distinct, hidden order that becomes detectable as soon as we learn to distinguish Third Wave changes' (Toffler, *The Third Wave*, 16). The way out of this particular dilemma, Gordon Kaufman has written, is through trust 'in One who is Lord of all history and whom history cannot destroy ...' (Kaufman, *Relativism, Knowledge and Faith*, 94). See also Mortimer J. Adler, *Six Great Ideas*, particularly 197–205.

37 See also Dorothy Nelkin, *Selling Science: How the Press Covers Science and Technology*; and Michael L. Smith, 'Selling the Moon: The u.s. Manned Space Program and the Triumph of Commodity Scientism,' 177–209.

Bibliography

In this bibliography, list I is composed of books, book chapters, monographs, theses, articles, and conference papers. List II is composed of consultants' reports, briefs, submissions, corporate reports, and annual reports. List III is composed of government documents.

I BOOKS, BOOK CHAPTERS, MONOGRAPHS, THESES, ARTICLES, CONFERENCE PAPERS

Adams, Walter, and James Brock. *The Bigness Complex.* New York: Pantheon 1986
Adler, Mortimer, J. *Six Great Ideas.* New York: Macmillan 1981
Allard T.J. *Straight Up: Private Broadcasting in Canada, 1918–1958.* Ottawa: Canadian Communications Foundation 1979
– *The C.A.B. Story: Private Broadcasting in Canada.* Ottawa: Canadian Association of Broadcasters 1979
Allen, Lindsay Ross. 'Factors in the Development of the British Columbia Telephone Industry 1877–1930.' Unpublished manuscript, Department of Communication, Simon Fraser University, Burnaby, BC, 1981
Armstrong, Christopher, and H.V. Nelles. *Monopoly's Moment: The Organization and Regulation of Canadian Utilities 1830–1930.* Philadelphia: Temple University Press 1986
Audley, Paul. *Canada's Cultural Industries.* Toronto: Lorimer 1983
Averch, Harvey, and Leland Johnson. 'Behavior of the Firm under Regulatory Constraint.' *American Economic Review* 1961
Babe, Robert E. *Cable Television and Telecommunications in Canada: An Economic Analysis.* East Lansing: Bureau of Business and Economic Research, Michigan State University 1975

- *Canadian Television Broadcasting Structure, Performance and Regulation.* A study for Economic Council of Canada. Ottawa: Supply and Services 1979
- 'Copyright and Culture.' *Canadian Forum* (February/March 1988); also printed in Ian Parker et al., eds., *The Strategy of Canadian Culture in the 21st Century*, 57–65. Toronto: TopCat Communications 1988
- 'Public and Private Regulation of Cable Television: A Case Study of Technological Change and Relative Power.' *Canadian Public Administration* 17, no. 2 (1974)
- 'Vertical Integration and Productivity: Canadian Telecommunications.' *Journal of Economic Issues* 15, no. 1 (1981)

Babe, Robert E., and Conrad Winn. *Broadcasting Policy and Copyright Law: An Analysis of a Cable Rediffusion Right.* Ottawa: Department of Communications 1983

Barnouw, Eric. *The Sponsor: Notes on a Modern Potentate.* New York: Oxford University Press 1978

Barthes, Roland. *Mythologies,* New York: Hill and Wang 1972

Bateson, Gregory. *Mind and Nature: A Necessary Unity.* New York: Dutton 1979

Beke, A. John. 'Government Regulation of Broadcasting in Canada.' *Saskatchewan Law Review* 36 (1971)

Bell, Daniel. *The Coming of Post-Industrial Society.* New York: Basic Books 1973
- 'The Social Framework of the Information Society.' In Michael Dertouzos and Joel Moses, eds., *The Computer Age: A Twenty-Year View.* Cambridge, Mass.: MIT Press 1979
- 'Teletext & Technology: New Networks of Knowledge and Information in Post-Industrial Society.' *Encounter,* June 1977; printed also in *The Winding Passage: Essays and Sociological Journey, 1960–1980,* 34–65. New York: Basic Books 1980

Bell Canada Telephone Historical Collection. 'The Federal Telephone Company 1877–1891.' Unpublished monograph, October 1985.

Beniger, J.R. *The Control Revolution: Technological and Economic Origins of the Information Society.* Cambridge, Mass.: Harvard University Press 1986

Berle, Adolph, and Gardiner C. Means. *The Modern Corporation and Private Property.* New York: Harcourt, Brace and World 1967 (first published 1932)

Bernard, Elaine. *The Long Distance Feeling: A History of the Telecommu-nications Workers Union.* Vancouver: New Star Books 1982

Bernstein, Marver. *Regulating Business by Independent Commission.* Princeton, NJ: Princeton University Press 1955

Blackford, C.W. 'A Plan for the Settlement of Tolls Interchanged over the Proposed All-Canadian Transcontinental Telephone Line.' *Annual Proceedings of the Telephone Association of Canada 1928.* Reprinted in Peter S. Grant, ed., *Telephone Operation and Development in Canada, 1921–1971.* Toronto: Faculty of Law, University of Toronto 1974

Bloom, Allan. *The Closing of the American Mind: How Higher Education has Failed Democracy and Impoverished the Souls of Today's Students.* New York: Simon and Schuster 1987

Bode, H.W. *Synergy: Technical Integration and Technological Innovation in the Bell System.* Murray Hills, NJ: Bell Laboratories 1971

Boettinger, H.M. *The Telephone Book: Bell, Watson, Vail and American Life, 1876–1976.* New York: Riverwood Publishers 1977

Bonbright, James. *Principles of Public Utility Rates.* New York: Columbia University Press 1961

Borchardt, Kurt. *Structure and Performance of the U.S. Communications Industry.* Boston: Graduate School of Business Administration, Harvard University 1970

Boyer, J. Patrick. 'Should the Regulator Do Some Walking through the 'Yellow Pages'?: An Inquiry into the Unregulated Aspects of a Public Utility.' Research paper prepared for communications Law Seminar, University of Toronto, April 1975

Briggs, Asa. 'The Pleasure Telephone: A Chapter in the Prehistory of the Media.' In Ithiel de Sola Pool, ed., *The Social Impact of the Telephone.* Cambridge, Mass.: MIT Press 1977

Britnell, G.E. 'Public Ownership of Telephones in the Prairies.' MA thesis, University of Toronto 1934

Brooks, John. *Telephone: The First Hundred Years.* New York: Harper and Row 1975

Brothers, James. 'Telesat Canada: Pegasus or Trojan Horse?' MA thesis, Carleton University, Ottawa, 1979

Brown, R. Sutherland. 'A Bibliographic Review of the Canadian Telegraph Industry.' Unpublished manuscript prepared for Department of Communications, Ottawa, nd

Brzezinksi, Zbigniew. *Between Two Ages: America's Role in the Technetronic Era.* Harmondsworth: Penguin 1970

Buchan, Robert J., and C. Christopher Johnston. 'Telecommunications Regulation and the Constitution: A Lawyer's Perspective.' In Robert J. Buchan, et al., *Telecommunications Regulation and the Constitution*. Montreal: Institute for Research on Public Policy 1982

Burck, Gilbert. 'Knowledge: The Biggest Growth Industry of Them All.' *Fortune*, November 1964: 128–31

Cameron, Wendy. 'Erastus Wiman.' *Canadian Encyclopedia*. Edmonton: Hurtig 1985

Careless, J.M.S. *The Union of the Canadas: The Growth of Canadian Institutions, 1841–1857*. Toronto: McClelland and Stewart 1967

Carey, James. 'Technology and Ideology: The Case of the Telegraph.' *Prospects* 8 (1983): 303–25

Carey James, and John Quirk. 'The Mythos of the Electronic Revolution,' parts 1, 2. *American Scholar*, Spring, Summer 1970: 219–41, 395–434

Carr, Jack. 'Demand and Cost: An Empirical Study of Bell Canada.' In H.E. English, ed., *Telecommunications for Canada: An Interface of Business and Government*. Toronto: Methuen 1973

Carroll, Joy. *Pioneer Days, 1840–1860*. Toronto: Natural Science of Canada 1979

Cashman, Tony. *Singing Wires: The Telephone in Alberta*. Edmonton: Alberta Government Telephone Commission 1972

Chapman, John. *Upper Atmosphere and Space Programs of Canada*, Ottawa: Queen's Printer 1967

– 'Why Satellite Communications in Canada?' *In Search/En Quête*, Spring 1979

Charland, Maurice. 'Technological Nationalism.' *Canadian Journal of Political and Social Theory* 10, nos. 1, 2 (1986)

Clarke, Arthur C. *Profiles of the Future*. New York: Bantam Books 1964

Collins, Robert. *A Voice from Afar: The History of Telecommunications in Canada*. Toronto: McGraw-Hill Ryerson 1977

Cordell, Arthur J. *The Multinational Firm, Foreign Direct Investment, and Canadian Science Policy*. Science Council of Canada, special study 22. Ottawa: Information Canada 1971

– *The Uneasy Eighties: Transition to an Information Society*. Science Council of Canada, background study 53. Ottawa: Supply and Services 1985

Creighton, Donald. *British North America at Confederation*. Study prepared for the Royal Commission on Dominion-Provincial Relations. Ottawa: Queen's Printer 1963

– *Canada's First Century*. Toronto: Macmillan 1970

Czitrom, Daniel J. *Media and the American Mind: From Morse to McLuhan*. Chapel Hill: University of North Carolina Press 1982

Dalfen, Charles, 'Constitutional Jurisdiction over Interprovincial Telephone Rates.' *Canadian Communications Law Review* 2 (1970)

– 'Telecommunications and Regulation.' *Proceedings of the 6th Annual Meeting, Canadian Telecommunications Carriers Association* 1977

– 'The Telesat Canada Domestic Communications Satellite System.' *Canadian Communications Law Review* 1 (1969)

Danielian, N.R. *AT&T: The Story of Industrial Conquest*. New York: Arno Press 1974 (first published 1939)

Davis, John P. *Corporations: A Study of the Origin and Development of Great Business Combinations and of Their Relation to the Authority of the State*. New York: Capricorn Books 1961 (first published 1905)

Denny, M., A. de Fontenay, and M. Werner. 'Comparing the Efficiency of Firms: Canadian Telecommunications Companies.' In L. Courville et al., eds. *Economic Analysis of Telecommunications: Theory and Applications*. Amsterdam: North-Holland Press 1983

de Sola Pool, Ithiel. *Technologies of Freedom*. Cambridge, Mass.: The Belknap Press of Harvard University Press 1983

Dobell, Rodney, et al. 'Telephone Communications in Canada: Demand, Production and Investment Decisions.' *Bell Journal of Economics and Management Science*, April 1977

Dyer, Gillian. *Advertising as Communication*. London: Methuen 1982

Ellul, Jacques. *Perspectives on Our Age*, ed. William Vanderburg. Toronto: Canadian Broadcasting Corporation 1981

– 'The Power of Technique and the Ethics of Non-power.' In Kathleen Woodward, ed., *The Myths of Information: Technology in Post-Industrial Society*. Madison, Wis.: Coda Press 1980

Evans, Christopher. *The Mighty Micro: The Impact of the Computer Revolution*. London: Victor Gollancz 1979

Fetherstonaugh, R.C. *Charles Fleetford Sise, 1834–1918*. Montreal: Gazette Publishing Company 1944

Forsey, Eugene. 'The Telegraphers' Strike of 1883.' *Transactions of the Royal Society of Canada*, series 4, vol. 9 (1971)

Fortner, Robert S. 'Communication and Regional/Provincial Imperatives.' *Canadian Journal of Communication*, 6, no. 4 (Spring 1980)

Fox, Harold G. *The Canadian Law and Practice Relating to Letters Patent for Inventions*. 4th ed. Toronto: Carswell 1969

Fox, R.W., and T.J. Lears, eds. *The Culture of Consumption*. New York: Patheon 1983

Gabel, Richard. 'The Early Competitive Era in Telephone Communication, 1893–1920.' *Law and Contemporary Problems* 34, no. 2 (Spring 1969)

Galbraith, John Kenneth. *The Age of Uncertainty*. Boston: Houghton Mifflin 1977

Garfield, Paul J., and Wallace Lovejoy. *Public Utility Economics*. Englewood Cliffs, NJ: Prentice-Hall 1964

Garnham, Nicholas. 'Communication Technology and Policy.' In Michael Gurevitch and Mark R. Levy, eds., *Mass Communication Review Yearbook 5*. Beverly Hills: Sage 1985

Gelhaus, Robert, and Garry Wilson. 'An Earnings-Price Approach to Fair Rate of Return in Regulated Industries.' *Stanford Law Review*, January 1968

Glazebrook, J.P. de T. *A History of Transportation in Canada*. Toronto: Ryerson Press 1938

Globerman, Stephen. *Cultural Regulation in Canada*. Montreal: Institute for Research on Public Policy 1983

Godfrey, Dave. 'Preface' in Canadian Conference on Electronic Publishing *Selected Proceedings*. Vancouver 1986

Godfrey, Dave, and Douglas Parkhill, eds. *Gutenberg Two*. Toronto: Press Porcépic 1979

Goulden, Joseph C. *Monopoly*. New York: Pocket Books 1970

Grant, George. *Time as History*. Massey lectures, 9th series. Toronto: Canadian Broadcasting Corporation 1969

Green, Ernest. 'Canada's First Electric Telegraph.' *Papers and Records of the Ontario Historical Society* 24 (1927): 366–72

Gregory, John. 'Telephone Regulation in Quebec: A Study of the Quebec Public Service Board.' *Canadian Communications Law Review* 5 (1973)

Grindlay, Thomas. *A History of the Independent Telephone Industry in Ontario*. Toronto: Ontario Telephone Service Commission 1975

Guité, Michel. 'Requiem for Rabbit Ears: Cable Television Policy in Canada.' Stanford, Calif.: Institute for Communication Research, Stanford University 1977

Hallman, E.S., and H. Hindley. *Broadcasting in Canada*, Don Mills, Ont: General Publishing 1977

Hardin, Herschel. *Closed Circuits: The Sellout of Canadian Television*. Vancouver: Douglas and McIntyre 1985

Harlow, Alvin, F. *Old Wires and New Waves*. New York: Appleton-Century 1937

Hills, Jill. *Deregulating Telecoms: Competition and Control in The United States, Japan and Britain.* London: Frances Pinter 1986

Hopper, A.B., and T. Kearney. 'Canadian National Railways: Synoptical History of Organization, Capital Stock, Funded Debt and Other General Information as of December 31, 1960.' Montreal: Canadian National Railway Company 1962

Ide, Thomas Ronald. 'The Technology.' In Guenther Friedrichs and Adam Schaff, eds., *Micro-electronics and Society: A Report to the Club of Rome.* New York: Mentor 1982

Innis, Harold A. *Empire and Communications.* Revised by Mary Q. Innis. Toronto: University of Toronto Press 1972

– *A History of the Canadian Pacific Railway.* Toronto: University of Toronto Press 1972 (first published 1923)

International Telecommunications Union. *From Semaphore to Satellite.* Geneva: ITU 1965

Intven, Hank. 'Some Recent Court Decisions Related to the Functions and Operations of Canadian Regulatory Tribunals.' Notes for a presentation to the CAMPUT annual Regulatory Studies Training Programme, Montreal, 15 June 1987

Irwin, Manley. *Telecommunications America: Markets without Boundaries.* Westport, Conn.: Quorum Books 1984

– *The Telecommunications Industry: Integration versus Competition.* New York: Praeger 1971

Johnston, C. Christopher. *The Canadian Radio-television and Telecommunications Commission: A Study of Administrative Procedures in the CRTC.* Prepared for the Law Reform Commission of Canada. Ottawa: Supply and Services 1980

Josephson, Matthew. *The Robber Barons: The Great American Capitalists, 1861–1901.* New York: Harcourt, Brace and World 1934

Kahn, Alfred. *The Economics of Regulation.* 2 vols. New York: Wiley 1971

Kaiser, Gordon. 'Competition in Telecommunications: Refusal to Supply Facilities by Regulated Common Carriers.' *Ottawa Law Review* 13, no. 1 (1981)

Kaufman, Gordon D. *Relativism, Knowledge and Faith.* Chicago: University of Chicago Press 1972

Kern, Stephen. *The Culture of Time and Space, 1880–1918.* Cambridge, Mass: Harvard University Press 1983

Kesterton, W.H. *A History of Journalism in Canada.* Toronto: McClelland and Stewart 1970

King, Alexander. 'A New Industrial Revolution or Just Another Technology?' In Guenther Friedrichs and Adam Schaff, eds., *Micro-electronics and Society: A Report to the Club of Rome*. New York: Mentor 1982

Kiss, F., et al. 'Economies of Scale and Scope in Bell Canada.' In L. Courville, A. de Fontenay, and R. Dobell, eds., *Economic Analysis of Telecommunications: Theory and Applications*. Amsterdam: North Holland Press 1983

Koebberling, Ursel. 'The Application of Communication Technologies in Canada's Inuit Communities.' PhD thesis, Simon Fraser University, Burnaby, BC, 1988

Koestler, Arthur. *Janus: A Summing Up*. London: Pan Books 1979

Kroker, Arthur. *Technology and the Canadian Mind: Innis/McLuhan/Grant*. Montreal: New World Perspectives 1984

Kuptana, Rosemarie. 'Neutron Bomb Television.' *Article Policy Review* 12 (1983)

Lasch, N.M. 'Progress Report of the Study on a TransCanada Telephone Line.' *Annual Proceedings of the Telephone Association of Canada* 1923; reprinted in Peter S. Grant, ed., *Telephone Operation and Development in Canada, 1921–1971*. Toronto: Faculty of Law, University of Toronto 1974

Latham, Robert. 'The Telephone and Social Change.' In Benjamin D. Singer, ed., *Communications in Canada Society*. Toronto: Addison-Wesley 1983

Lears, T.J. Jackson. 'From Salvation to Self-realization: Advertising and the Therapeutic Roots of the Consumer Culture, 1880–1930.' In Richard Wightman Fox and T.J. Jackson Lears, eds. *The Culture of Consumption: Critical Essays in America History 1880–1980, 1–38*. New York: Pantheon Books 1983

Lederman, W.R. 'Telecommunication and the Federal Constitution of Canada.' In H.E. English, ed., *Telecommunications for Canada: An Interface of Business and Government*. Toronto: Methuen 1973

Lippmann, Walter. *The Public Philosophy*. New York: Mentor 1955

Lorenz, Konrad. *The Waning of Humaneness*. Boston: Little, Brown 1987

Loudon, W.J. *Sir William Mulock: A Short Biography*. Toronto: Macmillan 1932

Lowenthal, David. *The Past Is a Foreign Country*. Cambridge: Cambridge University Press 1985

Lukasiewicz, J. *The Railway Game*. Toronto: McClelland and Stewart 1976

Lyman, Peter. *Canada's Video Revolution*. Toronto: Lorimer 1983

Macdonald, J.S. *The Dominion Telegraph*. Battleford, Sask.: Canadian North-West Historical Society 1930

MacGibbon, Duncan Alexander. *Railway Rates and the Canadian Railway Commission*. Boston, Mass.: Houghton Mifflin 1917

Machlup, Fritz. *The Production and Distribution of Knowledge in the United States*. Princeton, NJ: Princeton University Press 1962

– *Knowledge: Its Creation, Distribution and Economic Significance*. Vol. 1, *Knowledge and Knowledge Production*. Princeton, NJ: Princeton University Press 1980

Mackay, Corday. 'The Overland Telegraph.' *Canadian Geographical Journal* 32, no. 4 (1946): 172–9

MacMurchy, Angus, and J. Shirley Denison. *The Canadian Railway Act*. 2nd ed. Toronto: Canada Law Book 1911

Mankumah, Emmanuel. 'An Investigation into Bell Canada's Incursions in Pioneer Radio Broadcasting in the 1920's.' Ottawa: Department of Communication, University of Ottawa 1985

Manno, Jack. *Arming the Heavens: The Hidden Military Agenda for Space 1945–1995*. New York: Dodd, Mead 1984

Mantell, Leroy. 'Some Estimates of Returns to Scale in the Telephone Industry.' In Arthur Hall, ed. *Digest of the Conference on the Economies of Scale in Today's Telecommunications Systems*. Washington, DC: IEEE 1973

Marr, William, and Donald Paterson. *Canada: An Economic History*. Toronto: Macmillan 1980

Marschak, Jacob. 'Economics of Inquiring, Communicating and Deciding.' *American Economic Review* 58, no. 2 (1968): 1–8

Marsh, James. 'Railway History.' *Canadian Encyclopedia*. Edmonton: Hurtig 1985

Marshall, Herbert, Frank Southard Jr, and Kenneth Taylor. *Canadian-American Industry: A Study in International Investment*. Toronto: McClelland and Stewart 1977 (first published 1936)

Mattelart, Armand. *Multinational Corporations and the Control of Culture*. Brighton, England: Harvester Press 1979

Mavor, James. *Government Telephones: The Experience of Manitoba, Canada*. New York: Moffat, Yard 1916

McCallum, Margaret E. 'Sir Hugh Allan.' *Canadian Encyclopedia*. Edmonton: Hurtig 1985

McLuhan, Marshall, *Culture is Our Business*. New York: McGraw-Hill 1970

– *The Mechanical Bride: Folklore of Industrial Man.* New York: Vanguard Press 1951
– *Understanding Media: The Extensions of Man.* New York: Mentor 1964
McLuhan, Marshall, and Quentin Fiore. *The Medium Is the Massage.* New York: Bantam 1967
McManus, John C. 'Federal Regulation of Telecommunications in Canada.' In H.E. English, ed., *Telecommunications for Canada: An Interface of Business and Government.* Toronto: Methuen 1973
McNulty, Jean. 'The Political Economy of Canadian Satellite Broadcasting.' *Canadian Journal of Communication* 13, no. 2 (1988)
– 'Satellite Broadcasting in Northern Canada.' In Duncan Cameron, ed., *Explorations in Canadian Economic History: Essays in Honour of Irene M. Spry.* Ottawa: University of Ottawa Press 1985
Meisel, John. 'An Audible Squeak: Broadcast Regulation in Canada.' In *Cultures in Collision: The Interaction of Canadian and U.S. Television Broadcast Policies.* New York: Praeger 1983
Melody, William. 'Direct Broadcast Satellites: The Canadian Experience.' Paper presented to the Symposium on Satellite Communication, Hans Bredou Institute for Radio and Television. University of Hamburg, Germany, 11 December 1982
– 'Satellite Communications.' *Canadian Encyclopedia.* Edmonton: Hurtig 1985
– 'Summary and Future Prospects.' In Royal Society of Canada, *Proceedings of the Twentieth Symposium: Hermes (The Communications Technology Satellite)*, vol. 3. Ottawa: Royal Society of Canada 1978
Milavsky, Barry. 'An Assessment of Telesat Canada and Its Canadian Domestic Satellite System with Respect to Canada's National Objectives.' MA thesis, University of Pennsylvania 1972
Morgan, Henry James, ed. *The Canadian Men and Women of the Time.* 2nd ed. Toronto: William Briggs 1912
Morton, Desmond, and Reginald H. Roy, eds. *Telegrams in the North-West Campaign 1885.* Toronto: Champlain Society 1972
Muir, Gilbert A. 'A History of the Telephone in Manitoba.' In C.J. Jaenen, ed., *Transactions of the Historical and Scientific Society of Manitoba*, series 3, no. 21 (1964–5)
Mumford, Lewis. *The Myth of the Machine: The Pentagon of Power.* New York: Harcourt, Brace, Jovanovich 1964
Murray, John. *A Story of the Telegraph.* Montreal: John Lovell and Son 1905

Myers, Gustavus. *A History of Canadian Wealth*. Toronto: James Lewis and Samuel 1972 (first published 1914)

Nader, George A. *Cities of Canada*. vol. 2, *Profiles of Fifteen Metropolitan Centres*. Toronto: Macmillan 1976

Naisbitt, John. *Megatrends*. New York: Warner 1982

Naylor, Tom. *The History of Canadian Business, 1867–1914*. 2 vols. Toronto: Lorimer 1975

Nelkin, Dorothy. *Selling Science: How the Press Covers Science and Technology*. New York: Freeman 1987

Nichols, M.E. *(CP): The Story of the Canadian Press*. Toronto Ryerson 1948

O'Brien, A.H. *A Digest of Canadian Cases Relating to Railway, Telegraph and Express Companies*. Toronto: Canada Law Book 1920

Ogle, E.G. *Long Distance Please: The Story of the TransCanada System*. Toronto: Collins 1979

Osborne, Brian, and Robert Pike. 'Lowering "the Walls of Oblivion": The Revolution in Postal Communications in Central Canada, 1851–1911.' *Canadian Papers in Rural History* 4 (1984)

Parkinson, C. Northcote. *The Rise of Big Business: From the Eighteenth Century to the Present*. London: Weidenfeld and Nicholson 1977

Patten, William. *Pioneering the Telephone in Canada*. Montreal: privately printed 1926

Pawlick, Thomas. 'Ma Bell: Exacting the Country Toll.' *Harrowsmith* 4, no. 32 (December 1980)

Peers, Frank. *The Politics of Canadian Broadcasting 1920–1951* Toronto: University of Toronto Press 1969

Pelton, Joseph. 'Life in the Information Society.' In Jerry L. Salvaggio, ed., *Telecommunications: Issues and Choices for Society*. New York: Longman 1983

Petrie, A. Roy. *Alexander Graham Bell*. Toronto: Fitzhenry and Whiteside 1983

Porat, Marc U. 'Communications Policy in an Information Society.' In Glenn O. Robinson, ed., *Communications for Tomorrow*. New York: Praeger 1978

– 'Definition and Measurement,' vol. 1, *The Information Economy*. Washington, DC: Government Printing Office 1977

– *The Information Economy*. Stanford, Calif.: Center for Interdisciplinary Research 1976

Reid, James D. *The Telegraph in America: Its Founders, Promoters and Noted Men*. New York: Arno Press 1974 (first published 1879)

Rens, Jean-Guy. 'La télégraphie.' Unpublished manuscript 1988

Richieson, D.R. 'The Electric Telegraph in Canada, 1846–1902.' In *Canada's Visual History*. Ottawa: National Museum of Man/National Film Board of Canada, nd

Robins, Kevin, and Frank Webster. 'Cybernetic Capitalism: Information Technology, Everyday Life.' In Vincent Mosco and Janet Wasko, eds., *The Political Economy of Information*. Madison, Wis.: University of Wisconsin Press 1988

Robinson, Gertrude J. 'Prologue: Canadian Communication Studies, a Discipline in Transition?' *Canadian Journal of Communication*, special issue (Winter 1987)

Ronaghan, Allen, 'The Telegraph Line to Edmonton.' *Alberta Historical Review*, no. 4 (1970)

Roszak, Theodore. *Where the Wasteland Ends*. Garden City, NY: Anchor Books, 1973

Rubin, Michael R., ed. *Information Economics and Policy in the United States*. Littleton, Colo: Libraries Unlimited 1983

Rutherford, Paul. *A Victorian Authority: The Daily Press in Late Nineteenth Century Canada*. Toronto: University of Toronto Press 1982

Salter, Liora, and Debra Slaco. *Public Inquiries in Canada*. Science Council of Canada, background study 47. Ottawa: Supply and Services 1981

Samuels, Warren J. 'Interrelations between Legal and Economic Processes.' *Journal of Law and Economics* 14, no. 2 (1971)

Schnebly, Clarence D. 'History of Northern Electric.' Montreal: Bell Canada Historical Collection, nd

Schumpeter, Joseph A. *Capitalism, Socialism and Democracy*. 3rd ed. New York: Harper Torch Books 1962

Serafini, Shirley, and Michel Andrieu. *The Information Revolution and Its Implications for Canada*. Ottawa: Supply and Services 1981

Shooshan, Harry M., ed. *Disconnecting Bell: The Impact of the AT&T Divestiture*. New York: Pergamon Press 1984

Singer, Benjamin, ed. *Communications in Canadian Society*. Toronto: Addison-Wesley 1983

Smith, Anthony. 'The Future of the Newspaper: The Waning of the Fourth Estate.' *Intermedia* 6, no. 4 (August 1978)

– *The Geopolitics of Information*. London: Faber and Faber 1979

– *Goodbye Gutenberg: The Newspaper Revolution of the 1980's*. New York: Oxford University Press 1979

Smith, Goldwin, *Canada and the Canadian Question*. Toronto: University of Toronto Press 1971 (first published 1891)

Smith, Michael L. 'Selling the Moon: the u.s. Manned Space Program and
the Triumph of Commodity Scientism.' In R.W. Fox and T.J. Jackson
Lears, eds., *The Culture of Consumption: Critical Essays in American
History 1880–1980*. New York: Pantheon 1983

Smith, William. *The History of the Post Office in British North America
1639–1870*. New York: Octagon Books 1921

Smythe, Dallas W. 'The Relevance of the United States Legislative-Regulatory Experience to the Canadian Telecommunications Situation.'
Study prepared for the Telecommission. Ottawa: Information Canada
1971

– 'A Study of Saskatchewan Telecommunications.' Study prepared for the
Department of Communications, Ottawa, July 1974

Stanley, Della. 'Andrew George Blair.' *Canadian Encyclopedia*. Edmonton: Hurtig 1985

Starr, Richard. 'A History of the Manitoba Telephone System.' Winnipeg
1974

Stigler, George J. *Memoirs of an Unregulated Economist*. New York: Basic
Books 1988

Stores, Paul B. *The Militarization of Space: U.S. Space Policy 1945–84*.
Ithaca, NY: Cornell University Press 1985

Strick, John. 'Socio-economic Influences of Satellite Communications
Technology.' In Rowland Lorimer and Donald Wilson, eds., *Com-
munications Canada: Issues in Broadcasting and New Technologies*.
Toronto: Kegan and Woo 1988

Switzer, Israel. 'How I Learned to Love the Satellite.' In Peter S. Grant,
ed. *New Developments in Canada Communications Law and Policy*.
Toronto: Law Society of Upper Canada 1980

Taylor, James R. 'The New Communication Environment.' Paper prepared
for Institute for Research on Public Policy, Ottawa, 1989

– 'The Twenty-First Century in the Rear View Mirror: A Critique of DOC's
1987 Discussion Paper.' *Canadian Journal of Communication* 13,
nos. 3, 4 (1988)

Thompson, Robert Luther. *Wiring a Continent: The History of the Telegraph in the United States*. Princeton, NJ: Princeton University Press
1947

Toffler, Alvin. *The Third Wave*. New York: Bantam 1981

Urquart, M.C., and K.A. Buckley, eds. *Historical Statistics of Canada*.
Toronto: Macmillan 1965

Waverman, Leonard. 'The Regulation of Intercity Telecommunications.'
In Almarin Philips, ed., *Promoting Competition in Regulated Markets*. Washington, DC: Brookings Institution 1975

Weinhaus, Carol L., and Anthony G. Oettinger. *Behind the Telephone Debates*. Norwood, NJ: Ablex 1988

Weizenbaum, Joseph. *Computer Power and Human Reason: From Judgement to Calculation*. Harmondsworth: Penguin 1984 (first published 1976)

– 'Once More: The Computer Revolution.' In Michael L. Dertouzos and Joel Moses, eds. *The Computer Age: A Twenty-Year View*. Cambridge, Mass: MIT Press 1979

Williams, Raymond. *The Year 2000*. New York: Pantheon 1983

Wilson, Kevin. *Technologies of Control: The New Interactive Media for the Home*. Madison, Wis.: University of Wisconsin Press 1988

Winner, Langdon. *Autonomous Technology: Technics-Out-of-Control as a Theme in Political Thought*. Cambridge, Mass.: MIT Press 1977

Woodrow, R. Brian, and Kenneth B. Woodside. *The Introduction of Pay TV in Canada*. Montreal: Institute for Research on Public Policy 1982

– 'Players, Stakes and Politics in the Future of Telecommunications Policy and Regulation in Canada.' In W.T. Stanbury, ed., *Telecommunications Policy and Regulation*. Montreal: Institute for Research on Public Policy 1986

Woodrow, R. Brian, et. al. *Conflict over Communications Policy*. Montreal: C.D. Howe Institute 1980

II CONSULTANTS' REPORTS, BRIEFS, SUBMISSIONS, CORPORATE REPORTS, ANNUAL REPORTS

Association of Competitive Telecommunications Suppliers. 'Application; before the Canadian Radio-television and Telecommunications Commission, between Association of Competitive Telecommunications Suppliers, Applicants, and British Columbia Telephone and Bell Canada, Respondents.' 7 April 1988

Babe, Robert, E. 'An Economic Analysis of Telecommunications in Manitoba.' Paper prepared for the provincial Position Paper on Communications, Winnipeg, 11 August 1973

– 'Performance Analysis of Selected Common Carriers.' Report to the Department of Communications, Ottawa, May 1976

– 'Theory of Cost Separations for the Telephone Industry.' Report to the National Branch, Department of Communications, Ottawa 1981

– 'Bell Canada Reorganization: Non-Financial Studies.' Paper prepared for CRTC, 14 January 1983

Babe, Robert E., and Philip Slayton. *Competitive Procedures for Broadcasting – Renewals and Transfers.* Study prepared for the Department of Communications, Ottawa, 1980

Bell Canada. *Form 10-K, Annual Report Pursuant to Section 13 or 15(d) of the Securities Exchange Act of 1934.* Annual

– 'Request for Increase in Rates.' Memoranda of Support, 3 November 1976
– 'Integrated Telecommunications Plant.' 21 February 1977
– 'Memorandum on the Technological and Cost Aspects of Integrated Distribution Plant.' March 1978
– 'Argument; CNCP Telecommunications Interconnection Case.' 29 May 1978
– 'Intervention in the Matter of an Application by Canadian Cablesystems (Ontario) Limited – to Provide a Communications Service of a Non-programming Nature, Namely a Teletext Service.' Before CRTC, 1 November 1978
– *The First Century of Service.* Montreal: Bell Canada 1980
– 'Evidence.' 15 November 1982
– 'Bell Canada's Presentation to the Task Force on Broadcasting Policy.' 18 November 1985
– 'Memorandum on Rate Rebalancing.' Updated, 17 March 1987
– 'Cost Inquiry Phase III 1986 Study Report.' September 1987

Bell Canada Enterprises (BCE). *Annual Reports*

Bell Telephone Company of Canada (Bell Canada). *Annual Reports*

Bolter, Walter. 'Bell Canada's Proposed Reorganization: Comparisons with U.S. Experience.' Report prepared for CRTC. nd

Booth, Peter, and Russel Wills. 'Telidon Synthesis Study: Regulatory, Industrial, Marketing and Social Issues' (vol. 4). Report prepared for the Department of Communications, March 1983

British Columbia Telephone Company. 'Cost Inquiry Phase III 1986 Study Report.' September 1987

Canadian Independent Telephone Association. *Official Report of the Proceedings of the First Annual Convention.* Toronto: Moore Bros. 1906

Canadian Telephone Company. *Annual Reports* (1880, 1881)

CNCP Telecommunications. *Crisis in Canadian Telecommunications Policy and Regulation.* nd

– 'Development of CNCP as a Telecommunications Carrier.' nd
– *Meeting the Challenge: The Proposal of CNCP Telecommunications to the CRTC for the Introduction of Competitive Long Distance Public Telephone Service.* nd
– 'Market Survey' 1977

- 'Exhibit CNCP 14 – Competitive Services vs. Non-Competitive Services.' 1978
- 'Application for Review of Telecom Decision CRTC 85–19.' Before CRTC, 19 December 1985
- 'Datapac Rates.' Before CRTC, Bell Canada Review of Revenue Requirements for 1985, 1986, and 1987, 25 June 1986
- 'Application in the Matter of Bell Canada's Rates for Competitive Network Services and British Columbia Telephone Company's Rates for Competitive Network Services and Competitive Terminals'. Before CRTC, 23 March 1988

Cox, Kenneth A. 'Statement Submitted to the Subcommittee on Antitrust and Monopoly of the Senate Committee of the Judiciary.' In *Hearing on S.1167, Part 2, The Communications Industry*. Washington, DC: U.S. Government Printing Office 1973

DCF Systems Limited. 'Brief Pertaining to Bill C-104. An Act Respecting The Bell Telephone Company of Canada.' Printed in House of Commons, Standing Committee on Transport and Communications, *Minutes of Proceedings and Evidence Respecting Bill C-104*. 1967

Goldenberg, Carl. *Government Commercial Enterprises Survey*. Winnipeg: King's Printer 1940

Institute of Applied Economic Research. 'A Study of the Productive Factor and Financial Characteristics of Telephone Carriers.' Study prepared for the Department of Communications, 1974

Irwin, Manley. 'Technology and Communications: A Policy Perspective for the 1980's.' Working paper for the Economic Council for Canada

Manitoba Telephone System. *People of Service: A Brief History of MTS*. Winnipeg: MTS nd

- *Annual Reports*

Maritime Telegraph and Telephone Company, Limited. 'Response of Maritime Telegraph and Telephone Company, Limited: Telecommunications in Nova Scotia, a Cost of Service Study for Maritime Telegraph and Telephone Company, Limited.' June 1983

Melody, William H. 'Report.' Before the Canadian Radio-television and Telecommunications Commission on Cost Inquiry, Phase III, 16 July 1982

- 'Telecommunications in Nova Scotia: A Cost of Service Study for Maritime Telegraph and Telephone Company, Limited.' Final Report prepared for the Board of Commissioners for Public Utilities, Province of Nova Scotia, June 1983

Merchants' Telephone Company (Limited). *Prospectus* 1887

- 'Report of Proceedings of the Annual Meeting.' Montreal, 2 October 1894
Niagara Television Ltd. and Power Corporation of Canada Ltd. 'Proposal for a Canadian TV Network and a Domestic Satellite Distribution System.' Before Board of Broadcast Governors, October 1966
Northern Electric Co. and Bell Canada. *Prospectus.* 7 October 1975
Porat, Marc. 'Definition of Measurement' (vol. 1 of *The Information Economy*). Washington, DC: U.S. Government Printing Office 1972
Robert E. Babe Associates, Consultants. 'A Study of Radio: Economic/Financial Profile of Private Sector Radio Broadcasting in Canada.' Study for the Task Force on Broadcasting Policy, 10 December 1985
Snavely, King and Tucker, Inc. *Report of the Consultants to Canadian Transport Commission Cost Inquiry.* Vol. 2, *Conduct of the Inquiry.* 1974
- *Report of the Consultants to Canadian Transport Commission Cost Inquiry.* Vol. 3, *Components and Factors of Cost.* 1974
- *Report of the Consultants to Canadian Transport Commission Cost Inquiry.* Vol. 5, *Characteristics of Telecommunications Costs.* 1974
Stanbury, William T. 'Comments on the Proposed Reorganization of Bell Canada.' Report prepared for CRTC, January 1983
- 'Evidence.' CRTC Telecom Public Notice 87–15, 21 August 1987
Sutherland, J.G. 'Telecommunications in Canada.' In CNCP Telecommunications, 'Statement of Evidence: Application for Interconnection to Bell Canada.' Before CRTC, 1978
TransCanada Telephone System. 'TransCanada Telephone System Brief to the Department of Transport and the Government of Canada.' 1962
- *History of Regulation and Current and Regulatory Setting.* Report prepared for the Telecommission. Ottawa: Information Canada 1971
TransCanada Telephone System and CNCP Telecommunications. 'Canadian Communications Satellite System.' May 1967

III GOVERNMENT DOCUMENTS

Canada
Board of Railway Commissioners for Canada. *Annual Reports*
- Official transcripts, case no. 955–71, 1926
- 'Application of the Bell Telephone Company for Local Exchange Services.' CRTC no. 6057, 1927

Board of Transport Commissioners for Canada. *Judgements, Orders, Rulings and Regulations,* (JOR&R). Annual
- 'In the Matter of the Application of the Bell Telephone Company of Canada for an Order under Section 374 and all Other Relevant Sections of the Railway Act, Approving to be Effective on December 1, 1949, the Revisions of Certain of the Applicant's Tariffs for Exchange and Long Distance Services: Case No.955–170.' Judgment. Ottawa 1950
- Decision, case no. 955–172, 15 March 1958
- Judgment, file no. 36730–4, 13 January 1964
- Judgment, Northern Telephone case, file no. 3839–1054, 3 June 1964
- Judgment, case no. 955–176, pamphlet 16, May 1966
Canadian Broadcasting Corporation. *TV and Radio: Figures That Count.* CBC 1985
Canadian Radio-television and Telecommunications Commission. *Annual Reports*
- 'Telecommunications Regulation – Procedure and Practices: Statement of the CRTC.' 20 July 1976
- 'Public Announcement: Rate Adjustment Formula, Cost Inquiry and Other Pending Proceedings.' 7 September 1976
- 'Bell Canada, Confidentiality and Other Preliminary Matters Concerning Support Structures Tariff Proceedings.' Telecom Decision CRTC 76–2, 31 December 1976
- 'Bell Canada, Tariff for the Use of Support Structures by Cable Television Licensees.' Telecom Decision CRTC 77–6, 27 May 1977
- 'Bell Canada, Increases in Rates.' Telecom Decision CRTC 77, 1 June 1977
- 'Telesat Canada, Proposed Agreement with TransCanada Telephone System.' Telecom Decision CRTC 77–10, 24 August 1977
- *Challenge Communications Ltd. v. Bell Canada.* Telecom Decision CRTC 77–16, 23 December 1977
- 'CRTC Procedures and Practices.' Telecom Decision CRTC 78–4, 23 May 1978
- 'Bell Canada, Increases in Rates.' Telecom Decision CRTC 78–7, 10 August 1978
- Committee of Inquiry, City of Prince Rupert, Connecting Agreement with B.C. Telephone Company. *Report.* 22 December 1978
- 'A Review of Certain Cable Television Programming Issues.' Public Announcement, 26 March 1979
- 'CNCP Telecommunications: Interconnection with Bell Canada.' Telecom Decision CRTC 79–11, 17 May 1979

- Committee to Annually Review Bell Canada's Construction Program. Telecom Public Notice 1979–27, 12 June 1979
- 'City of Prince Rupert, Connecting Agreement with B.C. Telephone Company.' 9 November 1979
- *Canadian Broadcasting and Telecommunications: Past Experience Future Options*. Study commissioned by the CRTC. Ottawa: Supply and Services 1980
- Committee on Extension of Service to Northern and Remote Communities. *The 1980's: A Decade of Diversity – Broadcasting Satellites and Pay-TV*. Ottawa: Supply and Services 1980
- 'Bell Canada, British Columbia Telephone Company and Telesat Canada: Increases and Decreases in Rates.' Telecom Decision CRTC 81–13, 7 July 1981
- 'Bell Canada Increase in Rates.' Telecom Decision CRTC 81–15, 28 September 1981
- 'CNCP Telecommunications: Interconnection with the British Columbia Telephone Company.' Telecom Decision CRTC 81–24, 24 November 1981
- 'Bell Canada: Articles of Continuance and Proposed Corporate Reorganization.' CRTC Telecom Public Notice 1982–31, 12 August 1982
- 'Attachment of Subscriber-Provided Terminal Equipment.' Telecom Decision CRTC 82–14, 23 November 1982
- *Report on the Proposed Reorganization of Bell Canada*. 18 April 1983
- 'Telesat Canada – Final Rates for 14/12 GHz Satellite Service and General Review of Revenue Requirements.' Telecom Decision CRTC 84–9, 20 February 1984
- *Report of the Inquiry Officer with Respect to the Inquiry into Telecommunications Carriers: Phase III Costing and Accounting Procedures*. 30 April 1984
- 'Enhanced Services.' Telecom Decision CRTC 84–18, 12 July 1984
- 'Inquiry into Telecommunications Carriers' Costing and Accounting Procedures: Phase II, Costing and Existing Services.' Telecom Decision CRTC 85–10, 25 June 1985
- 'Identification of Enhanced Services.' Telecom Decision CRTC 85–17, 13 August 1985
- *Interexchange Competition and Related Issues*. Telecom Decision CRTC 85–19, 29 August 1985
- 'Telesat Canada and Bell Canada – Amendments to Connecting Agreement between Telesat Canada and Telecom Canada.' Telecom Decision CRTC 86–9, 8 May 1986

- 'Application for Review of Telecom Decision CRTC 85–19.' Telecom Decision CRTC 86–18, 31 October 1986
- 'Bell Canada – 1988 Revenue Requirement, Rate Rebalancing and Revenue Settlement Issues.' Telecom Decision CRTC 88–4, 17 March 1988
Canadian Radio-Television Commission. 'Public Announcement: The Improvement and the Extension of U.S. Television Coverage in Canada by CATV.' 3 December 1969
- 'Public Announcement: Guidelines for Applicants Regarding Licences to Carry on CATV Undertaking.' 18 April 1970
- 'Policy Statement on Cable Television: Canadian Broadcasting, A Single System.' 16 July 1971
Canadian Transport Commission. *Annual Reports*
- *In the Matter of Whether the Canadian Transport Commission Should Award Costs to Parties That Appear Before It and More Particularly to Some Intervenors under Certain Circumstances*. Report, 19 August 1975
Committee on Broadcasting. *Report*. Ottawa: Queen's Printer 1965
Consultative Committee on the Implications of Telecommunications for Canadian Sovereignty (J.V. Clyne, Chairman). *Telecommunications and Canada*. Ottawa: Supply and Services 1979
Department of Communications. *Annual Reports*
- *Financial Statistics of Canadian Telecommunications Common Carriers*. Annual
- *A Review of the Public Message Telegraph Service in Canada*. Ottawa: Department of Communications 1970
- 'News Release: Statement by Minister of Communications, Jeanne Sauvé in Respect of an Order-in-Council to Vary CRTC Decision 77–10 and to Approve a Proposed Agreement for Membership by Telesat Canada in the TransCanada Telephone System.' 3 November 1977
- *The Canadian Space Program: Five Year Plan*. Ottawa: Supply and Services 1980
- *Spacebound*. Ottawa: Supply and Services 1982
- *Direct-to-Home Satellite Broadcasting for Canada*. Ottawa: Supply and Services 1983
- *Towards a New Broadcasting Policy*. Ottawa: Supply and Services 1983
- *Telidon Trials and Services* Ottawa: Supply and Services 1983
- *Vital Links: Canadian Cultural Industries*. Ottawa: Supply and Services 1987
- *Communications for the Twenty-First Century: Media and Messages in the Information Age*. Ottawa: Supply and Services 1987

- *(Communications Canada)*. 'Proposed Guidelines for Type 1 Telecommunications Carriers.' January 1988
Department of Industry. *White Paper on a Domestic Satellite Communication System for Canada*. Ottawa: Queen's Printer 1968
Department of Transport. 'Satellite Communications in Canada.' 5 vols. Unpublished
Director of Investigation and Research, Combines Investigation Act. *The Effects of Vertical Integration on the Telecommunications Equipment Market in Canada*. Ottawa: Department of Consumer and Corporate Affairs 1976
Federal Court of Appeal. 'Reasons for Judgement no. 1260–84: between CNCP Telecommunications Appellant and Alberta Government Telephones and Canadian Radio-television and Telecommunications Commission, Respondents, and Attorney General of Canada, Intervenor.' 4 December 1985
Federal Court of Canada, Trial Division. 'Affidavit between Alberta Government Telephones, Applicant and Canadian Radio-television and Telecommunications Commission, Respondent.' 17 September 1982
- 'Originating Notice of Motion under Section 18 of the Federal Court Act, between Alberta Government Telephones, Applicant, and Canadian Radio-television and Telecommunications Commission, Respondent.' 18 October 1982
- Order T-8340-82, 26 October 1984
Governor-in-Council. Order-in-Council, P.C. 1972–1569
- Order P.C. 1982–3253, 22 October 1982
House of Commons. *Debates*. 1880, 1902, 1903, 1904, 1905, 1906, 1917, 1918, 1919, 1932, 1946, 1968, 1969, 1978
- *Journals*. 1900, 1901, 1902, 1905, 1918, 1919
- Select Committee on Telephone Systems. *Proceedings*. Ottawa: King's Printer 1905
- Special Committee on the Railway Act. *Minutes of Proceedings and Evidence* 1917
- Standing Committee on Transport and Communications. *Minutes of Proceedings and Evidence* 1967
- Standing Committee on Transport and Communications. *Minutes of Proceedings and Evidence* 1968
- Standing Committee on Broadcasting, Films and Assistance to the Arts. *Minutes of Proceedings and Evidence* 1969
- Standing Committee on Communications and Culture. *Minutes of Proceedings and Evidence* 1985

Minister of Communications (Hon. Gérard Pelletier). *Proposals for a Communications Policy for Canada*. Ottawa: Information Canada 1973

Minister of Communications (Hon. Francis Fox). 'Statement in Respect of an Order-in-Council to Further Vary Telecom Decision 81–13.' 10 December 1981

– *Culture and Communications: Key Elements of Canada's Economic Future*. Ottawa: Supply and Services 1983

Mongeau, Jean-Pierre. *Federal-Provincial Examination of Telecommunications Pricing and the Universal Availability of Affordable Telephone Service*. Ottawa: Supply and Services 1986

Restrictive Trade Practices Commission. *Telecommunications in Canada, Phase I: Interconnection*. Ottawa: Supply and Services 1981

– *Telecommunications in Canada, Part III: The Impact of Vertical Integration on the Equipment Industry*. Ottawa: Supply and Services 1982

Royal Commission on Broadcasting. *Report*. Ottawa: King's Printer 1929

Royal Commission on Newspapers. *Report*. Ottawa: Supply and Services 1981

Science Council for Canada. *A Space Program for Canada*. Report no. 1. Ottawa: Queen's Printer 1967

– *Planning Now for an Information Revolution: Tomorrow Is Too Late*. Ottawa: Supply and Services 1982

Secretary of State. *1966 White Paper on Broadcasting*. Ottawa: Queen's Printer 1966

Senate of Canada. *Debates*. 1880, 1882, 1902

– Standing Committee on Transport and Communications. *Minutes of Proceedings and Evidence* 1976

Statistics Canada. *Cable Television*. Cat. no. 56–205. Annual

– *Radio and Television Broadcasting*. Cat. no. 56–204. Annual

– *Telephone Statistics*. Cat. doc. 56–203. Annual

– *Telecommunications Statistics*. Cat. doc. 56–201

Task Force on Broadcasting Policy. *Report*. Ottawa: Supply and Services 1986

Telecommunications Committee, Canadian Transport Commission. Decision, file no. 49645–1, 21 September 1972

– Decision, file no. 49616, 19 November 1973

– 'In the Matter of Amended Application "B" of Bell Canada.' Decision, file no. C-955-182-1, 15 August 1974

– 'Order no. T-474: Rate Adjustment Formula Procedure for Telecommuni-

cations Carriers under the Jurisdiction of the Canadian Transport Commission.' 15 August 1974
- Decision, file no. 49645-26, 14 April 1975
- Decision, file no. 49616-2, 15 October 1975
- Decision, 22 December 1975

Provincial
Alberta. Alberta Public Utilities Board. 'Manner of Regulation of Alberta Government Telephones.' Decision no. E76090, 8 July 1976
Manitoba, Department of Consumer, Corporate and Internal Services. *Broadcasting and Cable Television: A Manitoba Perspective.* Winnipeg: Queen's Printer 1974
Ontario. Ontario Telephone Service Commission. *Annual Report* 1986
- Rural Telephone Committee. *Report to the Hydro-electric Power Commission of Ontario Concerning Rural Telephone Service in Ontario* 1953
- Railway and Municipal Board. *Annual Reports* 1912, 1914, 1918, 1919
Quebec. *Quebec: Master Craftsman of Its Own Communications Policy.* Quebec: L'Editeur de Québec 1973

United States
Comptroller General. *Legislative and Regulatory Actions Needed to Deal with a Changing Domestic Telecommunications Industry.* CED-136. Gaithersburg, Md.: U.S. General Accounting Office 1981
Congress. House. Federal Communications Commission. *Investigation of the Telephone Industry in the United States.* House Document no. 340, 76th Congress, 1st Session. Washington, DC: U.S. Government Printing Office 1939
Congress. House. Subcommittee on Telecommunications, Consumer Protection and Finance of the Committee on Energy and Commerce. *Telecommunications in Transition: The Status of Competition in the Telecommunications Industry.* Washington, DC: U.S. Government Printing Office 1981
District Court for the District of New Jersey. Final Judgement, Civil Action no. 17–49, 24 January 1956

Index

fully allocated costing, 151

Galbraith, John Kenneth, 137
Gamble, Clarke, 37
Garnham, Nicholas, 242–3
Gary, Theodore, 112
Gellman, Dr H.S., 145, 152–3, 193
General Electric: patent pool, 201–2
General Telephone and Electronics
    Corp. (GTE): 30–1, 113; acquires
    BC Tel, 113
Geoffrion, Aime, 120
Gisborne, Fred, N., 38–40; and
    Atlantic cable, 51; and B.N.A.
    Telegraph Association, 45; and
    government telegraph, 51, 55; in
    Newfoundland, 50–1
Globe and Mail, 231
Godfrey, David, 230–1
Godfrey, O.J. and Company, 108
Gotlieb, A.E., 5, 223
Gould, Jay, 47–9, 56, 67
Government Telegraph and Signal
    Service, 55
Grand Trunk Pacific Railway, 119
Grand Trunk Railway, 42, 55, 59
Grand Trunk Telegraph Company,
    45
Grant, George, 256
Gray, Elisha, 67
Gray, John T., and costs to inter-
    veners, 165–6
Great North Western Telegraph
    Company: acquisition of, 60;
    formed, 49; links Winnipeg and
    Ontario, 56; and news services,
    58–9; take-over of Canadian teleg-
    raphy, 49–50
Great Western Railway, 35
Grindlay, Thomas, 82–4

Guité, Michel, 214

Halifax, NS: telegraph connec-
    tions to, 39–40, 75
Hall Beach, NWT, 140
Hallman, H., 6–7
Hamilton, Sir Frederick, 108
Hamilton, Ont., 37–8, 43, 199
Hamilton and District Telephone
    Company, 66
Hamilton Real Estate Board, 66
Hamilton *Spectator*, 41
Hamilton Street Railway Com-
    pany, 66
Harding Communications, 146–7,
    148
Harlow, Alvin, 201
Harris, Thomas Denne, 37
Harvard University, 248
Hazelton, BC, 54–5
Henderson, Rev. Thomas, 66, 69
Hertz, Heinrich, 200
Highgate, 199
historical analysis: to demytholo-
    gize, 4–5
Holland, Gordon, 107
Holmes: the mysterious Captain, 85
Homemaker's Magazine, 232
House of Commons. *See* Commons
Howe, C.D., 204
Hudson's Bay Company: fur trade,
    55
Hughes Aircraft, 223

IBM, 129, 243
incorporation: and corporate veil,
    176–95
indemnification: and CNCP case,
    130; for exclusive privileges at
    railway stations, 89; for long-

Maritime Telegraph and Telephone
Company (MT&T), 30, 161
Maritimes: railways in, 119. *See
also* New Brunswick, Nova
Scotia, Prince Edward Island
Marsh, James, 119
Masse, Marcel, 135, 240
Matane, Que., 81, 214
Mavor, Prof. James, 108, 288n1
Maxfield, Gordon, 124
Means, Gardiner, 175–6
Meisel, John, 211
Melody, Dr William, 226
Memotec Data Inc., 30
Merchant's Bank of Canada, 43
Merchants' Telephone Company
(Compagnie de Téléphone des
Marchands de Montréal), 77–8
message record services: decline in,
60–1. *See also* telegraph
Métis Telephone Company, 81
microwave: first coast-to-coast system, 129
military: interest in telecommunications, 54–6, 201–2, 219–20,
305n10
Mill, John Stuart, 137
Minc, Alaine, 243
mobile telephones, 147–8. *See also*
cellular telephones
monopolization: of telegraphs,
45–53, 59–62; of telephony, 66–9,
112
monopolization techniques:
acquisition premiums, 124, 141,
288n2; acquisitions, 45–53, 113;
cartels, 46, 202–3, 265n9; collu-
sion, 223; cost/price squeeze,
121–4; cross-subsidy, 45–6; court
battles, 146–7; deception, 184–7,
288n5; discrimination, 58–9;

extravagant claims, 130; franchises, 89; indemnification,
117–21; interconnection restrictions, 82, 84, 87, 102, 115–21,
127–35; intimidation, 6, 49–50,
82, 146–7, 167, 217–18, 225,
303n73; manipulation of
corporate form, 112; overcapacity, 129; patents, 66–8,
201–2; pricing, 67–8, 48–9, 75,
78–9, 150–7; public relations,
85–6; rate rebalancing, 121–6;
reciprocity, 46, 48; refusal to
supply, 80; restrictive contracts,
82, 87–9; reversed rate rebalancing, 133–4
monopoly: government's complic-
ity, 16; oscillation between
competition and, 135–6. *See also*
natural monopoly
Montagamy, Que., 81
Montreal, Que.: economic conditions in 1840s, 40–1; population
in 1850s, 43; railway connections
to, 42; telephone competition in,
76–8; telephones in (1904), 80–1
Montreal and Troy Telegraph Company, 45
Montreal Board of Trade, 38
Montreal *Star*, 56, 214
Montreal Telegraph Company, 8,
15, 38, 43–4; exclusive railway
right-of-way, 42; expansion of,
45–9, 267–8n21; leases lines, 50;
sues Great North Western Telegraph Company, 271n41; telephone operations, 66–7, 71
Montreal Trust Company, 194,
234
Montreal *Witness*, 56
Morse, Samuel F.B., 35–6, 52